BOOK OF MAINTENANCE AND REPAIR OF
LUCAS
ELECTRONIC SYSTEMS FOR 1950's - 1970's BRITISH MOTORCYCLES

CONTENTS

Each of the individual publications in this compilation have their own index, the page numbers corresponding to that index are printed to the upper corner of each page. The number printed to the center bottom of the page is the page number within the book. The contents list below refers to the book page number.

Compensated Voltage Control Equipment (1950's - 1960's)..................page 1

Alternating Current Equipment (1950's - 1960's)......................................page 31

Electrical Equipment Service Manual (1970's Onwards)..........................page 65

Parts Catalog and Parts Interchange (1960 -1968).....................................page 119

Parts Catalog and Parts Interchange (1969-1977).....................................page 165

© 2021 Veloce Enterprises Inc., San Antonio, Texas USA
All rights reserved. This work may not be reproduced or transmitted in any form without the express consent of the publisher

ACKNOWLEDGEMENT

We would like to take the opportunity to extend our appreciation to Lucas Industries for the publications included in this compilation. It is important to remember that the company was founded in 1860 and their continuing research and development helped pave the way for the trouble free systems that are incorporated into today's motorcycles and automobiles. We are pleased to offer this reprint as a service to all British motorcycle owners and collectors worldwide, and we extend our thanks to Lucas Industries for its contribution to the British motorcycle industry.

INTRODUCTION

Welcome to the world of digital publishing ~ the book you now hold in your hand was printed using the latest state of the art digital technology. The advent of print-on-demand has forever changed the publishing process, never has information been so accessible and it is our hope that this book serves your informational needs for years to come. If this is your first exposure to digital publishing, we hope that you are pleased with the results. Many more titles of interest to the classic automobile and motorcycle enthusiast, collector and restorer are available via our website at www.VelocePress.com. We hope that you find this title as interesting as we do.

NOTE FROM THE PUBLISHER

The information presented is true and complete to the best of our knowledge. All recommendations are made without any guarantees on the part of the author or the publisher, who also disclaim all liability incurred with the use of this information.

TRADEMARKS

We recognize that some words, model names and designations, for example, mentioned herein are the property of the trademark holder. We use them for identification purposes only. This is not an official publication.

INFORMATION ON THE USE OF THIS PUBLICATION

This manual is an invaluable resource for those interested in performing their own maintenance. However, in today's information age we are constantly subject to changes in common practice, new technology, availability of improved materials and increased awareness of chemical toxicity. As such, it is advised that the user consult with an experienced professional prior to undertaking any procedure described herein. While every care has been taken to ensure correctness of information, it is obviously not possible to guarantee complete freedom from errors or omissions or to accept liability arising from such errors or omissions. Therefore, any individual that uses the information contained within, or elects to perform or participate in do-it-yourself repairs or modifications acknowledges that there is a risk factor involved and that the publisher or its associates cannot be held responsible for personal injury or property damage resulting from the use of the information or the outcome of such procedures.

WARNING!

One final word of advice, this publication is intended to be used as a reference guide, and when in doubt the reader should consult with a qualified technician.

Maintenance Instructions for

LUCAS

ELECTRIC LIGHTING
and
IGNITION EQUIPMENT
With Compensated Voltage Control

for motor-cycles

JOSEPH LUCAS LIMITED · BIRMINGHAM · ENGLAND

Publication No. 820H.   J/456/L   LHZ/756/L   Printed in England

Foreword

Lucas Electrical Equipment is designed and manufactured to give long periods of service with the minimum of attention. As with other parts of the motor cycle, however, occasional minor adjustments, lubrication of moving parts and cleaning should be carried out to ensure that the equipment will operate with the utmost reliability and efficiency.

This Manual gives general information on the various items of equipment fitted to motor cycles having D.C. generators and describes the small amount of attention which is required. In addition the recommended procedure is set out for a systematic examination to be adopted in the event of the electrical equipment not functioning correctly.

By reference to the Contents overleaf you will be able to locate the information relating to the compensated voltage control dynamo equipment fitted on your motor cycle.

Any further information will be supplied on application to Joseph Lucas Ltd., Great King Street, Birmingham 19, England.

CONTENTS

	Page
Battery	3
Generator	5
Magnetos, rotating armature	8
Magnetos, rotating magnet	11
Coil Ignition Equipment	13
Headlamps	16
Parking Lights	19
Rear Lights	21
Horns	24
Wiring	25
Location and Remedy of Faults :	26

BATTERY

Topping-Up.

During charging, water is lost by gassing and evaporation. Fortnightly, or more often in warm climates, check the electrolyte level in the battery cells; if necessary, add distilled water to raise the electrolyte level with the top edges of the separators. Do not use tap water as it may contain impurities detrimental to the battery. With the smaller capacity five-plate batteries, e.g., model PU5E, fitted to certain lightweight motor cycles, make this examination weekly.

Batteries with Correct-Acid-Level Devices.

The correct acid level device consists of a central tube with a perforated flange which rests on a ledge in the filling orifice. When topping-up a battery fitted with these devices, pour distilled water round the flange (not down the tube) until no more drains through into the cell. This will happen when the electrolyte level reaches the bottom of the central tube and prevents further escape of air displaced by the topping-up water. Lift the tube slightly, to allow the small amount of water in the flange to drain into the cell. The electrolyte level will then be correct.

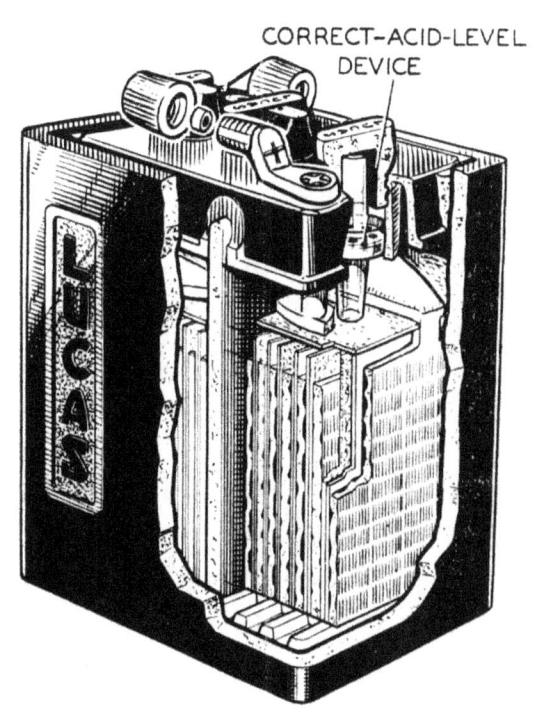

Fig. 1. Battery model PU7E/9.

Batteries without Correct-Acid-Level Devices.

Remove the battery lid, unscrew the filler plugs, and, if necessary, add distilled water carefully to each cell to bring the electrolyte just level with the top edges of the separators.

The Lucas Battery Filler will be found helpful when topping-up, since it ensures that the correct electrolyte level is obtained automatically and also prevents distilled water from being spilled over the battery top.

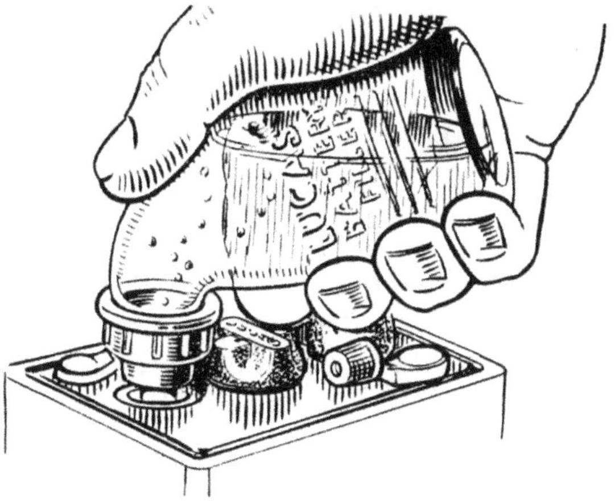

Cleaning.

Wipe away all dirt and moisture from the top of the battery.

Fig. 2. Using a Lucas Battery Filler.

Checking the Condition of the Battery.

Occasionally check the condition of the battery by taking measurements of the specific gravity of the electrolyte in each of the cells. A small-volume hydrometer is required for this purpose — this instrument resembles a syringe containing a graduated float which indicates the specific gravity of the acid in the cell from which the sample has been taken. Do not take measurements immediately after "topping-up" the cells as the electrolyte will not be thoroughly mixed. Before taking a sample, tilt the battery to bring sufficient electrolyte above the separators.

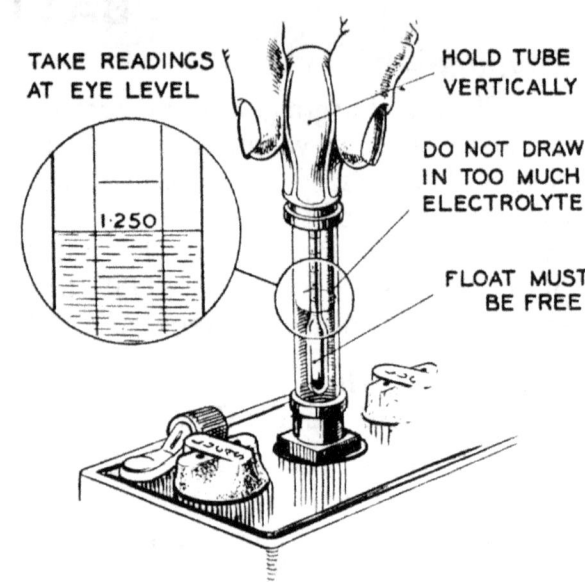

Fig. 3. Taking Hydrometer Readings.

Specific gravity readings and their indications are as follows :—

Climates below 90° F.		Climates above 90° F.
1·270—1·290 ...	Cell fully charged	1·210—1·230
1·190—1·210 ...	Cell about half discharged	1·130—1·150
1·110—1·130 ...	Cell completely discharged	1·050—1·070

The reading for each of the cells should be approximately the same. If one cell gives a value very different from the rest, it may be that acid has been spilled or has leaked from the particular cell, or there may be a short circuit between the plates, and in this case the battery should be examined by a Lucas Service Depot or Agent.

Never leave the battery in a discharged condition. If the motor cycle is to be out of use for any length of time, have the battery fully charged and every fortnight give it a short refreshing charge to prevent any tendency for the plates to become permanently sulphated.

Detachable Cable Connectors.

When connecting batteries with detachable cable connectors, unscrew the knurled nut and withdraw the collet or cone-shaped insert, noting that it is not interchangeable with the collet in the other terminal. Bare the end of the cable for about one inch and thread the bared end through the knurled nut and collet. Bend back the cable strands over the narrow end of the collet, insert the collet and cable into the terminal and secure the connection by tightening the knurled nut.

GENERATOR

Output Control.

The generator is either a two-brush or a four-brush shunt wound machine and works in conjunction with a regulator unit to give compensated voltage control. Although combined structurally, the regulator and cut-out are electrically separate. Both are accurately adjusted during manufacture and should not be tampered with.

The regulator provides a completely automatic control. It causes the generator output to vary according to the load on the battery and its state of charge. When the battery is discharged the generator gives a high output, but if the battery is fully charged then the generator gives only a trickle charge to keep the battery in a good condition. In addition to controlling the output of the generator according to the condition of the battery, the regulator provides for an increase of output to balance the current taken by the lamps when in use.

The purpose of the cut-out is to connect the generator to the battery only when the engine speed is high enough to permit charging. When the speed drops to a low value the cut-out contacts open and prevent the battery discharging through the generator windings.

The regulator and cut-out are accurately set during manufacture and in normal service the battery will be kept in a good condition. If due to special running conditions you should find that the battery is not kept in a charged condition or is being overcharged, we advise you to have the settings checked by a Lucas Service Depot or Agent. Do not attempt adjustment yourself.

Ammeter Readings.

Normally, during day-time running when the battery is in good condition, the generator gives only a trickle charge so that the ammeter needle should show only a small deflection to the "+" side of the scale.

A discharge reading may be observed immediately after switching on the headlamp. This usually happens after a long run when the battery voltage is high. After a short time the battery voltage will drop and the regulator will respond, causing the generator output to balance the lamp load.

Lubrication.

Models E3H and E3HM are fitted with a lubricator on the commutator end bracket which must be given a few drops of high quality thin machine oil every 1,000 miles. The bearing at the driving end is packed with grease and will last until the machine is taken down for a general overhaul.

Models E3L, E3LM, E3N, C35S and C35SD. No lubrication is required to these models as ball bearings are fitted at both ends. These bearings are packed with grease during assembly and will last until the machine is taken down for a general overhaul. Similarly, the gear drive to the distributor mounted at the driving end of the model C35SD generator should require repacking with grease only at overhaul.

Models MC45 and MC45L. Except in certain instances where the motor cycle manufacturer fits end-brackets to these models, no lubrication is necessary since the armature is mounted on a sleeve which fits over the end of the crankshaft, thus eliminating the need for bearings in the generator itself.

In order to prevent oil from the engine getting into the generator, an oil seal is fitted at the drive end of these generators. If required, replacement oil seals can be obtained from the engine manufacturer.

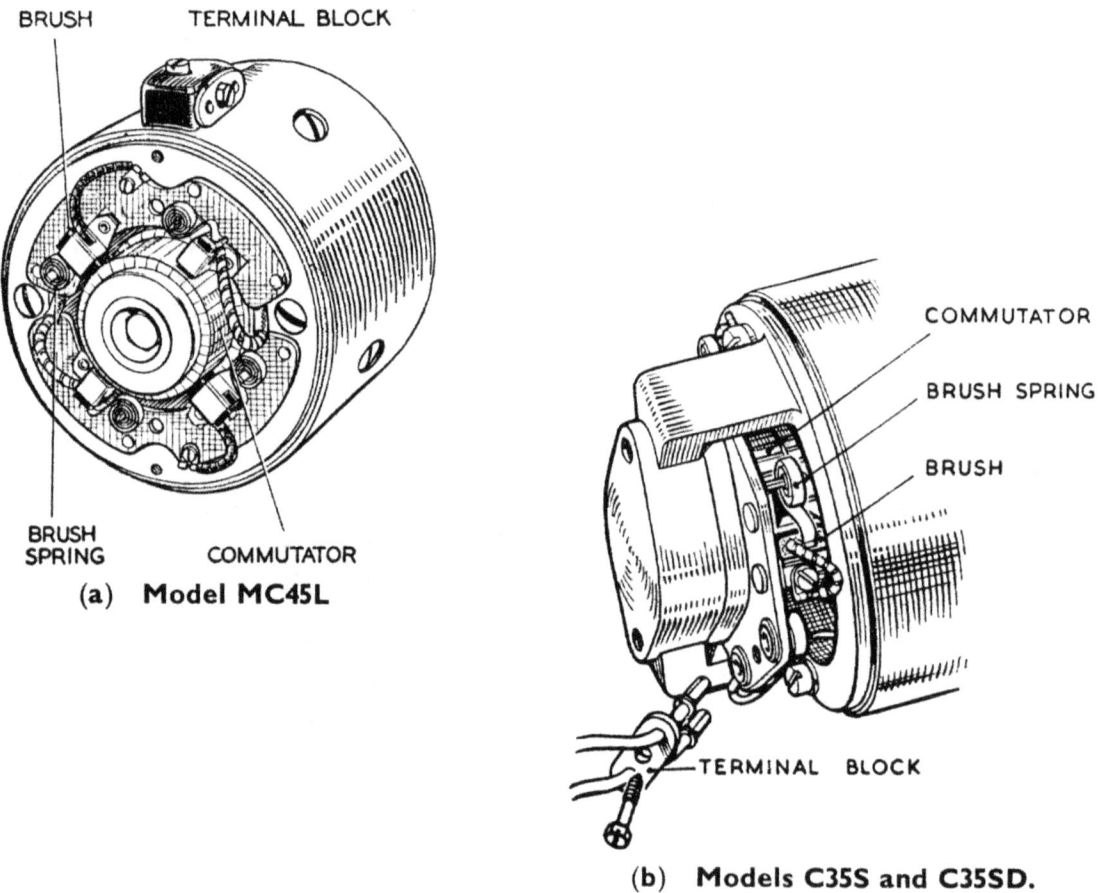

Fig. 4. Generators with Covers Removed.

Inspection of Commutator and Brushgear.

About every 6,000 miles remove the commutator cover and inspect the commutator and brushgear.

The brushes, which are held in boxes by means of springs, must make firm contact with the commutator. Move each brush to see that it is free to slide in its holder; if it sticks, remove it and clean with a petrol-moistened cloth. Care must be taken to replace the brushes in their original positions, otherwise they will not "bed" properly on the commutator. If after long service the brushes have become worn to $\frac{5}{16}$" (or $\frac{9}{32}$" with Models MC45 and MC45L) in length, replace them. Always use genuine Lucas brushes, which should be fitted by a Service Agent so that they can be properly bedded to the commutator.

Examine the commutator. It should be free from any trace of oil or dirt and should have a highly polished appearance. Clean a dirty or blackened commutator by pressing a clean dry cloth against it whilst the engine is slowly turned over by means of the kick starter crank. (It is

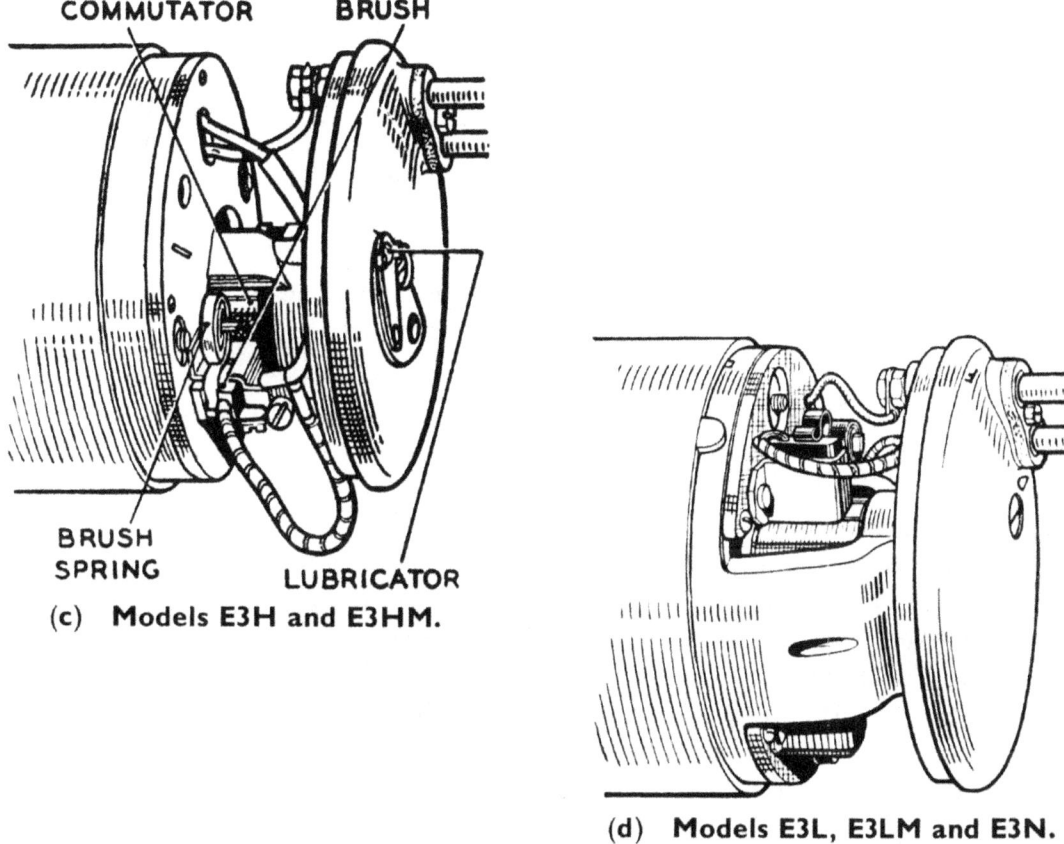

(c) Models E3H and E3HM.

(d) Models E3L, E3LM and E3N.

Fig. 5. Generators with Covers Removed.

best to remove the sparking plug before doing this). If the commutator is very dirty, moisten the cloth with petrol.

When replacing the cover on generators MC45 and MC45L, be careful to position the rubber seal between cover and yoke correctly.

Before tightening the cover of an E3L generator, a locating slot in the cover must first coincide with a projection on the generator body.

MAGNETOS
Rotating Armature Models

These magnetos have the magnet cast in the body and the armature and contact breaker rotate within the casting. Two designs of contact breaker are in common use. Single-cylinder magnetos usually employ the face cam type Fig. 6 while magnetos for twin-cylinder engines have the ring cam type shown in Fig. 7.

Ignition Timing Control.

Some magnetos are provided with a centrifugal timing device which varies the firing point according to the speed of the engine, thus relieving the rider of the necessity for adjustment of a hand ignition control.

If, however, automatic control is not provided, retard the hand ignition control for starting but advance it as soon as the engine is running at speed. For normal running, the control should be kept in the advanced position and retarded only when the engine is "labouring" on full throttle.

Any slackness in the cable can be taken up by sliding the water-proofing rubber shroud up the cable and turning the exposed hexagon adjuster. After adjusting, return the rubber shroud to its original position.

When renewing the cable control do not remove the cam from its housing.

Slide the water-proofing rubber shroud up the cable and remove the cable casing by unscrewing the control barrel at the base. Draw the cable and plunger upwards to the fullest extent and slip the nipple sideways out of the hole in the plunger.

Thread the replacement cable through the casing and solder the nipple to the end of it. Slip the nipple sideways into the hole in the plunger and screw the casing home. Replace the water-proofing shroud.

Every 3,000 miles.

Check the setting of the contact breaker gap. To do this, remove the contact breaker cover, slowly hand crank the engine until the contacts are fully open and insert a 0·012"—0·015" (0·3 mm.—0·4 mm.) feeler gauge in the gap. A gauge for this purpose is provided on the spanner supplied with each magneto. The gauge should be a sliding fit between the contacts.

To adjust the gap, slacken the lock nut and turn the contact screw by its hexagon head until the gap is set to the gauge thickness. Tighten the locknut and re-check the setting.

Lubricate the moving parts of the contact breaker as follows :—

Face Cam Type.

The cam face is lubricated from a wick contained in the base of the rotating contact breaker. To reach the wick, remove the screw securing the moving contact spring and lift off the backing spring and contact spring. Remove the screw carrying the lubrication wick and add a few drops of thin machine oil to the wick.

Unscrew the contact breaker securing screw and remove the contact breaker. Take the tappet which operates the contact spring from its housing and lightly smear with thin machine oil.

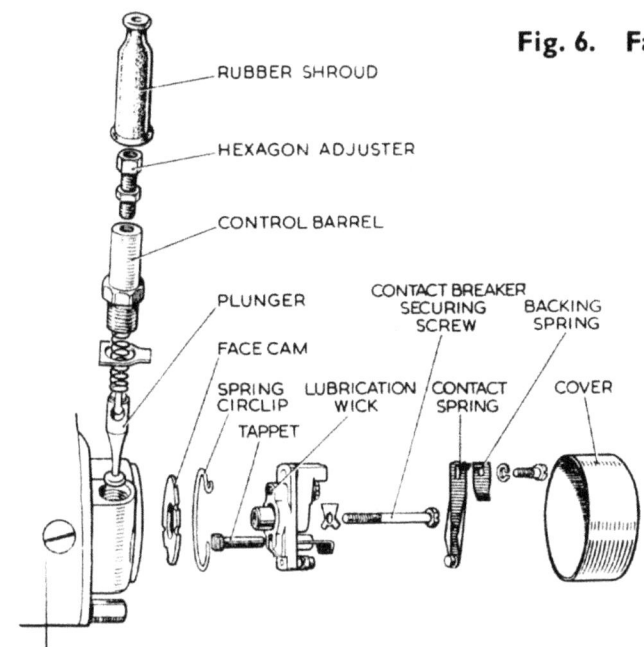

Fig. 6. Face cam type contact breaker.

Extract the spring circlip and remove the face cam. When a manual timing control is fitted, removal and refitting of the cam will be made easier if the control lever is half retarded, thus taking the cam away from its stop pin.

Remove any dirt from the surface of the cam and lightly smear both sides with Mobilgrease No. 2.

When refitting the contact breaker on magnetos having manual timing control, ensure that the stop peg in the housing and the plunger of the timing control engage with their respective slots. A recess is provided for the "eye" of the circlip. When refitting the spring arm, ensure that the backing spring is fitted on top with its bent portion facing outwards (see Fig. 6).

Ring Cam Type.

The cam is supplied with lubricant from a felt strip contained in a recess in the inside of the contact breaker housing. Oil from the felt strip is transferred through a circular wick, set in a small hole, to the surface of the cam.

Remove the contact breaker cover. Take out the hexagon-headed screw from the centre of the contact breaker and carefully lever the contact breaker from the tapered shaft.

Remove the cam ring which is a sliding fit in its housing. When a manual timing control is fitted, removal and refitting of the cam will be made easier if the control lever is half retarded, thus taking the cam away from its stop pin.

Wipe the cam clean and lightly smear the inside and outside surfaces with Mobilgrease No. 2. Add a few drops of thin machine oil to the felt strip and to the circular wick.

Push aside the rocker arm retaining spring, lift off the rocker arm, and apply sufficient Mobilgrease No. 2 to fill the grease retaining groove around the pivot pin.

Replace the rocker arm and rocker arm retaining spring. Replace the cam, taking care that, if fitted, the stop peg in the housing and the timing control plunger engage with their respective slots.

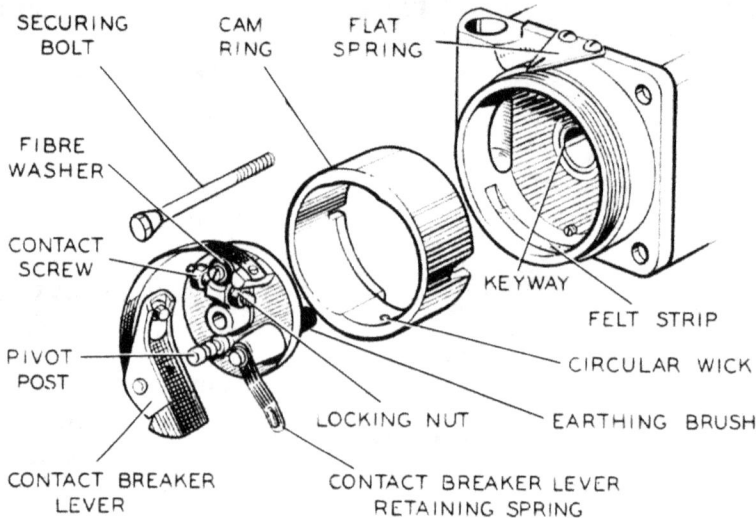

Fig. 7. Ring cam type contact breaker.

If an earthing brush is fitted at the back of the contact breaker base, ensure that it is clean and can move freely in its holder, before re-fitting the contact breaker.

When refitting the contact breaker, see that the projecting key on the tapered portion of the contact breaker base engages with the keyway cut in the magneto spindle, otherwise the timing of the magneto will be affected. Replace the contact breaker securing screw and tighten with care.

Every 6,000 miles.

Repeat the procedure carried out every 3,000 miles.

Remove the contact breaker cover and high tension pick-up mouldings. Thoroughly clean the inside and outside of the magneto using a clean dry fluffless cloth, if necessary, moistening it with petrol to remove any grease from the high tension pick-up mouldings and contact breaker contacts. Ensure that the pick-up brush moves freely in its holder. Renew the brush if it is worn to $\frac{1}{8}''$ above the shoulder. Clean the slip ring, track and flanges by pressing the cloth on them while the engine is cranked by hand.

Ensure that the gasket between the pick-up moulding(s) and the magneto body is in good condition before reassembling.

Examine the contacts when the contact breaker is removed for lubrication. If the contacts are pitted or piled, they should be trimmed with a carborundum stone, silicon carbide paper, or very fine emery cloth.

Contacts do not retain a polished appearance when in use and, if operating correctly, will have a dull grey appearance.

Every Two Years.

About every two years, or when the engine is given a general overhaul, the magneto should be dismantled at a Lucas Service Depot or Agent, where the weights, springs and toggles of the centrifugal timing control mechanism will be examined and lubricated, and the armature bearings repacked with grease.

Renewing High Tension Cable.

When high tension cable shows signs of cracking or perishing, replace it using 7 mm. p.v.c.-covered or neoprene-covered rubber insulated ignition cable. To replace a high tension cable proceed as follows :—

Remove the metal washer and moulded terminal from the defective cable. Thread the new cable through the moulded terminal and cut back the insulation for about $\frac{1}{4}''$. Pass the exposed strands through the metal washer and bend them back radially. Screw the terminal into the pick-up moulding.

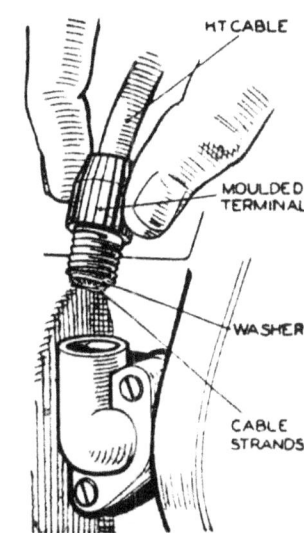

Fig. 8. Method of Fitting Cable to High Tension Pick-up.

Magneto-to-Engine Timing.

Always follow the engine manufacturer's instructions when re-timing a magneto to the engine. If, however, these instructions are not immediately available, the magneto-to-engine timing can (as a temporary measure only) be set as follows :—

Magnetos fitted with centrifugal timing control :
Contact breaker to open when the piston in the cylinder under compression is at T.D.C.

Magnetos fitted with manual timing control :
With the control lever set to the fully retarded position the contact breaker to open when the piston in the cylinder under compression is at T.D.C.

Rotating Magnet Models

In this magneto the less robust parts such as the coil, condenser, and contact breaker, remain stationary whilst the magnet and cam rotate. A centrifugal timing device is fitted on the driving shaft to vary the firing point according to the speed of the engine, thus relieving the rider of the necessity for adjustment of a hand ignition control.

After first 500 miles and, thereafter, every 3,000 miles.

Check the setting of the contact breaker gap. To do this, remove the cable cover, slowly hand crank the engine until the contacts are fully open and insert a 0·010"—0·012" (0·25 mm.—0·3 mm.) feeler gauge in the gap. The gauge should be a sliding fit between the contacts.

To adjust the gap, slacken the two screws securing the fixed contact plate and move the plate until the gap is set to the gauge thickness.

Apply a spot of clean engine oil to the visible end of the contact breaker pivot post. **No oil must be allowed on or near the contacts.**

Every 6,000 miles.

Remove the cable cover and clean the contacts. To do this, slacken the nut securing the low tension terminal assembly and withdraw the spring and contact breaker lever.

If the contacts are rough or pitted, polish them with fine carborundum stone, silicon carbide paper, or very fine emery cloth. Afterwards, clean the contacts with petrol or methylated spirits (denatured alcohol).

Smear the pivot post with Mobilgrease No. 2.

When refitting the contact breaker, see that the components are assembled in the order illustrated.

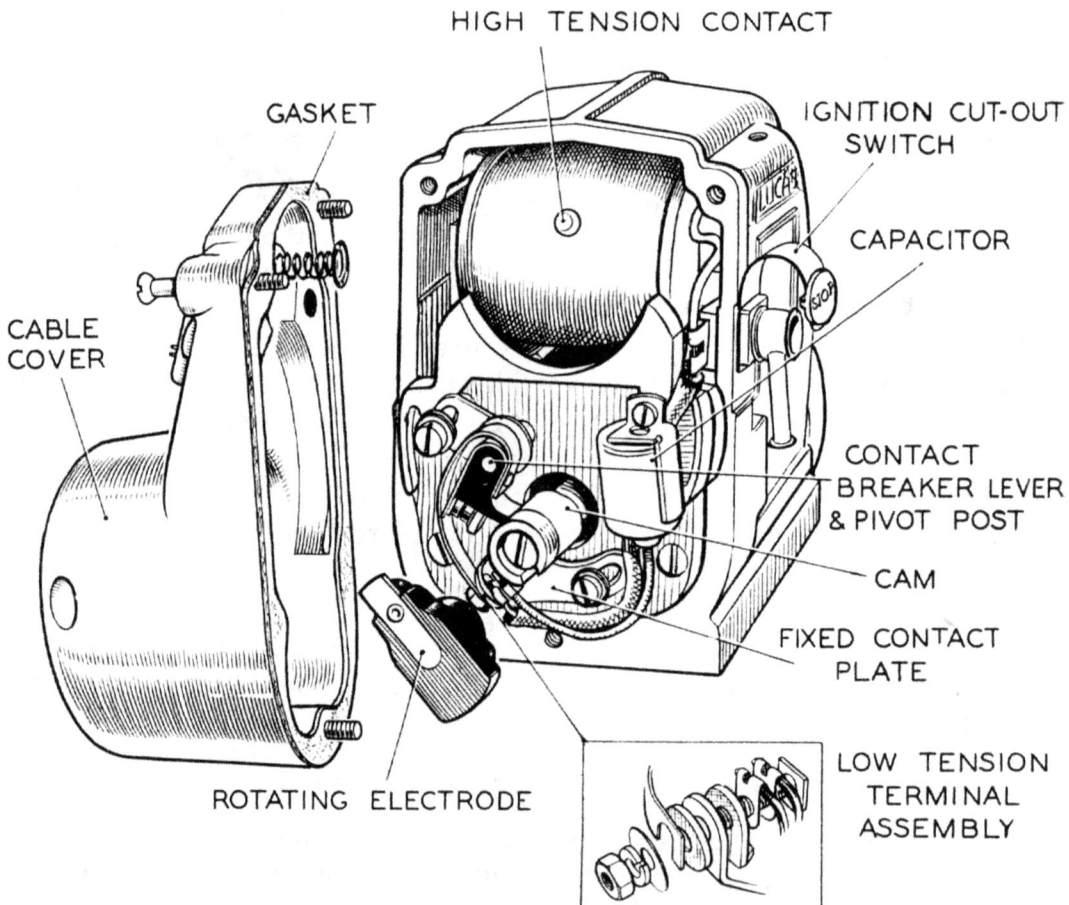

Fig. 9. Contact Breaker End View.

Every Two Years.

About every two years or when the engine is overhauled, the magneto should be dismantled at a Lucas Service Depot or Agent, where the weights, springs and toggles of the centrifugal timing control mechanism will be examined and lubricated with medium viscosity engine oil and the rotor bearings repacked with grease.

Renewing High Tension Cable.

When high tension cable shows signs of cracking or perishing, it must be replaced with 7 mm. p.v.c.-covered or neoprene-covered rubber insulated ignition cable. To do this, remove the cable cover, unscrew the cable securing screw and withdraw the defective cable. Cut the new cable to the required length and push one end well home into its terminal. Tighten the cable securing screw which will pierce the insulation and contact the cable core.

COIL IGNITION EQUIPMENT

Coil ignition equipment fitted to motor cycles comprises an ignition coil and a contact breaker, and in the case of twin and four-cylinder machines, a high tension distributor. Housed beneath the contact breaker base is a centrifugal timing control, which automatically varies the firing point according to the speed of the engine.

An ignition warning light is usually fitted in a prominent position (e.g., headlamp body) to remind the rider when the engine is stationary and the ignition is switched on. It will also light when the engine is idling. After long service the bulb may burn out. However, this will not affect the ignition system, but the bulb must be replaced as soon as possible as a safeguard for the ignition coil and battery.

When the lamp is mounted in an instrument panel it may be necessary to remove the panel front, when the bulb can be unscrewed from its holder. With other types the bulb can be removed when the chromium-plated bezel is unscrewed.

If the warning light is combined with the ammeter in the headlamp, remove the lamp front and reflector to gain access to the bulb.

Bulb replacement :—
    Lucas No. 998 6-volt 0·1-amp. M.E.S.

Note :—Earlier models were fitted with a 2·5-volt 0·2-amp. M.E.S. bulb, Lucas No. 970, which was used in conjunction with a series-wound resistor in the bulb holder.

After first 500 miles and, thereafter, every 6,000 miles.

Smear the surface of the cam very lightly with Mobilgrease No. 2 or, if this is not available, with clean engine oil.

Apply a spot of clean engine oil to the visible end of the contact breaker pivot post. **Do not allow oil or grease to get on or near the contacts.**

If a lubricator is fitted on the distributor shank, add a few drops of thin machine oil.

Lubricate the centrifugal timing mechanism as follows :—

D.K. types (similar to Fig. 10)
Unscrew the two screws securing the contact breaker base plate to the distributor, and lubricate with thin machine oil the centrifugal timing control thus exposed, paying particular attention to the pivots. Refit the base plate, and secure by means of the fixing screws.

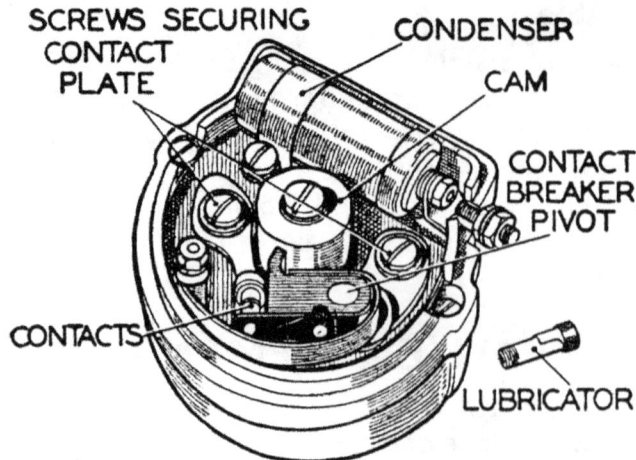

Fig. 10. Model DK type contact breaker.

Model DIA2 (Fig. 10)

Take the distributor off the machine and remove cover and rotor. Inject a little thin machine oil through the aperture between cam and contact breaker base plate.

To lubricate the cam bearing, remove the screw from inside the rotor boss and apply a few drops of thin machine oil to the tapped hole thus exposed. The spindle is drilled and cross-drilled to enable oil to find its way to the cam bearing.

Note :—If required, replacement oil seals, driving dogs or distance collars can be obtained from the engine manufacturer.

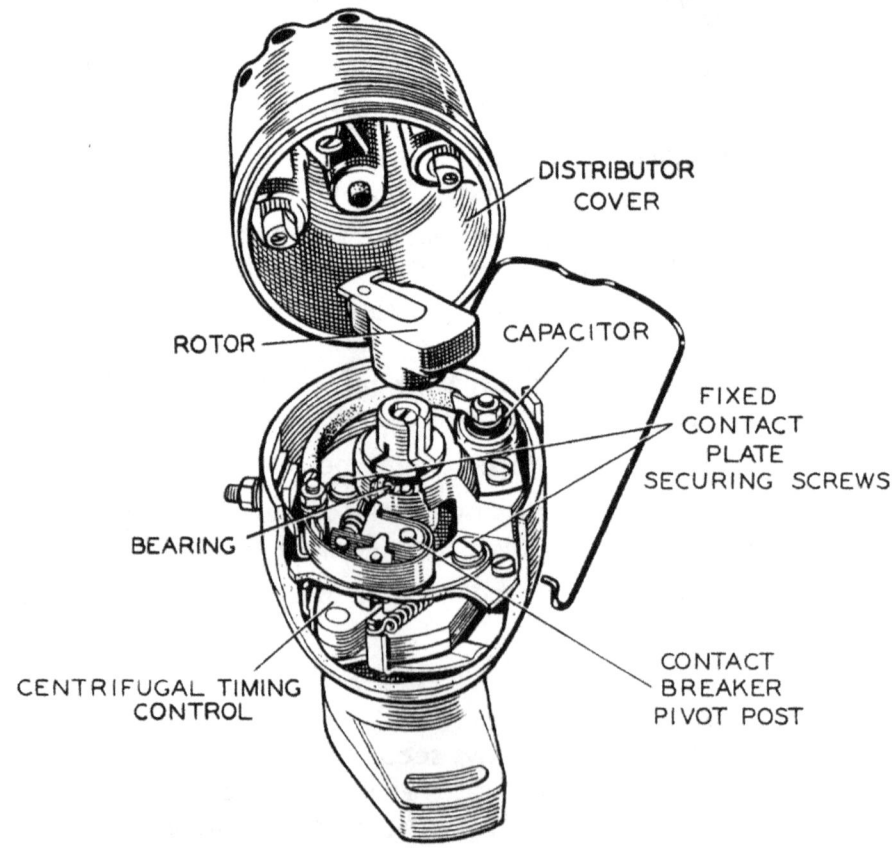

Fig. 11 Model DIA2 distributor sectioned to show centrifugal timing control.

Cleaning.

Thoroughly clean the inside and outside of the distributor using a clean dry fluffless cloth, if necessary moistening it with petrol to remove any grease from the high tension cover and contact breaker contacts. Ensure that the pick-up brush moves freely in its holder.

Examine the contacts. If they are rough or pitted, polish them with fine carborundum stone, silicon carbide paper or very fine emery cloth.

Afterwards, clean the contacts with petrol or methylated spirits (denatured alcohol).

After cleaning, check the contact breaker setting.

Contact Breaker Setting.

Check the contact breaker gap after the first 500 miles, running, and subsequently every 6,000 miles. To do this, remove the contact breaker cover, slowly hand crank the engine until the contacts are fully open and insert a 0·014"—0·016" (0·35 mm.—0·40 mm.) gauge in the gap. The gauge should be a sliding fit between the contacts.

To adjust the gap, slacken the two screws securing the fixed contact plate and move the plate until the gap is set to the gauge thickness. After setting the gap tighten the securing screws and on two and four-cylinder models check the gap for other positions of the cam.

Apply a spot of clean engine oil to the visible end of the contact breaker pivot post.

Renewing High Tension Cable.

When high tension cable shows signs of cracking or perishing, it must be replaced, using 7 mm. p.v.c.-covered or neoprene-covered rubber insulated ignition cable.

To fit new cable to a high tension cover having vertical outlets, proceed as follows :—

Remove the metal washer and moulded terminal from the defective cable. Thread the new cable through the moulded terminal and cut back the insulation for about $\frac{1}{4}"$. Pass the exposed strands through the metal washer and bend them back radially. Screw the terminal into the high tension cover.

To fit new cable to a high tension cover having horizontal outlets, proceed as follows :—

Slacken the screw on the inside of the high tension cover which secures the defective cable in the moulding.

Cut the new cable to the length required and push firmly home in the moulding. Tighten the cable securing screw, which will pierce the rubber insulation to make good contact with the cable core.

The Ignition Coil.

The coil requires no attention whatever beyond keeping its exterior clean, particularly between the terminals, and occasionally checking that the terminal connections are tight.

HEADLAMPS

There are a number of different models of Lucas headlamps. Briefly, they can be divided into the following groups :—

1. Separate lens and reflector. Bayonet-cap bulb.
2. Combined lens and reflector, *i.e.*, Lucas Light Unit. Bayonet-cap bulb.
3. Lucas Light Unit. Prefocus bulb.

The above combinations are incorporated in either a lamp body or a nacelle-type extension of the motor cycle forks.

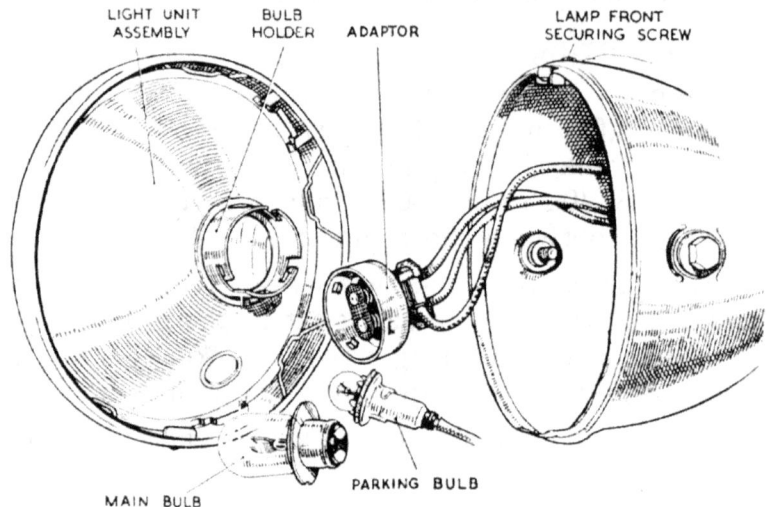

Fig. 12. Model SSU Headlamp with " Prefocus " Bulb and Light Unit.

Setting and Focusing.

Set the headlamp so that when the motor cycle carries its normal load the driving beam is projected straight ahead and parallel with the road surface.

Many garages possess a Lucas Beam Setter. These are scientific instruments enabling accurate beam setting to be effected. Motor cycle owners are strongly advised to make use of this service whenever possible. When such facilities are not available, the headlamp can be set by marking off a smooth blank wall and shining the lamp on it from a distance of twenty-five feet. Details are shown in Fig. 13.

On machines where the Light Unit is mounted in a nacelle or other special fitting, the motor cycle manufacturer's handbook should be referred to for instructions on setting the lamp.

The need to carry out focusing has been eliminated with headlamps carrying a " prefocus " bulb in the Light Unit assembly.

Other headlamps must be focused so that, when the main driving light is switched on, a uniform beam without a dark centre is given. If the bulb needs adjusting, remove the lamp front and reflector, as described on the next page, and slacken the bulb holder clamping clip at the back of the reflector. Move the bulb holder backwards and forwards until the correct position is obtained, and then tighten the clamping clip.

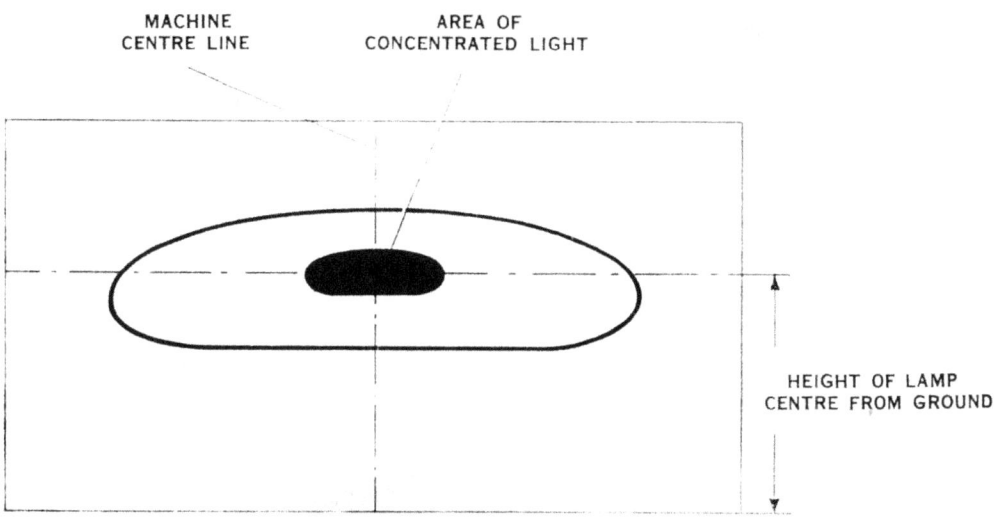

Fig. 13. Headlamp setting diagram.

(a) Front of motor cycle to be square with screen.

(b) Motor cycle to be carrying normal load and standing on level ground.

(c) Recommended distance for setting is at least 25 feet.

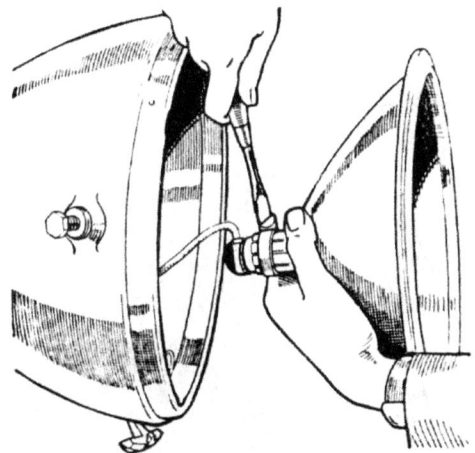

Fig. 14. Focusing Headlamp.

Removing Headlamp Front.

On earlier models, remove the lamp front by releasing the spring catch at the bottom of the lamp. The reflector is secured to the lamp body by means of a rubber bead, and can be withdrawn when the rubber is removed. When re-fitting, locate the thinner lip of the rubber bead between the reflector rim and the edge of the lamp body. To replace the front, locate the metal tongue in the slot at the top of the lamp, press the front on and secure by means of the fixing catch.

On later models, remove the lamp front by slackening the securing screw at the top or bottom of the lamp. It will then be possible to detach the front rim complete with Light Unit assembly. To replace, locate the

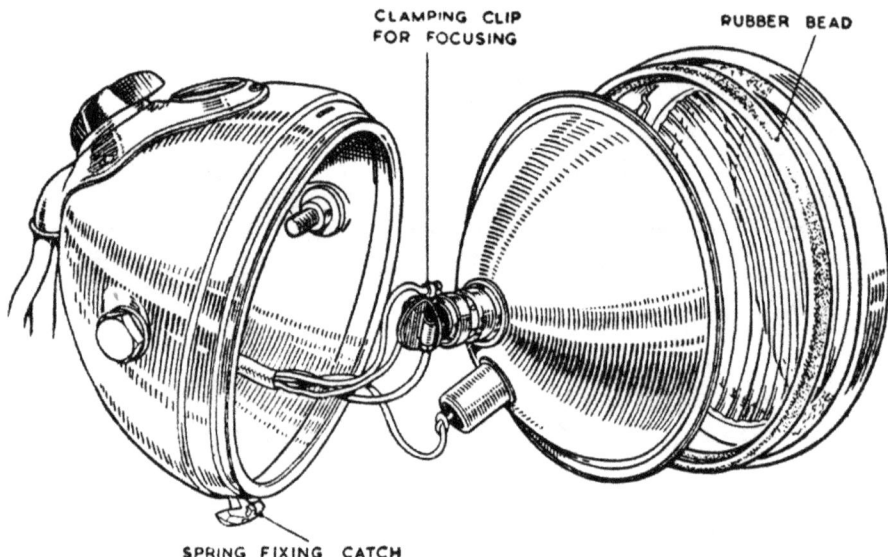

Fig. 15. "MU" Headlamp with Front and Reflector removed.

bottom of the Light Unit assembly in the lamp body, press the front on and secure in position by tightening the securing screw.

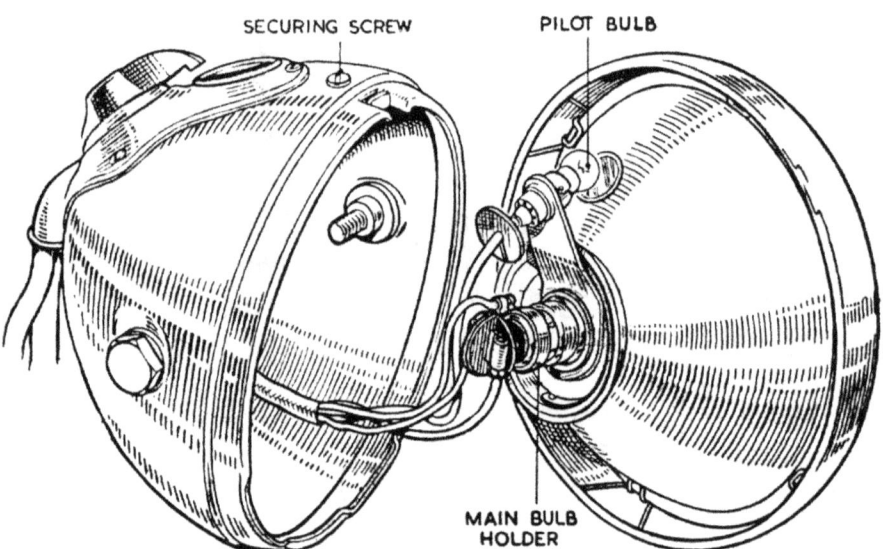

Fig. 16. An early Model "SSU" Headlamp with Light Unit and Bayonet Cap Bulb.

Replacement of Bulbs.

When the replacement of a bulb is necessary, it is important not only that the same size bulb is fitted, but also that it has a high efficiency and will focus in the reflector. Cheap and inferior replacement bulbs often have the filament of such a shape that correct focusing is not possible.

Lucas Authorised Spare Bulbs are specially tested to check that the filament is in the correct position to give the best results with Lucas lamps. To assist in identification, Lucas bulbs are marked on the metal cap with a number. When fitting a replacement, see that it has the same number as the original bulb.

When fitting a headlamp bulb, care must be taken to insert it the correct way round, *i.e.*, with the dipped beam filament above the centre filament. To assist, bulbs are usually marked TOP on the metal cap. In the case of " prefocus " bulbs, there is only one location for the bulb, to ensure correct positioning.

On lamps having separate lens and reflector the bulb is accessible for replacement when the front rim and glass are removed.

On lamps incorporating the Lucas Light Unit, the main bulb is accessible for replacement when the front rim and Light Unit are removed. To replace " prefocus " bulbs, twist the adaptor in an anti-clockwise direction and pull it off. The bulb can now be removed from the rear of the reflector. Place the correct replacement bulb in the holder, engage the projections on the inside of the adaptor with the slots in the bulb holder, press on and secure by twisting to the right. Lamps fitted with bayonet cap main bulbs have the bulb holder fitted into the rear of the Light Unit. Detach the bulb holder, held in position by two spring loaded pegs, fit the new bulb in the correct position, and refit the bulb holder.

After fitting a new bulb check the beam setting and, if necessary, re-adjust.

Cleaning.

Care must be taken when handling lamps with separate lens and reflector, to prevent the reflector from becoming finger-marked. If it does become marked, however, a transparent and colourless covering enables any finger marks to be removed by polishing with a chamois leather or a very soft dry cloth. Do not use metal polish on the reflector. The lamp body can be cleaned with a good car polish, and the plated rim polished with a chamois leather or soft dry cloth, after any dirt has been washed off with water.

Lucas Light Unit reflectors do not require cleaning and no attempt should be made to do so.

Dipper Switch.

Every 5,000 miles the moving parts of the dipper switch should be lubricated with a thin machine oil.

PARKING LIGHTS

On headlamps having separate lens and reflector, the parking light bulb is accessible for replacement when the front rim and lens assembly is removed.

On the majority of headlamps fitted with a Lucas Light Unit the parking light bulb is accessible for replacement when the front rim and Light Unit assembly is removed. The parking bulb is carried on a bracket on the main bulb holder, or on a small metal plate in the case of lamps with underslung parking lights. On more recent Light Units the parking light bulb holder is a push-fit in the reflector (see Fig. 12).

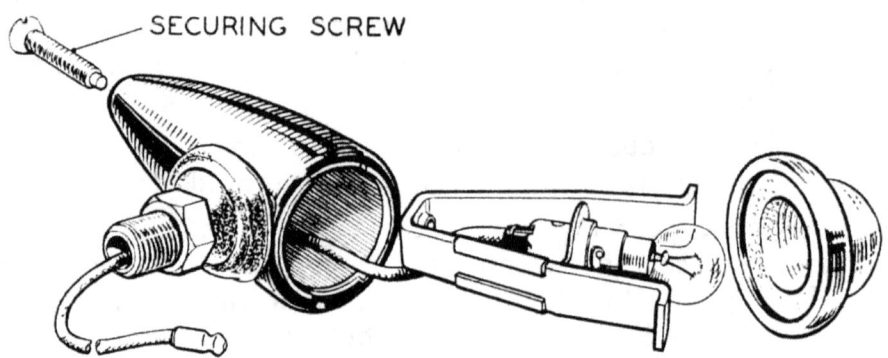

Fig. 17. Parking Light Model 516.

Certain motorcycles have parking lights of the type illustrated in Fig. 17. Access to the bulb in these lamps is gained by slackening the screw at the rear of the body shell and pulling the bulb holder rim and lens away from the lamp.

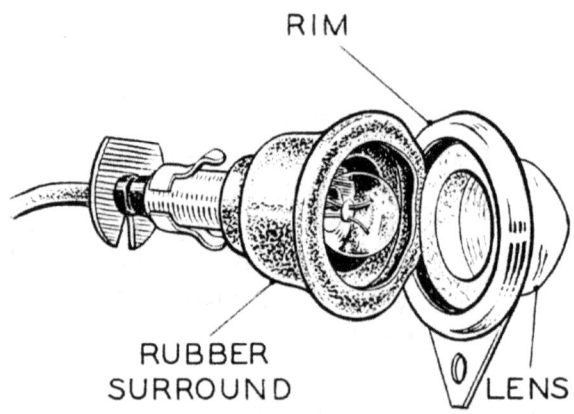

Fig. 18. Parking Light Model 550.

Certain motor cycles have flush-fitting parking lights (see Fig. 18), pressed into sockets in the headlamp nacelle. To reach the bulb in these lamps, remove the chromium-plated rim and peel back the rubber surround to release the frosted-glass lens.

Correct replacement bulbs are :—

Headlamps, Models "M" and "MU" (separate lens and reflector). Lucas No. 200. 6-volt 3-watt. Small bayonet cap, S.C.C.

All subsequent Headlamps, Models "SS," "SSU," etc. Lucas No. 988. 6-volt 3-watt. Miniature bayonet cap.

REAR LIGHTS

Replacement Bulbs.

In the United Kingdom, the correct size of bulb to be used for rear illumination is based on the cubic capacity of the engine. Solo machines of 250 c.c. or under may be fitted with 3-watt bulbs. Motor cycle combinations and solo machines exceeding 250 c.c. are required to be fitted with 6-watt bulbs.

Bulbs can be identified by a number, usually marked on the metal cap. When changing a defective bulb, the replacement should bear the same number as the original.

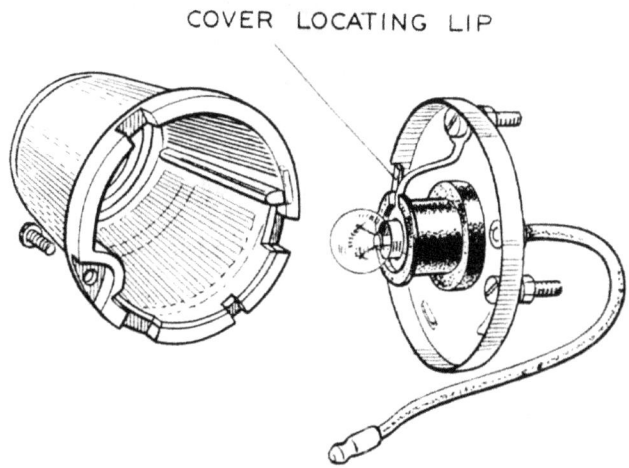

Fig. 19. Model 544 Tail Lamp.
Bulb type : Miniature Edison Screw.
Access to the bulb is gained by removing the screw on the bayonet fixing cover.

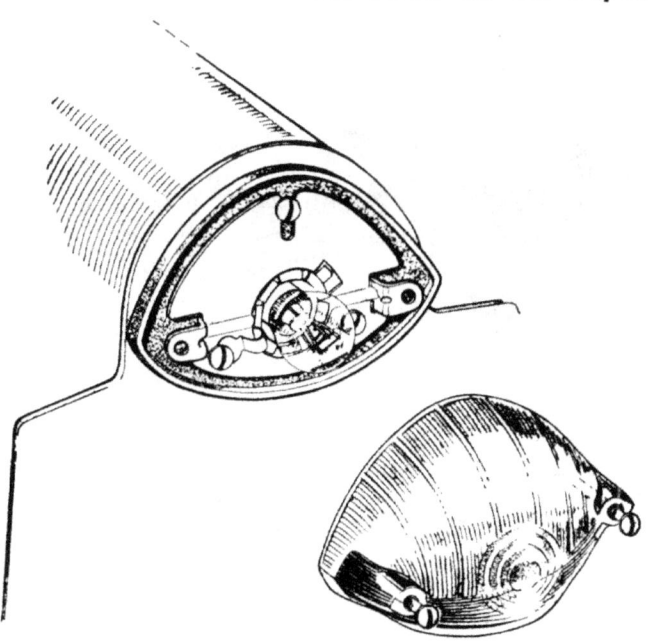

Fig. 20. Model 525 Stop-Tail Lamp.
Bulb type : Non-reversible Small Bayonet Cap.

(This lamp is also made for Tail illumination only. Bulb type : Miniature Bayonet Cap).

Fig. 21. Model 564 Stop-Tail Lamp with Reflex Reflector.

Bulb type : Non-reversible Small Bayonet Cap.

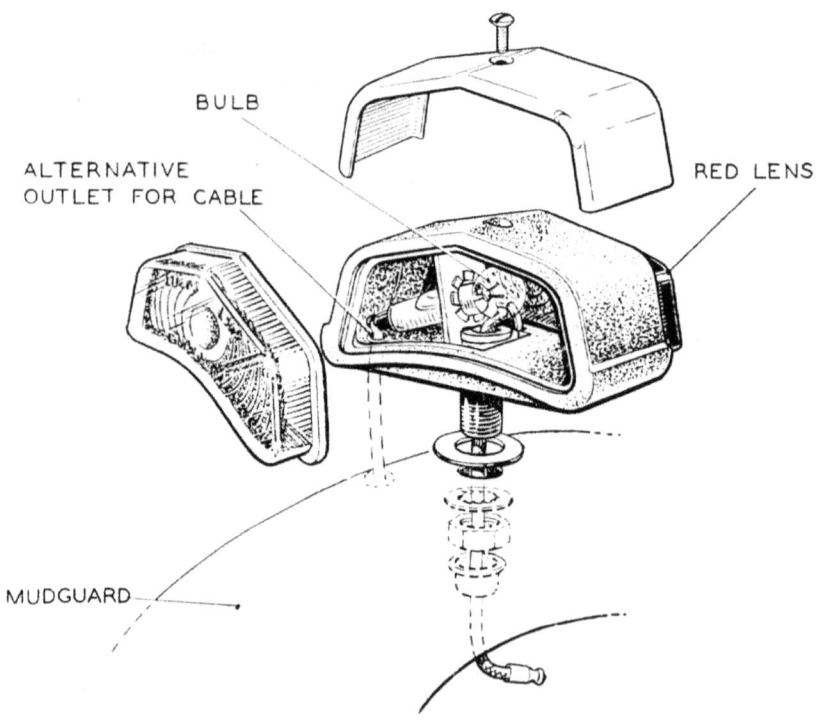

Fig. 22. Model 569 Sidecar Lamp.

Bulb type : Miniature Bayonet Cap.

HORNS

Horns are pre-set to give their best performance and, in general, no further adjustment is necessary.

If the horn becomes uncertain in its action, giving only a choking sound, or fails to vibrate, it does not follow that the horn has broken down. First ascertain that the trouble is not due to some outside source, e.g., a discharged battery, a loose connection, or short-circuit in the wiring of the horn. In particular, ascertain that the hornpush securing strap is in good electrical contact with the handlebars.

It is also possible that the performance of a horn may be upset by its mounting becoming loose.

Adjustment (Model HF1234 only).

The following adjustment will not alter the pitch of the note. It will take up any wear of the moving parts which, if not corrected, may result in roughness of tone and loss of power.

Accurate adjustment requires the use of specialised instruments, and tools, but the owner-rider, who may not possess these instruments, can carry out the following procedure if the horn performance is considered to have deteriorated:—

Operate the horn push and turn the adjustment screw anti-clockwise until the horn just fails to sound. Release the horn push and turn the adjustment screw clockwise for six notches, i.e., a quarter of a turn, when the original performance should be restored. If further adjustment seems to be necessary, turn the screw one notch at a time clockwise.

Note:—A few HF1234 horns made during 1950-51 were not provided with the above adjustment screw. No adjustment is therefore possible with these horns. Similarly, no adjustment is possible with Models HF1440 and HF1849 horns.

If the cause of the trouble cannot be found, do not attempt to dismantle the horn, but return it to a Lucas Service Depot for examination.

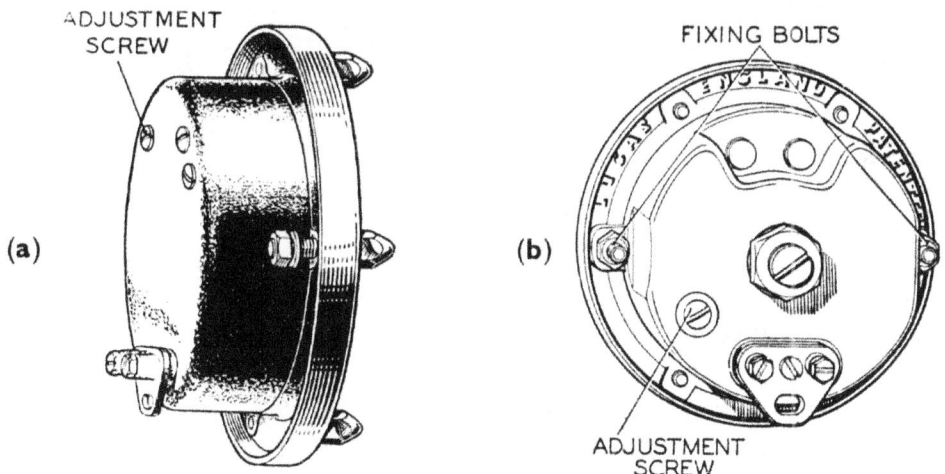

Fig. 23. Rear view of HF1234 horns, showing position of adjustment screw fitted to (a) Pre-1951 models and (b) Post-1951 models.

WIRING

On many older motor cycles the NEGATIVE terminal of the battery is earthed. More recent machines, however, have the POSITIVE terminal earthed.

Before making any alterations to the wiring or removing the switch from the headlamp or instrument panel, disconnect the battery to avoid the danger of short-circuits. Details of the terminal arrangement of King of the Road batteries are given on page 4. With other batteries a short length of cable is connected to the switch cable by means of a brass connector. The connector is insulated by a rubber sleeve which must be pushed back to enable the connector to be unscrewed. Take care to prevent the connector touching any metal part of the frame as this will short-circuit the battery. When connecting up again, refit the rubber sleeve over the connector.

All cables to "MU" and "SSU" headlamps are taken direct to the switch, incorporated together with the ammeter, in a small panel. The panel can be withdrawn when the three securing screws are removed.

The cables are identified by means of coloured braided insulation, coloured sleeving or coloured plastic insulation. The colour scheme and the diagram of connections are given on the wiring diagram. When making a connection to the switch, proceed as follows:—

Bare about $\frac{3}{8}''$ of the cable, twist the wire strands together and turn back about $\frac{1}{8}''$. Remove the grub screw from the appropriate terminal and insert the wire in the terminal post. Refit and tighten the grub screw.

To make a connection to the generator or regulator terminals, slacken the fixing screw on the terminal block and remove the clamping plate. Withdraw the metal ferrules from each terminal. Pass about 1" of cable through the holes in the clamping plate and bare the ends for $\frac{3}{8}''$. Fit the metal ferrules over the cables, bend back the wire strands over the ferrules and push them well home into their terminals. Finally screw down the clamping plate.

The cables connected to the "D" and "F" terminals of the generator and regulator units must not be reversed. To prevent this occurring, the screw in the generator terminal block is off-centre and the screws which secure the regulator terminal clamping plate are of different size.

Copies of wiring diagrams for many British motor cycles can be obtained on request to the Advertising Dept., Great King Street, Birmingham, 19. These diagrams are issued free on receipt of the appropriate information, namely, Make, Model, and Year of manufacture of the machine.

LOCATION AND REMEDY OF FAULTS

Although every precaution is taken to eliminate all possible causes of trouble, failure may occasionally develop through lack of attention to the equipment, or damage to the wiring. The following notes set out the recommended procedure for a systematic examination should an electrical fault be suspected.

If, after carrying out the examination, the cause of the trouble is not found, the owner is advised to get in touch with the nearest Lucas Service Depot or Agent.

CHARGING CIRCUIT

Battery in low state of charge.

(a) This state will be shown by poor light from the lamps and low hydrometer readings (see page 4). Check the ammeter reading when the motor cycle is running steadily in top gear with no lights in use. On motor cycles with coil ignition, the warning light will not go out if the generator fails to charge, or will flicker on and off in the event of intermittent output.

(b) Examine the charging and field circuit wiring, tightening any loose connections, or replacing broken cables.

(c) Examine the generator brushgear and commutator, cleaning if necessary. Have worn brushes replaced. (See page 7).

(d) If the cause of the trouble is still not apparent, have the equipment examined by a Lucas Service Depot or Agent.

Battery Overcharged.

This will be indicated by burnt-out bulbs, very frequent need for topping-up the battery, and high hydrometer readings.

Check the ammeter when the motor cycle is running steadily. With a fully charged battery and no lights or accessories in use, the ammeter needle should show only a small deflection to the "+" side of the scale.

If the ammeter reading is in excess of this value, it is advisable to have the regulator setting checked by a Lucas Service Depot or Agent.

LIGHTING CIRCUITS

Failure of lights.

(a) If only one bulb fails to light, replace with new bulb.

(b) If all lamps fail to light, test the state of charge of battery, re-charging it, if necessary, either by a long period of daytime running or from an independent charging supply.

(c) Examine the wiring for a broken or loose connection, and remedy.

Headlamp gives insufficient illumination.

(a) Test the state of charge of the battery, re-charging if necessary.

(b) Check the setting of the lamp. See if the bulb is in focus (when " prefocus " bulb is not used).

(c) If the bulb is discoloured as a result of long service it should be replaced. On lamps on which the reflector surface is accessible, see that the reflector is clean.

Lamps light when switched on, but gradually fade out.

Test the state of charge of the battery, re-charging if necessary.

Brilliance varies with speed of motor cycle.

Test the state of charge of the battery, re-charging if necessary.

Lights flicker.

Examine the wiring for loose connections.

MAGNETO IGNITION CIRCUIT

Engine will not fire or misfires.

(a) See that the controls are correctly set for starting, petrol turned on, etc.

(b) Remove the sparking plug (or plugs), and place on the cylinder head. If a spark occurs regularly at the plug points when the engine is slowly hand-cranked, the magneto is in order. Look for engine defects and check ignition timing.

(c) If a spark does not occur in (b), disconnect the high tension cable from the plug and hold the cable end about $\frac{1}{8}$" from a metal part of the engine. If a spark occurs regularly when the engine is cranked, the plug is faulty. If there is no spark, disconnect the high tension cable at the magneto, replace with a new length of cable and test again as before.

(d) Should there still be no spark, possible causes of trouble are : contact breaker gap out of adjustment or contacts dirty ; contact breaker rocker arm sticking (on ring cam types) ; pick-up brush worn or broken, or slip ring track dirty. Remedy as described.

Engine Misfires.

(a) Check as in para. (b) and (c) above to eliminate engine defects, faulty high tension cable and sparking plug.

(b) Check magneto as in para. (d) above.

COIL IGNITION CIRCUIT

Engine will not fire.

(a) See that the battery is in a charged condition, either by means of a hydrometer or by checking that the lamps give good light.
In emergency, a start can be obtained with two flash lamp batteries connected in series (i.e., the short terminal strip of the one

battery connected to the long strip of the second). On "positive earth" machines, connect the negative battery terminal (usually the long strip) to the coil terminal "SW" and the other battery terminal to the frame. As soon as the generator begins to charge, the flashlamp battery can be removed.

(b) See that the controls are correctly set for starting, ignition switched on, petrol turned on, etc.

(c) Remove the high tension cable from the sparking plug terminal and hold it about $\frac{1}{8}''$ away from some metal part of the engine while the latter is slowly turned over. If sparks jump the gap regularly, the ignition equipment is functioning correctly. Check for engine defects.

(d) If sparks do not occur in test (c), check for a fault in the low tension wiring. This will be indicated by (i) no ammeter reading when the engine is slowly cranked and the ignition switch is on, or (ii) no spark occurring between the contacts when quickly separated by the fingers with the ignition switched on. Examine all cables in the ignition circuit and see that all connections are tight.

(e) If the wiring proves to be in order, examine the contacts; if necessary, clean them and adjust the gap.

Engine misfires.

(a) Examine the contacts; if necessary, clean them and adjust the gap.

(b) Remove the sparking plug (or each plug in turn), rest it on the cylinder head and observe if a spark occurs at the plug points when the engine is turned. Irregular sparking may be due to dirty plugs, which should be cleaned and adjusted, or to defective high tension cables. Any cable showing signs of deterioration or cracking should be renewed.

(c) If sparking is regular at each plug when tested as described in (b), the trouble is probably due to engine defects, and the carburetter, petrol supply, etc., must be examined.

LUCAS SERVICE DEPOTS

BELFAST ... ... 51/55 Upper Library Street
Telephone: Belfast 25617   Telegrams: "Servdep, Belfast"

BIRMINGHAM, 18 ... ... Great Hampton Street
Telephone: Central 5050   Telegrams: "Lucaserve, Birmingham"

BRIGHTON, 4 ... ... 85 Old Shoreham Road, Hove
Telephone: Hove 38993   Telegrams: "Luserv, Brighton"

BRISTOL, 4 ... ... 345 Bath Road
Telephone: Bristol 76001   Telegrams: "Kingly, Bristol"

CARDIFF ... ... 54a Penarth Road
Telephone: Cardiff 28361   Telegrams: "Lucas, Cardiff"

CORK (Distribution Depot) ... ... 4 Caroline Street
Telephone: Cork 22868   Telegrams: "Luserv, Cork"

DUBLIN ... ... Portland Street North, North Circular Road
Telephone: Dublin 46195   Telegrams: "Luserv, Dublin"

EDINBURGH, 11 ... ... 60 Stevenson Road, Gorgie
Telephone: Edinburgh 62921   Telegrams: "Luserv, Edinburgh"

GLASGOW, C.3 ... ... 4/24 Grant Street (St. George's Road)
Telephone: Douglas 6591-6   Telegrams: "Lucas, Glasgow"

LEEDS, 8 ... ... 64 Roseville Road
Telephone: Leeds 28591   Telegrams: "Luserdep, Leeds 8"

LIVERPOOL, 13 ... ... 450/470 Edge Lane
Telephone: Stoneycroft 4721   Telegrams: "Luserv, Liverpool 13"

LONDON, W.3 ... ... Dordrecht Road, Acton Vale
Telephone: Shepherds Bush 3160   Telegrams: "Lucas, Dynomagna, London"

LONDON, E.10 ... ... 757-759 High Road, Leyton
Telephone: Leytonstone 3361   Telegrams: "Luserdep, Leystone, London"

MANCHESTER ... ... Talbot Road, Stretford
Telephone: Longford 1101   Telegrams: "Lucas, Stretford"

NEWCASTLE-ON-TYNE, 1 ... ... 64/68 St. Mary's Place
Telephone: Newcastle 25571   Telegrams: "Motolite, Newcastle-on-Tyne"

LONDON SALES OFFICE ... ... 319 Regent Street, W.1
Telephone: Langham 4311   Telegrams: "Guidepost, Wesdo, London"

LONDON EXPORT OFFICE   Lucas House, 46 Park Street, W.1
Telephone: Grosvenor 4491   Telegrams: (Inland) "Lucaslond, Audley, London"
                                                      (Overseas) "Lucaslond, London"

Maintenance Instructions for

LUCAS

ALTERNATING CURRENT EQUIPMENT

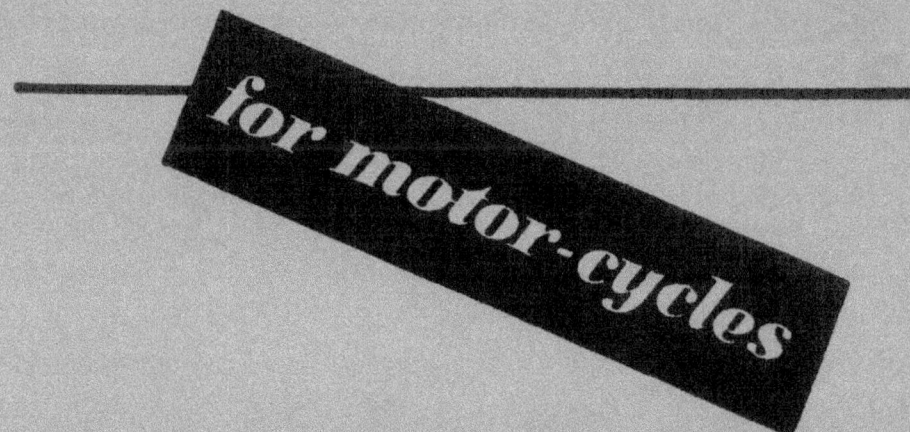

JOSEPH LUCAS LIMITED · BIRMINGHAM · ENGLAND

Publication No. 1093U   R/1160/D   R/661/D   Printed in England

FOREWORD

Lucas Electrical Equipment is designed and manufactured to give long periods of service with the minimum of attention. As with other parts of the motor cycle, however, occasional minor adjustments, lubrication of moving parts and cleaning should be carried out to ensure that the equipment will operate with the utmost reliability and efficiency.

This Manual gives general information on the various items of equipment fitted to motor cycles having A.C. generators and describes the small amount of attention which is required. Two alternator systems in current use are described, namely, A.C. Lighting-Ignition introduced in 1951 and Energy Transfer (" E.T.") Ignition introduced in 1959. Although the former system is normally specified for Roadster machines and the latter (with direct lighting) for Competition machines, some Roadster models have been fitted with "E.T." ignition and battery lighting, as described on page 4.

Information is also included on magnetos—both rotating armature and magnet rotor types—as fitted to machines in which the alternator is used only for battery charging.

In addition, the recommended procedure is set out for a systematic examination to be adopted in the event of the electrical equipment not functioning correctly.

Any further information will be supplied on application to Joseph Lucas Ltd., Great King Street, Birmingham 19, England.

INDEX

	Page
A.C. Lighting-Ignition Units	3
Energy Transfer (" E.T.") Ignition System	4
Alternator	5
Rectifier	6
Battery	6
Distributors and Contact Breaker Units	8
Magneto Ignition	13
Rotating Armature Magnetos	13
Rotating Magnet Magnetos	17
Starting Motor	19
Headlamp	19
Parking Light	19
Rear Lamps	22
How to Connect a Foglamp	24
Electric Horn	25
Location and Remedy of Faults	27
Addresses of Lucas Service Depots	31

Wiring diagrams for many Lucas equipped machines can be obtained on request to the Advertising Dept., Gt. King St., Birmingham 19. These diagrams are issued free on receipt of the appropriate information, namely, Make, Model and Year of Manufacture of motor cycle.

A.C. LIGHTING-IGNITION UNITS

Lucas A.C. Lighting-Ignition Units are 6-pole alternators consisting of a permanent magnet rotor rotating within a laminated wound stator. The rotor is driven by an extension of the engine crankshaft and is built into the crankcase or chain case.

A rectifier is included in the circuit, this being a device for converting the alternating current output of the alternator to uni-directional current which is essential for battery charging.

Normal Running.

Under normal running conditions (i.e., ignition switch in IGN position) electrical energy in the form of rectified alternating current passes through the battery from the alternator. When no lights are in use, the alternator output is sufficient only to supply the ignition coil and to charge the battery. When the lighting switch is turned, the output is automatically increased to meet the additional load. On some machines an increase occurs both when the parking light is switched on and again when the main bulb is brought into use; on other machines, only when the main bulb is switched on.

Emergency Starting.

An EMERGENCY starting position is provided on the ignition switch, for use if the battery has become discharged and a normal start cannot therefore be made. Under these conditions, the alternator is connected direct to the ignition coil, allowing the engine to be started independently of the battery. It should be noted that with the ignition switch at EMG and the engine running, the battery receives a charging current, so that its terminal voltage begins to rise. This rising voltage opposes the alternator voltage, and, on single-cylinder machines, in the event of a rider omitting to return the ignition key to IGN after an emergency start has been made, misfiring may occur. This will cease on turning the ignition key to the normal running position, IGN.

Alternator Models.

Two sizes of stator are made, one being of 5-in. diameter and the other, which is hexagonal, $5\frac{7}{16}$-in. A/F*. The smaller is used, in different thicknesses, in alternator models RM13, 13/15 and 15 and the larger in model RM14. Model RM13/15 has an RM13 stator with the larger rotor used in RM15 and its output falls between the two. Models RM13 and 13/15 are designed for small capacity machines having low top gear ratios, whilst models RM14 and 15 are for large capacity machines having high top gear ratios. The additional output available from these two latter alternators permits the continuous use of larger capacity batteries (SC7E, GU11E, etc.).

Model 5AF scooter alternators have RM13 stators and RM15 size rotors cast integral with the engine flywheel. The latter has cooling fins and, on 6-volt units, is fitted with an inertia ring, while on 12-volt units it carries a ring gear for engagement with the (model M3) starting motor.

* $5\frac{7}{8}$-in. spigot diameter.

Alternative Battery Charging Rates.

Lucas Motor Cycle Alternators are connected to ensure that the battery is maintained fully charged under all normal running conditions. Although alternators models RM13 and RM15 are very similar in outward appearance, the performance of the RM15 is considerably higher than that of the RM13. On some earlier machines fitted with the smaller model RM13 alternator, the charge rate may not always be found quite sufficient to meet the requirements of low-speed town work, the " running-in " period, short winter runs involving long periods of parking with the lights on, and similar conditions. In this event, the charge rate can be increased by interchanging two of the three alternator cables where these are joined by means of snap-connectors to the main harness. To do this, switch off the lighting and ignition switches and disconnect the Green-with-Black (formerly Dark Green) and Green-with-Yellow (formerly Medium Green) cables by pulling these cables from their snap-connectors. The Green-with-Black alternator cable must now be connected to the Green-with-Yellow harness cable, and the Green-with-Yellow alternator cable to the Green-with-Black harness cable. It should be noted, however, that with these modified connections emergency starting may be adversely affected. If this form of starting is required but found difficult, the cables should be re-connected colour-to-colour.

If, due to a change in running conditions, the battery is found to be overcharged, as indicated by excessive gassing of the electrolyte and a frequent need for topping-up, the original connections must be restored, colour-to-colour.

ENERGY TRANSFER ("E.T.") IGNITION SYSTEM

The Lucas " E.T." Ignition System is independent of a battery supply and its characteristics combine the differing advantages of former magneto and coil ignition systems and of the A.C. Lighting-Ignition Units described above. In the " E.T." System, windings on either two or four of the alternator stator limbs (of RM13 or RM15 design) are devoted to supplying a pulse of energy to the primary winding of an ignition coil each time the contact breaker opens. These low tension pulses are converted by an ignition coil of special design to the high tension voltages required at the sparking plug. How the remaining stator limbs are utilised depends on the type of machine to which the system is fitted. On Roadsters, for example, four carry coils for charging the battery through a rectifier. Battery-less Competition machines on the other hand may have lighting coils on only two limbs, to supply alternating current for a direct lighting set. When stop-lights are used with direct lighting, these are fed either from a third, independent coil, or from two coils of a four-coil ignition winding.

N.B. (i) Never try to improve the engine timing of an " E.T." equipped machine. Settings are critical and optimum performances are determined by the engine and ignition system designers at the development stages.

(ii) **Battery Lighting Models — safeguarding the rectifier.** If a machine is to be run with the battery disconnected, first disconnect the Green-with-White cable at the snap connector near the alternator, and tape up the bared end.

THE ALTERNATOR

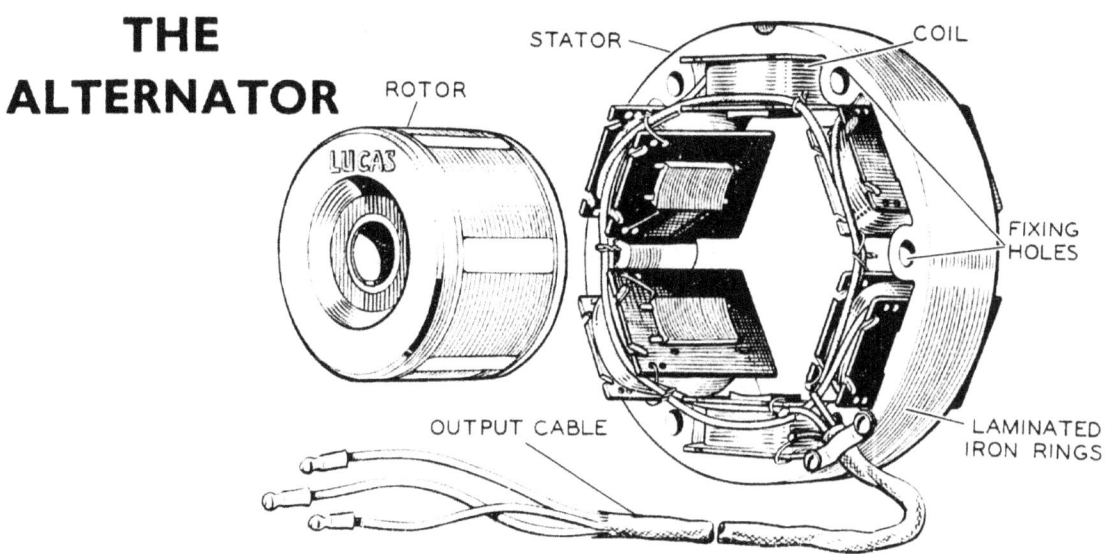

Fig. 1. Alternator Model RM15.

The alternator consists of a spigot-mounted 6-coil laminated stator with a rotor carried on and driven by an extension of the crankshaft. The rotor has an hexagonal steel core, each face of which carries a high-energy permanent magnet keyed to a laminated pole tip. The pole tips are riveted circumferentially to brass side plates, the assembly being cast in aluminium and machined to give a smooth external finish.

There are no rotating windings, commutator, brushgear, bearings or oil seals and consequently the alternator requires no maintenance apart from occasionally checking that the snap-connectors in the three output cables are clean and tight.

If removal of the rotor becomes necessary for any purpose, there is no necessity to fit keepers to the rotor poles. When the rotor is removed, wipe off any metal swarf which may have been attracted to the pole tips. Place the rotor in a clean place.

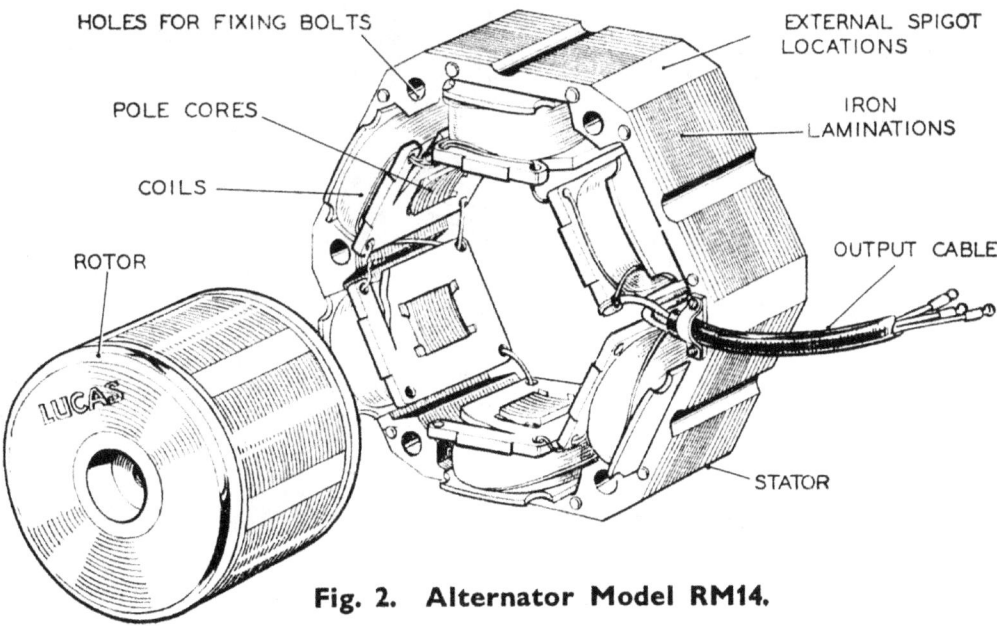

Fig. 2. Alternator Model RM14.

THE RECTIFIER

The rectifier is a device to allow current to flow in one direction only. It is connected to provide full-wave rectification of the alternator output current.

The rectifier requires no maintenance beyond checking that the connections are clean and tight. **The nuts clamping the rectifier plates together must not under any circumstances be slackened, as the pressure has been carefully set during manufacture to give correct rectifier performance.** A separate nut is used to secure the rectifier to the frame of the motor cycle and it is important to check periodically that the rectifier is firmly attached to its mounting bracket.

THE BATTERY

Topping-Up.

During charging, water is lost by gassing and evaporation. Fortnightly, or more often in warm climates, check the electrolyte level in the battery cells. This examination should be made weekly with battery models PU5E, MK9E, ML9E and SC7E as these are of reduced fluid capacity.

Remove the battery lid, unscrew the filler plugs, and, if necessary, **add distilled water carefully** to each cell **to bring the electrolyte just level with the separator guard or,** if visible, **with the top edges of the separators. DO NOT USE TAP WATER.**

Warning: Never top-up models ML9E and MLZ9E above the coloured line denoting the maximum filling level.

The use of a Lucas Battery Filler will be found helpful in this topping-up process, since it ensures that the correct electrolyte level is obtained automatically and also prevents distilled water from being spilled over the battery top. These Fillers cannot be used to top-up models MK9E, ML9E and SC7E batteries.

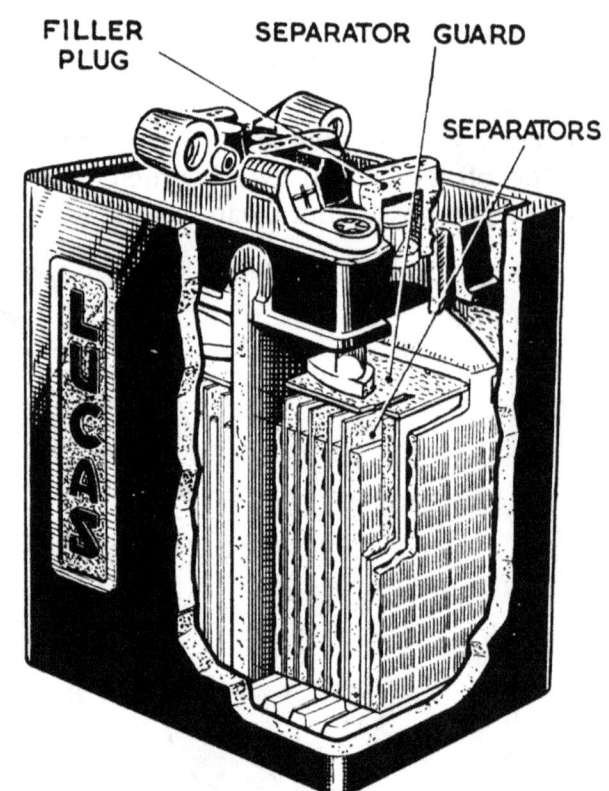

Fig. 3. Battery Model PU7E/11.

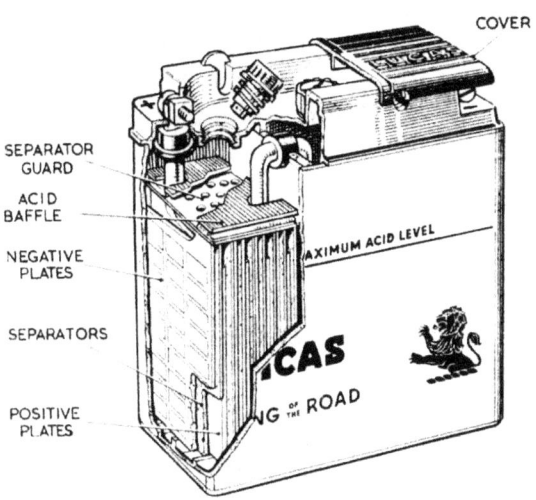

Fig. 4. Battery Model ML9E.

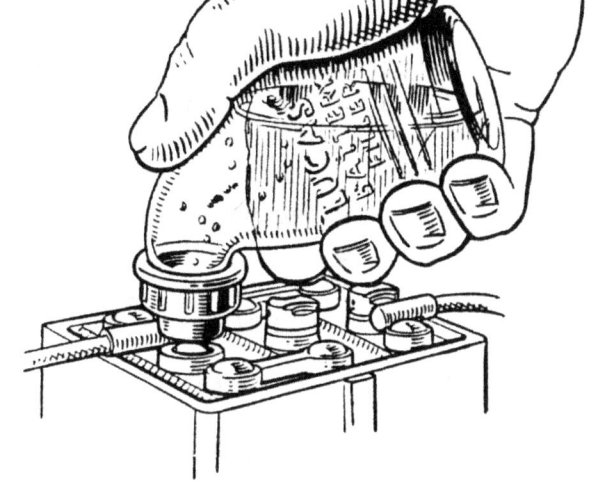

Fig. 5. **Using a Lucas Battery Filler.**
(Not applicable to MK9E, ML9E or SC7E batteries)

Cleaning.

Wipe away all dirt and moisture from the top of the battery.

Checking the Condition of the Battery.

Occasionally check the condition of the battery by taking measurements of the specific gravity of the electrolyte in each of the cells. A small-volume hydrometer is required for this purpose — this instrument resembles a syringe containing a graduated float which indicates the specific gravity of the acid in the cell from which the sample has been taken. Do not take measurements immediately after topping-up the cells as the electrolyte will not be thoroughly mixed.

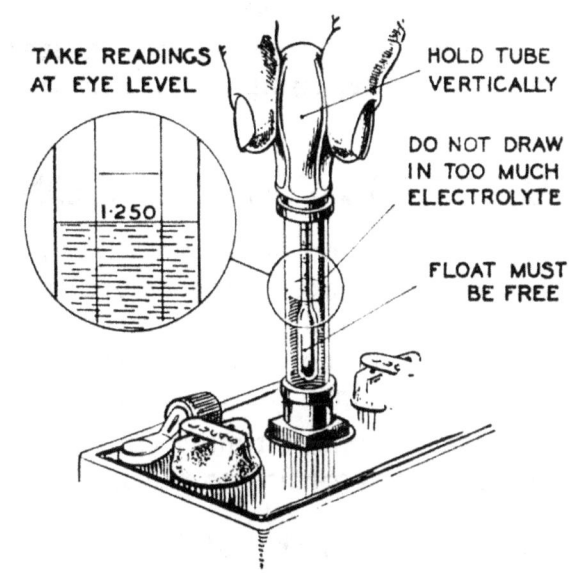

Fig. 6. **Taking Hydrometer Readings.**
(Not applicable to MK9E, ML9E or SC7E batteries)

Note:—The fluid capacities of some batteries, including models MK9E, ML9E and SC7E, preclude the use of a hydrometer, while others require tilting to make accessible sufficient electrolyte above the separator guards.

Specific gravity readings and their indications are as follows :—

Climates under 90°F.		Climates over 90°F.
1.270—1.290	Cell fully charged	1.200—1.220
1.190—1.210	Cell about half discharged	1.120—1.140
1.110—1.130	Cell completely discharged	1.040—1.060

The reading for each of the cells should be approximately the same. If one cell gives a value very different from the rest, it may be that acid has been spilled from this cell and the remaining acid been diluted by subsequent topping-up. In this event further stronger sulphuric acid must be added until the correct electrolyte strength is obtained. Alternatively, an incorrect reading may result from a leaky cell or from defective plates. In either event the battery should be examined at a Lucas Service Depot or by a Lucas Battery Agent.

Never leave the battery in a discharged condition. If the motor cycle is to be out of use for a considerable period have the battery fully charged and every fortnight give it a short freshening charge to prevent any tendency for the plates to become permanently sulphated.

Detachable Cable Connectors.

When connecting batteries with detachable cable connectors, unscrew the knurled nut and withdraw the collet. Bare the end of the cable and thread the bared end through the knurled nut and collet. Bend back the cable strands, insert the collet and cable in the terminal and secure the connection by tightening the knurled nut.

Battery Earth.

A.C. Lighting-Ignition and "E.T." Units have been designed for positive (+ve) earth systems. If battery connections are reversed the equipment will be damaged.

DISTRIBUTORS & CONTACT BREAKER UNITS

The ignition equipment comprises an ignition coil and a contact breaker unit and, in the case of twin and four-cylinder machines, either a high tension distributor or twin ignition coils. The contact breaker, together with an automatic timing control, may be housed in a separate unit or built into the engine timing case.

The automatic timing control is centrifugally operated and varies the firing point according to the speed of the engine.

Contact Breaker Setting — after first 500 miles and, thereafter, every 6,000 miles.

To check the contact breaker gap, turn the engine over slowly until the contacts are seen to be fully open and insert a feeler gauge between the contacts. The correct gap setting is 0.014"—0.016" (0.35—0.4 mm.). If the gap is correct, the gauge should be a sliding fit.

To adjust the gap on all models except 15D1, keep the engine in the position giving maximum contact opening and slacken the screw(s) securing the fixed contact plate. Adjust the position of the plate until the gap is set to the thickness of the gauge, and tighten the locking screw(s).

On model 15D1, keep the engine in the position giving maximum opening and slacken the screw at the side of the fixed contact plate. Slide the fixed contact carrier in its slotted hole, until the correct gap is obtained. Retighten the screw.

Warning: Before removing a distributor or contact breaker unit (or the centrifugal advance mechanism of the outrigger version of model 3CA), make careful note of the relative positions of the parts in order to preserve the ignition timing on **reassembly**.

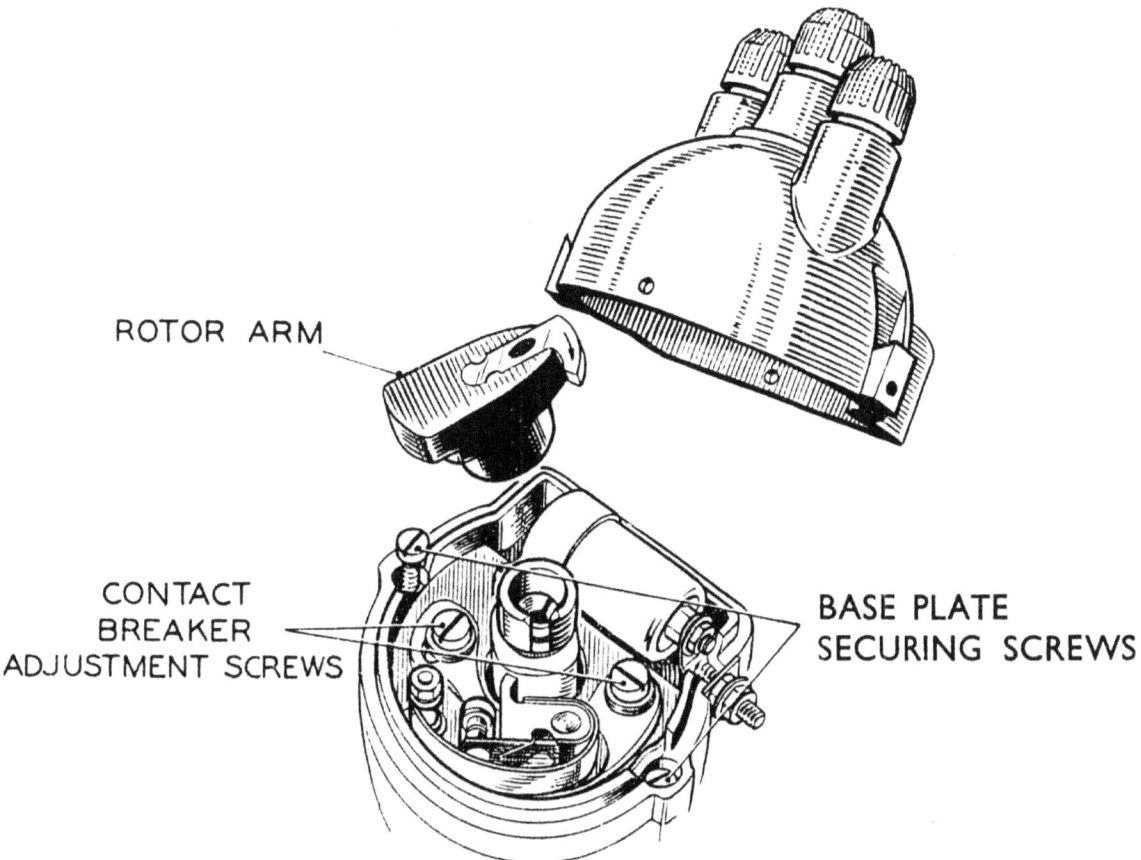

Fig. 7. Distributor Model DKX2A with cover removed.

Cleaning — every 6,000 miles.

Remove and clean the cover. On twin and four-cylinder units, pay particular attention to the spaces between the metal electrodes in the cover, and check that the small carbon brush moves freely in its holder.

Examine the contact breaker. The contacts must be free from grease or oil. If they are burned or blackened, clean with fine carborundum stone or very fine emery cloth, afterwards wiping away any trace of dirt or metal dust with a clean petrol-moistened cloth. Cleaning of the contacts is made easier if the contact breaker lever carrying the moving contact is removed.

To remove the moving contact from models DKX, CA1A, 2CA and 3CA, unscrew the nut securing the end of the spring and remove the capacitor connector (DKX excepted), spring washer and insulating bush. Lift the contact breaker lever off the pivot post. With model 2CA contact breaker unit, access to the contact breaker is gained by withdrawing the central bolt and removing the centrifugal timing control mechanism.

To remove the moving contact from model 15D1, remove the terminal

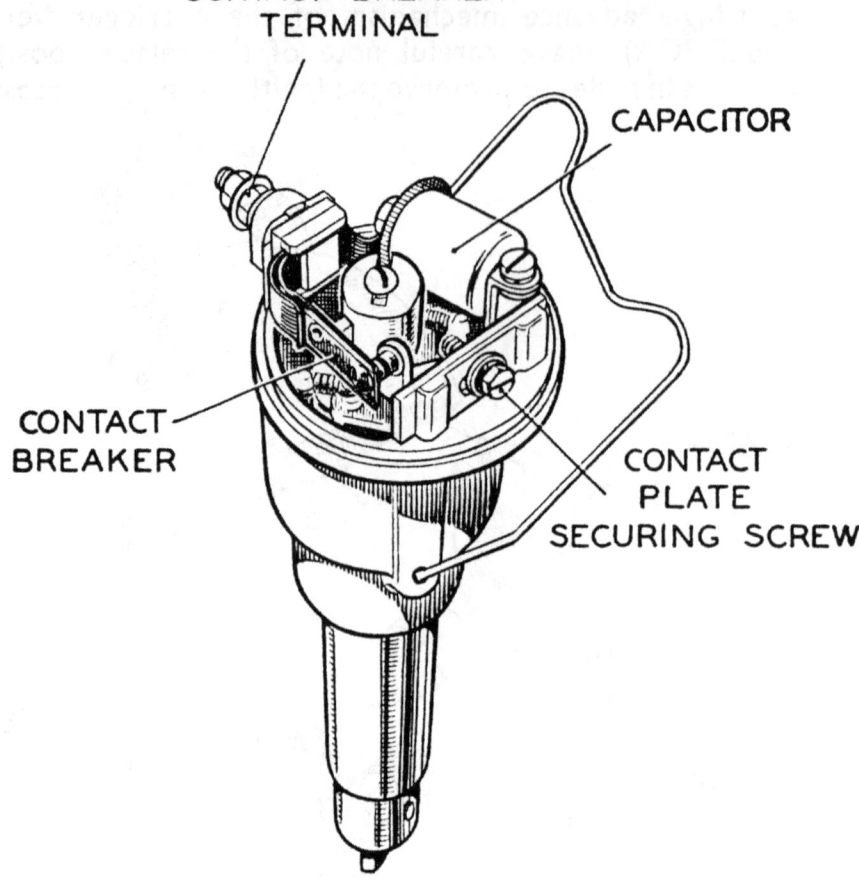

Fig. 8. Contact Breaker and Automatic Advance Unit, Model 15D1, with cover removed.

nut and withdraw the nylon washer. The contact breaker spring and heel can now be lifted out of the unit body.

To remove the moving contact from models 18D1 and 18D2, slacken the contact breaker terminal nuts and remove the nut and washers from the pivot post. Lift the contact breaker lever off the pivot post.

To remove the moving contact from models 4CC and 4CA, unscrew the nut from the capacitor terminal and withdraw the contact from the pivot post.

After cleaning, check the contact breaker setting.

Lubrication — to be carried out every 6,000 miles except where indicated.

No grease or oil must be allowed to get on or near the contacts when carrying out the following procedure.

Smear the surface of the cam very lightly with Mobilgrease No. 2, or, if this is not available, clean engine oil (S.A.E. 30—40) may be used.

Place a spot of clean engine oil on the contact breaker pivot post.

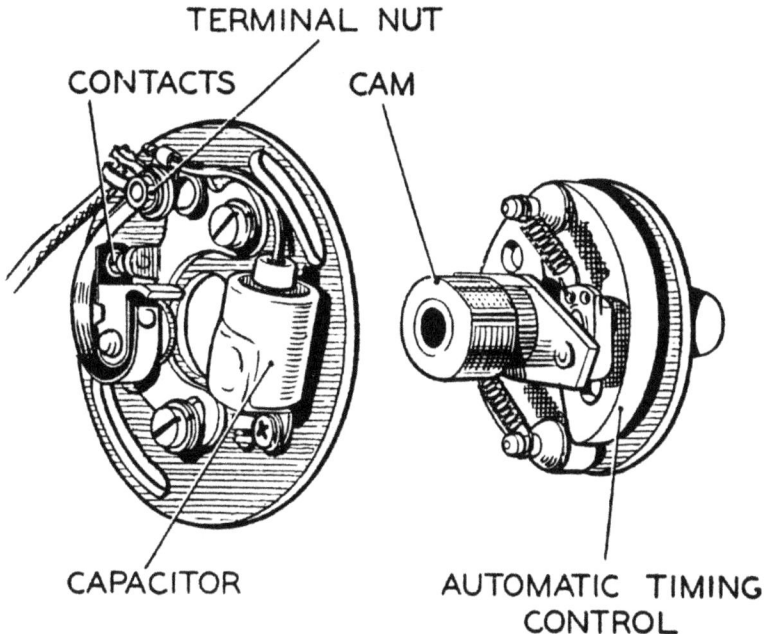

Fig. 9. Contact Breaker and Automatic Advance Mechanism, Model CAIA, removed from engine. (Other contact breaker units include Models 2CA, 3CA and 4CA. Also fixed ignition Model 4CC).

Automatic Timing Control.

Models DKX2A, DKX4A, 18D1 and 18D2: Lift off the rotor arm, and unscrew the two screws securing the contact breaker base plate to the distributor. Lubricate the automatic timing control, thus exposed, with clean engine oil, paying particular attention to the pivots. Refit the base plate, and secure by means of the fixing screws. Refit the rotor arm.

Model 15D1: Remove the contact breaker cover and use clean engine oil to lubricate the automatic timing mechanism in the base of the unit.

Models CAIA, 3CA: Every 3,000 miles remove the central fixing bolt and inject a small amount of clean engine oil into the hole thus exposed. When the fixing bolt has been replaced and the engine run for a few minutes, the oil will be forced out over the automatic advance mechanism by centrifugal force.

Model 2CA: Lightly lubricate the mechanism with clean engine oil.

Model 4CA: Turn engine to bring slot in cam uppermost and apply ONE drop of clean engine oil to slot. This will diffuse over the end of the cam and lubricate the cam spindle of this twin lever unit.

The Ignition Coil.

The coil requires no attention whatever beyond keeping its exterior clean, particularly the terminal moulding, and occasionally checking that the connections are tight.

Renewing High Tension Cables.

When the high tension cable shows signs of perishing or cracking it must be renewed, using 7 mm. p.v.c.-covered or neoprene-covered (vulcanised-rubber-insulated) ignition cable.

To fit new cable to ignition coils and distributors having vertical screw-type connectors, remove the metal washer and moulded terminal nut from the defective cable. Thread the new cable through the moulded terminal nut and cut back the insulation for about $\frac{1}{4}$-in. Pass the exposed strands through the metal washer and bend them back radially. Screw the terminal nut into the pick-up moulding.

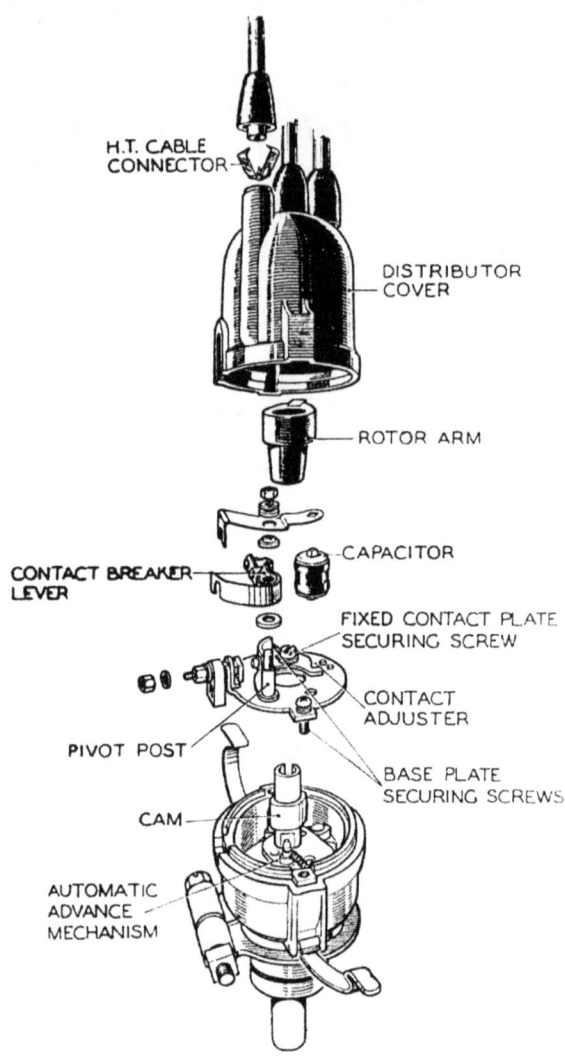

Fig. 10. Distributor Model 18D2.

To fit new cables to distributors having the horizontal type of outlet, remove the two screws securing the moulded cable cover on to the distributor cap. Cut the cables off flush to the required length and locate them in the recesses in the distributor moulding. Refit the cover. This presses the cables on to pointed metal studs which make good contact with the cable core.

With distributors having outlets similar to those illustrated in Fig. 10, pull the old cable and connector from the sockets in the distributor cap and fit the new cable and connectors in like manner.

MAGNETO IGNITION

When a magneto is fitted, the sole function of the alternator is to charge the battery by way of the rectifier.

Two types of magneto are in use. These are known as rotating armature and rotating magnet magnetos, by reason of their differing construction. In the former, the windings and capacitor rotate and the magnet is stationary, but in the latter the reverse is true.

Both types are often fitted with a centrifugally operated mechanism that automatically varies the point of firing to suit differing engine speeds. Alternatively, some rotating armature magnetos, particularly when fitted to competition machines, carry a manual control of ignition timing. Such a control should be moved to the Retard position for starting and when the engine labours on full throttle. At all other times the control should be in the Advance position.

ROTATING ARMATURE MAGNETOS (Model K2F, etc.).
Every 3,000 miles.
Checking Contact Breaker Gap.

To check the contact breaker gap, remove the contact breaker cover and turn the engine over slowly until the contacts are fully open. A flat steel gauge of thickness 0.012"—0.015" (0.305—0.381 mm.) should be a sliding fit between the contacts.

Adjusting Contact Breaker Gap.

Two types of contact breaker are in service. The present assembly, shown in Figs. 11 and 12, has a fixed contact plate secured by a single screw passing through a slotted hole in the plate. To adjust the gap, slacken this screw and, using a screwdriver in the manner shown in Fig. 12, move the fixed contact plate until the correct gap is obtained. Tighten the screw and recheck the gap.

The earlier assembly, shown in Fig. 13, has a contact screw and locking nut. To adjust the gap, slacken the locking nut and turn the contact screw by its hexagon head until the correct gap is obtained. Tighten the locking nut and recheck the gap.

Note:—The present contact breaker is interchangeable with the older pattern, provided the present shorter straight-shanked securing screw is fitted in place of the former longer screw, the shank of which has a 17° taper for $\frac{3}{16}$" (4.76 mm.) below the head.

Lubrication.

The cam ring is supplied with lubricant from a felt strip contained in a recess in the contact breaker housing. Oil reaches the inner surface of the cam ring by way of a small circular wick passing through the thickness of the cam ring.

Remove the contact breaker cover. Take out the central hexagon-headed securing screw and carefully withdraw the contact breaker from the tapered magneto spindle.

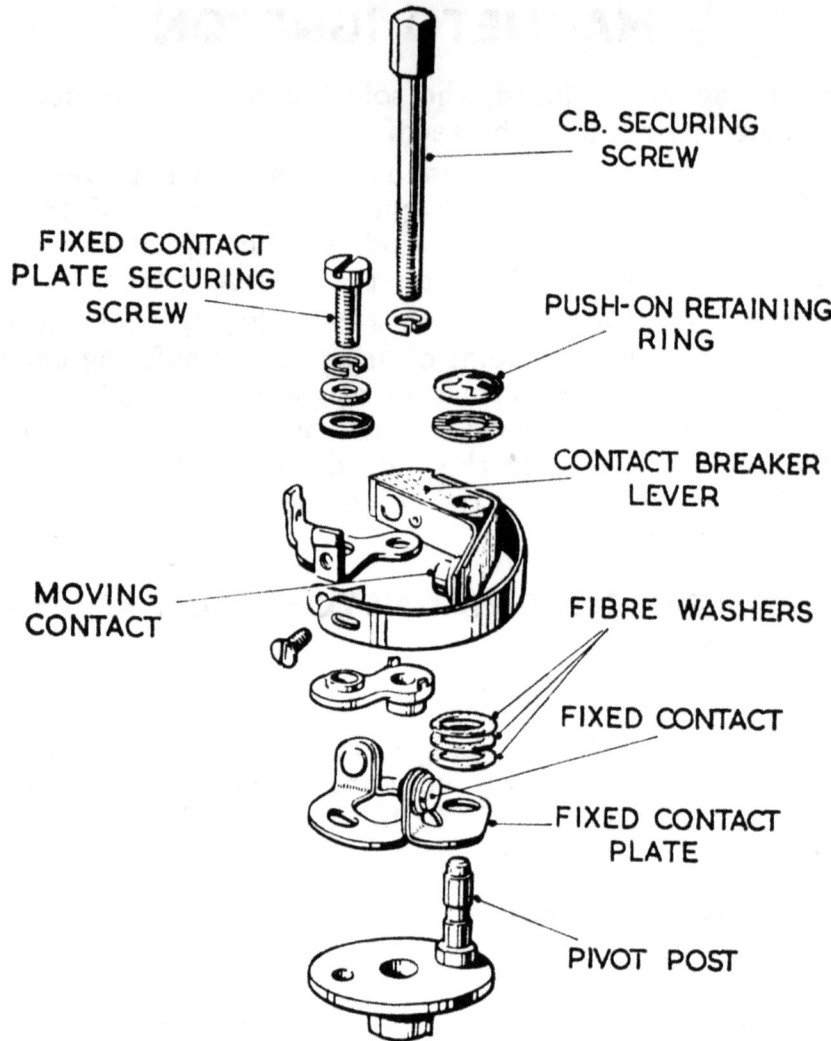

Fig. 11. Contact Breaker, dismantled.

Withdraw the cam ring. It is a sliding fit in the contact breaker housing.

Note:—If a manual control of ignition timing is fitted, withdrawal and refitting of the cam ring will be made easier if the handlebar control lever is moved to the half-Retard position, thus taking the cam ring from its stop peg.

Clean the cam and lightly smear the inside and outside surfaces with Mobilgrease No. 2.

Add a few drops of thin machine oil to the felt strip and to the circular wick.

Remove the contact breaker lever and smear the pivot with Mobilgrease No. 2, applying sufficient grease to fill the annular groove.

Note:—The method of removing the contact breaker lever will be apparent by reference to Figs. 11 or 13, depending on the type. Since the push-on retaining ring shown in Fig. 11 may need renewal after removal, an alternative form of lubrication for this pivot post is to

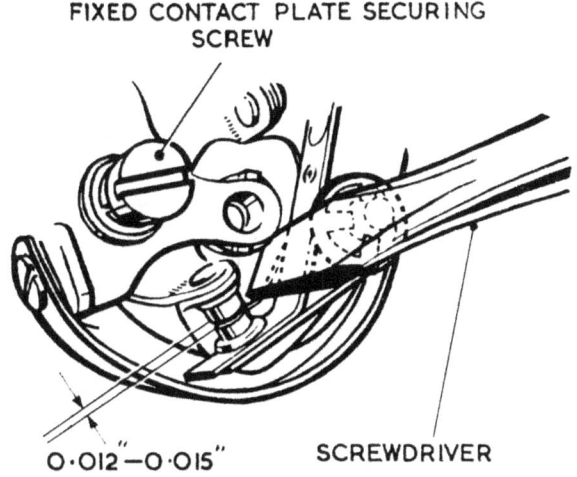

Fig. 12. Adjusting Contact Breaker gap.

apply a spot of clean engine oil to the tip of the post. While this will obviate the necessity of removing the lever, great care must be exercised to prevent any oil getting on or near the contacts.

The fibre washers shown in Fig. 11 are fitted below the contact breaker lever to ensure vertical alignment of the fixed and moving contacts.

Refit the contact breaker lever.

Refit the cam ring, taking care when manual timing control is fitted that the stop peg in the contact breaker housing and the spring loaded plunger engage with their respective slots.

If an earthing brush is fitted at the back of the contact breaker base plate, see that it is clean and can move freely in its holder before refitting the contact breaker assembly in the cam ring.

Refit the contact breaker assembly, ensuring that the projecting key on the tapered portion of the contact breaker base plate engages correctly with the spindle keyway.

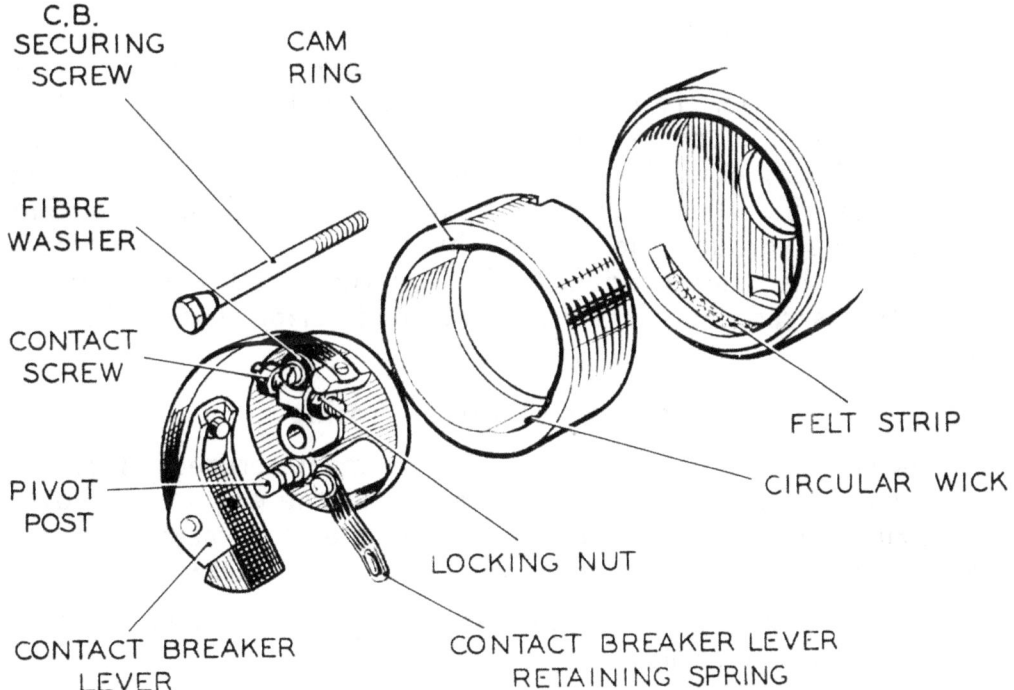

Fig. 13. Earlier type Contact Breaker, dismantled.

Every 6,000 miles.

Cleaning.

Remove the contact breaker cover and high tension pick-up mouldings. Thoroughly clean the inside and outside of the magneto using a clean dry fluffless cloth, if necessary, moistening it with petrol to remove any grease from the high tension pick-up mouldings and contact breaker contacts. Ensure that the pick-up brush moves freely in its holder. Renew the brush if it is worn to $\frac{1}{8}$" above the shoulder. Clean the slip ring track and flanges by pressing the cloth on them while the engine is cranked by hand.

Ensure that the gasket between the pick-up mouldings and the magneto body is in good condition before reassembling.

Examine the contacts when the contact breaker is removed for lubrication. If the contacts are pitted or piled, they should be trimmed with a carborundum stone, silicon carbide paper, or very fine emery cloth.

Contacts do not retain a polished appearance when in use and, if operating correctly, will have a dull grey appearance.

Every Two Years.

About every two years, or when the engine is given a general overhaul, the magneto should be dismantled at a Lucas Service Depot or Agent, where the weights, springs and toggles of the centrifugal timing control mechanism will be examined and lubricated, and the armature bearings repacked with grease.

Renewing High Tension Cables

When high tension cable shows signs of cracking or perishing, replace it using 7 mm. p.v.c.-covered or neoprene-covered vulcanised rubber-insulated ignition cable. To do this, pull back the rubber shroud (if fitted) and unscrew the moulded terminal from the pick-up moulding. Remove the split metal washer and moulded terminal from the defective cable. Prepare the new cable by cutting back the insulation for about $\frac{1}{4}$" (6.35 mm.). Thread the cable through the rubber shroud (if fitted) and the moulded terminal. Pass the cable conductor through the metal washer and bend back the strands radially. Screw the moulded terminal into the pick-up moulding.

Magneto-to-Engine Timing

Whenever possible, follow the engine manufacturer's instructions when re-timing a rotating armature magneto to the engine. If, however, these instructions are not immediately available, the magneto-to-engine timing can (as a temporary measure only) be set as follows :—

Magnetos fitted with or without centrifugal timing control (but excluding manual control) :

Contact breaker to open when the piston in the cylinder under compression is at T.D.C.

Magnetos fitted with manual timing control :
With the control lever set to the fully retarded position the contact breaker to open when the piston in the cylinder under compression is at T.D.C.

ROTATING MAGNET MAGNETOS (Models SR1, SR2, etc.).

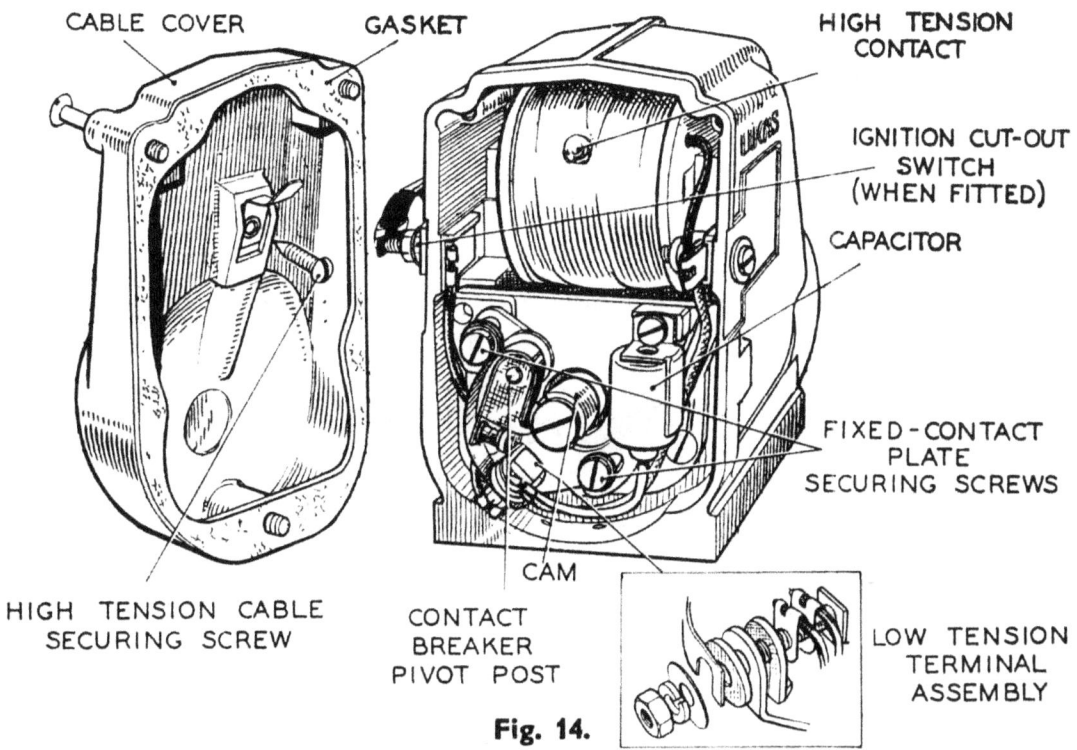

Fig. 14.

After first 500 miles and, thereafter, every 3,000 miles.

Check the setting of the contact breaker gap. To do this, remove the cable cover, turn the engine over slowly until the contacts are fully open and insert a 0.010"—0.012" (0.254—0.305 mm.) feeler gauge in the gap. The gauge should be a sliding fit between the contacts.

To adjust the gap, slacken the two fixed contact plate securing screws and move the plate until the gap is set to the gauge thickness.

Apply a spot of clean engine oil to the visible end of the contact breaker pivot post. **No oil must be allowed on or near the contacts.**

Every 6,000 miles.

Remove the cable cover and clean the contacts. To do this, slacken the nut securing the low tension terminal assembly and withdraw the spring and contact breaker lever.

If the contacts are rough or pitted, polish them with fine carborundum stone, silicon carbide paper or emery cloth. Afterwards, clean the contacts with petrol or methylated spirits (denatured alcohol).

Smear the pivot post with Mobilgrease No. 2 or an equivalent grease.

When refitting the contact breaker, see that the components are assembled in the order illustrated.

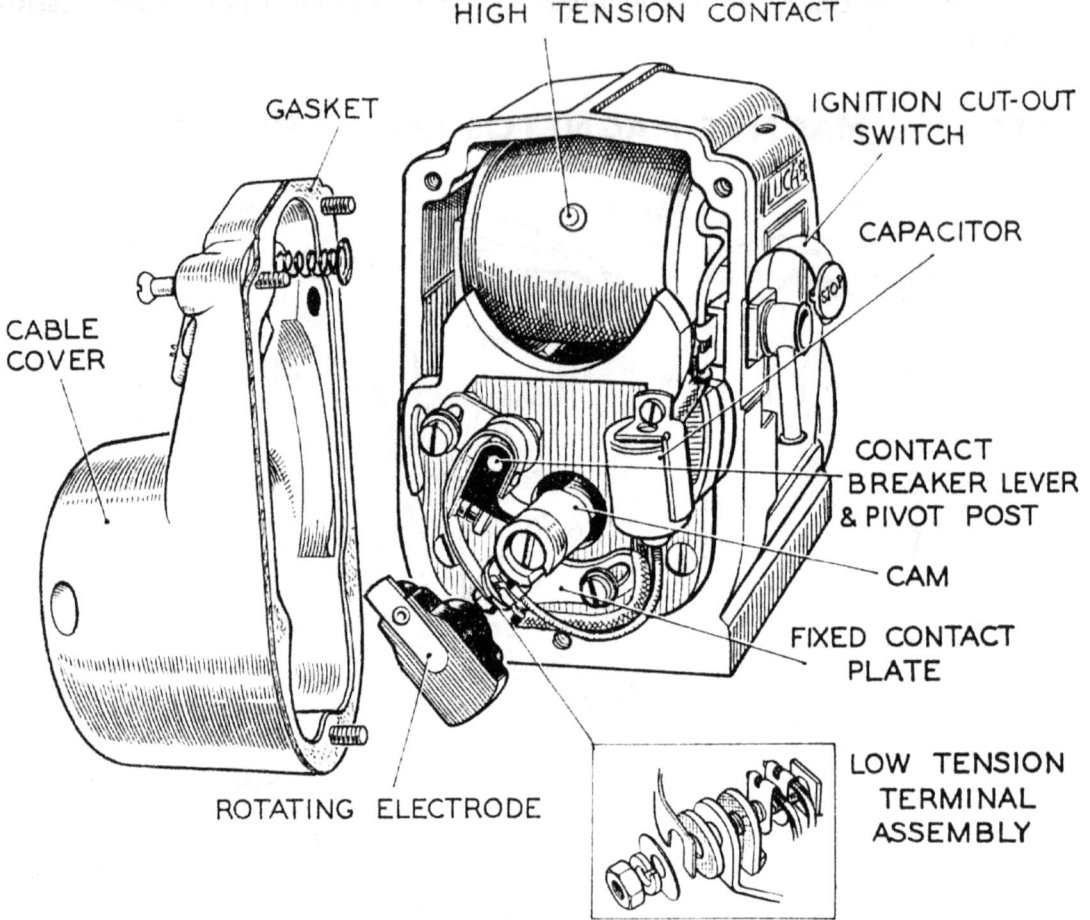

Fig. 15.

Note:—In some earlier magnetos, the rotating electrode shown in Fig. 15 was a common part with coil ignition distributors and the moulded portion carried the words "Remove to Oil." This instruction must be ignored on this magneto.

Every two years.

About every two years or when the engine is overhauled, the magneto should be dismantled at a Lucas Service Depot or Agent, where the weights, springs and toggles of the automatic timing control mechanism will be examined and lubricated with medium viscosity engine oil and the rotor bearings repacked with grease.

Replacing High Tension Cable.

When high tension cable shows signs of cracking or perishing, it must be renewed with 7 mm. p.v.c.-covered or neoprene-covered rubber insulated ignition cable. To do this, remove the cable cover, unscrew the cable securing screw and withdraw the defective cable. Cut the new cable to the required length and push one end well home into its terminal. Tighten the cable securing screw, which will pierce the insulation and contact the cable core.

Magneto-to-Engine Timing

Whenever possible, follow the engine manufacturer's instructions when re-timing a rotating magnet magneto to the engine. If, however, such instructions are not immediately available, the magneto-to-engine timing can (as a temporary measure only) be set so that the contact breaker opens when the cylinder under compression is at T.D.C.

STARTING MOTOR (Model M3)

The electric starter, fitted to certain machines, consists of a series wound electric motor having an extended armature shaft to carry, along straight splines, the engagement mechanism or drive assembly. The motor is of four-pole two-brush earth-return design, while the drive assembly includes, in addition to a pinion for meshing with the ring gear on the alternator rotor, a roller clutch to prevent the motor armature being driven by the engine after it has fired. The drive assembly is spring-loaded to the out-of-mesh position and an armature braking device is housed in the commutator end bracket. A starter switch, model 4S, is mounted on the motor yoke and actuated by the drive engagement lever. Except on occasions of tooth-to-tooth abutment, torque is developed by the rotor only when the pinion has engaged with the ring gear, and the current is automatically switched off before the pinion is withdrawn from engagement. Special provision, in the form of an overriding compression spring in the drive assembly, is made to counter tooth-to-tooth abutment.

Maintenance.

Occasionally inspect the switch terminal connection. This must be kept clean and tight.

No periodic lubrication is necessary, but when the machine is stripped down for overhaul the starting motor should be examined by a competent automobile electrician.

HEADLAMPS AND PARKING LIGHTS

Lucas motor cycle headlamps are all arranged to incorporate the Lucas Light Unit, which consists of a combined reflector and front lens assembly. A special "prefocus" bulb is used with the Light Unit, ensuring that when the bulb is fitted, the filament is correctly positioned in relation to the reflector, and no focusing is necessary. The parking light bulb holder is either a push fit in the rear of the Light Unit reflector, as shown in Figs. 16 and 18, or is carried in a separate lamp such as shown in Fig. 19.

On some machines a headlamp body is dispensed with and a nacelle type extension of the forks provides a housing for the Lucas Light Unit.

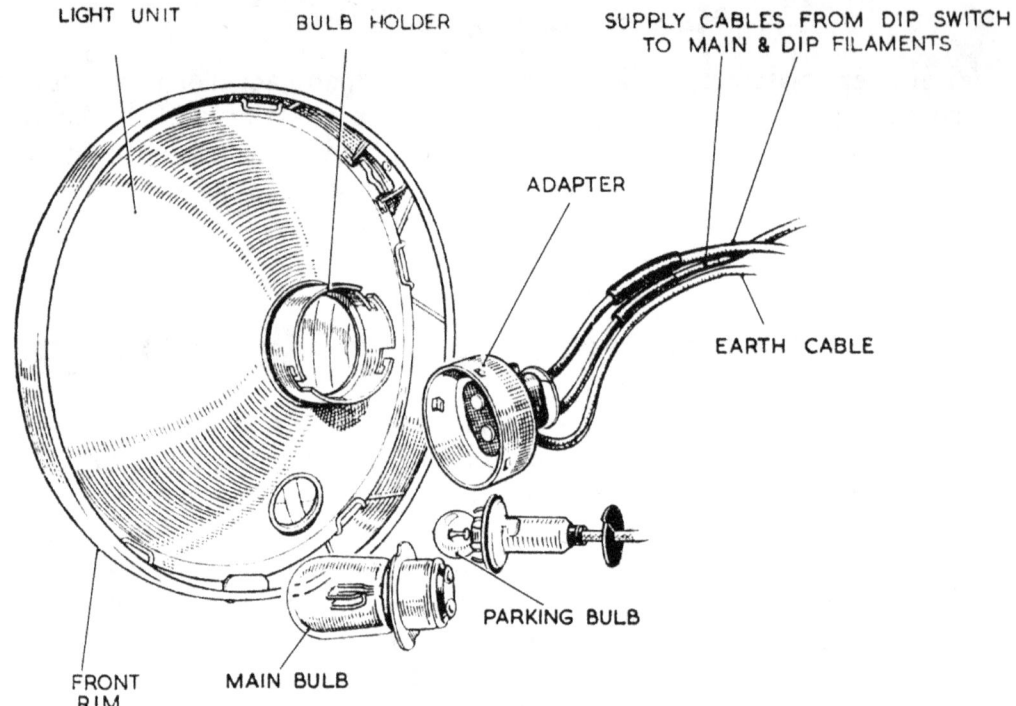

Fig. 16 Model F700P Light Unit and Rim removed from Lamp Body.

Setting.

Set the headlamp so that when the motor cycle carries its normal load the main or driving beam is projected straight ahead and parallel with the road surface.

Many garages possess a Lucas Beamsetter. This is a scientific instrument enabling accurate beam setting to be effected. Motor cycle owners are strongly advised to make use of this service whenever possible. When such facilities are not available, the headlamp can be set by marking off a smooth blank wall and shining the lamp on it from a distance of 25 feet. Details are shown in Fig. 17.

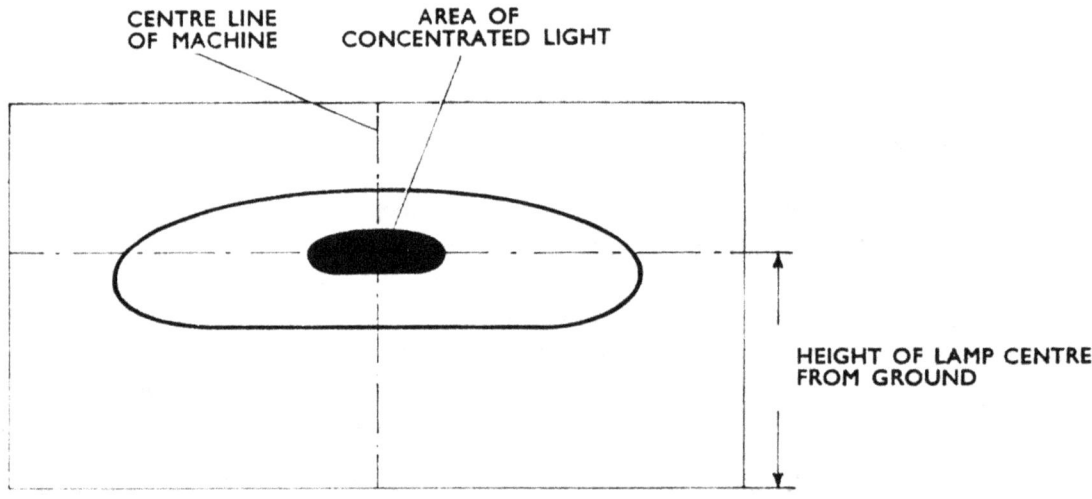

Fig. 17. Headlamp Main Beam Setting Diagram.

When setting :—

(a) Front of motor cycle to be square with screen.
(b) Motor cycle to be carrying normal load and standing on level ground.
(c) Recommended distance for setting is at least 25 feet.

On machines where the Light Unit is mounted in a nacelle or other special fitting, the motor cycle manufacturer's handbook should be referred to for instructions on setting the lamp.

Removing Headlamp Front.

Slacken the rim securing screw located at the top or bottom of the lamp body. On model MCF575 headlamps the securing screw at the bottom of the lamp must be unscrewed completely to release the lamp.

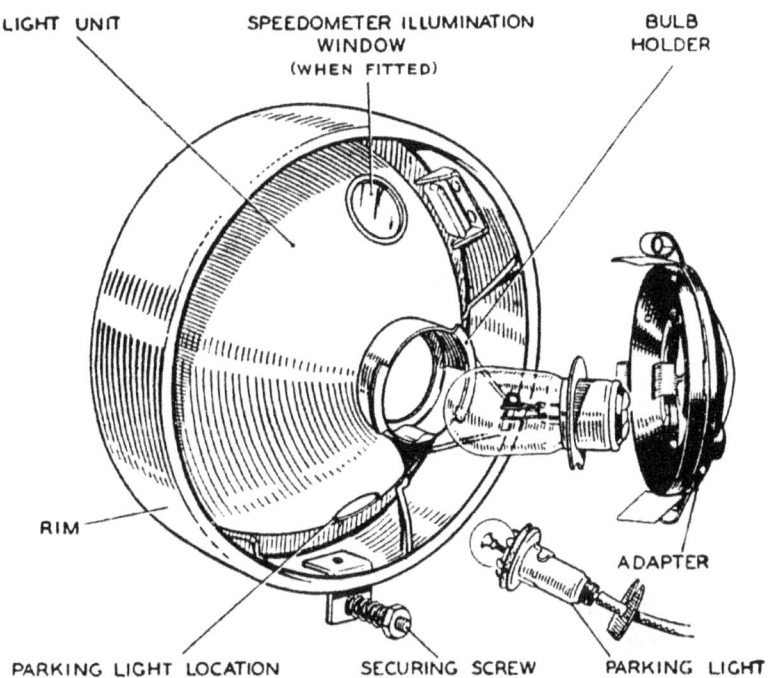

Fig. 18. Model F575P Light Unit and Rim removed from Lamp Body.

It will then be possible to detach the front rim complete with Light Unit assembly. To replace, locate the Light Unit assembly in the lamp body, press the front on and secure in position by tightening the securing screw.

Replacement of Bulbs.

When the replacement of a bulb is necessary, it is important not only that the same size bulb is fitted, but also that it has a high efficiency and will focus in the reflector. Cheap and inferior replacement bulbs often have the filament of such a shape that correct focusing is not possible ; for example, the filament may be to one side of the axis of the bulb, resulting in loss of range and light efficiency.

Lucas Genuine Spare Bulbs are specially tested to check that the filament is in the correct position to give the best results with Lucas lamps. To assist in identification, Lucas bulbs are marked on the metal cap with a number. When fitting a replacement, see that it has the same number as the original bulb.

To gain access to the headlamp bulb, remove the front rim and Light Unit assembly as previously described. Push on the adapter and twist it in an anti-clockwise direction to take it off. The bulb can now be removed from the rear of the reflector. Place the correct replacement bulb in the holder, engage the projections on the inside of the adapter, press on and secure by twisting to the right.

To gain access to the parking light bulb (if it is situated in the headlamp reflector) remove the front rim and Light Unit assembly and withdraw the bulb holder from the reflector in which it is a push-fit.

To gain access to the bulb in Model 550 (see Fig. 19), withdraw the rim securing screw and remove the rim. Peel back the rubber surround to release the lens.

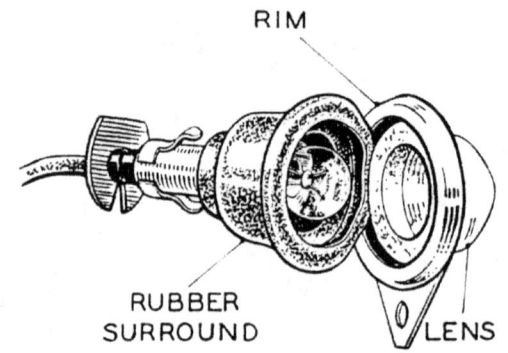

Fig. 19. Parking Light Model 550.

The correct parking light bulb replacement is Lucas No. 988 6-volt 3-watt miniature bayonet cap. The size of headlamp bulb varies with the type of alternator and the conditions under which the motor cycle is used.

Dipper Switch.

Every 5,000 miles the moving parts of the dipper switch should be lubricated with thin machine oil.

REAR LAMPS

Replacement Bulbs.

In the United Kingdom, the correct size of bulb to be used in rear lamps is based on the cubic capacity of the engine. Solo machines of 250 c.c. or less may be fitted with 3-watt bulbs. Combinations and machines exceeding 250 c.c. are required to be fitted with 6-watt bulbs.

Bulbs can be identified by number, usually stamped on the metal cap. When changing a defective bulb, the replacement should bear the same number as the original.

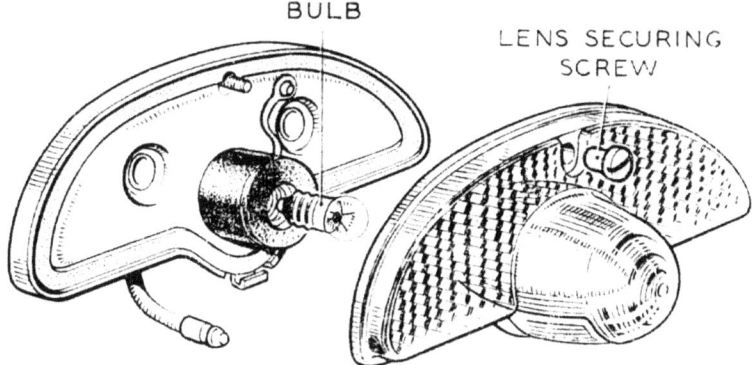

Fig. 20. Rear Lamp Model 590 incorporating Reflex Reflector.

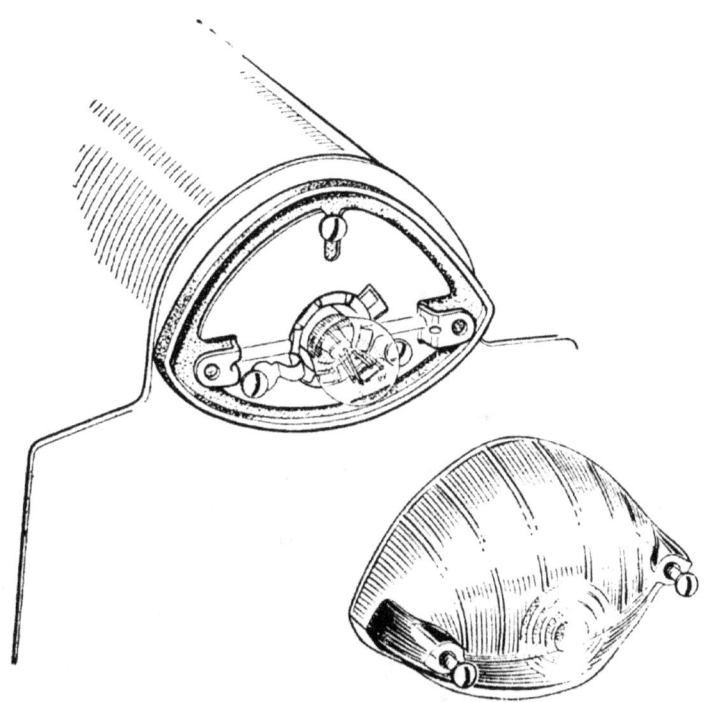

Fig. 21. Stop-Tail Lamp Model 529.

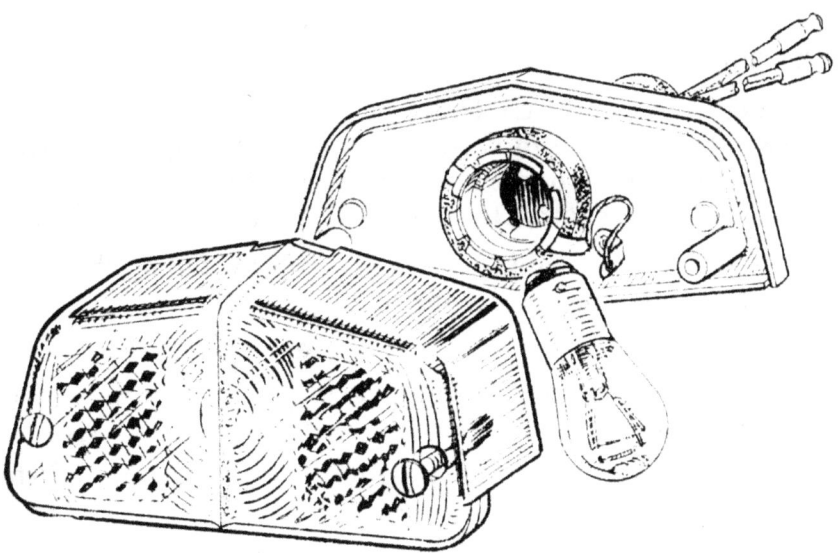

Fig. 22. Stop-Tail Lamp Model 564 incorporating Reflex Reflector.

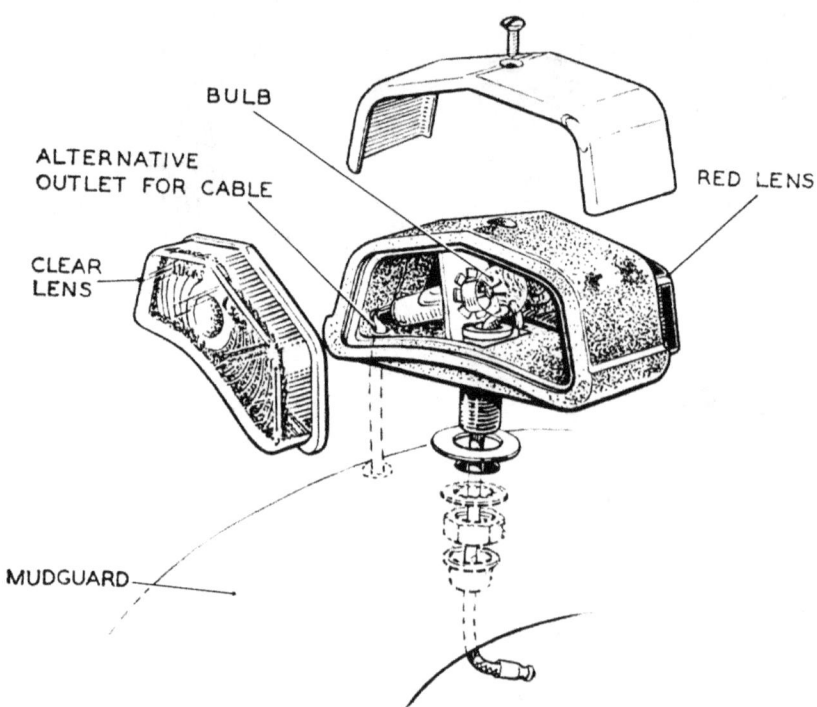

Fig. 23. Sidecar Lamp Model 569.

HOW TO CONNECT A FOGLAMP

As explained on Page 3, the alternator can only develop its maximum output when the lighting switch is turned to the 'H' position. This is because the alternator windings are switched to obtain the required charge rate by means of special contacts built into the lighting switch—the rate being least in the switch position 'Off' and most in 'H'.

It follows that a foglamp and its associated control switch should never be directly connected across the battery, since the alternator output in lighting switch position 'P' would be insufficient to balance the additional load and the resulting drain on the battery would soon cause the light from the foglamp to dim.

The correct method is to connect an additional dip switch (i.e., a single pole, two-way switch) in series with the existing dip switch in order to be able to select for operation either the headlamp or the foglamp, when the main lighting switch is turned to position 'H'. To do this:

(i) Disconnect the feed cable (normally blue) from the centre main terminal of the existing dip switch.

(ii) Connect this cable to the centre main terminal of the new switch.

(iii) Connect one of the two remaining terminals of the new switch to the centre main terminal of the existing switch.

(iv) Connect the third terminal of the new switch to one of the foglamp terminals.

(v) Connect the other terminal of the foglamp to earth.

An incidental advantage of this method of connection is that electrical overloading due to the simultaneous use of headlamp and foglamp is prevented and, further, the correct distribution of light to suit differing driving conditions is assured.

ELECTRIC HORNS

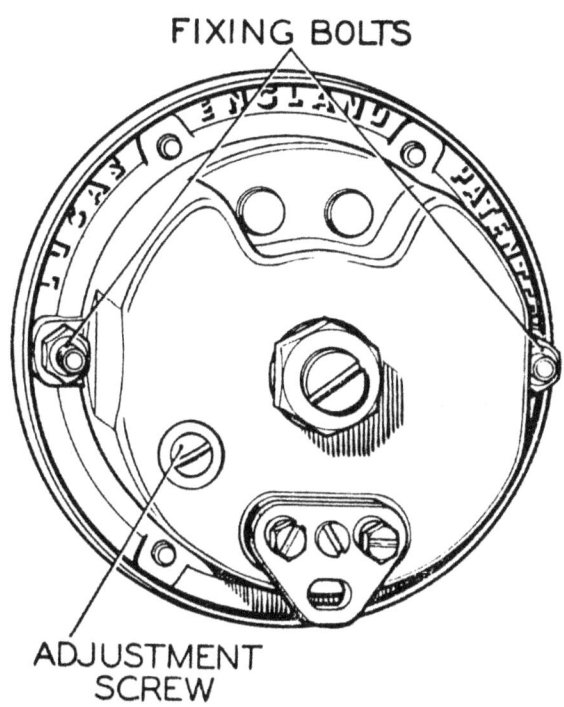

Fig. 24. Rear view of Horn Model HF1234.

Horns are pre-set to give their best performance and, in general, no further adjustment is necessary.

If the horn becomes uncertain in its action, giving only a choking sound, or does not vibrate, it does not follow that the horn has broken down — the trouble may be due to a discharged battery, a loose connection, or short-circuit in the wiring of the horn. In particular, ascertain that the horn push bracket is in good electrical contact with the handlebars.

It is also possible that the performance of a horn may be upset by its mounting becoming loose.

Adjustment of Models HF1234-5.

The following adjustment will not alter the note of the horn. It will take up any wear of the moving parts which, if not corrected, may result in roughness and loss of power.

Accurate adjustment requires the use of specialised instruments and tools, but the owner-rider, who may not possess these instruments, can carry out the following procedure if the horn performance is considered to have deteriorated :—

Operate the horn push and turn the adjustment screw anti-clockwise until the horn just fails to sound. Release the horn push and turn the adjustment screw clockwise for six notches, i.e., a quarter of a turn, when the original performance should be restored. If further adjustment is necessary, turn the screw one notch at a time.

If the original performance cannot be restored by adjustment, do not attempt to dismantle the horn, but return it to a Lucas Service Depot for examination.

Note:—A few HF1234 horns made during 1950-51 were not provided with the above adjustment screw. No adjustment is therefore possible with these horns. Similarly, no adjustment is possible with Models HF1440 and HF1441.

Adjustment of Model HF1849.

Service experience with this horn shows that a small amount of adjustment may be needed at infrequent intervals to ensure that the horn continues to give its best performance.

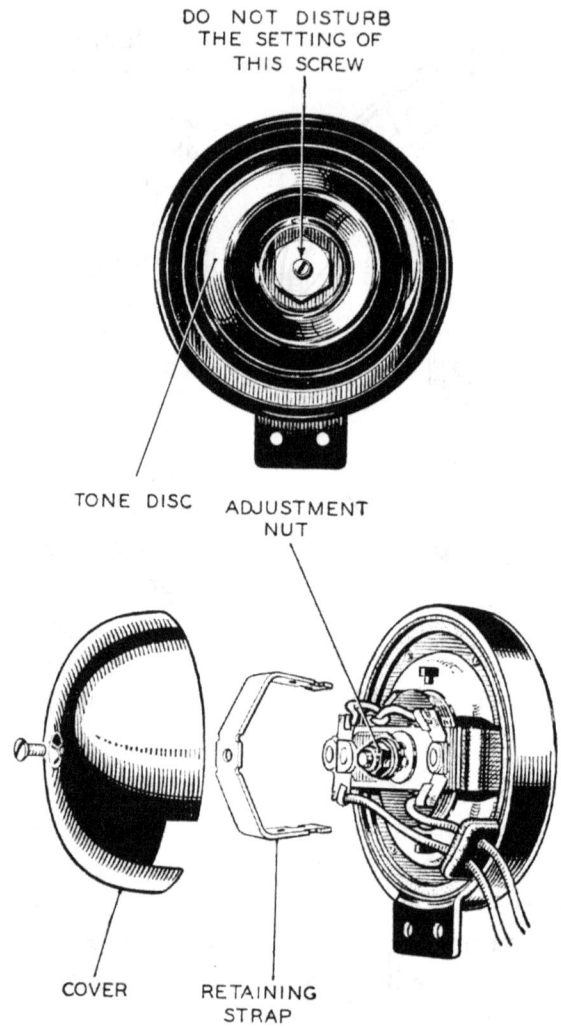

Fig. 25. Model HF1849 Horn with Rear Cover removed for Contact Breaker adjustment.

To make this adjustment, first remove the cover and retaining strap from the rear of the horn. Then, with the horn operating and using a 2BA spanner, turn the adjustment nut slowly in an anti-clockwise direction until the best performance is obtained. Usually, only a very small amount of movement will be necessary.

Important : The slotted screw in the centre of the tone disc on the front of the horn is accurately set during manufacture, and is secured in position by a locknut. This setting must not be disturbed.

LOCATION AND REMEDY OF FAULTS

Although every precaution is taken to eliminate all possible causes of trouble, failure may occasionally develop through lack of attention to the equipment, or damage to the wiring. The following pages set out the recommended procedure for a systematic examination to locate and remedy the causes of some of the more probable faults. The sources of many troubles are by no means obvious, and in some cases a considerable amount of deduction from the symptoms is needed before the cause of the trouble is disclosed.

When checking the continuity of circuits, a flashlamp battery and bulb should be used. On no account must the end of a live cable be flicked to earth against the motor cycle frame. This practice, known as " flashing," can cause heavy currents to flow round the alternator windings and result in the partial demagnetisation of the rotor and reduction of output. If a separate motor cycle battery is used, a low wattage test lamp must be included in the circuit.

If, after carrying out the examination, the cause of the trouble is not found, the owner is advised to get in touch with the nearest Lucas Service Depot or Agent.

A.C. LIGHTING-IGNITION UNITS.

Engine will not start in IGN Position.

(a) Turn switch to EMG position. If the engine will now fire, the alternator and rectifier are operating correctly and the indication is a discharged battery; this can be confirmed by poor light from the lamps and hydrometer readings below 1.200. Recharge the battery if necessary.

(b) Remove the H.T. cable from the sparking plug terminal and hold the cable end about $\frac{1}{8}$-in. away from some metal part of the engine while the latter is slowly turned over. If sparks jump the gap regularly, the ignition equipment is functioning correctly. Check for engine defects or examine sparking plug.

(c) If sparks do not occur in test (b), check for a fault in the low tension wiring, i.e., from battery to switch, coil and contact breaker. If the wiring proves to be in order, examine the contact breaker; if necessary clean the contacts and adjust the gap setting.

(d) If, after carrying out these checks, the ignition system is still inoperative, have it examined by a Lucas Service Depot or Agent.

Engine will not start in EMG Position.

(a) Remove the H.T. cable and test as described under (b) above: if sparks appear, then the trouble is due to engine defects, etc.

(b) If the ignition equipment is not operative in the above test, check the snap connectors, rectifier connections and other wiring. All connections must be clean and tight.

(c) Examine the contact breaker; if necessary clean the contacts and adjust the gap setting.
(d) Make sure ignition timing is correct to engine maker's specification.
(e) See that the alternator rotor is fitted the correct way round on the engine shaft.
(f) If the ignition system is still inoperative, have the equipment examined by a Lucas Service Depot or Agent.

Engine misfires.

(a) Examine the contact breaker; if necessary, clean the contacts and adjust the gap.
(b) Remove the sparking plug (or each plug in turn), rest it on the cylinder head and observe if a spark occurs at the plug points when the engine is turned. Irregular sparking may be due to dirty plugs, which may be cleaned and adjusted, or to defective high tension cables. Any cable on which the insulation shows signs of deterioration or cracking should be renewed.
(c) If sparking is regular at each plug when tested as described in (b), the trouble is probably due to engine defects, and the carburetter, petrol supply, etc., must be examined.
(d) If misfiring occurs after the engine has been running for some time, check that the ignition switch is in the normal IGN position. If run continuously in the EMG position, the rising voltage of the battery may eventually cause misfiring to occur.

ENERGY TRANSFER ("E.T.") IGNITION.

Important

1. Keep the contact breaker clean and its maximum opening correctly set to 0.014"—0.016".
2. Keep the sparking plug electrodes clean and correctly set.
3. Keep to the manufacturer's timing instructions.

Regarding notes one and three above, it is the magneto performance or spark energy developed by the alternator (in addition to the piston-to-spark relationship) that is involved. Since the rotor is keyed to the engine crankshaft which, in turn, is coupled through the connecting rod to the piston, any movement of the piston whilst timing will affect the position of the crankshaft and hence the magnetic timing position of the rotor. Thus the maximum magneto performance of the alternator can only be obtained with accurately set contact breaker and timing.

Engine will not start, difficult to start or misfires.

(a) Remove the H.T. cable from the sparking plug and hold the cable end about $\frac{1}{8}$" from the cylinder block. Sparks should jump this gap regularly when the engine is turned at kick-start speed.
(b) If sparks are obtained, check the sparking plug, reset and clean, or renew, as necessary.

(c) If no sparks are obtained, inspect the H.T. cable and renew, as necessary. Check contact breaker gap setting.

(d) If the sparking plug, H.T. cable and contact breaker gap setting are satisfactory, check for engine defects, faulty fuel supply, etc.

(e) If, after carrying out these checks, the ignition system is still unsatisfactory, have the equipment examined by a Lucas Service Depot or Agent.

MAGNETO IGNITION.

Engine will not start or difficult to start.

(a) See that the controls are correctly set for starting, petrol turned on, etc.

(b) Turn off the petrol tap. Remove the sparking plug (or plugs), and place on the cylinder head. If a spark occurs regularly at the plug points when the engine is slowly hand-cranked, the magneto is in order. Look for engine defects and check ignition timing.

(c) If a spark does not occur in (b), disconnect the high tension cable from the plug and hold the cable end about $\frac{1}{8}$" from a metal part of the engine. If a spark occurs regularly when the engine is cranked, the plug is faulty. If there is no spark, disconnect the high tension cable at the magneto, replace with a new length of cable and test again as before.

(d) Should there still be no spark, possible causes of trouble are : contact breaker gap out of adjustment or contacts dirty ; contact breaker rocker arm sticking ; or, with rotating armature magnetos, pick-up brush worn or broken, or slip ring track dirty. Remedy as described.

Engine misfires.

(a) Check as in para. (b) and (c) above to eliminate engine defects, faulty high tension cable and sparking plug.

(b) Check magneto as in para. (d) above.

(c) If the fault persists, have the magneto examined by a Lucas Service Depot or Agent.

CHARGING CIRCUIT.

Refer also to " Alternative Battery Charging Rates " on page 4.

Battery in low state of charge.

(a) This state will be shown by poor or no light from the lamps when the engine is stationary, with a varying light intensity when the motor cycle is running.

(b) If, with an A.C. Lighting-Ignition unit, the engine starts and runs in the EMG position, this indicates that the rectifier is functioning correctly.

(c) Check the condition of the battery with a hydrometer. Top up, if necessary, and have battery recharged.

(d) Check wiring from battery to switch, rectifier and alternator, tightening any loose connections or replacing broken cables.

(e) If the cause of the trouble is still not apparent, have the equipment examined by a Lucas Service Depot or Agent.

Excess Circuit Voltage.

(a) This will be indicated by burnt-out or blackened bulbs, and possibly poor engine performance due to burned ignition contacts.

(b) Examine all wiring for loose or broken connections.

(c) Check the earthing of battery and rectifier.

(d) Examine the battery, removing any traces of corrosion.

(e) If the ignition is affected (A.C. Lighting-Ignition units only) clean the contact breaker contacts or, if necessary, renew them.

(f) If the fault persists, have the equipment examined by a Lucas Service Depot or Agent.

THE BATTERY POSITIVE (+ve) TERMINAL IS EARTHED TO THE MACHINE. UNDER NO CIRCUMSTANCES MUST THE NEGATIVE (—ve) TERMINAL BE EARTHED.

LIGHTING CIRCUITS.

Failure of lights (machine stationary).

(a) If only one bulb fails to light, replace with new bulb.

(b) If all lamps fail to light, test the state of charge of battery, recharging it if necessary either by a long period of daytime running or by connecting to a suitable battery charger.

(c) Examine the wiring for a broken or loose connection, and remedy.

Lamps light when switched on, but gradually fade.

Test the state of charge of the battery, recharging if necessary.

Brilliance varies with speed of motor cycle.

Test the state of charge of the battery, recharging if necessary.

Lights flicker.

Examine the wiring for loose connections, or short circuits caused by faulty cable insulation.

Headlamp illumination insufficient.

(a) If the bulb is discoloured or filaments have sagged as a result of long service, a new bulb of the same type should be fitted.

(b) Check the setting of the lamp.

SERVICE DEPOTS

BELFAST, 1 ... ... 51-55 Upper Library Street
Telephone: Belfast 25617   Telegrams: "Servdep, Belfast"

BIRMINGHAM, 18 ... ... Great Hampton Street
Telephone: Central 5050   Telegrams: "Lucaserv, Birmingham"

BRIGHTON, 4 ... ... 85 Old Shoreham Road, Hove
Telephone: Hove 38993   Telegrams: "Luserv, Brighton"

BRISTOL, 4 ... ... 345 Bath Road
Telephone: Bristol 79311   Telegrams: "Kingly, Bristol"

CAMBRIDGE ... ... Newmarket Road
Telephone: Cambridge 51251   Telegrams: "Luserv, Cambridge"

CARDIFF ... ... 54a Penarth Road
Telephone: Cardiff 28361   Telegrams: "Lucas, Cardiff"

CORK ... ... Bachelors Quay
Telephone: Cork 21911 (3 Lines)   Telegrams: "Luserv, Cork"

COVENTRY ... ... Coventry Road, Exhall
Telephone: Bedworth 3077   Telegrams: "Luserv, Coventry"

DUBLIN ... ... Portland Street North, North Circular Road
Telephone: Dublin 46195-8   Telegrams: "Luserv, Dublin"

EDINBURGH, 11 ... ... 60 Stevenson Road, Gorgie
Telephone: Donaldson 2311   Telegrams: "Luserv, Edinburgh"

GLASGOW, C.3 ... ... 4-24 Grant Street (St. George's Road)
Telephone: Douglas 6591-7   Telegrams: "Lucas, Glasgow"

LEEDS, 8 ... ... 64 Roseville Road
Telephone: Leeds 28591   Telegrams: "Luserdep, Leeds"

LIVERPOOL, 13 ... ... 450/470 Edge Lane
Telephone: Stoneycroft 4721   Telegrams: "Luserv, Liverpool 13"

LONDON W.3 ... ... Dordrecht Road, Acton Vale
Telephone: Shepherds Bush 3160   Telegrams: "Lucas Dynomagna, London"

LONDONDERRY   147 Strand Road, Londonderry, N. Ireland
Telephone: Londonderry 3985

MANCHESTER ... ... Talbot Road, Stretford
Telephone: Longford 1101   Telegrams: "Lucas, Stretford"

NEWCASTLE-ON-TYNE, 1 ... ... 64-68 St. Mary's Place
Telephone: Newcastle 25571   Telegrams: "Motolite, Newcastle-on-Tyne"

WOODFORD GREEN   Southend Road, Woodford Green, Essex
Telephone: Crescent 6711-5   Telegrams: "Luserv, Woodford-Green, London"

LONDON SALES OFFICE ... ... 319 Regent Street, W.1
Telephone: Langham 4311   Telegrams: "Guidepost, Wesdo, London"

JOSEPH LUCAS (EXPORT) LTD. ... 46 Park Street, W.1
Telephone: Grosvenor 4491   Telegrams: (Inland) "Lucaslond, Audley, London"
                      (Overseas) "Lucaslond, London"

NOTES

LUCAS SERVICE INFORMATION

MOTOR CYCLE ELECTRICAL EQUIPMENT
SERVICE MANUAL

37p

JOSEPH LUCAS (SALES & SERVICE) LTD., BIRMINGHAM B18 6AU

LUCAS

motor cycle
electrical equipment

SERVICE MANUAL

JOSEPH LUCAS (SALES & SERVICE) LTD · BIRMINGHAM B18 6AU

Publication No. 3152   10M/1270/DL   Printed in England

Contents

Section 1
WORKING PRINCIPALS:

	Pages
A.C. ignition	12
A simple alternator	5
Controlling the alternator output	8
Emergency starting	8
Full-wave rectification	7
Half-wave rectification	7
Importance of correct timing for emergency ignition	11
Poor starting on emergency	11
Producing an E.M.F.	5
Special application	8
12-volt charging system and capacitor ignition	13

Section II
EQUIPMENT AND MAINTENANCE:

Batteries:
Maintenance in service	16
Preparation in service	16

Charging equipment:
Alternator	20
Ammeter	21
Rectifier	20
Zener diode	21

Coil ignition:
Ignition coil	18
Warning light	19
2CP capacitor pack	18
2MC capacitor	19
4CA and 4CC contact breaker	18
6CA contact breaker	17
7CA contact breaker	17

Component box	25
Horns	22

Lighting equipment:
Flashing indicators	22
Head and parking lights	21
Rear lights	22
Replacement bulbs	22

Starters	22

Switches:
Handlebar switches	24
Ignition/lighting switch	25

57SA lighting switch	24
118SA stop lamp switch	24
Wiring:	
Cable harness	23
Fused battery lead	23
H.T. cables	24
Suppressed cable (General)	24

Section III
GENERAL INFORMATION:

Anti-theft switch	31
Clipper diode	30
Lucar connectors	32
Twin horns	31
2MC capacitor ignition system	29
12-volt conversion	26

Section IV
TEST PROCEDURE:

Unit tests	
Equipment required	33
Batteries	33
Charging	33
Emergency circuit	36
Energy transfer (A.C. ignition)	37
Ignition	35
Ignition coil bench test	37
Rectifier	34
Zener diode	35
2MC capacitor system	36
3ET coil bench test	37

Section V
LOCATION AND REMEDY OF FAULTS:

A.C. ignition system	39
Charging equipment	39
Coil ignition system	39
Lighting equipment	39

TYPICAL WIRING DIAGRAMS:

6-volt system with PRS8 switch	42
6-volt system with 88SA switches	43
12-volt two-charge rate	44
12-volt full output	45
Energy transfer single	46
Energy transfer twin	47
Capacitor ignition	48
Three-cylinder motor cycle	49
Component box motor cycles	50
Anti-theft switch circuit	51

© JOSEPH LUCAS (SALES & SERVICE) LTD., 1971

INTRODUCTION

For many years Lucas have supplied electrical equipment for the majority of British motor cycles. During this time electrical equipment has developed through 6-volt charging systems, coil ignition and A.C. ignition to 12-volt systems with starting motors and capacitor igintion.

This Service Manual describes the operating principles of present day motor cycle equipment, and maintenance necessary at normal service intervals. By following the systematic test procedure time spent on fault diagnosis will be reduced to an absolute minimum.

Older motor cycles can often be modified to the latest specification. Details of the conversion to 12-volt electrical system, capacitor ignition etc. have been included. Wiring diagrams of the circuits are provided.

The scope of this edition of the SB519 has been extended to include ignition, lighting and auxillary equipment, so that the title has been changed to "Motor Cycle Electrical Equipment Service Manual".

WORKING PRINCIPLES

How an E.M.F. is Produced

When a conductor is moved through a magnetic field, an electro-motive force or E.M.F. is induced in it. If the conductor forms a loop or closed circuit, an electric current will register on a sensitive meter connected in the conductor circuit. When the conductor is moved downwards, as shown in the illustration Fig. 1A, the needle swings in a direction corresponding to the direction of current flow. If the conductor is moved upwards, Fig. 1B, the needle will swing in the opposite direction, indicating that the current flow is also in the opposite direction.

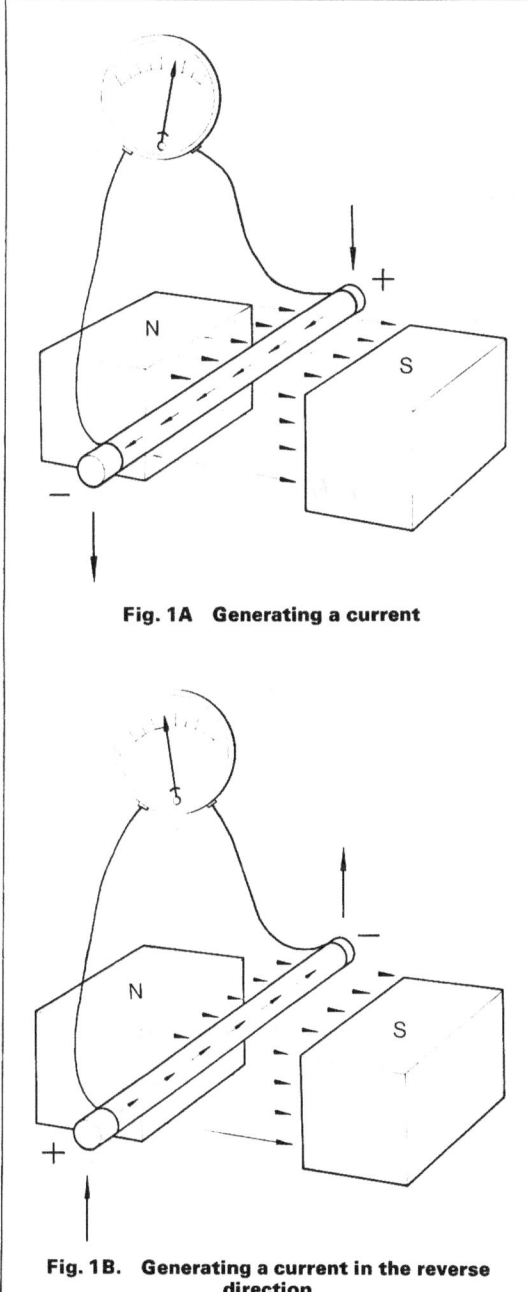

Fig. 1A   Generating a current

Fig. 1B.   Generating a current in the reverse direction

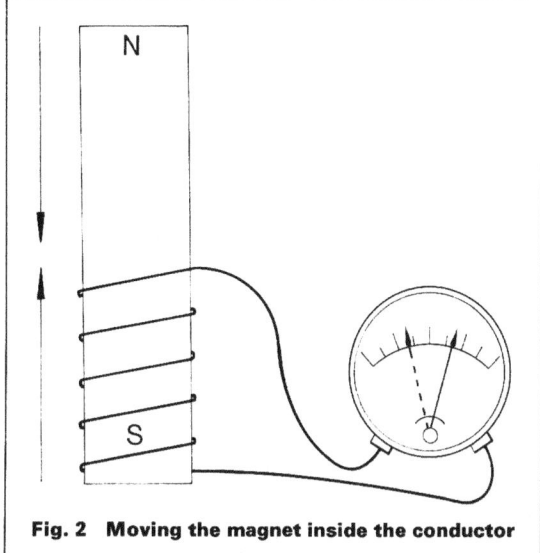

Fig. 2   Moving the magnet inside the conductor

The amount of movement of the needle will depend upon the speed at which the conductor is moved up and down, and the density of the magnetic field. The same effect can be obtained by moving a magnet in and out of a coil of wire, Fig. 2. Induction will again take place and current flows in the wire coil. This time, because the coil consists of several turns of wire, instead of one single conductor, the induction will be increased, thereby giving a greater output. The sensitive meter, if connected across the ends of the coil, will register in exactly the same manner as it did with the single conductor, except a larger deflection will occur.

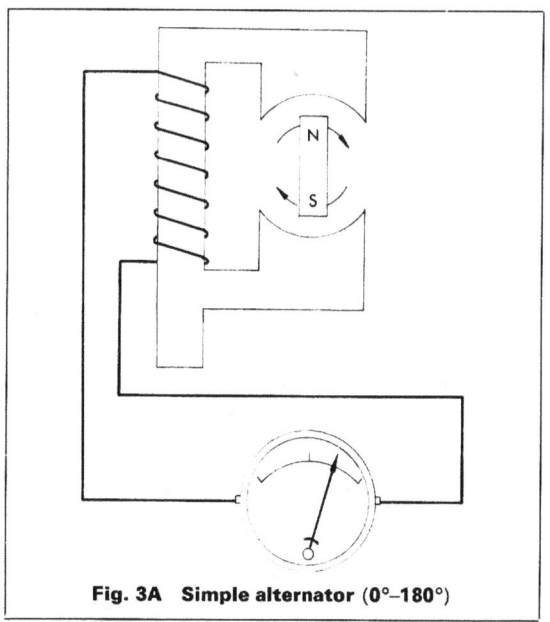

Fig. 3A   Simple alternator (0°–180°)

A Simple Alternator

Figures 3A and 3B show an alternator in its simplest form. The coil has now been wound round an iron yoke which concentrates the magnetic field around the coil. In the centre of the yoke a bar magnet is rotated.

The direction of the magnetic field will change every 180° of rotation of the magnet. In 3A illustration the north pole is at the top, but after the magnet has rotated 180°, 3B, the south pole is at the top. The magnetic field has been reversed. The direction of current flow in the coil has also been reversed. Induction has taken place due to movement of the magnet in close proximity to the coil, and alternating current has been produced.

The sine wave shown in Fig. 4 is a simple representation of the current output from an elementary alternator. It shows the current output during one complete revolution of the bar magnet alternator illustrated in Figs. 3A and 3B.

The vertical line represents the current in amperes, which is positive, above the neutral point or horizontal line; and negative below the neutral line. Starting from the left side, this line is divided into 360°, that is, one complete revolution of the bar magnet. From 0° the current gradually builds up to its maximum value at 90°; then gradually decreases until it is zero again at 180°. It now continues in the

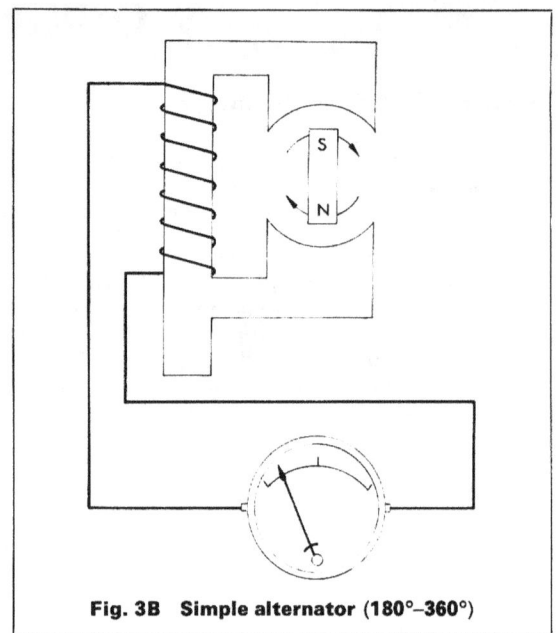

Fig. 3B Simple alternator (180°–360°)

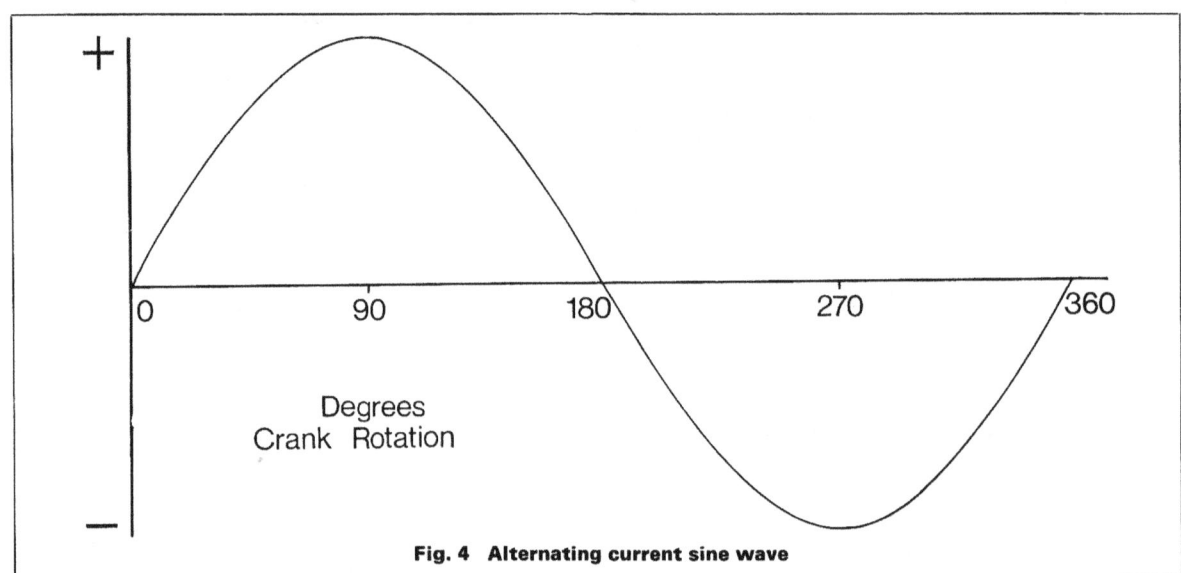

Fig. 4 Alternating current sine wave

negative direction reaching a maximum at 270°, then gradually reduced again, becoming zero at 360°. This cycle is repeated as long as the magnet is rotated.

Exactly the same thing happens with the motor cycle alternator. The current generated in the coils is used for lighting, and ignition purposes, etc. This type of alternator uses a magnetic six-pole rotor to cause the flux reversals, Fig. 5. The coils are stationary, being fixed to the stator assembly.

Rectifier for Battery Charging

Because of the alternating characteristic of the current produced by the alternator it cannot be connected directly to a battery for charging purposes. A battery can only be charged by a D.C. current. If a battery is to be charged by the alternator, then a rectifier must be incorporated in the circuit.

A rectifier is a device for converting an alternating current, Fig. 6A, B and C, into a direct current either by the suppression or inversion of alternate half-waves.

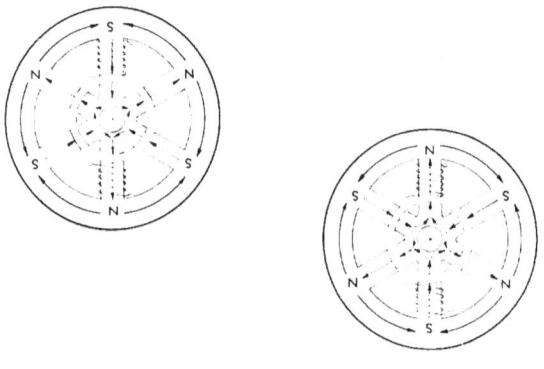

Fig. 5 Lucas alternator arrangement

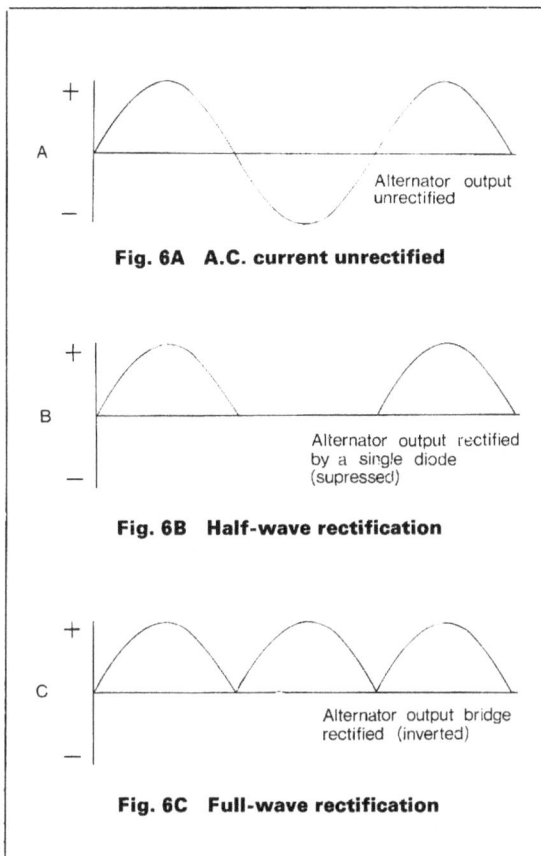

Fig. 6A A.C. current unrectified

Fig. 6B Half-wave rectification

Fig. 6C Full-wave rectification

Silicon diode rectifiers are used with Lucas A.C. equipment. The rectifier consists of 4 diodes, which act as one-way valves. Each consists of two small blocks of pure silicon specially treated by the addition of certain impurities. The blocks are then joined as shown in Fig. 7. Current then flows in the direction of the arrow. The symbol for the diode is shown.

With a diode of this type in the circuit, the generator can be connected so as to charge the

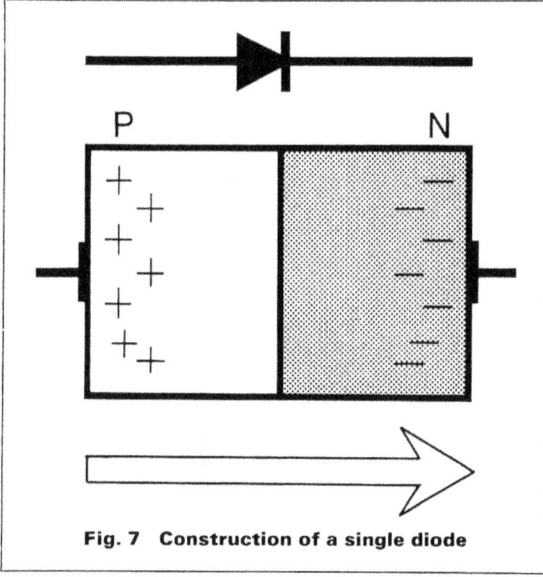

Fig. 7 Construction of a single diode

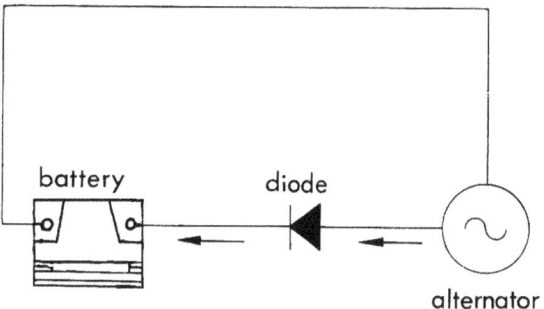

Fig. 8 Half-wave rectification

battery. The alternating output, which in effect would try to flow round the circuit, first in a clockwise direction and then in an anti-clockwise direction, becomes D.C., and current therefore will always flow through the battery in the same direction, Fig. 6B. The negative half-waves, which are shown below the horizontal line, have been suppressed, and only the positive half waves above the line are allowed to pass through the rectifier and round the circuit. This arrangement is known as half-wave rectification. as shown in Fig. 8.

In using this method of battery charging, however, one half-cycle of our generator output is unused. In practice this problem is overcome by the use of a full-wave rectifier.

Full-Wave Rectification

A full-wave rectifier consists of four elements, of the type shown in Fig. 7, connected so as to allow the full output from the alternator to pass through to the battery.

The illustrations in Fig. 9 show the bridge rectifier connected in circuit with an alternator and battery. The left-hand illustration (A) shows the circuit when

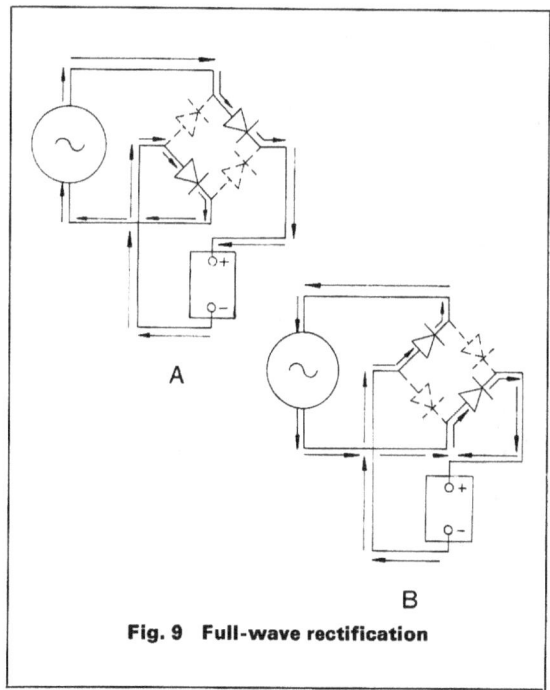

Fig. 9 Full-wave rectification

current is flowing in a clockwise direction; the right-hand illustration (B) an anti-clockwise direction. With this arrangement the full output from the generator is utilised. That is, both the positive half waves and the negative half waves are used to charge the battery, shown by the graph C in Fig. 6, by inversion of the negative half wave.

The silicon diode bridge rectifier incorporates four diodes, each mounted on a small circular plate which acts as a heat-sink.

Controlling the Alternator Output

The simple alternator described previously is, of course, not satisfactory for normal requirements, and in practice the alternator contains several coils, and the bar magnet becomes a multi-pole unit. The ampere output from such an alternator is considerably more than would be obtained from the unit with the single coil and bar magnet. Some form of output control is therefore necessary, otherwise the generator output would remain at a maximum irrespective of load requirements and the battery would become overcharged. The alternator stator carries six coils, one on each pole. These are three pairs of coils, each connected in series. The first pair have a green/black cable connected to them, the other two pairs are

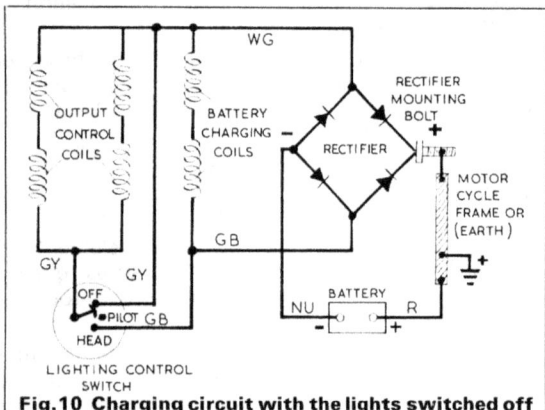

Fig. 10 Charging circuit with the lights switched off

linked together and connected to a green/yellow cable. All the coils have the remaining terminals connected to a common white/green cable.

The single pair of coils connected permanently across the bridge rectifier provide some charging current for the battery, whenever the engine is running.

Connections to the remaining coils vary according to the positions of the lighting and ignition switch, with the ignition key in the IGN position, for coil ignition the basic output control circuits are shown in Figs. 10, 11 and 12.

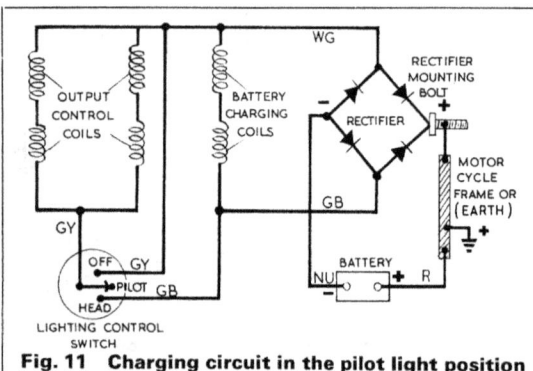

Fig. 11 Charging circuit in the pilot light position

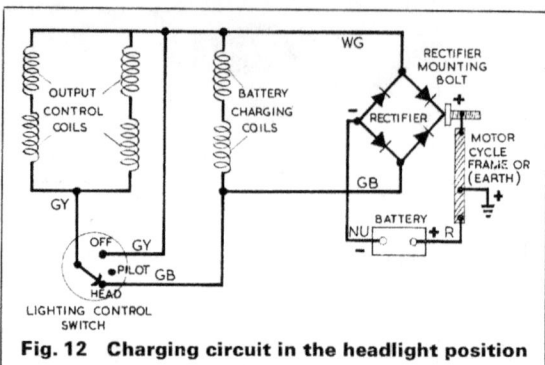

Fig. 12 Charging circuit in the headlight position

With the lighting switch in the OFF position, the output control coils are short-circuited, as shown in Fig. 10, and the alternator output is regulated to its minimum value by the interaction of the coil flux, set up by the heavy current circulating in the short-circuited coils, with the flux of the magnet rotor. Trickle-charging is provided by the permanently connected charging coils.

In the PILOT position, Fig. 11, the control coils are disconnected and the regulating fluxes are consequently reduced. The alternator output therefore increases and compensates for the additional parking light load. On certain applications the short circuit lead is omitted in the OFF position giving the higher output for both OFF and PILOT positions.

In the HEAD position, Fig. 12, the alternator output is further increased by connecting the control coils in parallel with the charging coil. Maximum output is now obtained.

Special Applications

AA and Police machines fitted with two-way radio do not have a short circuit lead in the OFF position. They also incorporate a separate "boost" control switch, which can be used at any time, irrespective of the position of the main lighting switch. When in the "boost" or closed position, maximum output is obtained from the alternator, see Fig. 13. When the switch is open, the output from the alternator depends upon the position of the lighting switch.

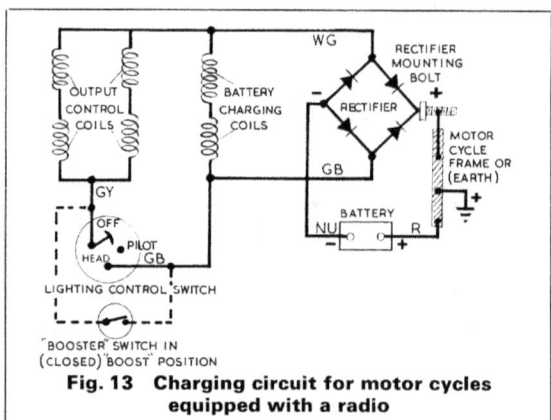

Fig. 13 Charging circuit for motor cycles equipped with a radio

Emergency Starting

Motor cycles fitted with coil ignition and the alternator-rectifier battery charging system are normally provided with a means of starting the engine when the battery is badly discharged. For this purpose, a three-position ignition switch is used, marked IGN, OFF and EMG. On switching to

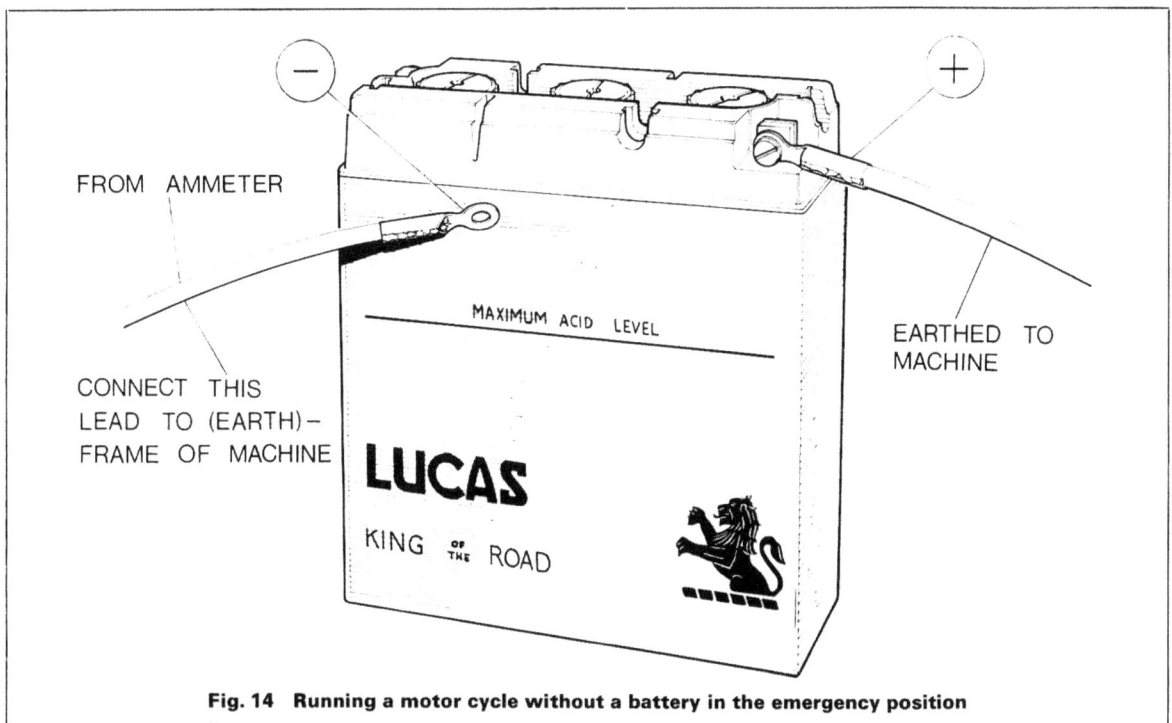

Fig. 14 Running a motor cycle without a battery in the emergency position

EMG and kick-starting the engine, the battery receives a high charging current, and after running for a while, the ignition switch should be turned back to the normal running position IGN. (In the case of single-cylinder machines and twins fitted with two ignition coils, the appropriate time to change back to normal ignition is indicated by a tendency for the engine to misfire. This is because the rising battery voltage is in opposition to the alternator voltage, and consequently the amount of energy available for transfer to the ignition coil is reduced).

The emergency starting feature also enables short journeys to be made (if absolutely essential) without battery or lighting. This is done by connecting the cable normally attached to the battery negative terminal to an earth point on the machine, Fig. 14, and kick-starting the engine with the ignition switch in the EMG position.

Thus a rider can return home even if his battery has failed completely. It must be emphasised, however, that continuous running in these conditions would result in badly burnt contacts in the distributor or contact breaker unit and cannot therefore, be recommended. Also the lighting system must not be switched on.

Single-Cylinder Machines

When current flows through the windings in the direction indicated by the arrows in Fig. 15 and the contacts are closed, the main return circuit to the alternator is through one arm of the rectifier bridge. As the contacts separate the built-up electromagnetic energy of the alternator windings quickly discharges through an alternative circuit provided by the battery and the ignition coil primary winding. This rapid transfer of energy from the alternator to coil causes H.T. to be induced in the ignition coil secondary windings and a spark occurs at the plug.

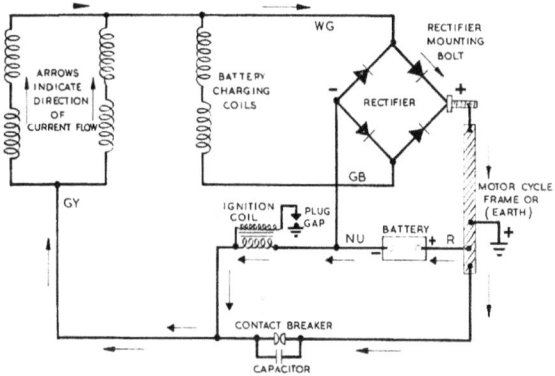

Fig. 15 Emergency start circuit for single cylinder motor cycles

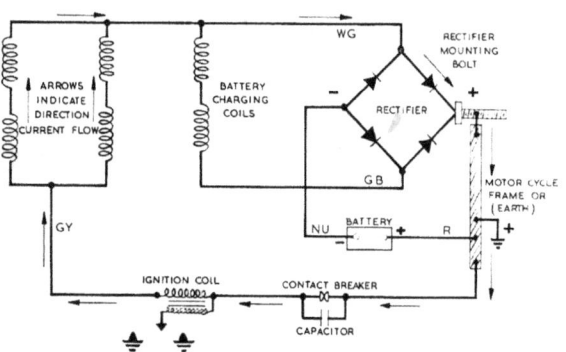

Fig. 16 Emergency start circuit for twin cylinder motor cycles with a distributor

Twin-Cylinder Machines
(single ignition coil and distributor)

Fig. 16 shows that the ignition coil primary winding and the contact breaker are connected in series, and not in parallel as for single cylinder machines. This enables a simpler harness and switching system to be used on twin cylinder machines, but it is unsuitable for use with single cylinder machines due to "idle" sparking before the contacts separate. Twin engines, fitted with a distributor, are unaffected by this premature sparking.

With single cylinder machines connected as shown in Fig. 15 "idle" sparking occurs after the contacts have separated and so does not affect these engines.

The machine should not run continuously with the switch in the emergency start position, because the rising voltage of the battery opposes that of the alternator and gradually the energy available for transfer to the ignition coil is reduced.

The engine will misfire, reminding the rider that he has not returned the ignition key to the IGN position.

Twin-Cylinder Machines (twin ignition coils and twin contact-breakers)

When the ignition switch is in the normal running position IGN, each coil, with its associated pair of contact-breaker contacts, serves one of the cylinders – each functioning as an ordinary battery coil ignition circuit. On switching to EMG, however, one of the ignition coils functions on the energy transfer principle.

The illustration (Fig. 17) shows the circuit used for emergency starting. The No. 1 contact-breaker is arranged to open when the alternating current in the windings reaches a maximum in the direction shown by the large arrows.

The system functions as follows:—

With the contacts closed, the main return circuit to the alternator is then via one arm (diode) of the rectifier bridge and the closed contacts. In effect the four output control windings have been short-circuited allowing a heavy current to build up and circulate through them.

As soon as the contacts separate, this built-up energy discharges through an alternative circuit provided by the battery and primary winding of the No. 1 or EMG ignition coil. The rapid transfer of current from alternator to the ignition coil primary winding results in H.T. being induced in the secondary winding and an efficient spark at the plug.

The efficiency of the energy transfer ignition is quite high because the alternative path through the battery, when the contacts are opened, is virtually a short-circuit. The "flat" battery has little or no potential difference across it, and consequently very little energy is lost at this point.

However, as the current surges pass through the battery, and there are two charging coils also in circuit, a potential difference is formed across the battery terminals. After several current pulses (assuming the engine has fired and is running on one cylinder), the amount of energy available for the ignition coil is reduced, causing the engine to misfire. This will remind the rider to return the ignition key to the IGN position. The contact points will be badly burnt if the switch is kept in the EMG position for long periods.

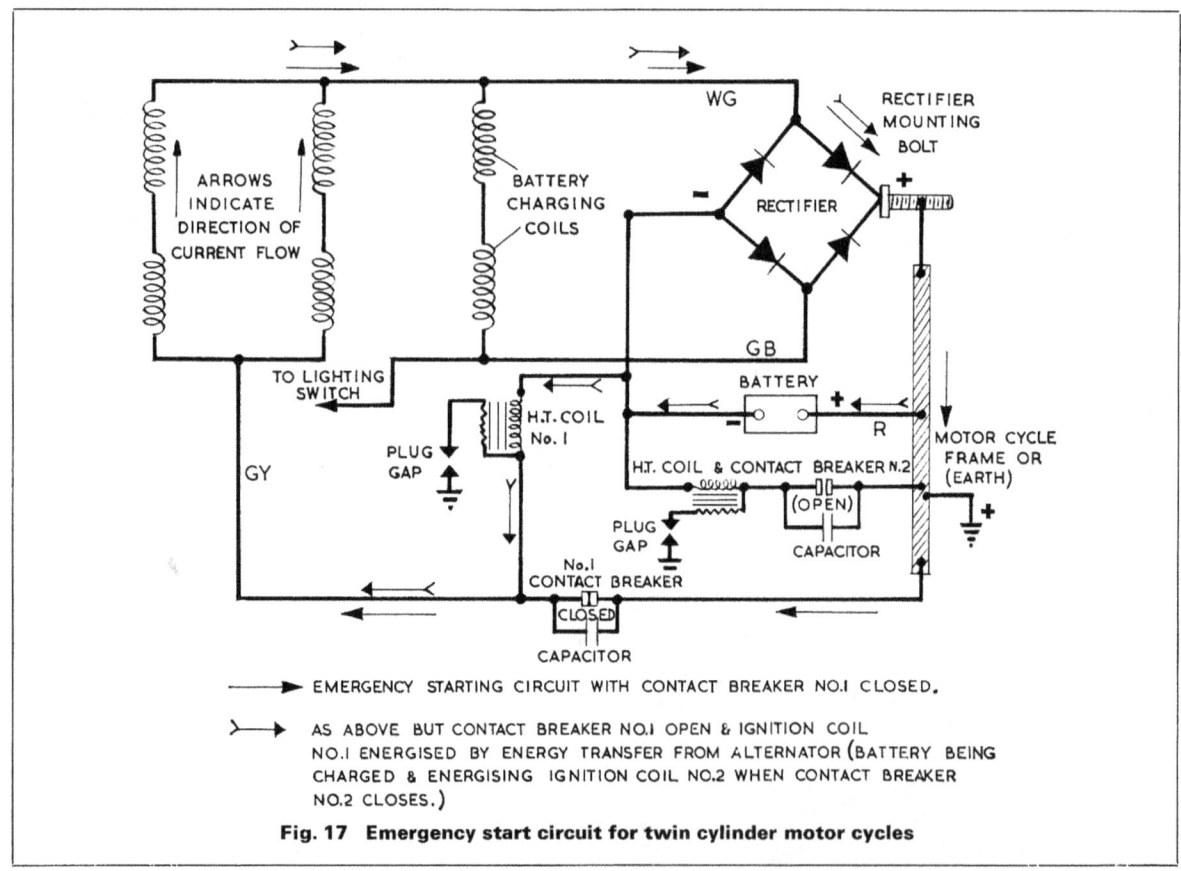

Fig. 17 Emergency start circuit for twin cylinder motor cycles

Another feature of the system is that the coil No. 2 eventually comes into operation during emergency starting, so that after a few seconds running on one cylinder, number two cylinder cuts-in and the engine functions as a normal twin-cylinder unit. It will not operate on both cylinders after a few more seconds because the rising battery voltage causes misfiring on the one cylinder.

Although the No. 2 coil "SW" terminal is linked to the same feed cable as the "SW" terminal of No. 1 coil, it does not pass any of the energy transferred from the alternator, during the "energy transfer" pulse, at this particular instant the No. 2 contact-breaker points are open, open-circuiting the No. 2 primary circuit. As the alternator current passes through the battery, the voltage rises. Further, while the No. 1 coil is fed by energy pulses from the alternator, the No. 2 coil, when its associated contacts close, will receive current direct from the battery which is gradually becoming charged. This results in the engine firing on both cylinders. It will not run at full power until switched to the IGN position, because the energy now available for the No. 1 coil is being reduced and misfiring will still occur.

Actually, when both coils are functioning, their primary windings are being fed in opposite directions. The No. 1 coil is receiving pulses from the alternator, via the battery, the insulated side of the circuit, through the primary from "SW" to "CB" and back to the alternator. The No. 2 coil is fed by a steady current direct from the battery, via earth, through No. 2 contacts to "CB" through primary to "SW" and back to battery "—ve".

Ignition performance under emergency starting conditions should be equivalent to that of a magneto at kick-start speeds.

NOTE: Where a "boost" control switch is fitted, the switch must be in the off position before attempting an EMG starting. As the switch short circuits the emergency starting system.

The Importance of Correct Timing for Emergency Ignition

Correct ignition timing, both electrically and mechanically, is a very critical factor with the A.C. sets, particularly in relation to emergency starting. As already stated, in the emergency start position the alternator supplies current direct to the ignition circuit. The timing is so arranged that the contacts are opened when the peak of the voltage wave coincides with each firing point of the engine, illustrated graphically in Fig. 18 (A).

If the contacts do not open at the precise instant required, emergency starting performance will be affected. Electrically, the timing position is fixed by the manufacturer, i.e., the alternator rotor is keyed on to the crankshaft in a position consistent with peak voltage, and cannot be altered. It is on the mechanical side that variations in timing can arise. The engine ignition timing must be accurately set to the figures specified for the particular machine. The contact breaker gap must also be set to, and maintained at, the specified figure as any variation in the gap setting will affect the timing position in relation to spark energy. If the timing at the distributor or contact breaker is advanced or retarded excessively either through a timing error, incorrect contact gaps, or weak automatic advance springs, the contacts

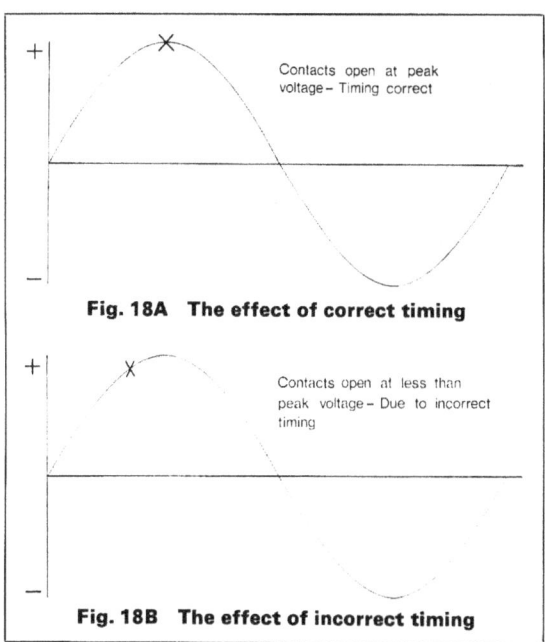

Fig. 18A The effect of correct timing

Fig. 18B The effect of incorrect timing

will not open at the peak of the voltage curve, see Fig. 18 (B) and consequently the spark will be weak. REMEMBER, IGNITION TIMING IS CRITICAL.

Poor Starting on Emergency

Faulty or dirty connections in the alternator electrical circuit will obviously have a bad effect on performance. Check the earth connections at the battery and rectifier. Both units are connected to the frame of the machine and a periodic check should be made to see that the connections are tight. Remember that the battery "+ve" terminal is the one earthed to the frame of the machine.

Dirty Contacts or Incorrect Gap Setting

The contact-breaker points should be periodically checked and cleaned, if necessary, and the gap should be maintained at its correct setting, i.e. 0·014"–0·016". This applies to both contact-breaker units.

Dirty Plugs or Incorrect Gap Setting

Plug gaps should be periodically checked and, if necessary, adjusted to the required gap, as specified by the manufacturer. It is also very important that the external insulator is kept clean and dry. Plugs should be replaced, if the electrodes are badly worn.

Faulty Rectifier

A rectifier may be faulty, even though its external appearance suggests it is in good working order. Where any doubt exists, the test procedure should be followed as detailed in Section 4. Do not flash connections to check the circuitry, as the rectifier and alternator could be damaged.

Rectifiers should be kept clean and dry and fitted to allow free passage of air through the plates for ventilation.

Dirty or Corroded Battery Terminals

Battery connections should be kept clean and tight, particularly the earth lead to the frame of the machine. Ensure that the top of the battery is clean and dry.

Sulphated Battery

A sulphated battery is usually the result of lack of maintenance, i.e. failure to maintain the electrolyte at the specified level, and allowing the battery to remain for long periods in a partially charged or discharged condition. A regular check on each cell should be made to see if "topping-up" is required. Distilled water should be added to the electrolyte to bring it up to the correct level.

A.C. Ignition

The alternator designed for A.C. ignition has the ignition generating coils connected in series with each other and with the primary winding of a special ignition coil, model 3ET.

This special ignition coil (Fig. 19) employs a closed iron circuit and has a primary winding whose impedance is closely matched to that of the ignition generating coils of the alternator. As a result of this electrical matching, the ignition performance combines the good top speed characteristics of the magneto with the good low speed performance of the conventional ignition coil.

The A.C. Ignition System functions as follows:

The contacts of a contact-breaker unit or distributor are connected in parallel with the ignition coil primary windings, since one end of the stator winding, one end of the ignition coil primary winding and one side of the contact-breaker is earthed, as shown in Figs. 20 and 21.

When the contact-breaker contacts close, the primary winding of the ignition coil is short-circuited and, at the same time, the stator ignition windings form a closed circuit. As the magnetic rotor turns, voltages are induced in the stator coils resulting in alternating currents while the contacts are closed. When the contacts open, a pulse of electromagnetic energy (developed in the stator while the contacts are closed) is discharged through the ignition coil primary winding. The effect of this energy pulse in the primary winding is to induce a high tension voltage in the ignition coil secondary winding which is then applied either directly or by way of a distributor to the appropriate sparking plug.

Timing Considerations

Since the magnetic rotor of the alternator is keyed (or otherwise located) on the crankshaft, the

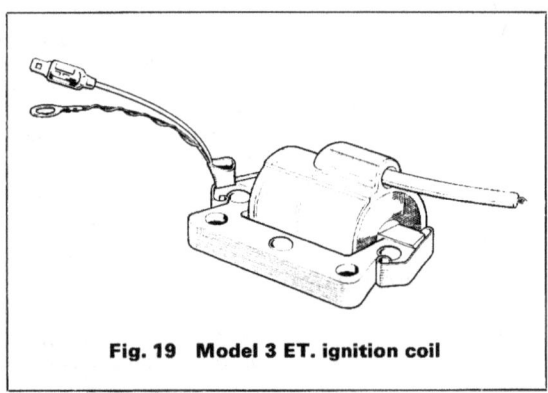

Fig. 19 Model 3 ET. ignition coil

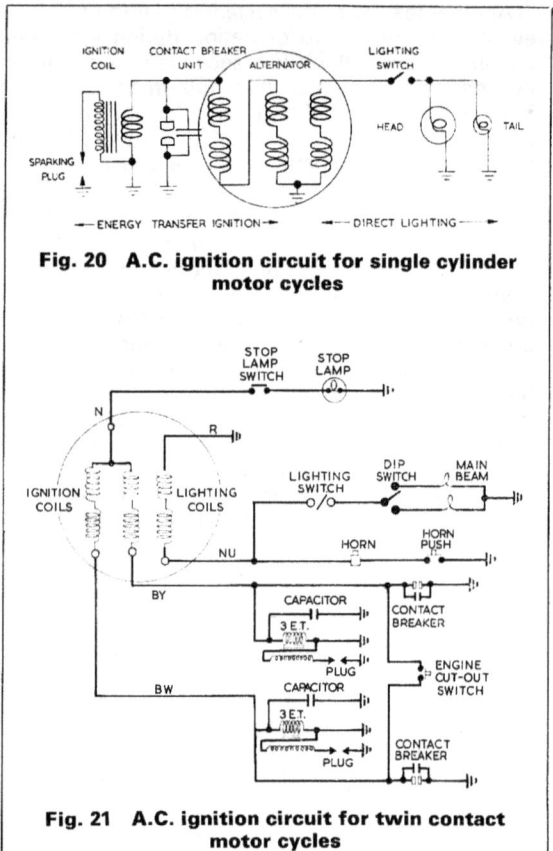

Fig. 20 A.C. ignition circuit for single cylinder motor cycles

Fig. 21 A.C. ignition circuit for twin contact motor cycles

magnetic pulse in the alternator stator, which produces the energy pulse to feed the ignition coil primary winding, must be timed to occur at the firing point of the engine.

The magnetic pulse occupies several degrees of crankshaft (and therefore of rotor) rotation. A fairly wide angular tolerance would thus be available for a fixed ignition engine.

However, it is desirable that most four-stroke engines should incorporate an ignition timing control (usually centrifugally operated) giving a range of advanced and retarded sparking. The magnetic relationship of the alternator rotor to its stator must therefore be governed by the fact, that the engine firing point will vary by several degrees between the fully retarded starting condition and the fully advanced running condition.

This is exactly the same problem which obtains with a manually controlled magneto and gives rise to the same characteristics, i.e. the available sparking voltage for a given kick-start speed reduces progressively with the retard angle. A magneto, however, is a self-contained unit and will produce a spark even though seriously mistimed to the engine, because a magneto contact-breaker is always in the correct relationship to the magnetic geometry of the unit. With an alternator, however, the position of the magnetic rotor with respect to the stator, and to the engine piston at the instant of firing, is pre-determined by its position on the engine crankshaft.

The range of retarded magnetic timing that can be used with a particular engine depends in part on that engine's starting performance, since the required plug voltage is influenced by many factors of engine design. The speed at which it can be kicked over in attempting to reach this voltage will depend on piston and bearing friction, kick-starter ratio, etc.

Fig. 22 shows how the available plug voltage varies with different magnetic timing positions and for different speeds of rotation. The reference point is known as the Magnetic Neutral position, where the interpolar gaps of the rotor are situated on the centre-lines of the stator limbs.

It will be seen that although the optimum magnetic position is just past the Magnetic Neutral at 300 rev/min, it changes to several degrees past at 2,000 rev/min, due to distortion of the magnetic flux.

It will also be seen that the sparking performance deteriorates rapidly a few degrees before the Magnetic Neutral position. Hence commercial tolerances on keyways, etc., dictate the inadvisability of approaching too near to this critical point in the advanced or running position of engine timing.

As previously stated, the extent to which the retard timing can be used depends on plug voltage requirements at starting and on kick-starter speed.

For example, if the required plug voltage is 6 kilo-volts, the retarded timing would be restricted to about 20° (engine) if the kick-starting speed was to be limited to 300 rev/min — in practice, a fairly low speed. On the other hand, at the fairly normal kick-starting speed of 500 rev/min, the timing range could be widened considerably with plug voltages up to about 8 kilo-volts.

Accurate ignition timing is an important requirement in the operation of an energy transfer system. The optimum conditions are determined by the engine designers during the development and should always be maintained to ensure the highest performance, both from the engine and from the ignition system designed to work with it.

It will also be appreciated that amateur tuning will not improve the performance of a highly developed engine. Indeed, in certain circumstances, it may be harmful. Indifferent sparking outside the prescribed range will almost certainly indicate tampering and may well serve as a warning to the would-be tuner.

12 Volt Charging System and Capacitor Ignition

The Lucas R.M. series alternator is voltage conscious, but, to avoid overcharging the battery, was used with 6 volt equipment. However, with the introduction of the Zener diode it became possible to control the output for all conditions using 12 volt equipment. Many advantages were gained. Extra output from the alternator, more accurately controlled charge rates and better headlight efficiency.

The Zener diode is constructed from similar materials to the diode used in the rectifier and it will pass current in one direction only. However, when connected in the reverse direction, it will act as an insulator while the voltage is below approximately 14 volts. Above this it will start to conduct current,

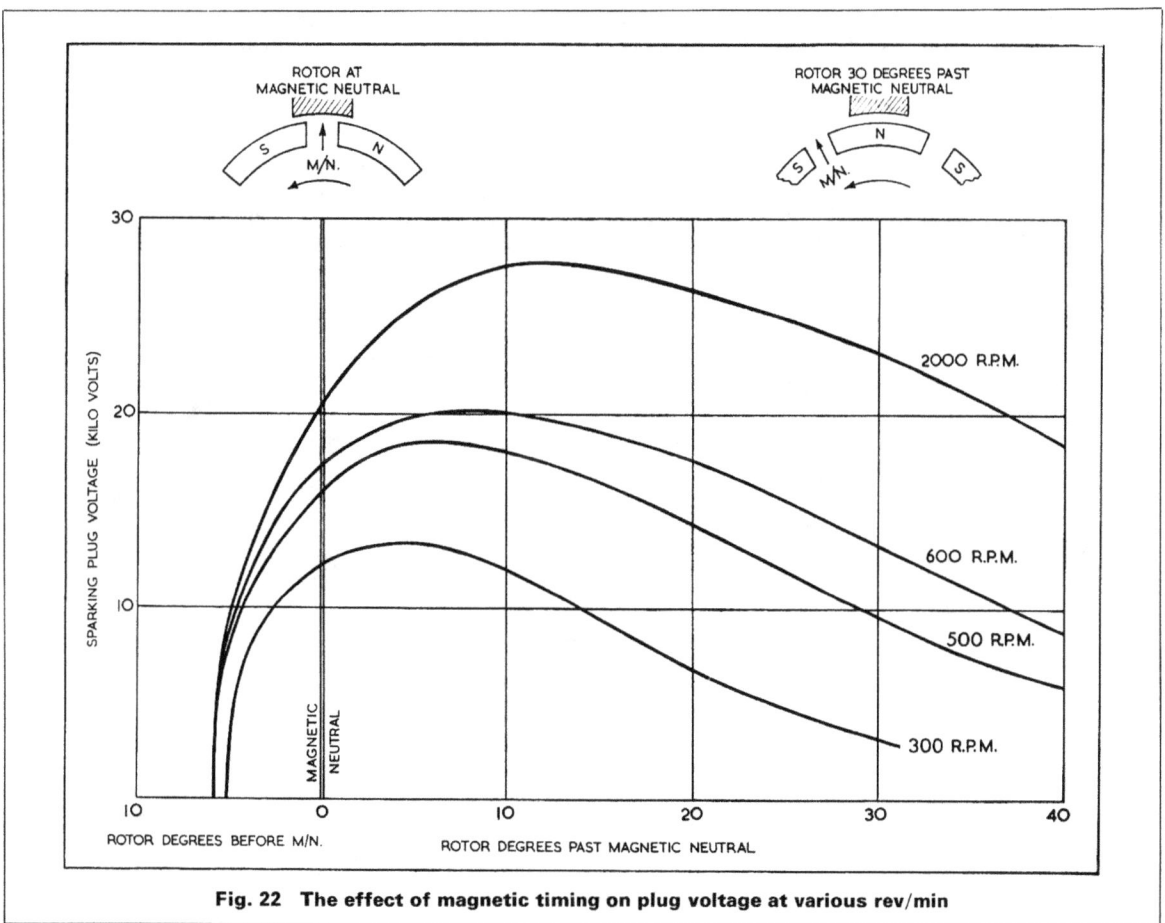

Fig. 22 The effect of magnetic timing on plug voltage at various rev/min

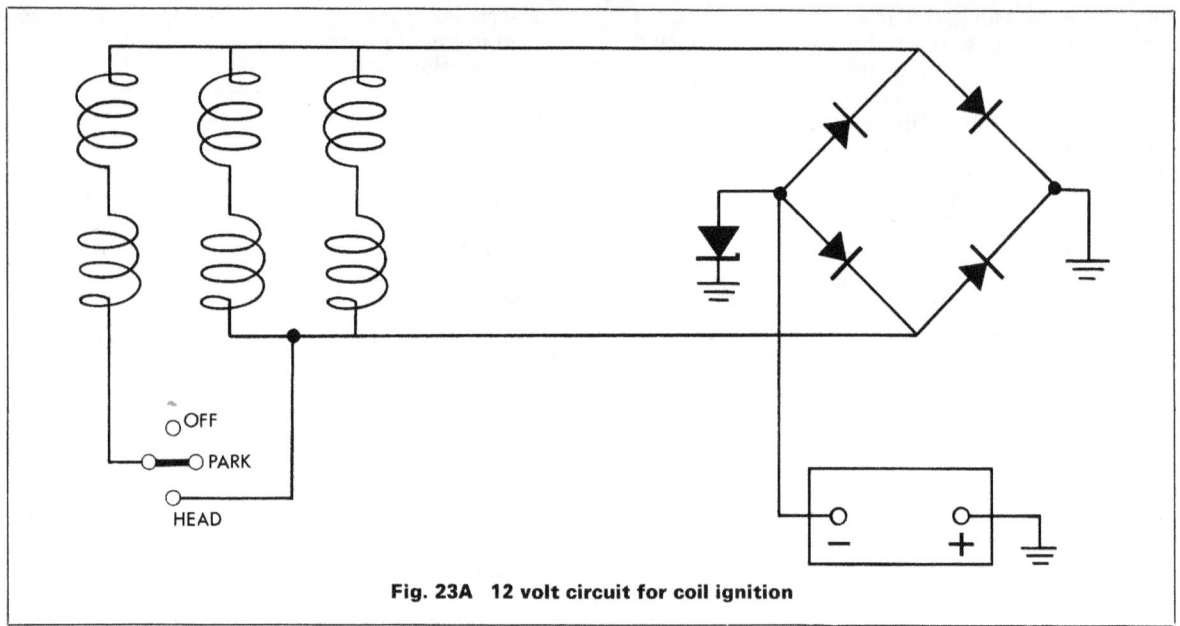

Fig. 23A 12 volt circuit for coil ignition

slowly at first, until at approximately 15 volts it becomes fully conductive. If the Zener diode is connected in parallel with the battery in the charging circuit, as shown in Fig. 23A, it will act as a regulator. When the battery is discharged, its terminal voltage is low and the system voltage is low, and the Zener diode acts as an insulator. All the output from the alternator is then directed through the battery. As the battery is charged, its terminal voltage rises and the system voltage rises accordingly, until approximately 14 volts is reached. At this point the battery requires less charge, so the Zener diode starts to break down and conducts part of the charging current away from the battery. When the battery voltage reaches approximately 15 volts, the Zener diode breaks down completely and conducts all the charging current away. When lighting equipment is switched on, the system voltage falls until it becomes an insulator again, at approximately 14 volts, and the output from the alternator is available to balance the lighting load.

As the Zener diode conducts excess current a large quantity of heat is produced by the diode and in order to keep the temperature within the operating limits, a heatsink is required. The maximum current the diode can carry is limited by the efficiency of the heatsink. In order to remain within this limit the switching arrangements were as shown in Fig. 23 A and B. Later heatsinks have a surface area of at least 72 square inches and are mounted in a good air stream. The full output from the alternator can now be permanently connected across the rectifier. The circuit for this system is shown in Fig. 24 and as the charging system requires no switching arrangement,

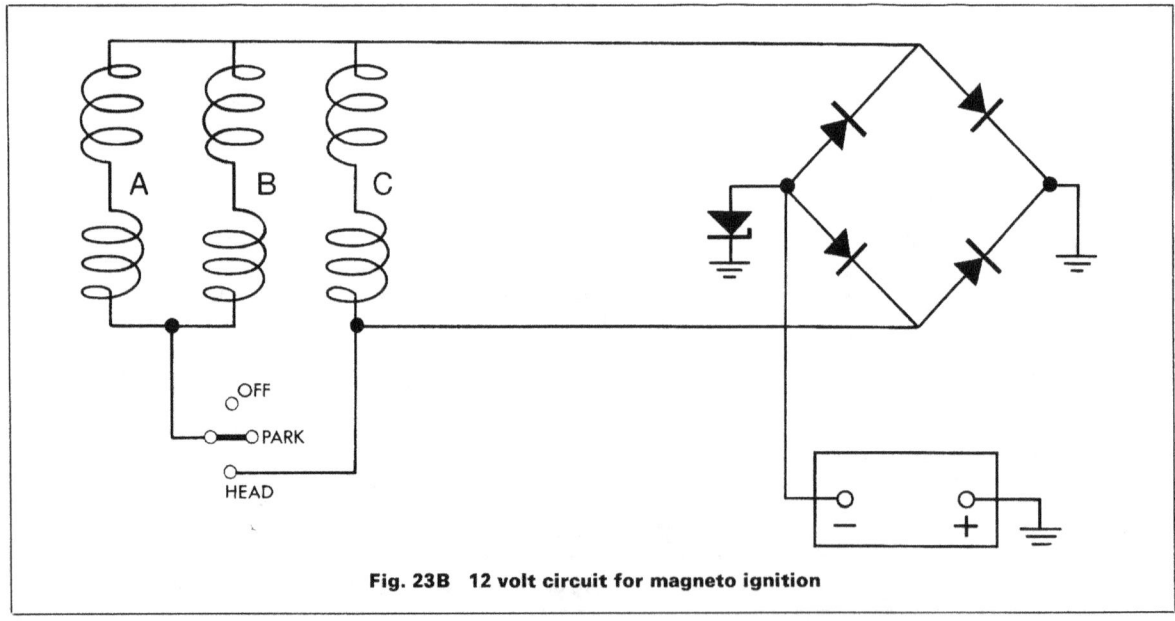

Fig. 23B 12 volt circuit for magneto ignition

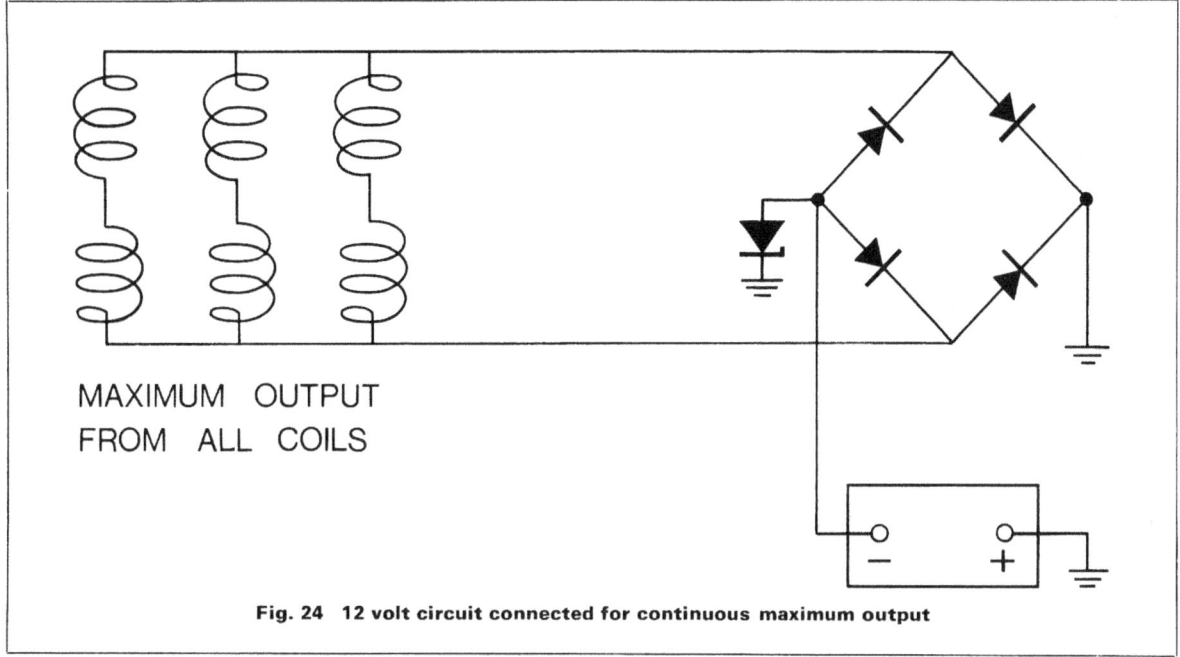

Fig. 24 12 volt circuit connected for continuous maximum output

car type ignition and lighting switches are used.

When the R.M. series alternator is used for 12 volt operation the maximum output is raised from approximately 60 watts on 6 volts to approximately 104 watts. The increased output on kick-over is enough to charge the battery sufficiently to start the machine on third or fourth kick. Consequently, no emergency start is necessary allowing the simple coil ignition circuit to be used.

It may be preferable to remove the battery for sporting events. The Zener diode will then maintain the system voltage at a safe level, but there will be insufficient output from the alternator to start the machine on kick-start. Consequently the 2MC capacitor is connected in parallel with the battery, as in Fig. 25. When the battery is removed, the capacitor stores the impulses from the alternator when the points are open and discharges when the points close to enable other impulses from the alternator to start the machine. The machine will, therefore, operate without the battery, and the full lighting load may be supplied while the engine is running. However, when the engine is not running there will be no lights available for parking etc.

Modern circuitry has now simplified the wiring system considerably and a typical 12 volt charging and ignition circuit is shown on page 45. (Wiring diagram).

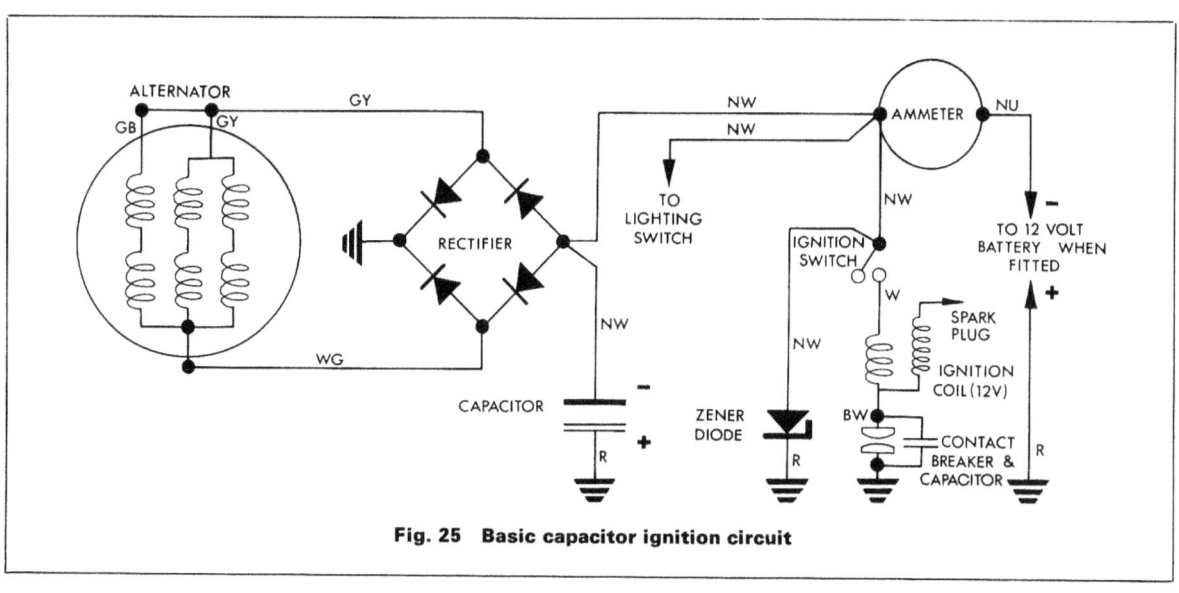

Fig. 25 Basic capacitor ignition circuit

LUCAS EQUIPMENT AND MAINTENANCE

The Battery

Preparation of PUZ5A Batteries for Service

The general instructions for putting dry-charged batteries into service are as follows:

Fill batteries, ensuring that acid and batteries are between 60°F (15·5°C) and 100°F (40°C).

In temperate climates (normally below 80°F – 29°C) the filling acid S.G. must be 1·260.

In tropical climates (normally above 80°F – 29°C) the filling acid S.G. must be 1·210.

Twenty minutes after filling the battery, the S.G. and temperature of the acid is checked and unless there is a fall of more than 10 points in S.G. or a rise of more than 10°F (5·5°C) in temperature, batteries are ready for service. If these limits are exceeded batteries should be charged at the normal recharge rate until S.G. and voltage remain constant for three successive hourly readings and all cells are gassing freely.

Owing to the limited amount of free electrolyte available in PUZ5A the above procedure has been modified, as follows:

With batteries and acid at a temperature of between 60°F (15·5°C) and 100°F (40°C), fill with acid S.G. 1·260 (temperate) or 1·210 (tropical). Read electrolyte temperature a few seconds after filling by inserting a thermometer into each individual cell in turn.

After standing for 20 minutes, individual cell temperatures are again noted.

The open-circuit voltage of the battery is then read using a good grade voltmeter.

If the temperature rise in any one cell or cells is not greater than 10°F (5·5°C) and the open circuit voltages not below 12·4v, the battery is ready for immediate service.

If these limits are exceeded the battery should be charged at 0·8A until the on-charge voltage remains

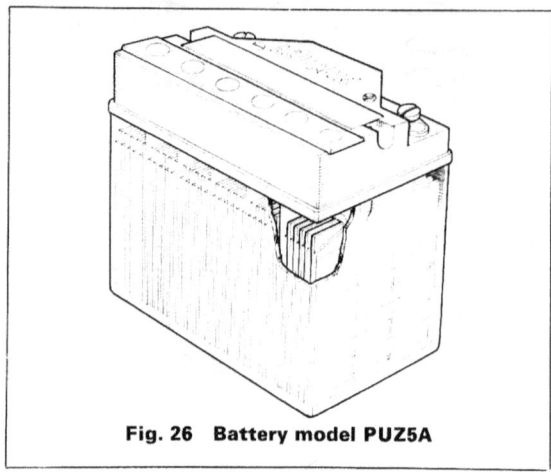

Fig. 26 Battery model PUZ5A

constant over three successive hourly readings and all cells are gassing freely.

Batteries which are more than 12 months old, before being filled for service should be charged at 0·4A until on-charge voltage remains constant for three successive hourly readings and all cells are gassing freely.

NOTE: Dry-charged batteries are delivered with a blanking plug fitted in the vent overflow pipe. This must be removed before filling.

Topping-up

During charging, water is lost due to gassing. Every week the electrolyte level of each cell should be checked and, if necessary, should be topped up.

USE ONLY DISTILLED WATER, NOT TAP WATER.

Remove the lid and if necessary, unscrew the filler plugs. Add distilled water until the electrolyte reaches the maximum level line on the casing. If there is no maximum level line, ensure that the electrolyte is level with the top of the separator guard.

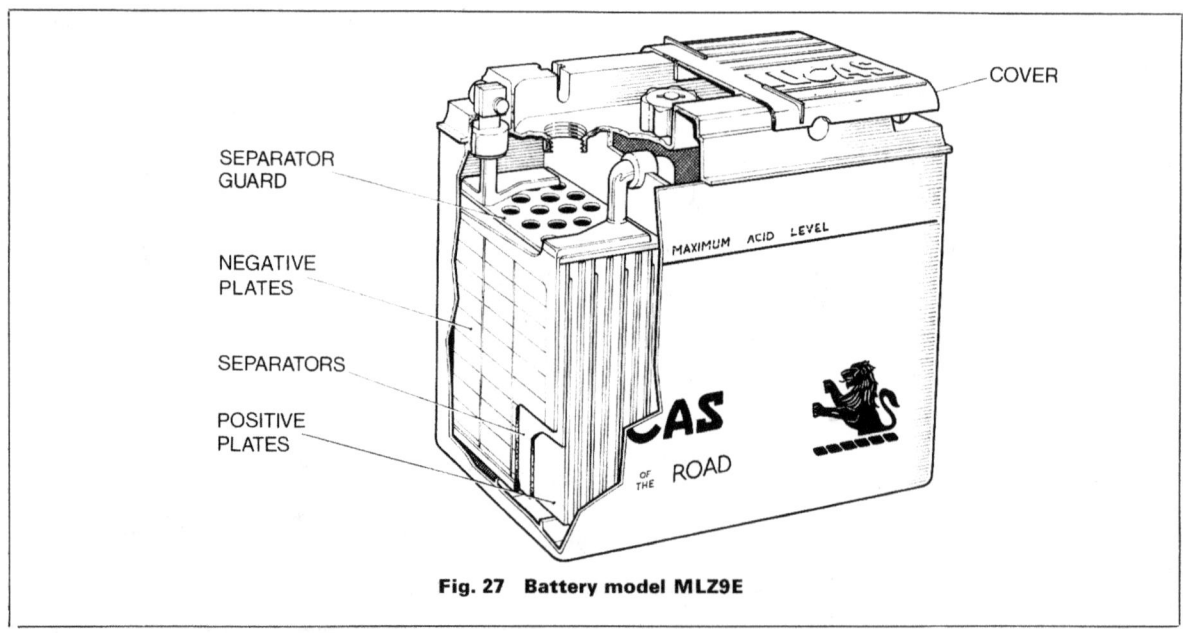

Fig. 27 Battery model MLZ9E

Occasionally, wipe away any dirt or moisture from the top of the battery, ensuring that the terminals are clean and tight. Never leave the battery in a discharged condition.

If the motor cycle is not to be used for a considerable period, the battery should be fully charged and a short refreshing charge given every two weeks, to prevent "sulphation". When a battery is fitted to the machine, ensure that the correct polarity is observed, as reversed battery connections will cause serious damage to other electrical equipment.

COIL IGNITION

6CA Contact Breaker Assembly

The assembly is adjustable for both contact breaker gap and individual timing for each cylinder. Adjustment is made by means of eccentric screws.

Adjustment of the Contact Gap

(i) Turn the engine until the contact breaker gap is at its maximum.

(ii) Slacken the screw (A) which secures the angle plate (fixed contact).

(iii) Turn the eccentric cam screw (B) and adjust the contact point gap between the limits 0·014" to 0·016" (0·35–0·40 mm).

(iv) Tighten the securing screw (A) and recheck the gap setting.

On twin cylinder applications this procedure is repeated for the second contact set.

Engine Timing

(i) Ensure the contact breaker gap is to the recommended setting.

(ii) Lock the cam in the fully advanced position by inserting a $\frac{7}{16}"$, (0·4375 ins – 11 mm) internal diameter washer between the existing washer and cam. Retighten the securing bolt with the cam fully advanced against the springs.

(iii) Turn the engine to the fully advanced timing position recommended by the manufacturer.

(iv) Slacken the two screws securing the base plate to the engine.

(v) Select the appropriate contact breaker associated with the cylinder being timed.

(vi) Rotate the base plate till the above contacts are just opening and tighten the screws securing the base plate.

(vii) To obtain fine adjustment, slacken the two screws (C) securing the contact breaker plate and rotate the eccentric cam screw (D), adjusting the position of the contact heel until the points are just opening. (A low wattage bulb of the same voltage as the machine, connected between the contact breaker spring and earth will, when the ignition is switched on, illuminate instantly as the points open. Retighten the two securing screws (C).

On twin cylinder applications, rotate the engine to the second position in accordance with the manufacturer's recommendations, and repeat operations (iii), (v) and (vii).

NOTE: When the timing procedure is completed, remove the $\frac{7}{16}"$ (0·4375 ins – 11 mm) washer locking the cam in the fully advanced position (ref. operation (ii)) and retighten the bolt.

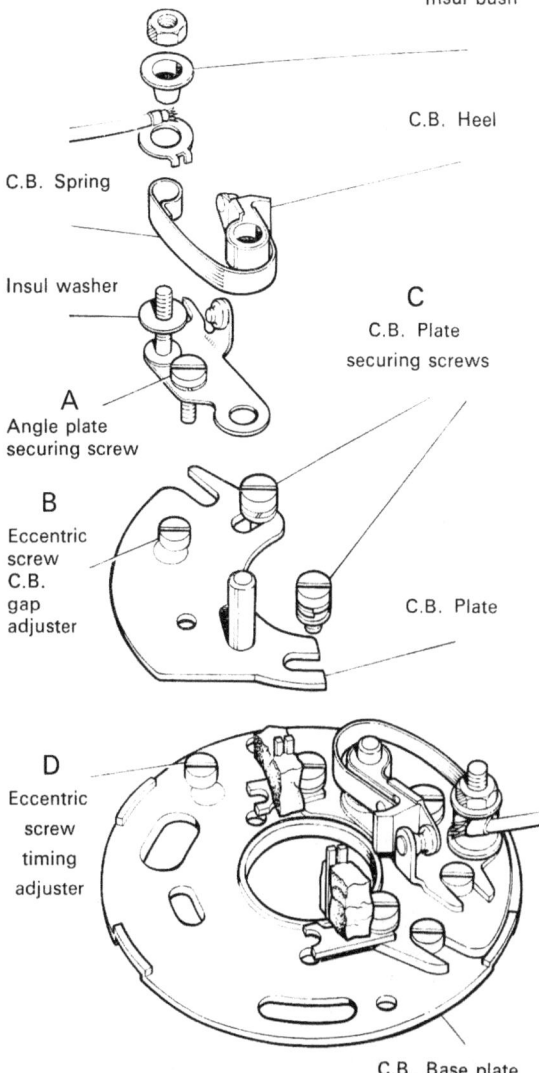

Fig. 28 Contact breaker model 6CA

7CA Contact Breaker Assembly

Adjustment of Contact Gap

Adjust as 6CA on all three sets.

Engine Timing

Adjust as 6CA for the first cylinder then repeat operation (iii), (v) and (vii) for other two cylinders.

Maintenance (6CA and 7CA)

(i) After 500 miles (800 km). Check contact breaker gap and re-adjust if necessary.

(ii) Every 3,000 miles (4,800 km). Add two drops of engine oil to the rear of the cam lubricating wick(s).

(iii) Every 6,000 miles (9,600 km). Release the contact breaker base plate by removing the securing screws. Draw the plate clear of the cam giving access to the auto-advance unit. Lubricate the pivot points B and C (Fig. 30) with one drop of engine oil, wiping away any surplus.

Inspect the condition of the contact surfaces of the contact breakers. If burned or blackened, clean with fine emery cloth or carborundum stone. Replace the plate, check the contact gap and retime the engine.

Warning

Unless otherwise stated in the manufacturer's handbook: Do not apply any form of lubrication to the bearing surface point A. This surface has been lubricated with a special lubricant during manufacture, and no further attention is required.

THE USE OF OTHER LUBRICANTS COULD CAUSE THE MECHANISM TO SEIZE.

2CP Capacitor Pack

The 6CA and 7CA contact breaker units are not fitted with capacitors. The capacitors are mounted separately on their own base plate. A rubber cover is used to prevent damage from water and road dirt. There is no maintenance required beyond the occasional check to ensure that the connections are clean and tight and also the base plate makes good contact to earth.

4CA and 4CC Contact Breaker Assembly

The model 4CA incorporates an auto advance unit, while the model 4CC is designed for fixed ignition motorcycles.

Contact Breaker Gap Adjustment

(i) Turn the engine until the contact breaker is open to its fullest extent.

(ii) Slacken the nut securing the fixed contact plate.

(iii) Adjust the position of the plate until the gap setting is between the limits of 0·014"–0·016" (0·35–0·40 mm) by inserting a screwdriver into the slot provided.

(iv) Tighten the locking nut and recheck the gap setting.

On twin cylinder applications the above process is repeated for the second contact breaker.

Engine Timing

Refer to manufacturer's handbook.

Maintenance

(i) After 500 miles (800 km). Check the contact gap setting and adjust, if necessary.

(ii) Every 6,000 miles (9,600 km). Inspect the contact surfaces and if burned or blackened, clean with fine emery cloth or carborundum stone. Check the gap setting and adjust, if necessary. Turn the engine until the slot in the cam is uppermost and apply one drop of engine oil to the slot. Place one drop of oil on each contact breaker pivot post and smear the surface of the cam very lightly with Mobilgrease No. 2 or equivalent.

NO OIL OR GREASE MUST BE ALLOWED TO GET ON OR NEAR THE CONTACTS.

Ignition Coil

The ignition coil requires no attention, but the exterior should be kept clean. Ensure that all connections are clean and tight. When an ignition coil is replaced, do not overtighten the clamp bolt, as damage to the casing could result in failure of the coil.

The high tension produced by the ignition coil is limited by the spark plug gap. If this gap is excessive or there is an open circuit in the plug lead, the

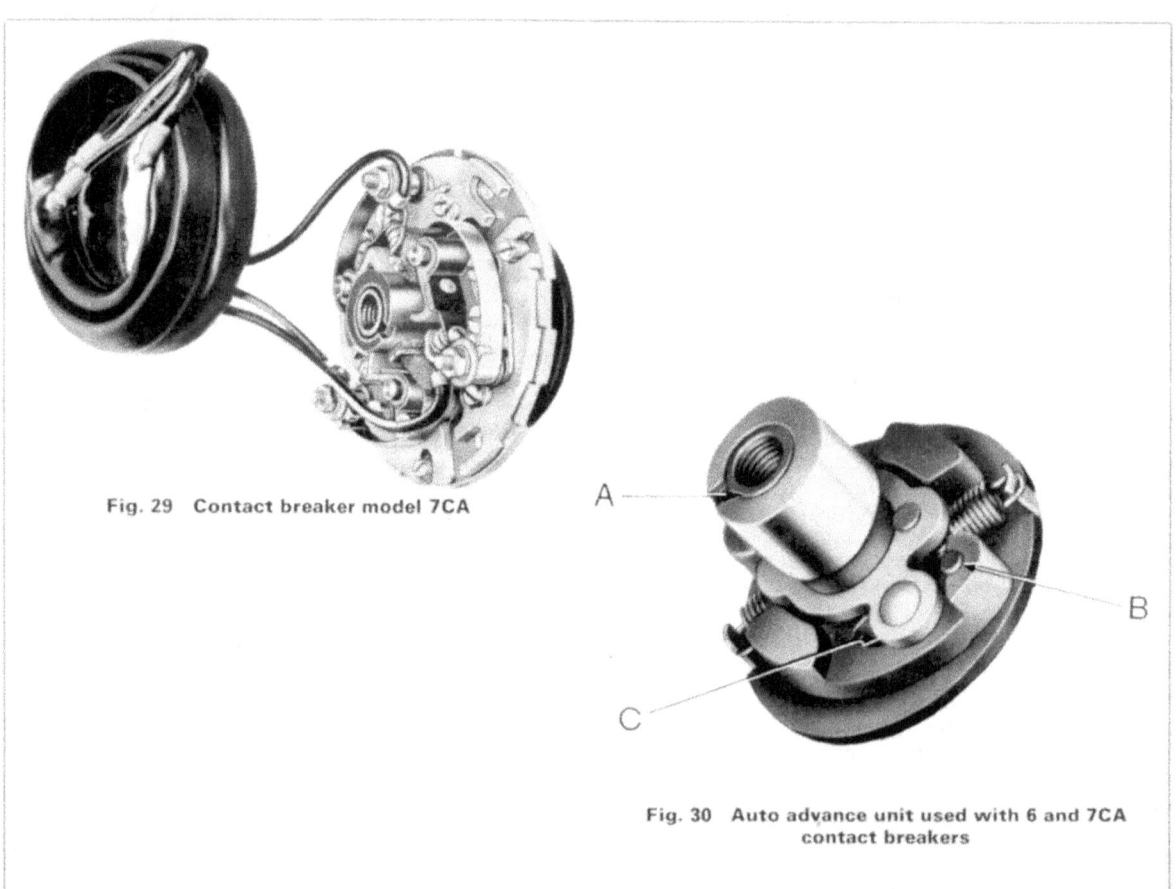

Fig. 29 Contact breaker model 7CA

Fig. 30 Auto advance unit used with 6 and 7CA contact breakers

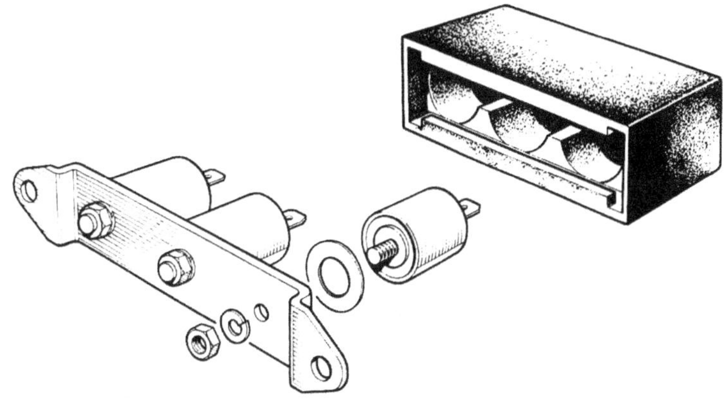

Fig. 31 Capacitor pack model 2CP

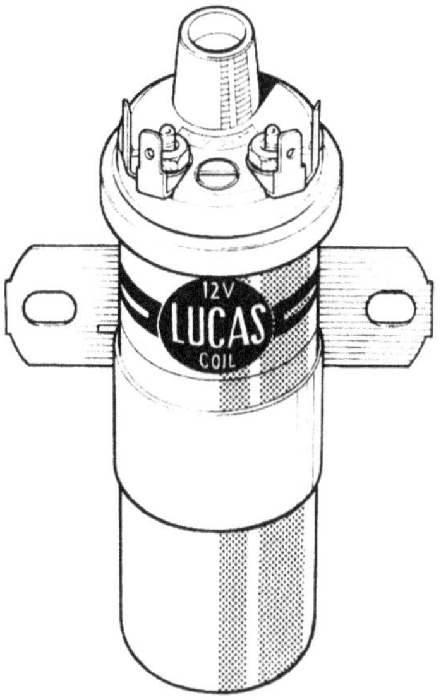

Fig. 33 Ignition coil model 17M12

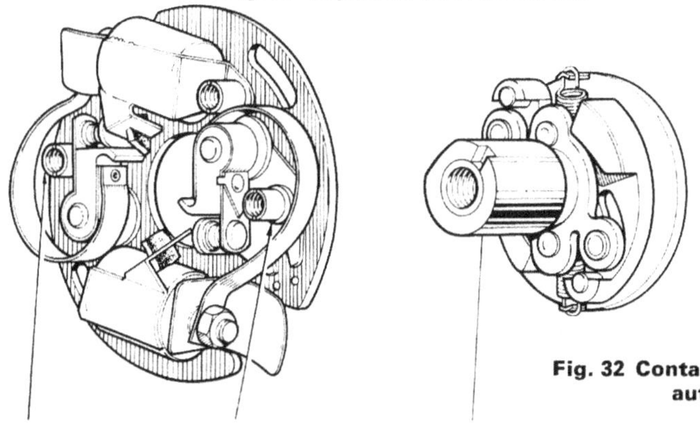

Fig. 32 Contact breaker model 4CA and auto advance unit

CONTACT LOCKING   PLATE NUTS   CAM

voltage could rise to 21,000 volts and normal insulation would break down especially in damp conditions. Ensure the chimney is clean and the H.T. connections are tight.

2MC Capacitor (when fitted)

The 2MC capacitor has been specially designed to withstand engine vibrations. It must be mounted in a spring with the terminals pointing downwards. It is only suitable for use with the 12 volt full output system.

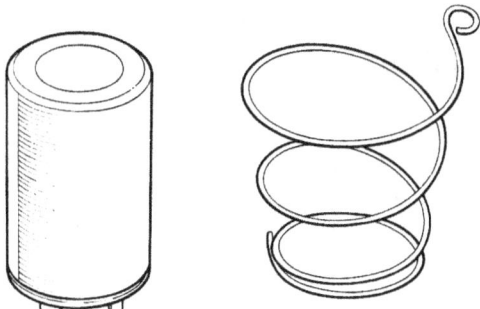

Fig. 34 Capacitor model 2MC and mounting spring

The capacitor requires no maintenance beyond an occasional check to ensure the connections are clean and tight.

NOTE: Ensure correct polarity is observed when connecting up the 2MC capacitor. The single $\frac{3}{16}$" (1·88 ins – 4·8 mm) Lucas blade is positive (+) and should be connected to earth.

When the capacitor is used in conjunction with a battery, occasionally check that the capacitor is operating by disconnecting the battery and starting the machine.

Ignition Warning Light

The ignition warning light only indicates that the ignition is "on". Consequently the light does not extinguish while the engine is running. However, on later machines the ignition and oil pressure warning lights are combined in a single unit. Therefore, the light will extinguish when the engine starts and runs.

If the light from the standard bulb is considered too brilliant and tends to dazzle the rider, the following are recommended for replacement purposes.

Motor cycle voltage	Recommended Bulb
6 volt	Part No. 281 (12 volt, 2 watt)
12 volt	Part No. 283 (24 volt, 2 watt)

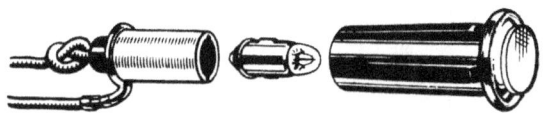

Fig. 35 Warning light model WL15

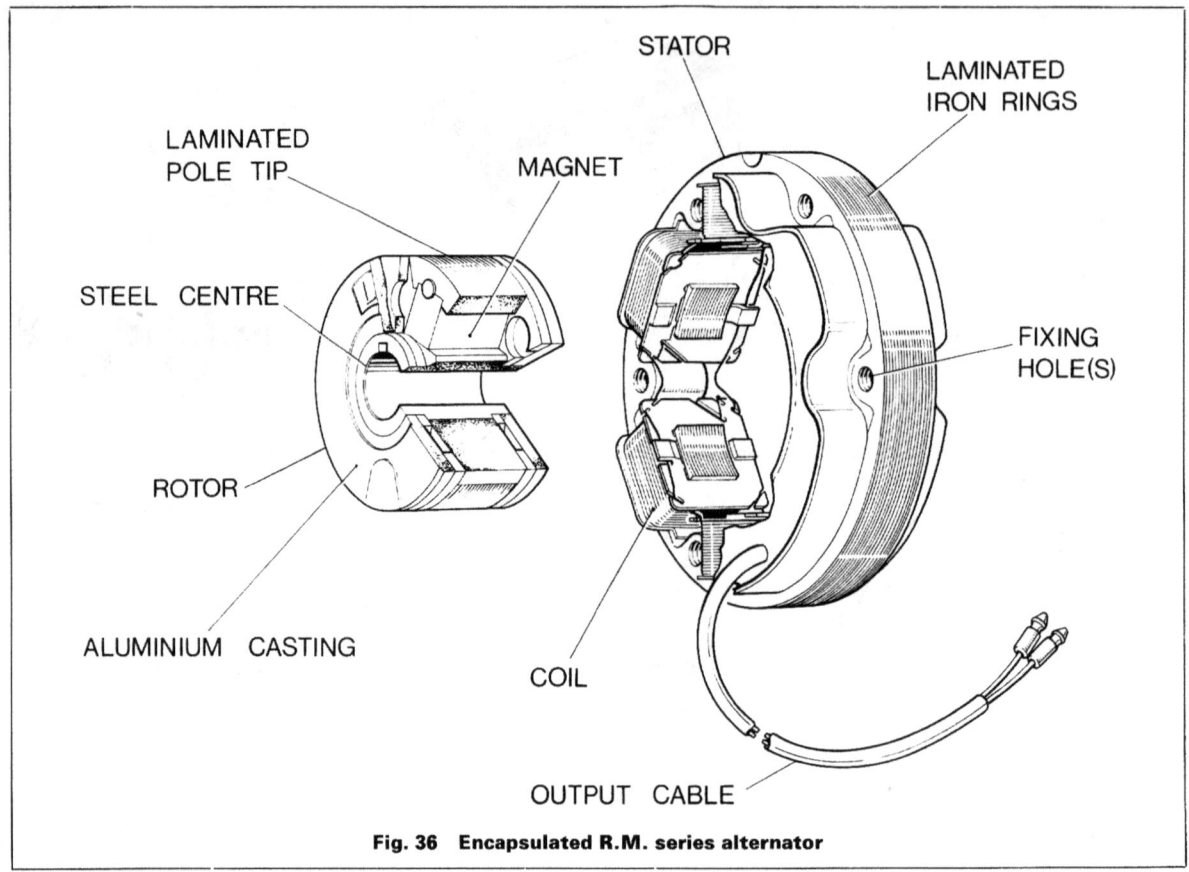

Fig. 36 Encapsulated R.M. series alternator

CHARGING EQUIPMENT

The Alternator

The Stator:

The stator consists of six coils mounted on circular six pole laminations. The assembly is encapsulated to protect the windings from damage by metallic swarf or vibration. There are two types of stators used:

1. The three lead stator, suitable for both six and twelve volt systems
2. The two lead type, which is similar in construction to the three lead version, except that it is internally connected for full output and is only suitable for twelve volt operation.

The Rotor:

The rotor has an hexagonal steel centre with a high energy magnet mounted on each face. Each magnet is keyed to a laminated pole tip and the complete assembly is cast in aluminium and machined to give a smooth external finish. The rotor is driven by an extension of the engine crankshaft, and revolves inside the stator. The alternator requires no maintenance beyond checking that the connectors are clean and tight.

The Rectifier

The rectifier consists of four semiconductor diodes connected in a bridge formation, each diode being mounted on its own heatsink. As the diodes get hot during operation, the rectifier must be mounted in a good airflow and kept clean and free from road dirt or corrosion. If the rectifier has to be removed for any purpose, two spanners should be employed, one for the head of the through bolt and the other for the securing nut.

NOTE: The nut clamping the plates together should not be disturbed, otherwise damage to the diode connections may occur.

The rectifier requires no regular maintenance beyond checking the connections are clean and tight, especially the earth connection through the mounting bolt.

Zener Diode

The Zener diode regulates the charge rate to the battery by diverting the excess charging current away from the battery, through the diode. During this process a large quantity of heat is produced. This would destroy the diode if it were not conducted away.

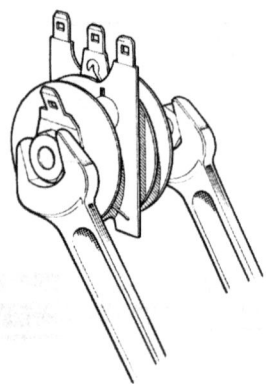

Fig. 37 Silicon diode rectifier

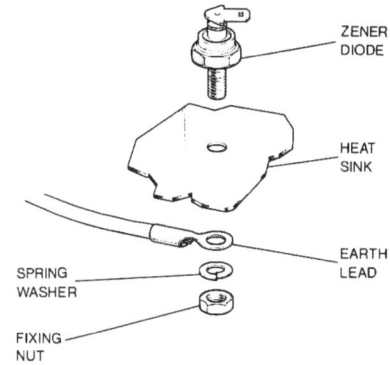

Fig. 38 Zener diode and heatsink

Fig. 39 Ammeter model 2AR

The diode is consequently mounted on a heatsink supplied by the manufacturer of the machine. To ensure efficient operation the diode base must make good metal-to-metal contact with the heatsink as dirt or corrosion under the diode, or a loose diode, would cause overheating and failure.

The Ammeter

The motor cycle ammeter is especially damped to steady the readings and has a scale of 12 – 0 – 12A. It is connected between the rectifier and the battery. The complete unit is factory sealed to prevent the entry of water and consequently requires no maintenance apart from occasionally checking that the connections are clean and tight.

LIGHTING EQUIPMENT

Head and Parking Lights

Lucas motor cycle headlamps incorporate the Lucas light unit which consists of a combined reflector and front lens assembly. A "prefocus" bulb is used with this light unit ensuring that the filament is always correctly positioned in relation to the reflector. Certain headlamps fit into a nacelle type extension of the forks which forms a housing for the headlamp.

Setting the Headlamp

Set the headlamp so that the main or driving beam is projected straight ahead, parallel to the road surface, when the machine carries its normal load.

Many garages possess a Lucas Beamsetter. This is an instrument which enables the beam to be

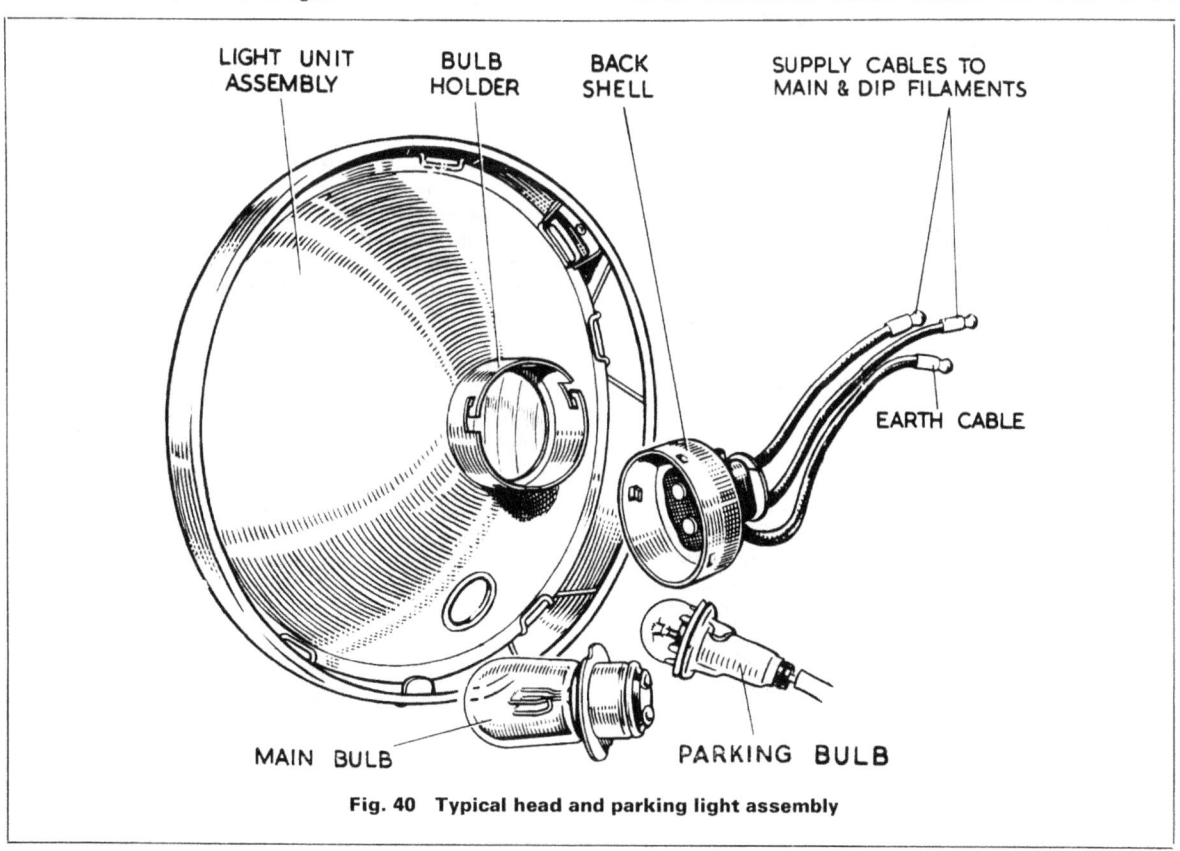

Fig. 40 Typical head and parking light assembly

set accurately. Motor cyclists are strongly advised to make use of this service.

If these facilities are not available, the headlamp may be set by marking off a smooth blank wall as shown in Fig. 41 and shining the lamp on it from a distance of 25 feet.

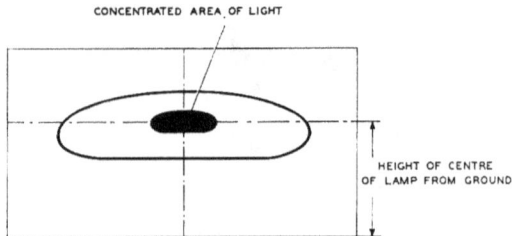

Fig. 41 Headlight adjustment

When setting the headlamp, the motor cycle must be:
(i) Square with the screen.
(ii) Carrying its normal load and standing on level ground.
(iii) At the recommended distance of 25 feet.

On machines where the headlamp is mounted in a nacelle or other special fitting, the instructions laid down by the manufacturer of the motor cycle should be followed.

Bulb Replacement

Slacken the rim retaining screw located at the top or bottom of the lamp body. (On model MCF headlamps the securing screw must be unscrewed completely to release the rim). It will then be possible to detach the rim and light unit complete. To gain access to the headlamp bulb, push the adaptor and twist it in an anti-clockwise direction. The bulb can now be removed from the reflector. Place the correct bulb in the light unit, engage the projections on the inside of the adaptor, press on and secure by turning clockwise. To replace the light in the headlamp, locate the assembly in the lamp body, press the front on and secure in position by tightening the securing screw.

To gain access to the parking light bulb, remove the front rim and light unit assembly and withdraw the parking light bulb holder which is a push fit in the reflector.

Rear Lamps

Motor cycle rear lights incorporate the number plate illumination. They require no regular maintenance but occasionally check that the snap connectors and bulb contacts make a good clean connection.

To replace the bulb, unfasten the screws retaining the lens and carefully remove the lens. The bulb is then removed by pushing inwards and rotating anti-clockwise. When replacing the lens, ensure that the lens body locates correctly with the rubber housing before the retaining screws are tightened. Otherwise, water will enter the lamp causing premature failure. Do not overtighten the retaining screws, or the lens may be cracked.

Flashing Direction Indicators

The flashing indicator set fitted to certain machines consists of four indicator lamps, a flasher unit, together with mounting spring, a warning light and operating switch. Some applications, particularly scooters, use a model 94SA switch incorporating a warning light. If the warning light does not operate, it indicates a fault in the system, for instance, the failure of one of the indicator bulb filaments.

If the system incorporates the later 8FL flasher unit and a signal light fails, the warning light will remain on but will not flash.

Checking a Faulty Operation

If a fault occurs in the system, the following procedure should be adopted:
(i) Check that the bulb filaments are not broken.
(ii) Check that all flasher circuit connections are clean and tight.
(iii) Switch on ignition and check with a voltmeter that the flasher terminal 'B' is at battery voltage.
(iv) Connect together flasher unit terminals 'B' and 'L' and operate the indicator switch. If the flasher lamps on the respective side now light without flashing, the flasher unit is faulty and should be replaced with the same type of unit as was originally fitted.

Replacement Bulbs

When a bulb needs replacement, check that the new bulb is the same wattage as the original. Avoid the use of non-branded bulbs as the filament is often so shaped that correct focusing is impossible; for example, the filament may be to one side of the axis of the bulb resulting in loss of range and efficiency.

LUCAS GENUINE REPLACEMENT BULBS are specially tested to ensure maximum life and efficiency. To assist in identification, Lucas bulbs are marked with a part number. When fitting a replacement, see that it has the same part number as the original bulb.

STARTING MOTOR

Model M3 Starting Motor

The model M3 pre-engaged starting motor is an earth return machine with series connected field coils. A lever operated drive assembly is carried on a straight splined extension of the armature shaft. The starter switch is mounted on the yoke and its contacts close when the drive is almost fully engaged, causing the starter to operate.

Maintenance

Ensure that the battery cable terminal on the starter is clean and tight. If the connection becomes dirty, clean the contacting surfaces and smear with petroleum jelly. No lubrication is necessary until the engine is due for major overhaul. The starting motor should then be examined by the local Lucas agent. Occasionally check the mounting bolts to ensure the starting motor is firmly fixed.

HORNS

Models 6H and 9H Horns

The above horns are pre-set during manufacture and in general no further adjustment is necessary.

If the horn becomes uncertain in its action, giving only a choking sound, or does not vibrate, the horn may not necessarily be faulty. The trouble could be due to a discharged battery, loose connection or

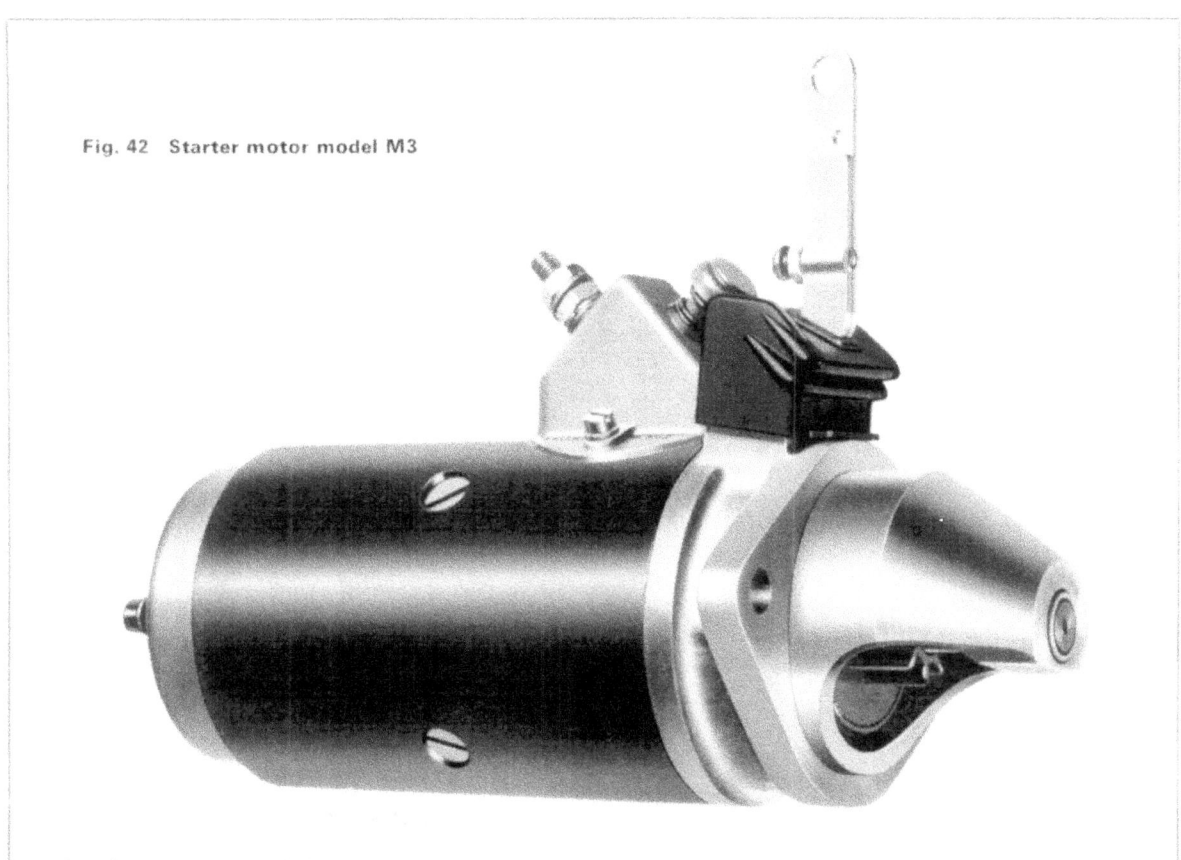

Fig. 42 Starter motor model M3

short-circuit in the wiring to the horn. In particular, ascertain that the horn push bracket is in good electrical contact with the handlebar. The performance of the horn may also be upset by its mounting bracket becoming loose.

Adjustment

The following adjustment will not alter the note of the horn. It will take up any wear on the moving parts, which if not corrected, would result in roughness and loss of performance.

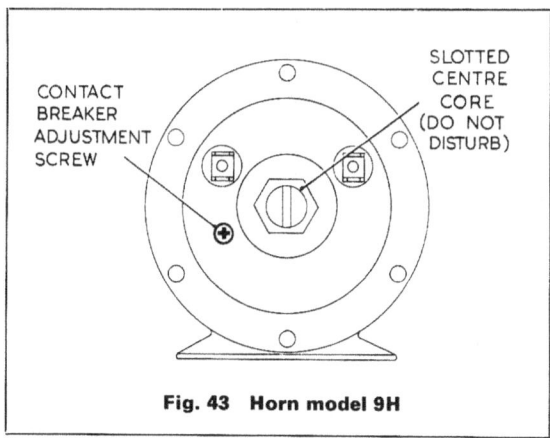

Fig. 43 Horn model 9H

Operate the horn push and slowly turn the adjustment screw anti-clockwise until the horn just fails to sound. Release the horn push and turn the adjustment screw clockwise one notch at a time until the original performance is restored. This usually entails a clockwise motion of one quarter to three-quarters of a turn. The centre locking nut must not be disturbed. If the original performance cannot be obtained do not attempt to dismantle the horn but return it to the local Lucas service centre for examination.

WIRING

Cable Harness

The cable harness requires no maintenance beyond checking that there are no signs of chafing along its length, especially around the steering head where the harness is continually flexing. The harness must not be stretched at any point and the terminals must be clean and tight.

Fused Battery Lead

On 12 volt motor cycles a fuse is fitted in an in-line fuse holder incorporated in one of the battery leads. If this fuse fails, it indicates a fault in the electrical system (such as a short-circuit). The cause of failure should therefore be ascertained before fitting a replacement fuse.

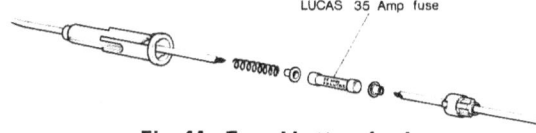

Fig. 44 Fused battery lead

The correct rating of the fuse is 35A. This rating must not be exceeded, neither must the fuse holder be by-passed to overcome fuse failure.

NOTE: When refitting the battery, ensure that the fused lead is not stretched to reach the battery terminal, as this may cause an open circuit at the fuse holder.

H.T. Cables

When the high tension cable shows signs of perishing or cracking it must be renewed with 7 mm p.v.c. or neoprene-covered cable, as detailed below.

Coil Ignition Models:

(i) Pull the defective cable from H.T. terminal.
(ii) Remove the metal terminal from the cable by opening the securing tags. Also, remove p.v.c. cover.
(iii) Fit the p.v.c. cover on the new cable then fit the metal clip.
(iv) Push the new cable firmly into the H.T. terminal moulding and ensure the p.v.c. cover fits tightly.

A.C. Ignition Models:

(i) Pull the defective cable from the H.T. terminal.
(ii) Before inserting the new cable, smear the outer casing with Bostik No. 1 (Clear) adhesive along the length of cable to be inside the coil housing.
(iii) Ensure that the coil H.T. terminal pin is located in the cable conductor and push the cable fully home.

General:

Some coil ignition machines are equipped with self-suppressed high tension cables to reduce radio and television interference. These cables are designed to suit each application individually and therefore, only the correct replacements should be fitted.

SWITCHES

Handlebar Switches Model

Two versions of the handlebar switch are used for right- and left-hand fitting. Each switch has different functions, although they outwardly appear similar. Both switches have one lever, two push buttons, and they are sometimes cast to form the pivot for the clutch and brake levers.

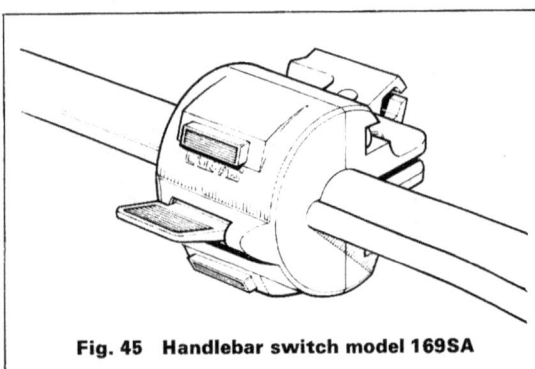

Fig. 45 Handlebar switch model 169SA

The left-hand switch controls headlight dipping on the lever, headlamp flash on the upper push button, and horn on the lower push button. The right-hand switch controls the direction indicators on the lever, the starter solenoid on the upper push button, and the ignition cut-out (or kill) on the lower push button.

Both switches are pre-wired and may have either female Lucar connectors or bullet snap connectors. The circuitry for these switches is shown in the typical wiring diagram for machines fitted with the electrical component box in Fig. 84.

Headlight Switch Model 57SA

This switch is used on the majority of 12 volt motor cycles. It is a toggle type switch, having three positions, "Off", "Parking" and "Headlight". The toggle lever action enables a rider to operate the switch easily with a gloved hand. The circuitry used with this switch is shown in the basic lighting circuit diagram Fig. 79.

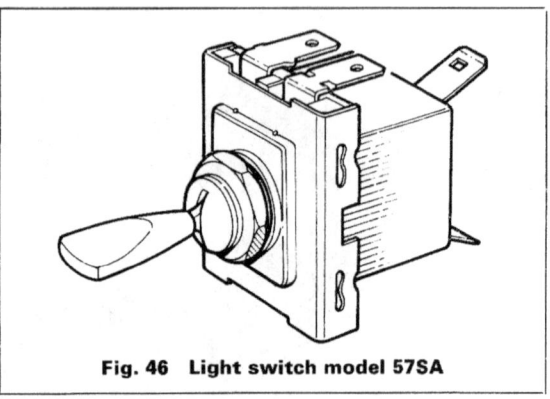

Fig. 46 Light switch model 57SA

Model 118SA Stop Lamp Switch

If the 118SA stop lamp is misaligned when the brake is adjusted, the excessive pressure from the operating mechanism will probably damage the fixing base of the switch. The following procedure should therefore be adopted after brake adjustment.

(i) Slacken the two bolts securing the switch.
(ii) With the brake in the fully off position (brake lever against front stop), insert a $\frac{1}{32}"$ (0·793 mm) spacer between the contacting brake mechanism and the switch plunger. Adjust the switch position so that the plunger is fully depressed (see Fig. 47).
(iii) Lock fixing bolts in this position.
(iv) Remove spacer and check the switch is operating correctly.

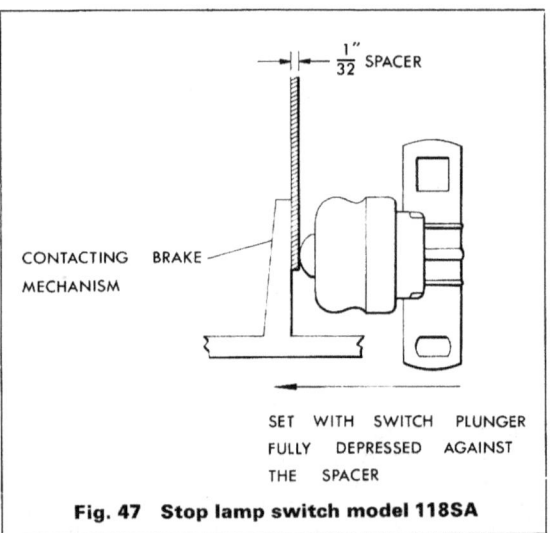

Fig. 47 Stop lamp switch model 118SA

Ignition/Lighting Switch

The model 149SA switch acts as the master switch for both the ignition and the lights. It is key operated and has four positions:

Position 1 Lights only: The key may be removed in this position enabling the machine to be parked safely at night.

Position 2 Off position: Again the key may be removed leaving everything isolated.

Position 3 Ignition only: The key cannot be removed. This position is used during normal daytime riding.

Position 4 Ignition and lights: Again, the key may not be removed. This position is used for all riding after dark.

THE ELECTRICAL COMPONENTS BOX

Certain motor cycles now incorporate the majority of the electrical components in a die-cast aluminium box. As the components are now close together the circuitry differs slightly from previous arrangements. The test procedure has been modified accordingly.

The following components are installed in the box.

1. The ignition capacitor.
2. The 8FL flasher unit.
3. The 2MC capacitor.
4. The ignition/lighting switch.
5. The Zener diode.
6. The rectifier.
7. A 9-pin plug and socket.
8. The ignition coil.
9. 2 reflex reflectors.

These parts are arranged as shown in Fig. 49.

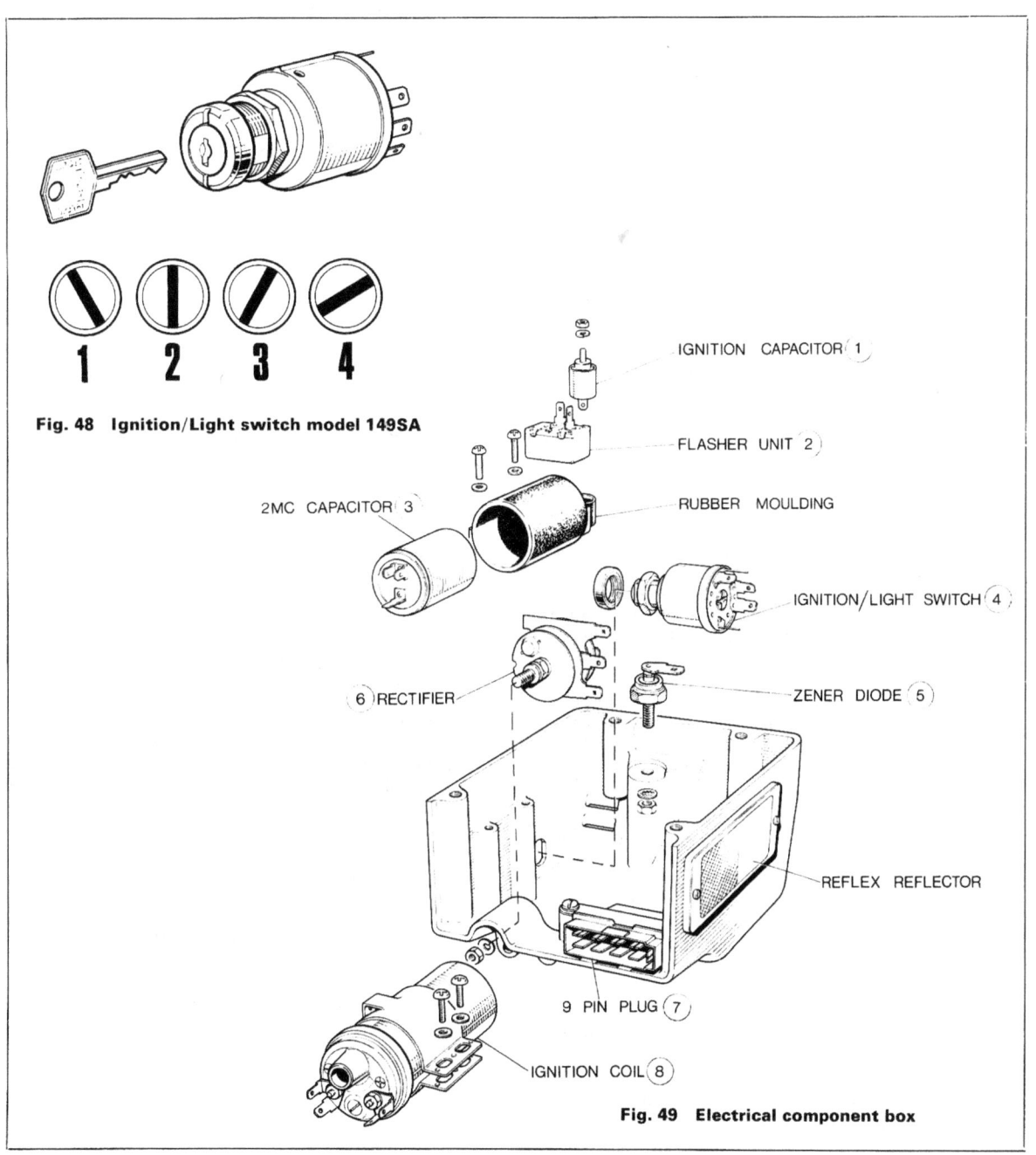

Fig. 48 Ignition/Light switch model 149SA

Fig. 49 Electrical component box

GENERAL SERVICE INFORMATION

Converting 6 Volt Alternator Equipped Motor Cycles to 12 Volt

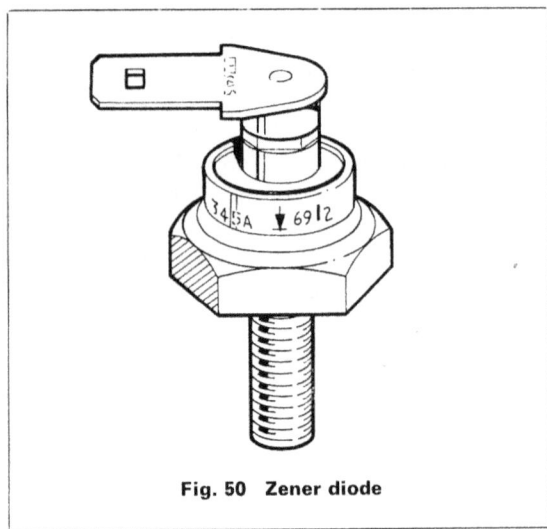

Fig. 50 Zener diode

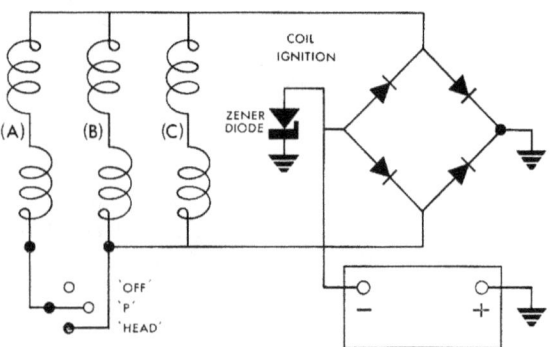

Fig. 51A Charging circuit showing Zener diode connection

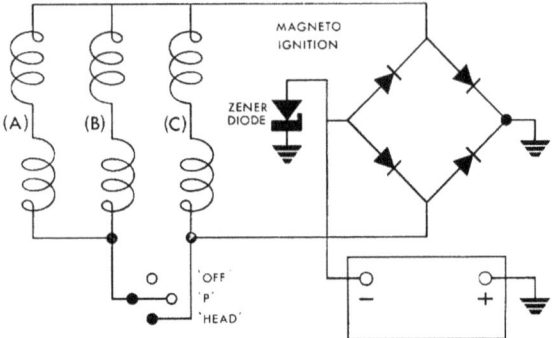

Fig. 51B Charging circuit for magneto equipped motor cycles

Function of Zener Diode as a Charging Current Regulator

Fig. 51A shows how the diode is connected in the alternator circuit. It is in parallel with (or shunted across) the battery, and operates as follows:

When the battery is in a low state of charge, its terminal voltage will be low (and the same voltage is across the diode). The maximum charging current then flows into the battery from the alternator. At first current is not-passed by the diode, the latter being non-conductive due to the low battery terminal voltage. However, as the battery voltage rises, the system voltage also rises until, at approximately 14 volts, the Zener diode becomes partially conductive, and an alternative path is provided for a small part of the charging current. Small increases in battery voltage result in large increases in Zener conductivity until, at approximately 15 volts, about 5 amperes of the alternator output is by-passing the battery. The battery will receive only a portion of the alternator output while the system voltage is relatively high.

As the system voltage falls, due to the use of headlamp or other lighting equipment, the Zener diode current decreases and the balance is diverted and consumed by the component in use. If the electrical loading is sufficient to cause the system voltage to fall below approximately 14 volts, the Zener diode will become non-conductive and the full generated output will be used to meet the demands of the system.

To prevent overloading the Zener diode some form of switching is required. When the lighting switch is in the positions "Off" and "P", four coils of the stator are permanently connected across the rectifier for coil ignition circuits, and two coils for magneto circuits, Fig. 51B. In the "Head" position full alternator output is obtained by connecting all six coils across the rectifier.

New Equipment Required

When converting a Lucas motor cycle alternator circuit from 6-volt to 12-volt the electrical units which must be considered are: battery, Zener diode and its associated heat sink, in-line fuse, rectifier, ignition coil, distributor (or contact breaker unit), horn, lighting equipment, and any extra electrical accessories that may be fitted. The original stator and rotor except energy transfer units, are retained in every application providing they are in good working condition. Each of these units is considered below.

Battery

Use the new 12-volt motor cycle battery type PUZ5A which is resistant to vibration and petrol. The special design features are a chamber venting system, with a one-piece manifold for easy topping up, and a transparent container allowing easy checks on acid levels.

Another method of obtaining a 12-volt supply is to connect another 6-volt battery in series with the existing battery. Providing the two batteries are of the same type and capacity, and the old one is in a charged and healthy condition, this arrangement will function satisfactorily. The battery capacity should be at least six or seven ampere-hours. Two batteries model MKZ9E, connected in series would give a 12-volt capacity of 8AH at the 10-hour rate. Two of these batteries occupy approximately the same space as one PUZ7E battery.

Two MLZ9E batteries having a capacity of 12 ampere-hours at the 10-hour rate, or one 12-volt

PUZ5A battery with a capacity of 8 ampere-hours at the 10-hour rate, could be used, depending on space available.

For sidecar use, one of the smaller car batteries such as model BHN5A/7/8 could be installed in the sidecar.

Battery Model	Voltage per Unit	Ampere-Hour Capacity (10-Hour Rate)
MKZ9E	6	8
MLZ9E	6	13
PUZ5A	12	10
BHN5/7A-8.85	12	22

Zener Diode and Heat Sink

A stud-mounted Zener diode, Part Number 49345, will be required. The diode must be mounted on a heat sink to prevent its working temperatures from rising above the designed operating range. The heat sink must be made of copper or aluminium sheet approximately $\frac{3}{8}$" (3·2 mm) thick, have a minimum area of 25 square inches, and be as square as space limitations permit. In practice, it is found that an area of 6" (152 mm) x $4\frac{1}{4}$" (108 mm), (as shown in Fig. 52), can most readily be accommodated. The diode must be mounted as near to the centre of the heat sink as possible. Care must be taken to see that the metal of the heat sink is clean, free from enamel and flat around the diode fixing hole to ensure maximum heat conduction from the diode.

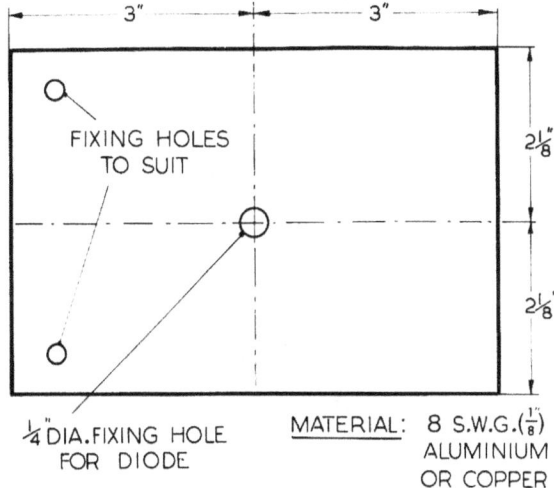

Fig. 52 Suitable heat sink dimensions

Fused Earth Lead

Available under Part Number 54938986 and connected between the positive terminal of battery and earth as shown in Fig. 53. Replacement 35A fuses are available (Part Number 188218).

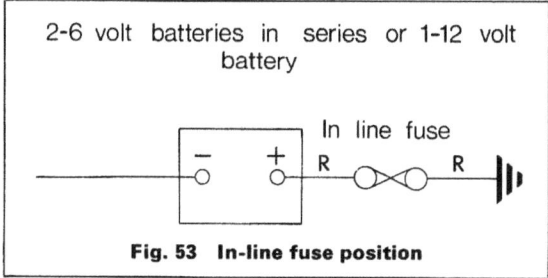

Fig. 53 In-line fuse position

Rectifier

Several types of rectifier have been used on alternator equipped machines but only the latest design, Part Number 49072, is suitable for the conversion. This is a silicon diode bridge unit, which functions in either 6 or 12-volt circuits. IF THE EXISTING RECTIFIER IS A SQUARE SELENIUM UNIT, OR ONE OF THE EARLIER TYPES, IT SHOULD BE REPLACED BY PART NUMBER 49072.

Ignition Coil(s)

The existing ignition coils will be 6-volt units. These must be replaced by the equivalent 12-volt unit.

Replace model MA6 with 17M12, Part Number 45223.

Distributor and Contact Breaker

The capacitor fitted in the model 18D1 and 18D2 distributor is unsuitable for 12-volt operation. It must therefore be removed and a new capacitor, Part Number 54441582, fitted externally.

All other original capacitors are suitable.

Horn

Several 12-volt horns are available, including the more powerful high frequency model 6H, and the car type horn, model 9H, which can be used either singly, or as a matched pair (high and low note). A relay will be required if horns are fitted. This limits the current passing across the horn button contacts.

Horn model 6H: Part No. 70183
Horn model 9H, Low Note: Part No. 54068087
Horn model 9H. High Note: Part No. 54068086
Relay model 6RA: Part No. 33188 (for use with twin horns).

Headlamp

On machines fitted with 7-inch dip left light units (Marked "RIGHT-HAND DRIVE"), replace the bulb with Lucas No. 414, 12-volt 50/40 watt.

On machines fitted with dip right headlamps (Marked "LEFT-HAND DRIVE"), replace the bulb with Lucas No. 415, 12-volt 50/40 watt.

On machines fitted with 7-inch vertical dip light units (Marked "MOTOR CYCLE"), replace the bulb with Lucas No. 446 12-volt 50/40 watt.

The total driving lamp(s) loading should be between 50 and 75 watts.

On machines fitted with $5\frac{3}{4}$-inch vertical dip lights (Marked "MOTOR CYCLE LIGHTWEIGHT"), replace the bulb with Lucas No. 446, 12-volt 50/40 watt.

Replace parking light bulb with No. 989 12-volt 6 watt.

12-volt speedometer bulbs are obtainable from Smiths Motor Accessories Ltd.

Stop-Tail Lamp

If the bulb holder is designed to accept non-reversible bulbs, use No. 380, 12-volt 6/21 watt (with off-set pins). If the bulb holder accepts reversible bulbs, fit bulb No. 381, 12-volt 6/21 watt. (Ensure the bulb is inserted the correct way round).

Sidecar Lamp

For the Lucas sidecar lamp model 569, use bulb No. 989, 12-volt 6 watt.

Electrical Accessories

The manufacturer of any electrical accessories fitted to your machine should be consulted about their suitability for 12-volt operation before connecting them to the converted circuit.

In the case of lamps, it will be necessary to fit a suitable 12-volt bulb.

Installing the New Equipment

With the exception of the battery and the Zener diode, the new equipment will replace existing units and fitting should present no difficulty.

Battery

The most difficult problem will probably be how to accommodate an extra battery on the motor cycle. Unfortunately, as each machine requires a different approach, it is not possible to make comprehensive recommendations. However, the following suggestions may be helpful:

If machines are equipped with the black "Milam" cased PUZ7E battery, two MKZ9E batteries (these occupy approximately the same space as the PUZ7E) can usually be accommodated. Where a plastic cased MLZ9E battery is in use, an additional MLZ9E battery may be fitted alongside the original or in some adjacent position.

NOTE: The earlier versions of some machines now equipped with MLZ9E batteries were originally fitted with PUZ7E batteries. In these instances, the original PUZ7E battery carrier may be obtained through your motor cycle dealer.

The batteries could also be mounted in the boot of a sidecar or in a suitably modified pannier.

Ensure that batteries are fixed firmly, as insecure mounting will cause failure due to vibration. If the two batteries are mounted side by side, a thin sheet of rubber should be placed between them (see Fig. 54) to prevent chafing.

Zener Diode

The diode and its heat sink must be mounted so that a good air stream passes over both sides of the plate to ensure efficient cooling. At the same time its location must be such that the diode will remain reasonably dry and clean.

On many machines these requirements will be met by mounting the heat sink underneath the front of the petrol tank, on the tank mounting bracket. Efficient operation of the diode depends upon the existence of a good earth connection. A separate cable link between the heat sink and the frame of the machine is, therefore, recommended.

CAUTION: The body of the Zener diode is made of copper to ensure maximum heat conductivity. This means that the fixing stud has a relatively low tensile strength, and must be subjected to a tightening torque within the limits of 24–28 lb.f.-ins. (2·72–3·16 Nm).

Connecting-Up

The new units must now be connected into the circuit. (All additional cable used in the conversion should be 28/·012" or equivalent, unless otherwise stated).

Battery

The two batteries should be connected in series by means of a short link wire which must join the +ve terminal of one battery to the —ve terminal of the other, as shown in Fig. 54.

The remaining +ve terminal should be connected to the Red fused earth wire, and the —ve terminal to the Brown/Blue wire to the ammeter or lighting switch.

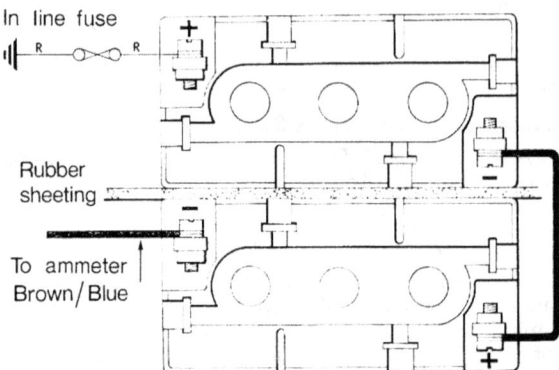

Fig. 54 Two 6 volt batteries connected for 12 volt operation

Zener Diode

The connection from the Lucar terminal of the diode should be made to a point along the Brown/White, Brown/Purple, Purple or Brown/Blue cable from the rectifier centre terminal.

NOTE: The method of fitting Lucar connectors to cables is shown stage-by-stage in Fig. 63.

Rectifier (When applicable)

The terminals of the silicon bridge rectifier have the same arrangement as the earlier selenium types, the connections should therefore be as shown in Fig. 55.

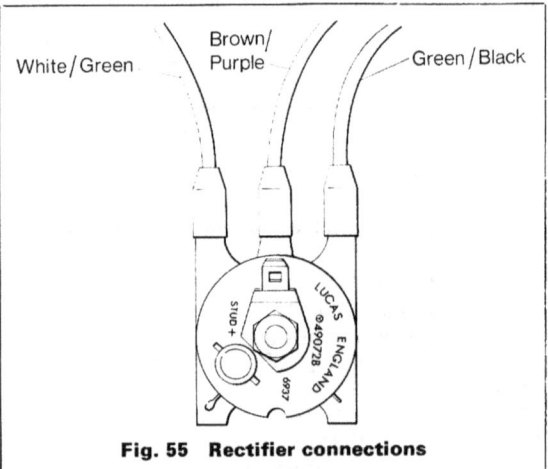

Fig. 55 Rectifier connections

If the original circuit includes a White/Green (Green/White or Light Green) cable connecting a rectifier terminal to the lighting switch, this must be disconnected at the switch and taped up.

When fitting the rectifier to the machine remember the earth connection should be made to the Lucar on the bolt head.

Ignition Coil

The terminal arrangement of the replacement coil is identical to the original coil. The White cable should be connected to the "SW" or "—ve" terminal, and the Black/White cable to the "CB" or "+ve" terminal.

Capacitor (When applicable)

Connect the capacitor either to the L.T. terminal of the contact breaker unit (or distributor), or to the ignition coil terminal "CB" (or "+"). The body of the capacitor must be in good electrical contact with earth.

Horn

Connect in the same manner as the original, or as directed in the fitting instructions supplied with the new horn(s).

Replacing 8H Horn with 6H Type

Generally the 8H horn can be replaced with the larger 6H type, but where the 6H will not fit into the same position, an additional mounting bracket may be required. These should be obtained from the motor cycle manufacturer concerned or their agents.

To extend the horn leads, the two Lucar terminals should be removed from the leads and replaced with single snap connectors and nipples (Part Nos. 900288 and 900269) using 14" ·010" cable for the extension, refitting or replacing the Lucar terminals and sleeves (Part Nos. 54942078 and 54190042), for connecting to the horn.

Alternator

With coil ignition machines four of the six alternator coils should be permanently connected across the rectifier and the remaining two coils brought into circuit when the headlamp is switched on. As shown in Fig. 56 two of the three alternator-to-wiring-harness connections (Green/Yellow and Green/Black) are transposed at the snap connectors.

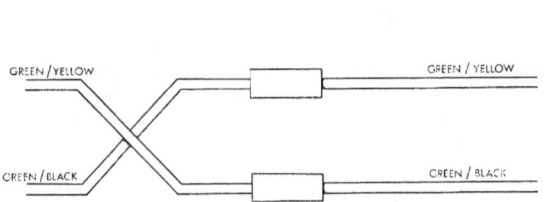

Fig. 56 Alternator connections for coil ignition motor cycles

NOTE: In two-colour cables, the first named is the main colour and the second the tracer. The colours at present used have been chosen for their permanency (they do not discolour with age and normal service). For reference, the four transistional colour coding schemes used with 3-lead motor cycle alternators are given below:

1	2
Light Green	Light Green
Mid Green	Green-with-Yellow
Dark Green	Dark Green
3	**4**
Green-with-White	White-with-Green
Green-with-Yellow	Green-with-Yellow
Green-with-Black	Green-with-Black

With magneto equipped machines there is no ignition coil load so the output from four alternator coils would be too high for the diode to control. Thus only two of the alternator coils are permanently connected across the rectifier, and the remaining four coils are brought into circuit by the lighting switch. This is done by connecting the alternator output cables colour to colour, as shown in Fig. 57.

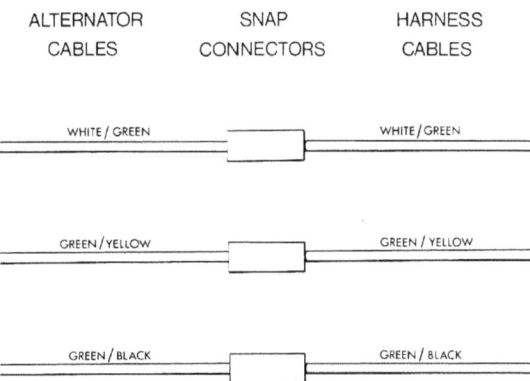

Fig. 57 Alternator connections for magneto ignition motor cycles

CONVERSION TO CAPACITOR IGNITION

Object of the System

The object of this system is to enable a motor cycle to be run, with or without a battery, enabling the rider to use the machine for competition work, and then re-fit the battery for normal road use.

Starting and lighting are equally effective with or without the battery, but additional accessories or parking lights cannot be used if the battery has been disconnected.

How the System Works

The capacitor stores the energy pulses from the alternator and supplies the ignition coil with sufficient energy to ensure adequate plug sparking for starting and running at all speeds throughout the engine operating range.

New Equipment Required

In the case of motor cycles already fitted with Lucas 12-volt systems, it is only necessary to purchase the 2MC capacitor complete with mounting spring.

Earlier machines wired to give partial generator output in "Off" and "Pilot" positions will not have heat sinks of sufficient size. These must, therefore, be replaced. Minimum dimensions of the heat sink are given below.

Energy transfer equipped machines, however, will further require a battery charging alternator stator, wiring harness, lighting and ignition switches, and contact breaker unit.

CAUTION: The minimum size for the Zener diode heat sink, when used with the 2MC capacitor system is 6 in. x 6 in. x $\frac{1}{8}$ in., aluminium or copper plate (or an alternative shape of equivalent total surface area, i.e. 72 square ins.). The Zener diode should be centrally mounted, flat on its base, **which must make direct metal-to-metal** contact with the plate. The assembly should be mounted on the machine so that it is in an unobstructed air stream, avoiding as far as possible, dirt or water thrown up by the road wheels.

Mounting the Capacitor

Two types of springs are available for mounting the capacitor, one for fixing underneath a vertically positioned bolt, the other for a horizontal fixing point. Whickever spring is used the capacitor **must** be positioned with its terminals pointing downwards, as in Fig. 58.

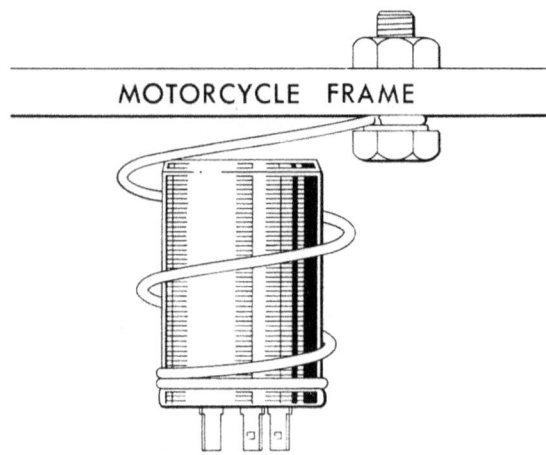

Fig. 58 Capacitor mounting

To fit the spring to the capacitor, insert the capacitor into the widest coil end and push it down until the small coil at the other end locates in the groove on the capacitor body.

Wiring Connections

CAUTION: The 2MC is an electrolytic **polarised** unit which may be irreparably damaged if incorrectly connected.

It will be seen that there are two sizes of Lucar connector on the unit. The small $\frac{3}{16}$ inch Lucar is the **positive** (earth) terminal, the rivet of which is marked with a spot of **red** paint. The double $\frac{1}{4}$ inch Lucar forms the **negative** terminal.

The capacitor negative terminal **and** Zener diode must be connected to the rectifier centre (D.C.) terminal or to a convenient point on the Brown/White lead. (This would be the Brown/Purple, Brown/Blue or Purple lead on some models). **They must not be connected to the ignition coil.**

Modifying Alternator Cable Connections

The alternator should be reconnected to give full output in all lighting switch positions. This can be done by joining the alternator external leads Green/Black and Green/Yellow using a double snap-connector, Part No. 850641.

Running with Battery Disconnected

Before running the machine with the battery disconnected THE BATTERY NEGATIVE LEAD MUST BE INSULATED to prevent it from shorting to earth (touching frame of machine).

Do not run the machine with the Zener diode disconnected as excessive voltage will damage the 2MC capacitor.

Periodic Check for Faulty Capacitor

A faulty capacitor may not be apparent when used while the battery is connected in circuit. Periodically check that the unit is serviceable by disconnecting the battery and starting the machine in the normal manner.

CLIPPER DIODE

A common fault experienced with machines equipped with Direct Lighting is the blowing of bulbs. This may be due to faulty dipper switches, causing momentary voltage surges, bad connections or intermittent earths. Whichever is the cause, the Clipper diode effectively protects bulbs against excessive voltage, but of course will not prevent failure caused by vibration, filament fractures or faulty bulb manufacture. The Clipper diode is available under Part No. 83137.

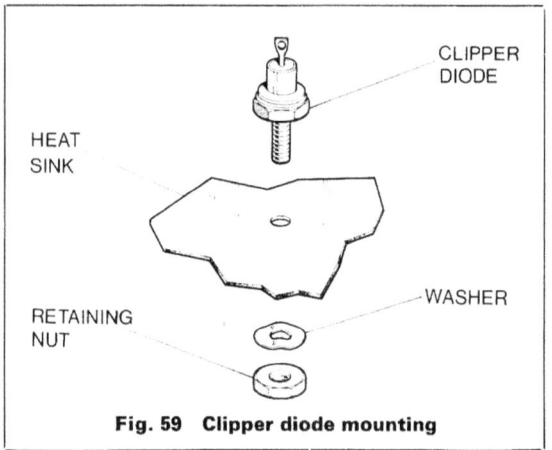

Fig. 59 Clipper diode mounting

Installation

The diode is wired into the circuit so that when the lights are switched on, the generator also supplies the diode. This can be achieved by connecting either into the tail-lamp feed or the wire supplying the dipper switch. If no dipper switch is used, the connection could be made directly to the headlamp bulb feed. (Fig. 60).

Either an aluminium or copper plate not less than 16 gauge in thickness and measuring 2 in. x 3 in. (50 x 76 mm) is required. Mount the diode on the plate by drilling a $\frac{3}{16}$ (0·1875) in. (4·77 mm) hole approximately in the centre of the plate, ensuring that all burrs are removed from round the edges of the hole so that the base of the diode bears flat on the plate.

Mount the plate on the machine in a convenient position so that air circulates around the diode and plate when the motor cycle is in motion. Do not position the unit too close to the ground or wheels since salt-contaminated mud and water may corrode the diode body. Ensure that the diode is properly earthed to the machine.

Operation

While the generator is below the safe maximum value for the bulbs, the diode does not absorb any of the output, so there is no loss of light. This is of prime importance when travelling at low speeds.

When the voltage has increased to the safe maximum value, the diode begins to absorb part of the output, and prevents further increase in voltage. Thus, the bulb load can be adjusted to give the best possible light output at all speeds without having to overload the generator, to keep down the voltage.

Limitations

The diode is normally recommended for use with generators whose rated output does not exceed 21 watts. If the diode is for use on higher output machines, the size of the mounting plate (heat sink) should be increased as follows:

Output	Heat Sink
25 watts	3 in. x 3 in.
30 watts	3 in. x 4 in.

The diode should not be used on generators having an output greater than 30 watts. Maximum working temperature, measured at the side of the diode, must not exceed 115°C.

WARNING: As the mounting stud is made of copper, care must be taken not to overtighten when bolting to the mounting plate.

TWIN HORNS

High speed motor cycles require a more effective warning system. The Lucas twin horns meet this requirement and as they are used intermittently they have no adverse effect on the electrical system. Twin horns are available for 6 or 12 volt operation. Model 9H horns together with the required relay are available from the local Lucas Agent or Service Centre and must be connected as shown in Fig. 61.

ANTI-THEFT SWITCH FOR COIL IGNITION MOTOR CYCLES

One of the most usual methods of thief-proofing a machine has been the use of a concealed switch which isolates the lighting and ignition circuits. By using model 45SA switch, Part No. 31923, not only are the ignition/lighting circuits isolated as before but, in addition, the horn is sounded when there is any attempt to start the motor cycle.

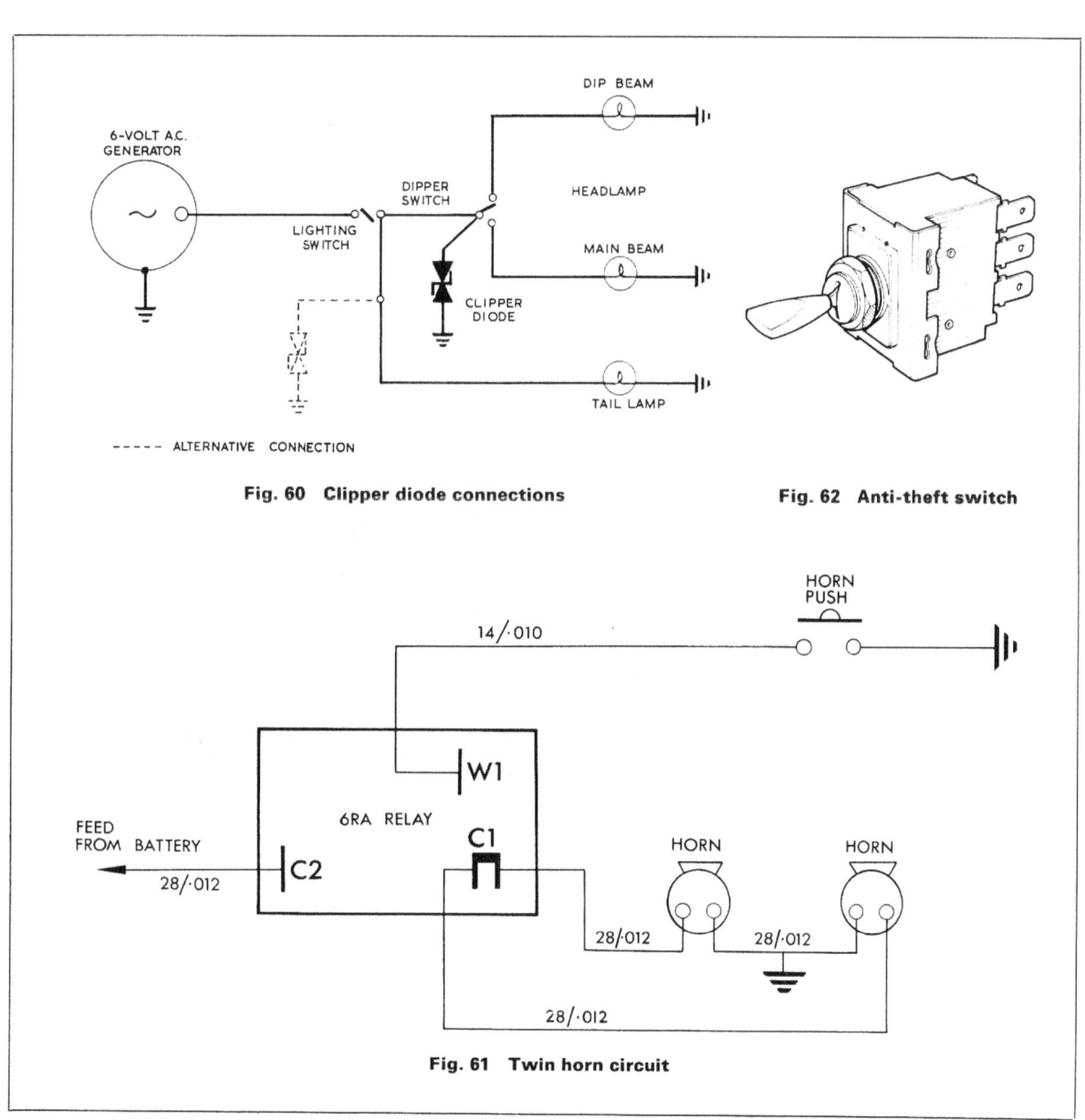

Fig. 60 Clipper diode connections

Fig. 62 Anti-theft switch

Fig. 61 Twin horn circuit

To fit the 45SA switch the connection between the positive (+) terminal of the battery and earth must be disconnected. The positive (+) terminal is connected to the No. 2 terminal of the 45SA switch, using 28/·012 cable. The No. 1 terminal is then connected to earth using the same type of cable. Disconnect the horn feed cable from the horn, and tape up. (If two cables are connected to the horn feed cable, these must be connected together before taping).

Make up another length of 14/·010 cable to connect the feed terminal of the horn to the No. 5 terminal of the 45SA switch. (It may be necessary to extend this cable). A double snap connector is fitted in the horn-to-horn push cable and an additional cable inserted from here to the No. 3 terminal of the 45SA switch. The feed from the ignition switch to the SW terminal on the coil is disconnected at the coil and reconnected to the No. 5 terminal of the 45SA switch along with the feed cable to the horn. Finally, No. 4 terminal is connected to the SW terminal of the coil. (Fig. 85 page 51).

With the switch in the normal position, the electrical system behaves normally. However, when the switch is in the "on" position, any attempt to start or short-circuit the ignition switch will cause the horn to operate.

FITTING A LUCAR CONNECTOR

It is essential that the Lucar connector is fitted in accordance with the following instructions to ensure the efficient operation of the associated equipment.

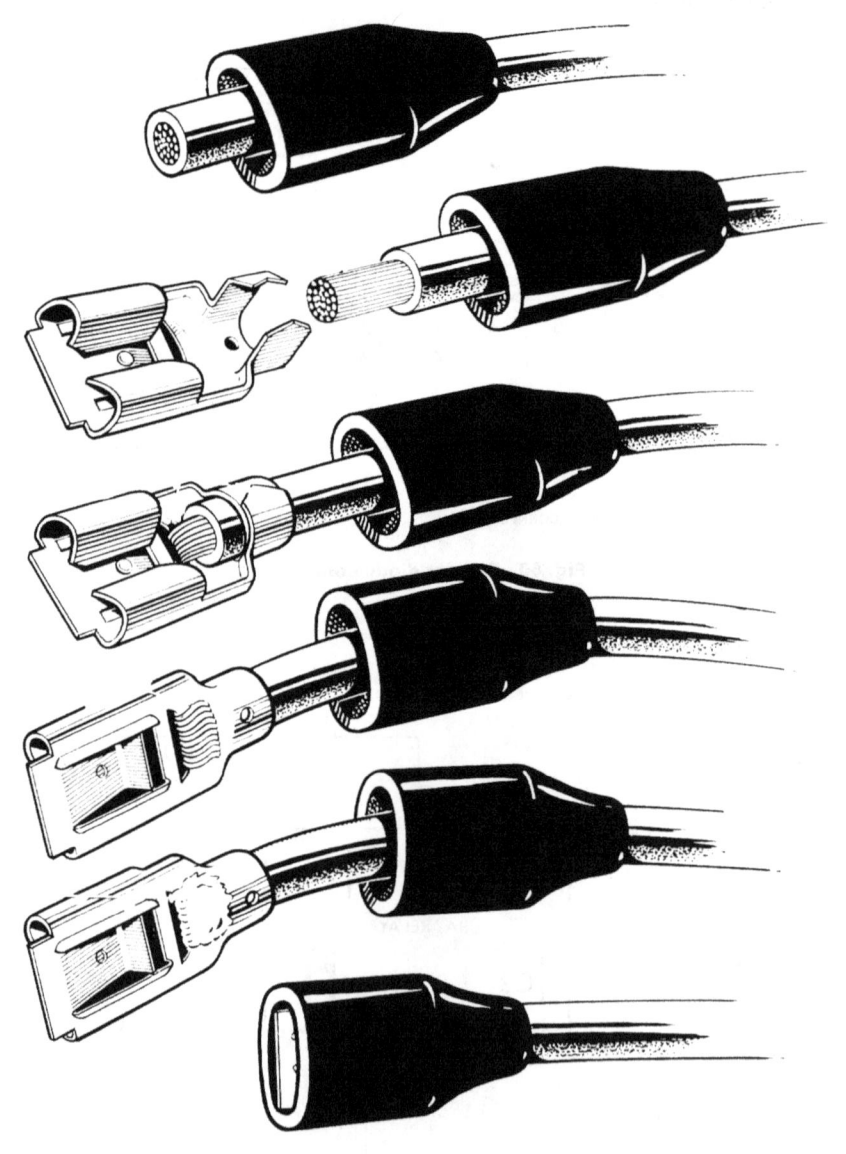

STAGE 1
Thread the insulating cover over the cable

STAGE 2
Strip the insulation neatly from the conductor

STAGE 3
Feed conductors through the aperture and grip the cable firmly in the tags

STAGE 4
Splay conductors back towards the cable and spread flat

STAGE 5
Solder securely and neatly to the connector. Do not allow solder to run through the aperture

STAGE 6
Allow the joint to cool. Slide the cover over the connector

Fig. 63 Fitting instructions for Lucar connectors

TEST PROCEDURE

In order to carry out systematic checking of the electrical circuitry the following test equipment is required.

(i) A.C. moving coil voltmeter scale 0–15 V
(ii) D.C. moving coil voltmeter scale 0–18 V
(iii) D.C. moving coil ammeter scale 5·0–25 A
(iv) Load resistor of 1 ohm capable of carrying 15 A
(v) Load resistor of 0·5 ohm capable of carrying 24 A
(vi) Length of cable having a small crocodile type clip at each end.

The "Wilkson" test box (Fig. 64) contains all the above units in a metal case which is compact and easy to use.

In addition a suitable hydrometer, scale 1·000–1·300 will be required.

NOTE: Certain motor cycles are now fitted with an electrical component box and special instructions are marked with (*). Otherwise normal instructions apply.

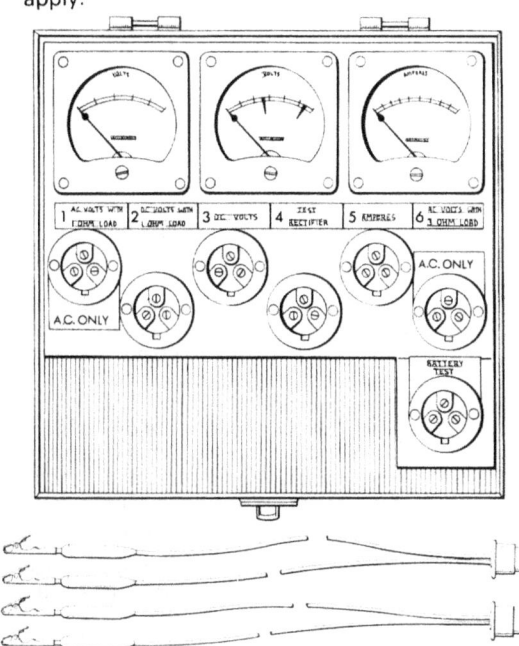

Fig. 64 Wilkson test box

Test I. Battery

Where possible a hydrometer test should be taken and the table below indicates the readings obtained with given battery conditions. The figures quoted are accurate at 15°C (60°F) and the results must be corrected to this figure. This is done by adding 0·007 to the reading for every 10°C (18°F) above 15°C (60°F), and subtracting for every 10°C (18°F) below. A variation of 0·040 between the readings obtained from each cell indicates a faulty battery, which should be checked by a Lucas battery agent.

(b) High Rate Discharge

As a battery ages its capacity is reduced. This may be due to the formation of heavy sulphate or the shedding of the active material from the plates. The high discharge test should be carried out after the battery has been recharged to at least 70% Connect.

	Specific Gravity (corrected to 15°C (60°F))	
	Climates normally Below 25°C (77°F)	Climates normally Above 25°C (77°F)
Fully charged	1·270 – 1·290	1·210 – 1·230
70% charged	1·230 – 1·250	1·170 – 1·190
Discharged	1·110 – 1·130	1·050 – 1·070

the D.C. voltmeter and one ohm load across the battery, as shown in Fig. 65, and keep in position for 15 seconds. The table below gives the minimum voltage for a healthy battery. Directly after 15 seconds the reading should remain steady, as a falling or low voltage indicates that the battery is faulty and must be taken to the local Lucas battery agent for examination.

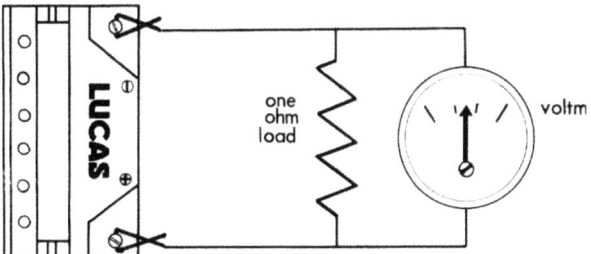

Fig. 65 High rate discharge test

Battery Voltage	Voltmeter Reading
12	9·4
6	4·8

Test II. Charging Circuit

(a) D.C. Input to the Battery

Disconnect the battery negative terminal and connect the ammeter between the battery post and the cable terminal (Fig. 66). If a Zener diode is fitted, it must be disconnected and the lead insulated to obtain full output from the alternator.

*Special Instructions for the Electrical Components Box

The Zener diode is disconnected by removing the straight Lucar connector with a Brown/Blue cable from the 2MC capacitor.

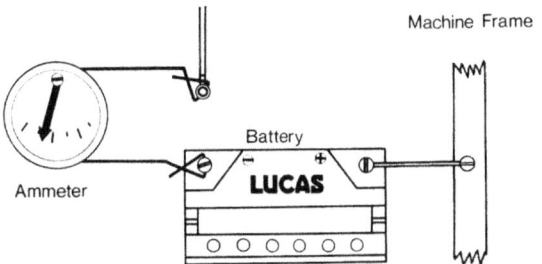

Fig. 66 Maximum charge rate test

Start the engine and increase speed to approximately 3,000 rev/min and note the ammeter readings. The following readings are obtained when the battery and charging system are in good condition.

Lighting switch position	Minimum Current Reading	
	Three-lead stator	Two-lead stator
Off	2·5 amp	4·5 amp
Headlamp Main beam	1·0 amp	1·0 amp

The readings may be higher provided there are no signs of over charging. If the readings are lower, a possible fault is indicated.

(b) Connections

On 6-volt and early 12-volt machines the cable connections to and from the lighting switch must be clean and tight. Check the alternator, rectifier, and battery terminals before proceeding with (c).

(c) Alternator Output

Disconnect the alternator output leads at the snap connectors and connect an A.C. voltmeter with a 1 ohm load resistor in parallel (Fig. 67). If the results are as shown in the following table the alternator is in good condition.

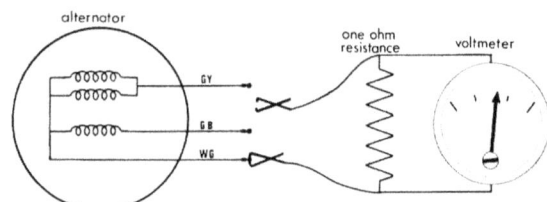

Fig. 67 Alternator output test

Voltmeter and Resistor between		Minimum Voltage Readings		
		Three-lead stators		Two-lead stators
		RM20	Others	RM21
White/Green	Green/Black with Green/Yellow	10	8·5	—
White/Green	Green/Yellow	—	—	9
Any one lead and stator (earth)		No reading		

Faults	
Voltmeter Reading	Diagnosis
All readings low	Demagnetised rotor. Return to Lucas agent for remagnetising
Low reading on one connection	Faulty coil
Zero reading	Open-circuit

NOTE: There should be no reading between any output lead and earth. A reading would indicate a breakdown of the insulation, and the stator should be replaced.

Test III. The Rectifier

Reconnect the alternator leads to the main harness. Disconnect the cable from the centre terminal of the rectifier and connect the D.C. voltmeter with the 1 ohm load as shown in Fig. 68. Start the engine and increase speed to approximately 3,000 rev/min. Turn the light switch to the headlamp position and take a reading from the voltmeter. This should read not less than 7·5 volts, which indicates the rectifier is operating satisfactorily. A lower reading indicates that the rectifier is faulty. This can be confirmed by checking each diode individually.

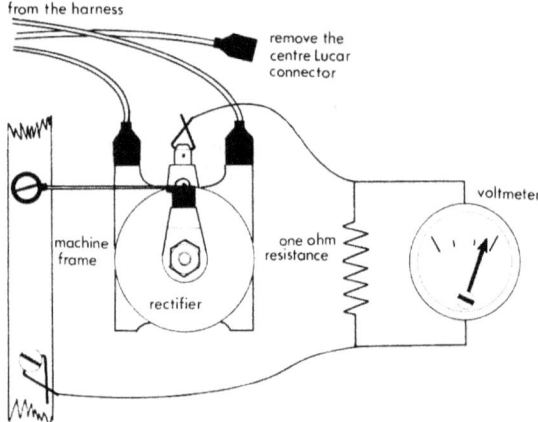

Fig. 68 Rectifier test in position

To check individual diodes a battery and a headlamp bulb are used. Remove the rectifier from the machine and connect the bulb and battery as shown in Fig. 69A. Then reverse the connections. If the bulb lights in one direction only the diode is satisfactory. If the bulb lights in both directions the diode is short-circuit. If the bulb will not light in either direction the diode is open-circuit. The test should then be repeated in the other three positions (Fig. 69B).

If any diode is faulty, the rectifier must be replaced.

NOTE: The silicon diode rectifier is interchangeable with the selenium type and should be tested in the same manner.

*Special Instructions for the Electrical Components Box

As the connections are not easily reached, the following method must be used:

(i) Disconnect the Zener diode as in Test II and reconnect the alternator cables into the main harness.

(ii) Disconnect the snap connector junction for the Brown/Blue cable at the box.

(iii) Connect a D.C. voltmeter (with the 1 ohm load in parallel) with the Red lead to earth and the Black lead to the Brown/Blue cable from the box.

(iv) Locate the White/Yellow cable in the other snap connector junction from the box, and using a jumper lead connect the cable from the box to the negative (—) terminal of the battery.

(v) Start the motor cycle and run at approximately 3,000 rev/min. A reading of 7·5 volts should be obtained, otherwise proceed with the rectifier bench test.

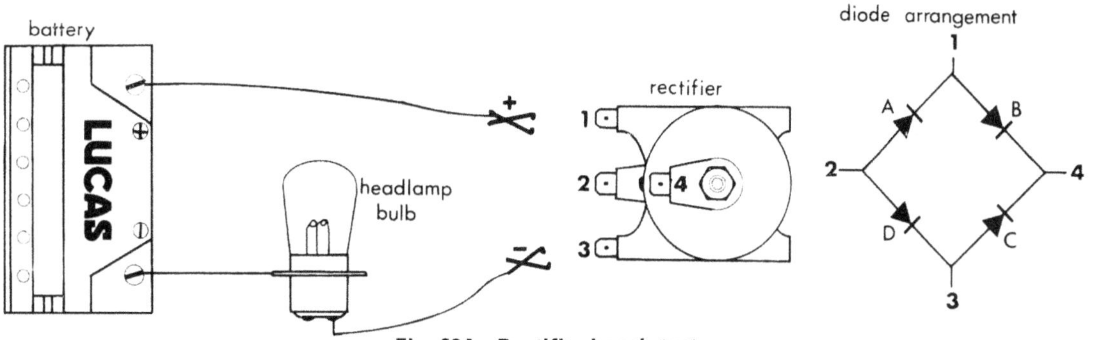

Fig. 69A Rectifier bench test

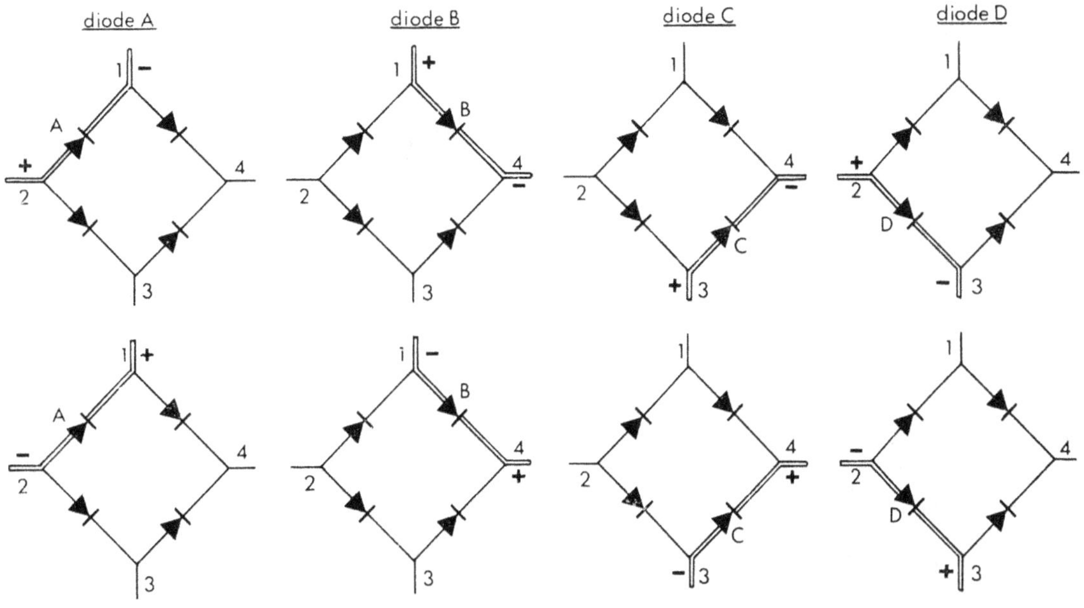

Fig. 69B Rectifier bench test (individual diode circuits)

Test IV. The Zener Diode

Replace the rectifier and connect correctly. Ensure the battery is fully charged before starting the motor cycle. Pull the cable off the Zener diode and connect the D.C. ammeter Red (+) lead to the Zener diode terminal and the Black (−) lead to the cable disconnected from the Zener diode. Connect the D.C. voltmeter without the 1 ohm load, with the Red lead to earth and the Black lead to the Zener Lucar blade, as shown in Fig. 70. Check that the electrical load except the ignition is switched off, increase speed to approximately 3,000 rev/min and note the readings. As the system voltage rises to approximately 12·75 volts, there should be no reading on the ammeter.

Above approximately 12·75 volts a reading should start on the ammeter. When the ammeter rises to 2 amps, the voltmeter should read between 13·5 and 15·5 volts. If the readings do not come within this specification the diode must be replaced.

NOTE: When refitting a Zener diode, the contact between the diode and the heat sink must be clean and free from corrosion. Also the retaining nut must not be tightened beyond 24–28 lbs.f.ins. (2·72–3·16 Nm).

*Special Instructions for the Electrical Components Box

Disconnect the Zener diode as in Test II, connect a D.C. voltmeter Black lead to the straight Lucar with the Brown/Blue cable (at 2MC capacitor) and the Red lead to earth. Connect a D.C. ammeter Black lead to the straight Lucar with the Brown/Blue cable and the Red lead to the right-angle Lucar with a Brown/Blue cable. Otherwise the test follows the normal procedure.

Test V. Ignition

Connect the D.C. voltmeter, without the 1 ohm load, with the Black lead to the 'CB' or '+' terminal of the coil and the Red lead to earth (Fig. 71). Turn the engine until the contacts open. When the ignition is switched on, the voltmeter should read battery

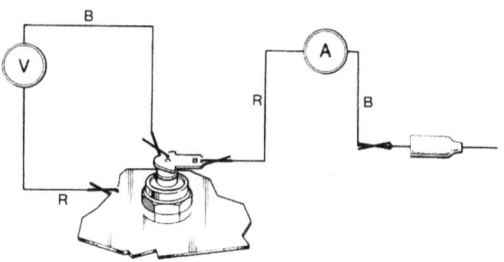

Fig. 70 Zener diode test

volts. No reading indicates either an open-circuit ignition switch, cable, coil primary winding or a short-circuit across the contacts. This can be confirmed by disconnecting the coil/contact breaker lead at the coil. If battery voltage is then indicated the fault is due to either the contacts or the wiring from the coil to the contacts. Failure of this sort is very often caused by incorrect assembly of the contact breaker insulating washers.

Turn the engine until the contacts close. The voltmeter should then read zero. Any reading indicates the contacts are burnt or dirty and should be cleaned or stoned flat.

engine and switch on the full lighting complement. A faulty capacitor will result in difficult starting. Remove the capacitor from the machine and connect to a 12-volt battery.

IMPORTANT: Correct polarity must be observed. Ensure the small single Lucar blade is connected to the positive (+) terminal and the larger double blade to the negative (−) terminal. After 5 seconds disconnect the battery and allow the capacitor to stand for 5 minutes. Connect the voltmeter across the terminals. An initial reading of not less than 9 volts should be obtained. (Some voltmeters may show an instantaneous overswing. This should be ignored). If an initial reading of less than 9 volts is obtained, the capacitor is leaking and should be replaced.

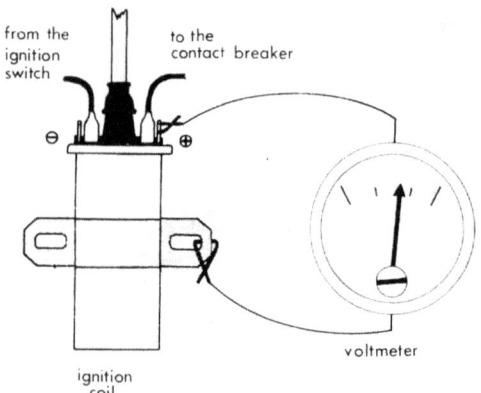

Fig. 71 Coil and contact breaker circuit test

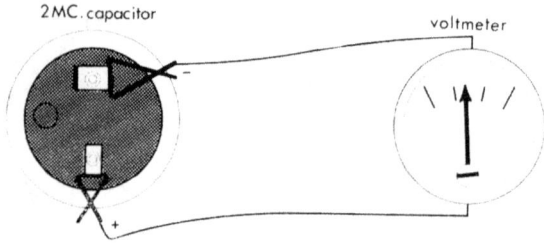

Fig. 73 Capacitor bench test

Test VII. Emergency Start Circuit (6-Volt Applications)

Ignition timing must be accurately set to the manufacturer's recommendations after checking the contact gap and alternator output.

Ensure all leads are connected correctly. Connect the D.C. voltmeter, without the 1 ohm load, with the Red lead to earth and the Black lead to the contact breaker coil terminal. Turn the engine until the points open. Then switch on the ignition switch and check the voltmeter readings. The following readings should be obtained.

Transfer the voltmeter Black lead to the Green/Yellow harness lead at the alternator connector when the ignition switch is on the emergency position, the voltmeter should register battery volts.

Connect the voltmeter with the Red lead to earth and the Black lead to the 'SW' or '−' terminal of the coil (Fig. 72). Ensure the contacts are closed and switch on the 'ign' switch. Observe the voltmeter reading. Then quickly transfer the Black lead to the battery '−' terminal and again observe the reading. The difference between the two readings should not exceed 0·5 volts. Readings in excess of this indicate a high resistance in the ignition feed circuit, i.e. faulty ignition switch, cut-out button or wiring.

Test VI. 2MC Capacitor

The operation of the 2MC capacitor should be checked at normal service intervals. Disconnect and insulate the battery negative terminal. Start the

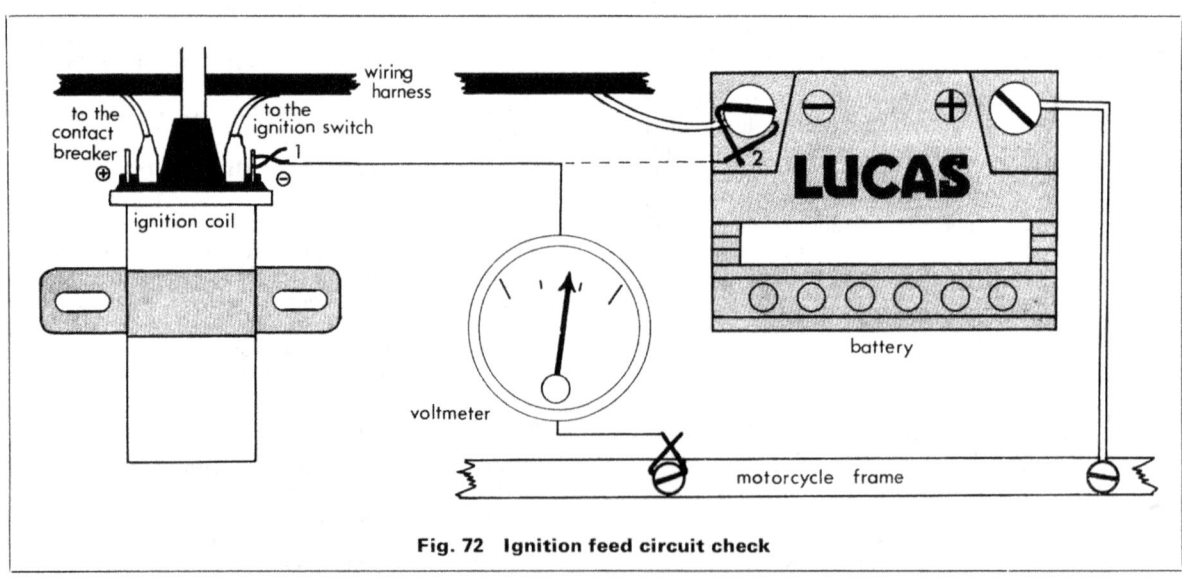

Fig. 72 Ignition feed circuit check

Test VIII. Energy Transfer (A.C.) Ignition – Direct Lighting

NOTE: Tests which necessitate running the engine, can only be performed if the ignition system is operating correctly, i.e. ignition timing, contacts and plug gap settings etc., are in accordance with the manufacturer's recommendations.

If the alternator timing and plugs etc., are satisfactory and the E.T. ignition coil is suspect, but a replacement is not immediately available, the following procedure will enable further tests to be carried out.

To enable the motor cycle to be started a substitute ignition system is used. This comprises of a 6-volt battery and a standard type motor cycle ignition coil. Connect as follows:

(1) Positive battery lead to frame of machine (earth).
(2) Negative battery lead to substitute ignition coil ('SW' or '—').
(3) Connect ignition coil ('CB' or '+') to contact-breaker on machine, removing the existing lead from contact-breaker.

(A) Alternator

(i) Disconnect all alternator cables from main harness – Red, Brown/Blue, Black, White (and Brown when fitted).
(ii) Run engine at fast idling speed.
(iii) Connect A.C. voltmeter (with 1 ohm resistor in parallel) across coils as follows:

Connect Voltmeter between	Voltmeter Reading (*minimum*)
Red and Brown/Blue	5·0 volts
Black/Yellow and Black/White	1·5 volts
Red and Brown (when fitted)	3·5 volts
Any lead and stator (earth)	No reading

CONCLUSIONS:

If all readings are low it indicates that the rotor is demagnetised.

A low reading across any coil (when the remainder are satisfactory) indicates a short-circuited coil.

A zero reading indicates open-circuited coil(s).

A reading between any lead and stator indicates earthed coil(s).

(B) The E.T. Ignition Coil

There is no method of checking the output of the coil in situ. When a coil is suspect, it should first be checked by substitution, and then bench-tested.

Test Equipment Required

A four-cylinder car-type contact-breaker (distributor) is required, having closed periods of not less than 42° and an operating range of up to 750 rev/min. Also, a 12-volt battery, a three-point rotary spark gap and a 1 ohm resistor (approximately 15 watt).

Test Procedure

(a) Connect the 12-volt battery, contact-breaker and 1·0 ohm resistor in series with the primary winding of the ignition coil. Connect the negative side of the battery to the earthed end of the primary winding, as shown in Fig. 74.
(b) Connect the spark gap electrode which is farthest from the ionising electrode, to the negative side of the circuit, by means of a jumper lead.
(c) Connect the H.T. lead from the ignition coil to the three-point spark gap, at the main electrode nearest to the ionising electrode.
(d) Run the contact-breaker at 750 rev/min. Regular sparking should occur between the main electrodes when set to 8 mm (approximately 14kV). Do not continue this test for more than 30 seconds because there will be considerable arcing at the contact-breaker points due to slow running and the low resistance of the primary winding.

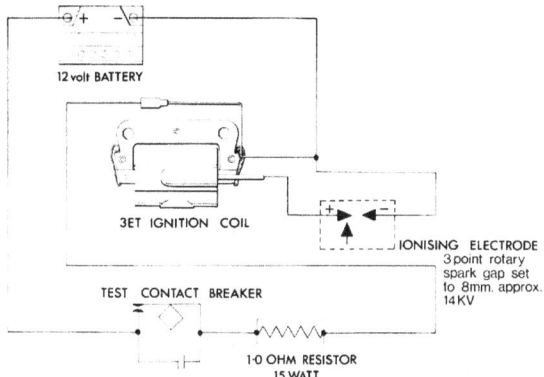

Fig. 74 Model 3 E.T. ignition coil bench test

Test Conclusions

If there is intermittent sparking or no sparking, replace the coil.

Ignition Coil Bench Test

A standard model 23D6 distributor (or a model 25D6 distributor fitted with a model 23D contact breaker plate assembly) is used to make and break the primary circuit of the coil under test. A contact set with a spring tension of 28–32 oz., Part Number 544 135 68, must be fitted in place of the standard unit. The closed period (dwell angle) is modified to 38°–40° by adjusting the contact gap. The capacitor should be 0·18–0·25 microfarads.

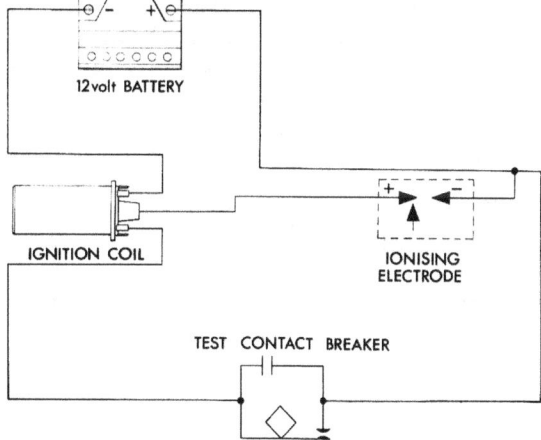

Fig. 75 Ignition coil bench test circuit

The three-point test gap should be connected so that the auxiliary electrode is adjacent to the H.T. electrode. The auxiliary electrode causes the gap to break down at a lower voltage with more consistent sparking. It is therefore essential that the coil test circuit is wired correctly and that the correct battery terminal is earthed.

Coil Position

While under test the coil should be mounted at an angle of 45° with the 'CB' (+) terminal uppermost. The coil case must be earthed during the test.

Saddle Screw Torque

All coils except
MA6, MA12, 17M6
and 17M12   10–14 lbf.in. (1·13–1·58 Nm)
MA6 and MA12   5–7   lbf.in. (0·56–0·79 Nm)
17M6 and 17M12 8–12 lbf.in. (0·90–1·36 Nm)

Insulation Resistance

Between either L.T. terminal and the coil case, the insulation resistance should be at least 20 megohms at 500V.

Low Speed Test (Stationary Gap)

For this test a three-point gap is adjusted to the appropriate setting. Run the distributor at 100 rev/min.

It is not possible to specify a gap at which no missing at low speeds will occur, since contact breaker conditions are not sufficiently consistent at these speeds. The test specification calls for not more than 5% missing. This may be regarded as not more than 30 misses in one minute.

This test should be carried out with the coil cold, at 20°C (68°F).

High Speed Test

(a) **Setting Rotary Gap** (Fig. 2)

Set the gap between the H.T. electrode and the earth electrode of the rotary gap to approximately 4·75 mm.

Start the rotary gap.

Connect an LA12 ignition coil to a 6-volt supply of the correct polarity, and the test contact breaker (Fig. 75).

Set a peak voltmeter to negative position then connect it between the H.T. terminal and the earth terminal of the battery.

Increase the speed of the contact breaker unit until the rotary gap is just sparking irregularly.

Reset earth electrode if necessary until voltage is 8kV and the rotary gap is just sparking irregularly.

THIS SETTING IS MOST IMPORTANT.

(b) **Test**

Remove the peak voltmeter from the circuit.

Replace the calibration coil with the coil to be tested.

Ensure the supply voltage, earth polarity and contact breaker speed are as quoted in the table below.

If irregular sparking occurs on the rotary gap the coil is faulty.

TEST CIRCUIT

The standard test circuit, Fig. 75, is suitable for all coils marked '+' and '—' and positive earth coils marked 'CB' and 'SW'. The following results should be obtained:

Model	Primary Resistance (ohms) 20°C	Low Speed Test Gap (mm)	(ins)	High Speed Test (rev/min)	Supply Voltage (min)	(max)
LA6	1·0 – 1·1	11	0·44	2750	6·0	6·5
LA12	3·0 – 3·4	10	0·40	3000	12·0	12·5
*MA3	0·6 – 0·7	7·5	0·30	2500	6·0	6·5
MA6	1·8 – 2·1	8	0·32	2250	6·0	6·5
MA12	3·0 – 3·4	9	0·35	3000	12·0	12·5
17M6	1·7 – 1·9	8	0·32	2250	6·0	6·5
17M12	3·3 – 3·8	9	0·35	3000	12·0	12·5

* The MA3 coil is tested with a 0·5 ohm ballast resistor in series.

LOCATION AND REMEDY OF FAULTS

Although every precaution is taken to ensure trouble-free running, electrical faults may sometimes arise and the following test procedure is recommended.

When checking the continuity of circuits, a flashlamp battery and bulb should be used. Do not "flash" the end of a live cable to earth, as this may cause heavy currents which damage the equipment. If a vehicle battery is to be used, a low wattage bulb of similar voltage must be connected in series with the circuit to be checked. Never check the continuity of alternator stator windings when the rotor is in position. The rotor should be removed to avoid demagnetisation and reduced output.

If, after carrying out the following checks, the owner cannot trace the cause of trouble, he is advised to contact the local Lucas agent or service centre.

Battery Charging Systems

Engine will not start on IGN position:

(i) Turn the switch to EMG position if provided. If the engine now starts, the battery is probably discharged.
If there is no EMG position, check the condition of the battery and recharge, if necessary.

(ii) Remove the H.T. cable from the sparking plug and hold the cable end about $\frac{1}{8}$" from a metal part of the engine while the latter is turned over. If sparks occur regularly, the ignition system is functioning correctly. Check for engine defects after examining the sparking plug.

(iii) If sparks do not occur in test (ii), check for a fault in the low tension circuit. Check the wiring from battery to fuse, switch, coil and contact breaker. If the circuit is continuous, examine the contact breaker and if necessary clean and adjust the contacts. Also, check the engine timing.

Engine will not start on EMG position:

Carry out previous tests (ii) and (iii), check that the alternator rotor is the correct way round on the engine shaft (the name "Lucas" should face away from the engine).

Engine misfires:

(i) Examine the contact breaker. If necessary, clean the contacts and adjust the gap.

(ii) Remove the sparking plug (or each plug in turn), rest it on the cylinder head and observe if a spark occurs at the plug points when the engine is turned. Irregular sparking may be due to dirty plugs (which may be cleaned and adjusted) or to defective high tension cables. If the insulation of any cable shows signs of deterioration or cracking it should be renewed.

(iii) If sparking is regular at each plug when tested as described in (ii), the trouble is probably due to engine defects, and the carburetter, petrol supply, etc., must be examined.

(iv) If misfiring occurs after the engine has been running for some time, check that the ignition switch is in the normal IGN position. If run continuously in the EMG position, the rising voltage of the battery may eventually cause misfiring to occur.

A.C. Ignition

Important:

1. Keep the contact breaker clean and ensure the maximum opening is set at 0·014"–0·016".
2. Keep the sparking plug electrodes clean and correctly set.
3. Keep to the manufacturer's timing instructions.

Engine will not start or misfires:

(i) Remove the H.T. cable from the sparking plug and hold the cable end about $\frac{1}{8}$" (3 mm) from the cylinder block. Sparks should jump this gap regularly when the engine is turned at kick-start speed.

(ii) If sparks are obtained, check the sparking plug, reset and clean, or renew as necessary.

(iii) If no sparks are obtained, inspect the H.T. cable and renew, as necessary. Check contact breaker gap setting.

(iv) If the sparking plug, H.T. cable and contact breaker gap setting are satisfactory, check for engine defects, faulty fuel supply, etc.

Charging Equipment

Battery in low state of charge:

(i) This will be indicated by poor or no lights when the engine is stationary, and varying light intensity when the engine is running.

(ii) Check the condition of the battery, and recharge if necessary.

(iii) Check the wiring from the battery to switch, rectifier, and alternator. Ensure all connections are clean and tight.

Excessive circuit voltage:

(i) This will be indicated by burnt out or blackened bulbs and possibly burned ignition contacts.

(ii) Examine the wiring for loose or broken connections.

(iii) Check the earth connections to the battery, rectifier and Zener diode.

(iv) Examine the battery, checking the electrolyte level and removing any corrosion.

Lighting Equipment

Failure of lights:

(i) If one bulb fails to light, replace with a new bulb.

(ii) If all lamps fail to light, check the fuse (if fitted) and check the battery condition, recharging if necessary.

(iii) Examine the circuitry and replace broken or loose connections.

Lights fade when switched on:

Check the battery condition, and recharge if necessary.

Brilliance varies with engine speed:

Check the battery condition, and recharge if necessary.

Lights flicker:

Examine the wiring for loose connections or damaged cable insulation. Check the battery condition.

Headlamp illumination insufficient:

(i) If the bulb is discoloured or filaments have sagged as a result of long service, replace with a new bulb of the same type.

(ii) Check the setting of the lamp and the condition of the reflector.

NOTES

WIRING DIAGRAMS

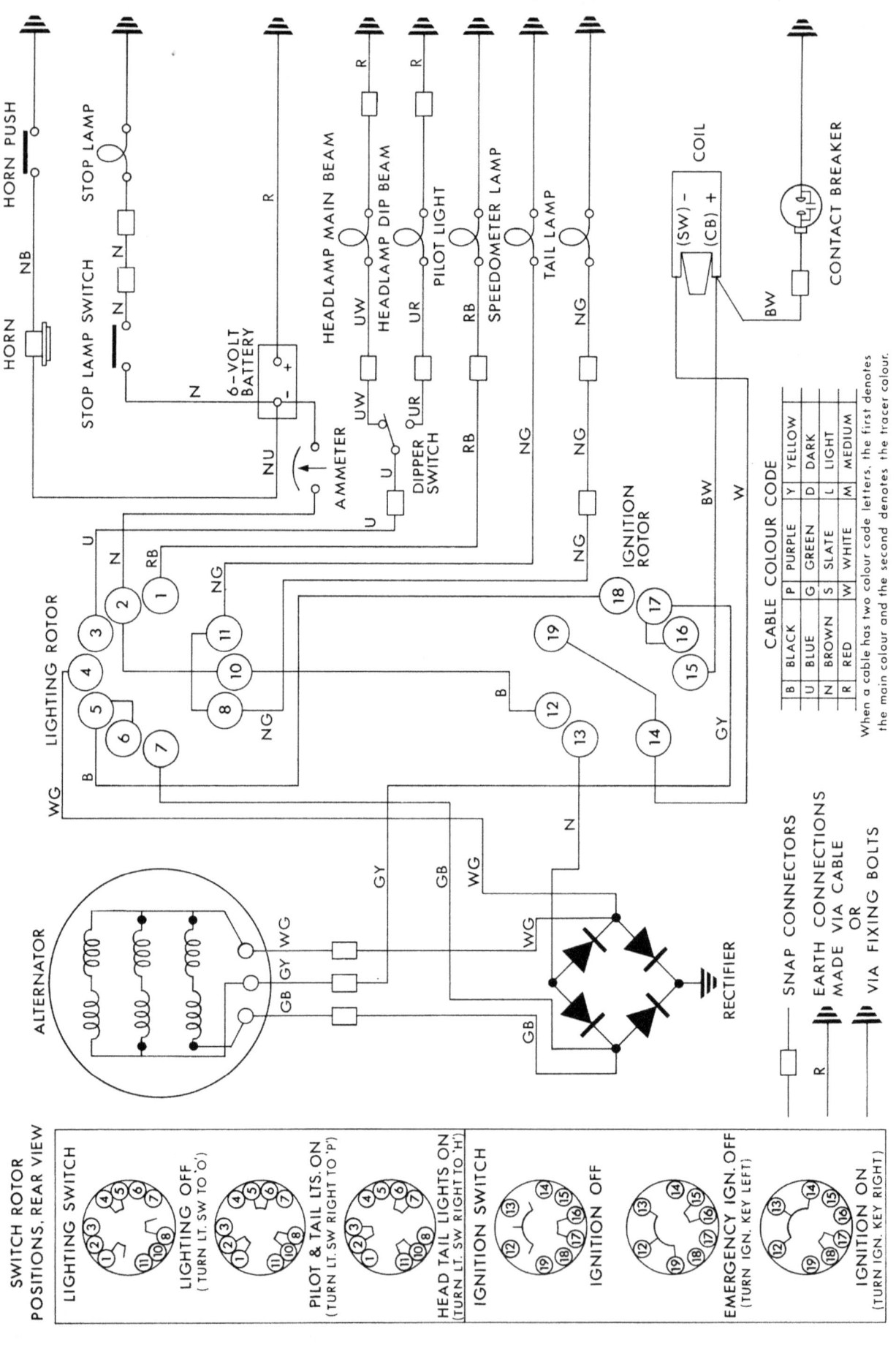

Fig. 76 Typical 6 volt system using PRS8 switch in a single cylinder machine

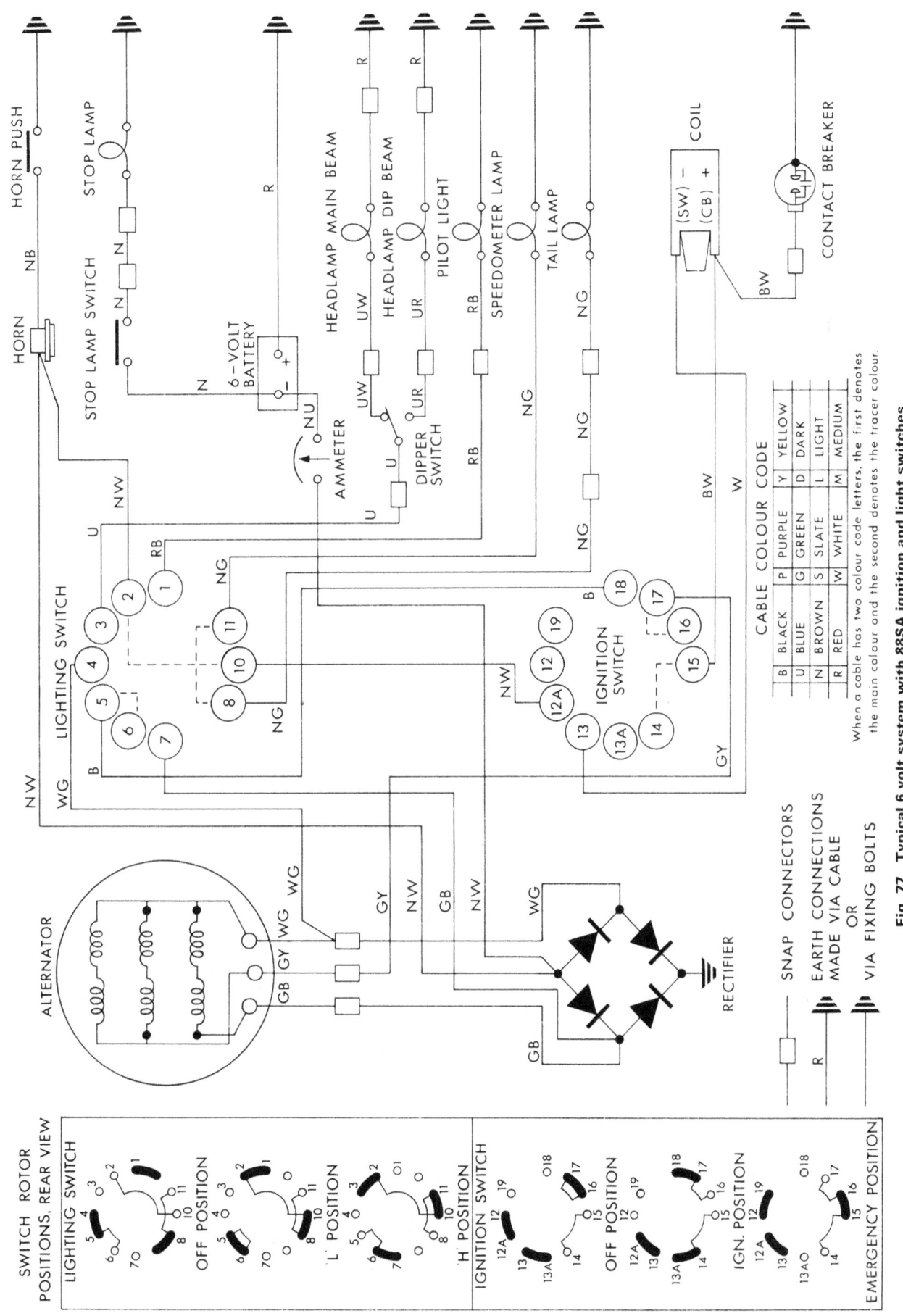

Fig. 77 Typical 6 volt system with 88SA ignition and light switches

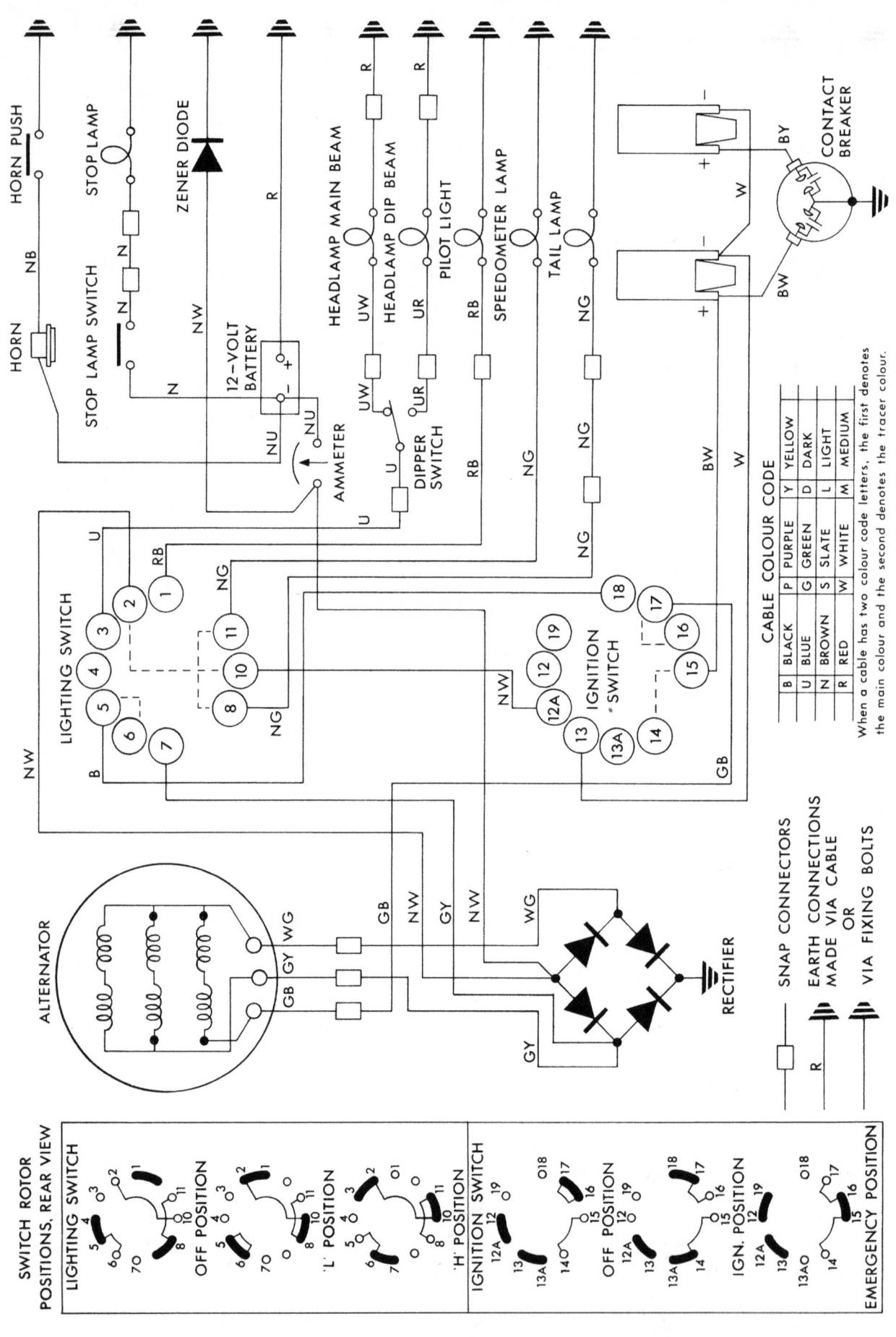

Fig. 78 Typical 12 volt 2 charge rate

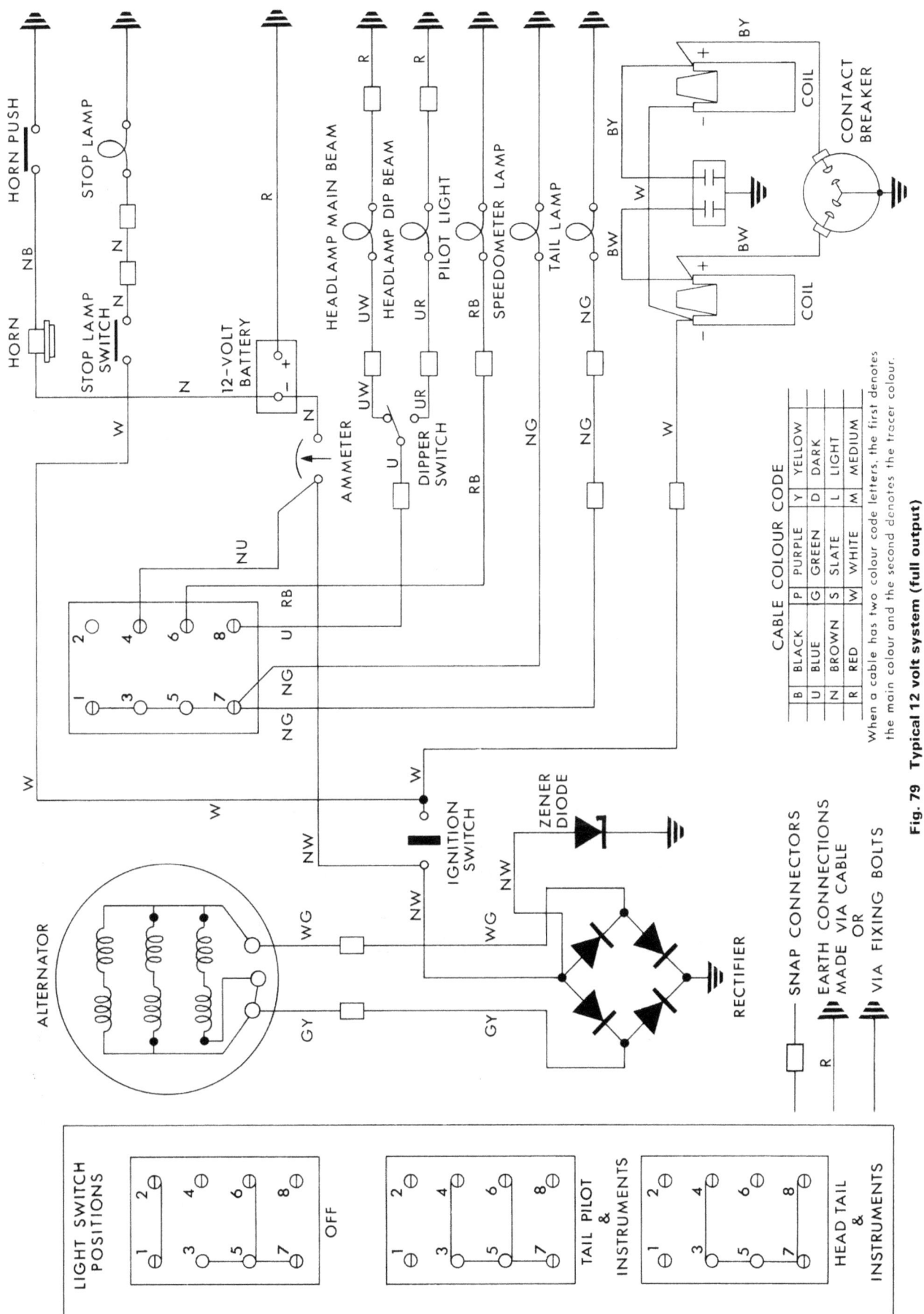

Fig. 79 Typical 12 volt system (full output)

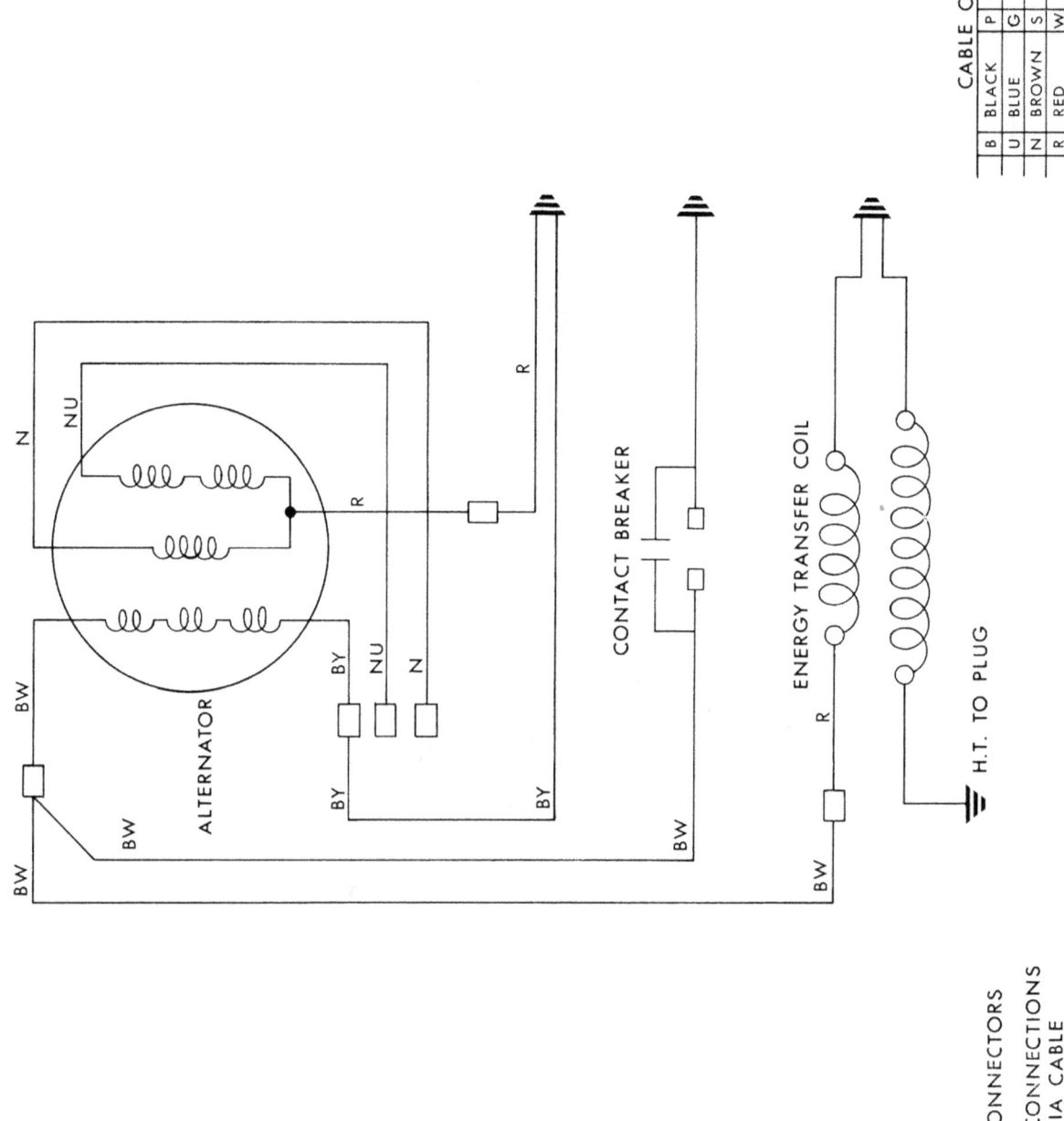

Fig. 80 Typical energy transfer for single cylinder machines (without lights)

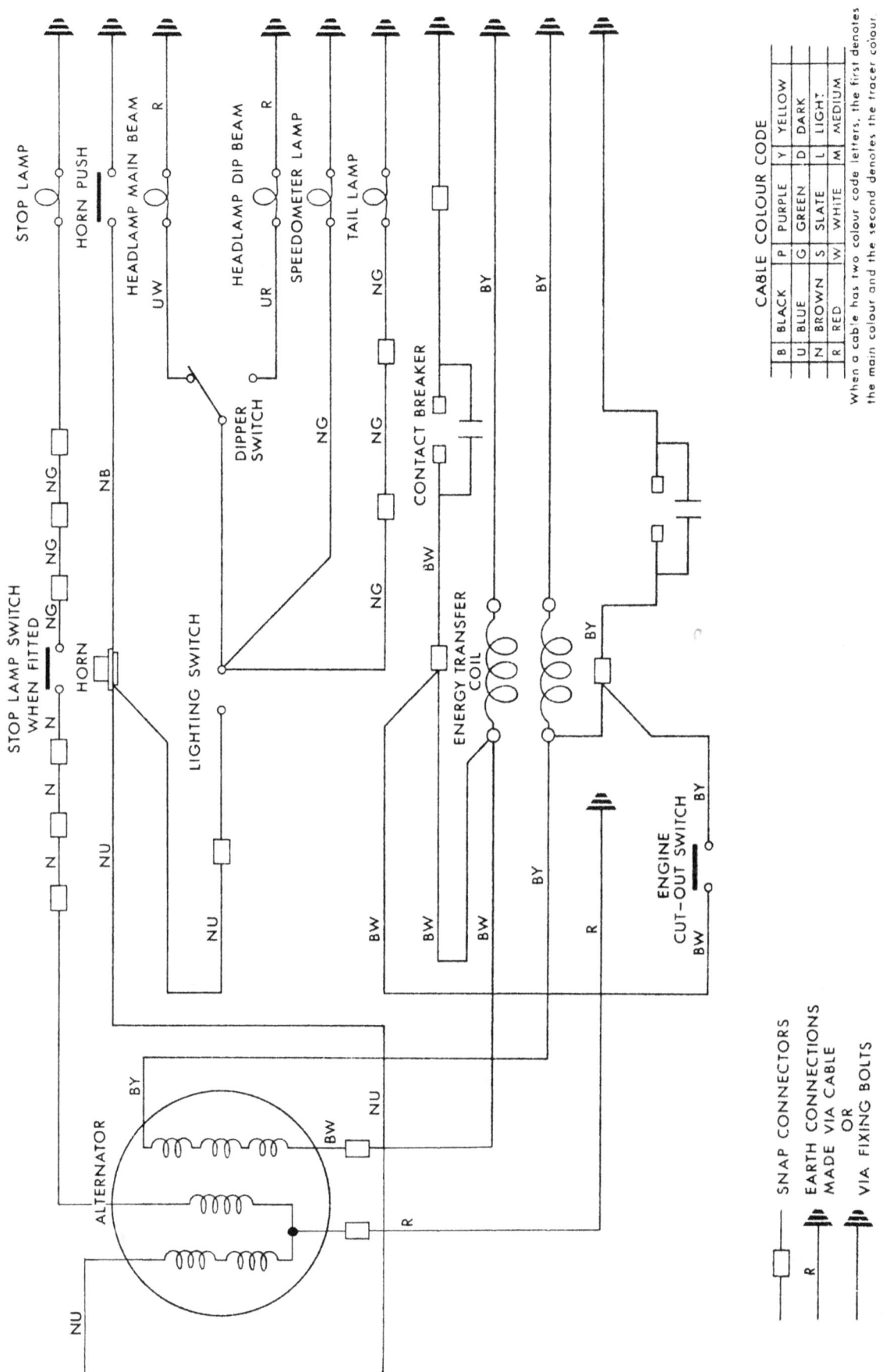

Fig. 81 Typical energy transfer system for twin cylinder machines (with lighting)

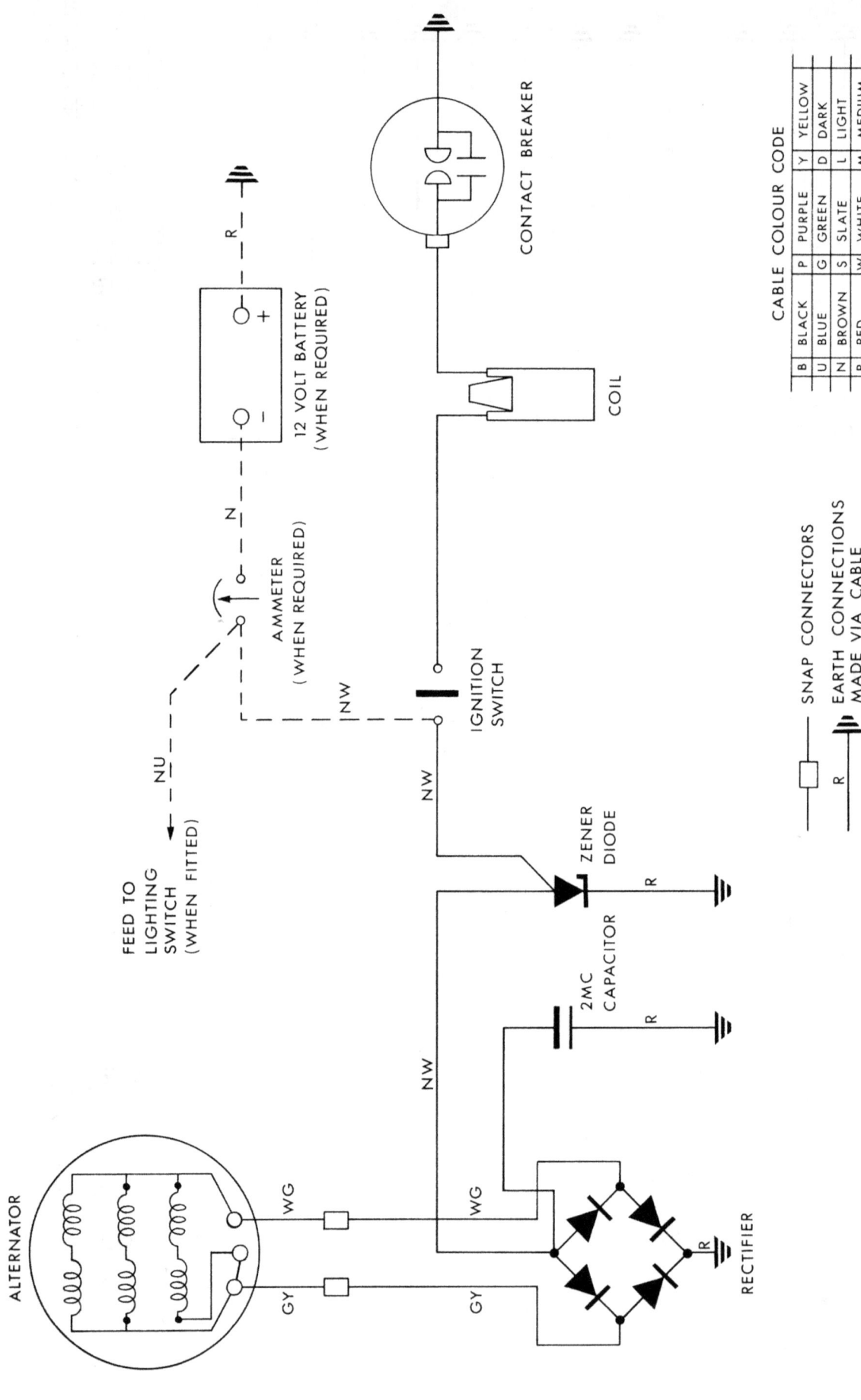

Fig. 82 Basic capacitor ignition system

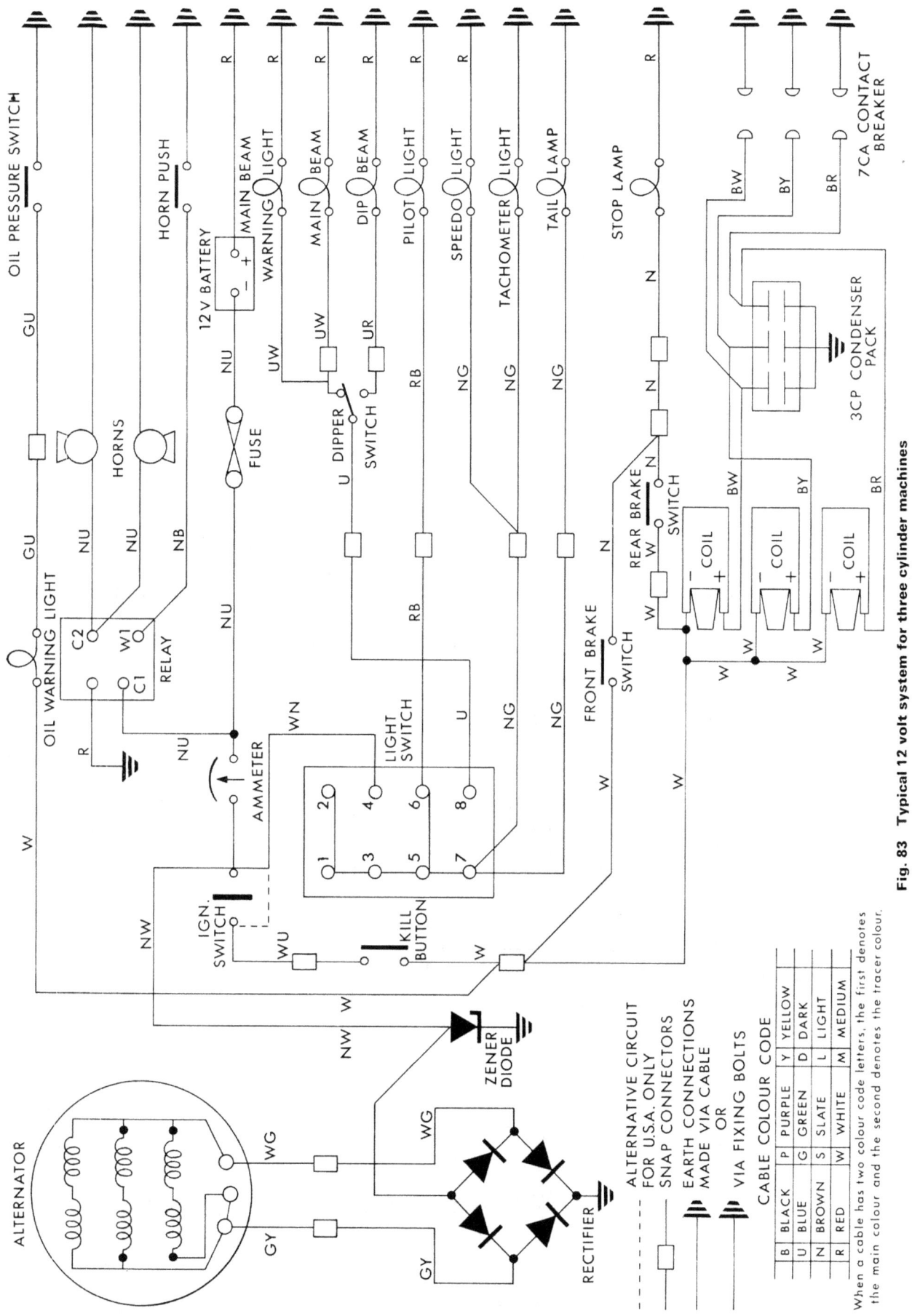

Fig. 83 Typical 12 volt system for three cylinder machines

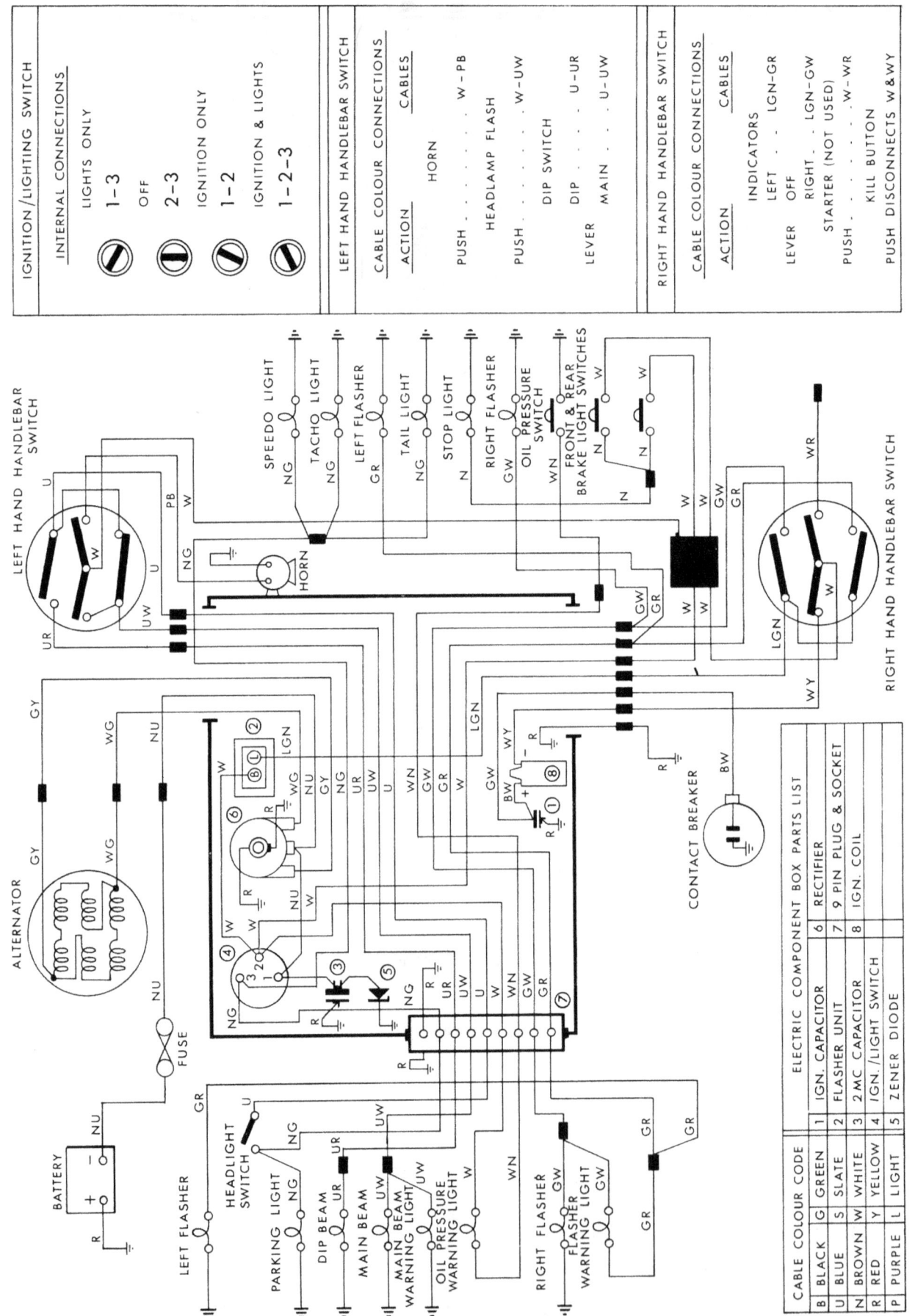

Fig. 84 Typical circuit for machines fitted with the electrical component box

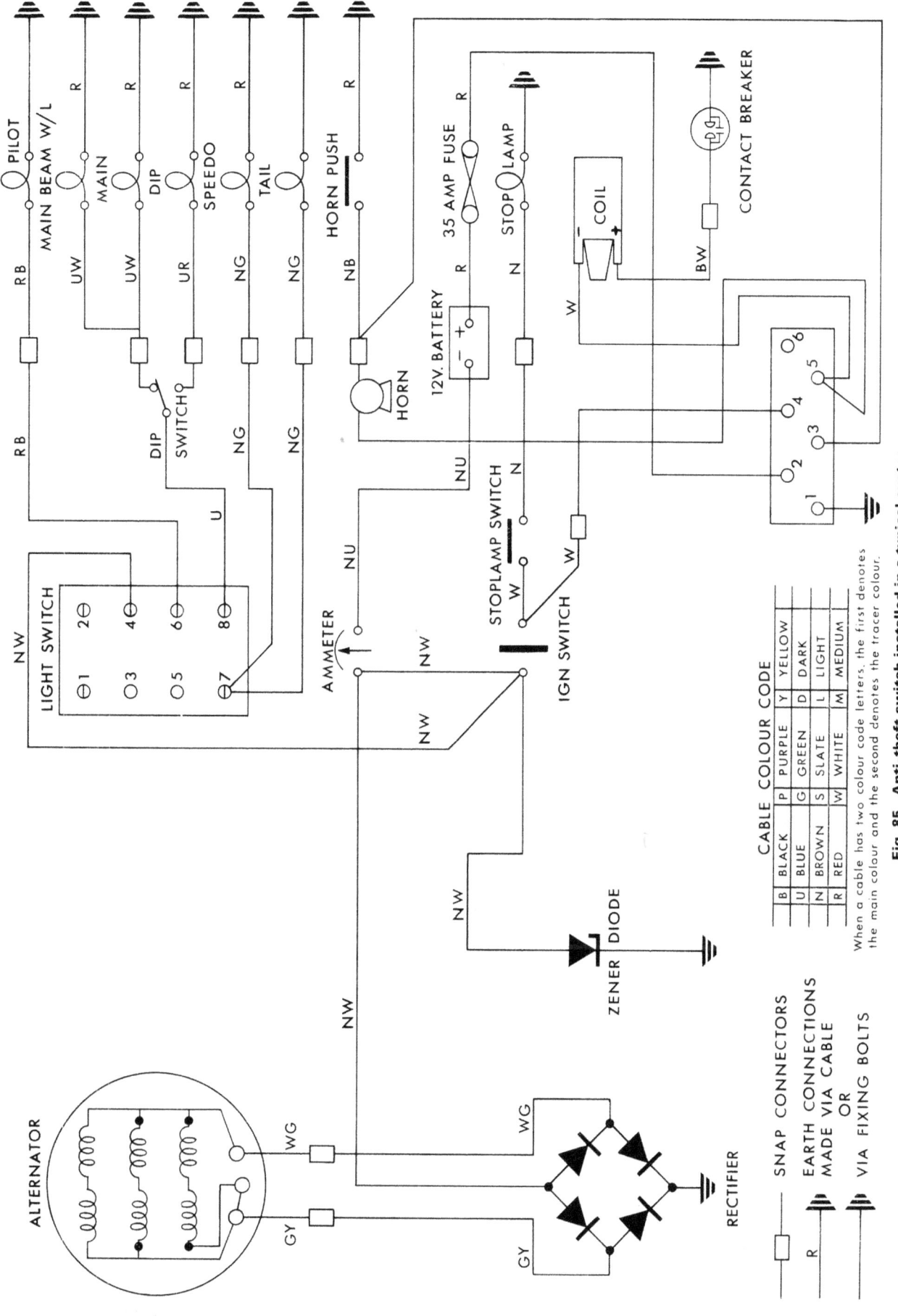

Fig. 85 Anti-theft switch installed in a typical system

NOTES

LUCAS

GIRLING

ELECTRICAL AND SUSPENSION PARTS

1960–1968
MOTORCYCLES

LUCAS ELECTRICAL SERVICES, INC.

LUCAS AND GIRLING EQUIPMENT FOR 1960-1968 MOTORCYCLES

INDEX

Alternators and Parts	Pages 38 – 40
Ammeters	Pages 10 – 17
Batteries	Pages 18 – 23
Bulbs (Except Stop Tail Lamp Bulbs)	Pages 10 – 17
Bulbs (For Stop Tail Lamps)	Pages 18 – 23
Capacitors (Charging Circuit)	Pages 38 – 40
Capacitors (Ignition Circuit)	Pages 32 – 37
Coils, Ignition	Pages 32 – 37
Contact Breaker Units and Parts	Pages 32 – 37
Control Boxes and Parts	Pages 28 – 29
Diodes, Zener	Pages 38 – 40
Distributors and Parts	Pages 32 – 37
Girling Equipment (Suspension Units)	Page 41 – 43
Generators and Parts	Pages 28 – 29
Headlamps and Parts	Pages 10 – 17
Horns and Parts	Pages 2 – 9
Horn Pushes	Pages 2 – 9
Ignition Coils	Pages 32 – 37
Lamps (Head and Parking) and Parts	Pages 10 – 17
Lamps (Stop Tail and License Plate) and Parts	Pages 18 – 23
Magdynos and Parts	Pages 30 – 31
Magnetos and Parts	Pages 24 – 27
Parking Lamps and Parts	Pages 10 – 17
Rectifiers	Pages 38 – 40
Reflex Reflectors	Pages 18 – 23
Regulators and Parts	Pages 28 – 29
Starters and Parts (Including Starter Switches)	Pages 30 – 31
Stop Tail and License Plate Lamps and Parts	Pages 18 – 23
Suspension Units and Parts	Pages 41 – 43
Switches (Except Starter Switches)	Pages 2 – 9
Switches and Solenoids for Starters	Pages 30 – 31
Warning Lights	Pages 10 – 17
Zener Diodes	Pages 38 – 40

SPECIFICATIONS SUBJECT TO ALTERATION WITHOUT NOTICE

Published by

LUCAS ELECTRICAL SERVICES, INC.

30 Van Nostrand Avenue, Englewood, N.J. 07631. Phone 201-567-6400

Factory Branches at

ATLANTIC COAST
    670 Moravia Park Drive, Baltimore, Md. 21237. Phone 301-488-4040
    30 Van Nostrand Ave., Englewood, N.J. 07631. Phone 201-567-6400
    400 South Edgewood Ave., Jacksonville, Fla. 32205. Phone 904-388-7607
    Southwest Pk. Rte. 1 at Rte. 128, Westwood, Mass. 02091. Phone 617-329-0960

MIDWEST
    5001 West Belmont Ave., Chicago, Ill. 60641. Phone 321-282-3161

PACIFIC COAST
    5025-5029 W. Jefferson Blvd., Los Angeles, Calif. 90016. Phone 213-735-1111
    171 Beacon St., S. San Francisco, Calif. 90480. Phone 415-589-4292
    5516 First Avenue South, Seattle, Wash. 98108. Phone 206-762-0950

SOUTHWEST
    6055 Armor Drive, Houston, Texas 77011. Phone 713-928-5255

WEST
    6001 East 38th Avenue, Denver, Colo. 80207. Phone 303-388-4241

1960-1968 SPECIFICATIONS

HORN / SWITCHES

	MAKE AND MODEL	YEAR	HORN	BRACKET	LIGHTING	KNOB, LIGHTING	IGNITION	COVER OR KNOB (IGNITION)	CUTOUT
	A.J.S.								
(1)	250cc 14 Sapphire and 14CS Scorpion	1960-61	70146B						
(2)	250cc 14 Sapphire 14S Sapphire Sports and 14CS Scorpion	1962	70163A	54680850					
(3)	350cc 16C Experts	1960-61	069446	703232	31754A				
(4)	350cc 16C Experts	1962-63	70163A	54680850	31754A	351815			
(5)	500cc 18 Statesman	1960-61	70137A	701851	54033109		54033027		
(6)	500cc 18 Statesman	1962-65	70163A/B	54680850	34289A	54330934	34427B	54336178	
(7)	500cc 18CS Southerner	1960-61	70137A	701851	31784A				
(8)	500cc 18CS Southerner	1962-63	70163A	54680850	31784D	351815			
(9)	500cc 18CS Southerner	1964	70163A/B	54680850	34289A	54330934			
(10)	500cc 18CS Southerner	1965-66	70163D	54680850	31784D				
(11)	650cc 31 Swift	1960-61	70137A	701851	54033028		54033056		
(12)	650cc 31 Swift	1962-63	70163A	54680850	34289A	54330934	34287B	54332498	*76204D
(13)	650cc 31 Swift	1964-65	70159B/D		34289A	54330934	34427B	54336178	*76204D
(14)	650cc 31 Tourer	1966	70163D		34289A	54330934	34427B	54336178	
(15)	650cc 31 De Luxe	1960-61	70137A	701851	54033028				76204A
(16)	650cc 31CS and 31CSR Hurricane	1960-61	70137A	701851	31754A				76204A
(17)	650cc 31CS and 31CSR Hurricane	1962-63	70163A	54680850	34289A *31784D	54330934			76204D
(18)	650cc 31CSR Hurricane	1964-65	70159B/D		34289A	54330934			76204D
(19)	650cc 31CSR Hurricane	1966	70163D		34289A	54330934			
(20)	750cc 33 and 33CS	1965	70159B/D		34289A	54330934			76204D
(21)	750cc 33 and 33CS	1966	70159B/D		34289A	54330934			
(22)	750cc 33 and 33CS	1967	70197A		34289A	54330934			76204D
	B.S.A.								
(23)	250cc C15 Star and 350cc B40 Star	1960-61	70146B		54033004	54330934 *54330485	54033003	54331351 *54330576	
(24)	250cc C15 Star SS80 Sports Star, 350cc B40 Star and SS90 Sports Star	1962-65	70169B/D	54680850	34289A	54330934 *54330576	34427A	54336178 *54330576	
(25)	250cc C15S and C15T Competition	1960-62	70145D		31276B				76204D
(26)	250cc C15S and C15T Competition	1963	70145D		31356A				76204D
(27)	250cc C15S and C15T Competition	1964			31356A/B				76204D
(28)	250cc C15S and C15T Competition and 350cc B40ES	1965			31356A/B				
(29)	250cc C15 Star, C15S Sportsman and 350cc B40 Star	1966	70197A		34289A	54330934	34427A	54336178	
(30)	250cc C15 Star	1967	70196A		34289A	54330934 *54330576	34427B	54336178 *54330576	
(31)	250cc Starfire 250	1967	70197A		34289A	54330934 *54330576	31899B		
(32)	250cc Starfire 250	1968	70197A		35710A		31899B		
(33)	350cc B32 Gold Star and Competition and 500cc B34 Gold Star and Competition	1960-61	069483	700168	31754A				
(34)	350cc B32 Gold Star and Competition and 500cc B34 Gold Star and Competition	1962	70169A	54680850	31754A	351815			
(35)	441cc B44 Victor Special	1966-67			31356B				
(36)	441cc B44 Victor Special	1968	70197A		35710A		31899B		
(37)	441cc Shooting Star 441	1966-67	70197A		34289A	54330934 *54330576	31899B		
(38)	441cc Shooting Star	1968	70197A		35710A		31899B		
(39)	500cc A7, A7SS Shooting Star and 650cc A10 Golden Flash	1960-61	70137A	701851	31754A				76204A
(40)	500cc A7, A7SS Shooting Star and 650cc A10 Golden Flash	1962	70169A	54680850	31754A	351815			
(41)	500cc B34 Gold Star and Competition	1963	70169A	54680850	31763A				76204D
(42)	500cc A50 Star and 650cc A65 Star (6 volt)	1963-64	70169A	54680850	34289A	54330934 *54330485	34427A	54336178	
(43)	500cc A50 Star and 650cc A65 Star (6 volt)	1965	70186A	54680822	34289A	54330934 *54330576	34427A	54336178 *54330576	
(44)	500cc A50 Cyclone and 650cc A65 Spitfire Hornet	1964			31356A/B				31071D
(45)	500cc A50 Cyclone A50CC Cyclone Clubman and A502C Cyclone Road	1965	70186A	54680822	34289A	54330934 *54330576	34427B	54336178 *54330576	
(46)	500cc A50 Wasp and 650cc A65 Spitfire Hornet	1966							31071D
(47)	500cc A50 Royal Star	1966	70169D	54680850	34289A	54330934	31899B	54336178	
			*later †Airflow ‡12 volt ††650cc only		*later †Airflow ‡Lighting and ignition	*Escutcheon plate †later	*Airflow ‡Non-starter version only	*Escutcheon plate	*When fitted

SWITCHES

	STOP LAMP	SPRING, STOP LAMP	HORN PUSH & DIPPER	HORN PUSH	DIPPER	PANEL
(1)						
(2)						
(3)	31384B	315543		76204A	31482A	
(4)	31384B	315543	31563D			
(5)	31384B	315543	31563D			
(6)	31383A/B		31563D			
(7)	31384B	315543		76204A	31620A	
(8)	31384B	315543	31563D			
(9)	31384B	315543	31563D			
(10)	54033235		31563D			
(11)	31384B	315543	31563D			
(12)	31384B *31383A	315543	31563D			
(13)	31383A/B		31563D			
(14)	31383A/B		31563D			
(15)	31384B	315543	31563D			
(16)	31384B	315543		76204A	31482A	
(17)	31384B	315543	31563D			
(18)	31383A/B		31563D			
(19)	31383A/B		31563D			
(20)	31383A/B		31563D			
(21)	31383A/B		31563D			
(22)	31383B		31563D			
(23)	31827A		*31563D			
(24)	31827A					
(25)	31827A			76204D	31620E	
(26)				76204D	31620E	
(27)				*76204D	31620E	
(28)				76204D	31620E	
(29)	31827B					
(30)	31827B					
(31)	31827B					
(32)	34815A					
(33)	31437 *34257			76204D †76206A	31549B	
(34)	34257A			76204D †76205E	31549B	
(35)					31620F	
(36)	34815A			76204D	31620F	
(37)	31827B					
(38)	34815A					
(39)	34257A					
(40)	34257A					
(41)	31437A			76204D †76206E	31549B	
(42)	34448B					
(43)	34448B					
(44)	34448A/B			76204A/B	31620A/E	
(45)	34448B					
(46)						
(47)	34448B					
	*later		*-1960 only	*Optional †Clubman ‡Sports	‡Sports †Starter Motor	

1960-1968 SPECIFICATIONS

HORN | SWITCHES

	MAKE AND MODEL	YEAR	HORN	BRACKET	LIGHTING	KNOB, LIGHTING	IGNITION	COVER OR KNOB (IGNITION)	CUTOUT
	B.S.A. (Continued)								
(1)	500cc A50 Royal Star	1967	70197A		34289A	54330934	31899B		
(2)	500cc A-50 Royal Star	1968	70197A		35710A		31899B		
(3)	650cc A10 Super Rocket	1960-61	069482	703349	31340A				76204A
(4)	650cc A10 Super Rocket	1962	069482	703349	31340A	351815			76204A
(5)	650cc A10 Super Rocket	1963	069482	703349	31763A				76204D
(6)	650cc Rocket Gold Star	1963	069482A		31763A				76204A
(7)	650cc A10 Golden Flash	1963	70169A	54680850	31763A	*351803			76204D
(8)	650cc A65 Star (12 volt)	1964	70164A/B	54680850	34289A	54330934 *54330485	34427A	54336178	
(9)	650cc A65R Rocket and A65 Lightning Rocket	1964	70161E		34289A	54330934 *54330485	34427A	54336178	
(10)	650cc A65R Rocket (6 volt), A652L Lightning Rocket, A651T Thunderbolt Rocket, A65L Lightning and A65LC Lightning Clubman	1965	70186A	54680822	34289A	54330934 *54330576	34427B	54336178 *54330576	
(11)	650cc A65R Rocket (12 volt)	1965	70187A	54680822	34289A	54330934 *54330576	34427A	54336178 *54330576	
(12)	650cc A65 Thunderbolt, A65 Lightning and A65 Spitfire Mk II Special	1966	70169D	54680850	34289A	54330934	31899B	54336178	
(13)	650cc A65 Hornet	1967							31071D
(14)	650cc A65 Firebird	1968	70197A		35710A		31899B		
(15)	650cc A65 Thunderbolt, A65 Lightning and A65 Spitfire Mk III Special	1967	70197A		34289A	54330934 54330576	31899B	54336178	
(16)	650cc A65 Thunderbolt Lightning and Spitfire Mark IV	1968	70197A		35710A		31899B		
	ENFIELD								
(17)	500cc Fury Scrambler	1960-61	069424	703185	31491A				76204D
(18)	500cc Meteor Minor, De Luxe and Sports	1960	70142D		31491A †31784A		34093B		
(19)	500cc Meteor Minor, De Luxe and Sports – later	1960-61	70142D		31491A †31784A		34093B		
(20)	500cc Meteor Minor, De Luxe and Sports	1962	70142D *70163A		31491A †31784A	351567 351815	34093B		
(21)	500cc Bullet	1960	069424	703185	31491A †31784A		34093B		
(22)	500cc Bullet – later	1960-62	069424	703185	31491A †31784A		34093B		
(23)	500cc Sports Twin	1963	70163A	54680850	31491A †31784D *34289A	351567 351815 54330934	34093B *34427A ‡34093B		
(24)	700cc Super Meteor and Constellation	1960	069424	703185	31491A †31784A		34093B		*76204D
(25)	700cc Super Meteor and Constellation	1961	069424	703185	31491A †31784A		54033056	54331351	*76204D
(26)	700cc Super Meteor	1962	069424		31491A †31784A	351567 331815	34427A	54336178	*76204D
(27)	700cc Constellation	1962	069424		31491A †31784A	351567 361815	54033056	54331351	*76204D
(28)	700cc Constellation (6 volt) and 736cc Interceptor	1963	069424		31491A †31784A/D *34289A	351567 351815 54330934	34427A 34093B 54033056	54336178 54331351	*76204A
(29)	700cc Contellation (12 volt)	1963	54068075	54680686	34289A		34427A/B		
(30)	736cc Interceptor (6 and 12 volt)	1964	70163A ‡69133A	54680850	31491A †31784A/D *34289A	351567 351815 54330934			76204D 76204D 76204D
(31)	736cc Interceptor (6 and 12 volt)	1965-66	70163B/D ‡69133A/D	54680850	34289A 34289A	54330934 54330934			76204D 76204D
(32)	736 Interceptor (12 volt)	1967-68	70197D		31788D		31899B		
	MATCHLESS								
(33)	250cc G2 Monitor and G2CS Messenger	1960-61	70146B						
(34)	250cc G2 Monitor G2S Monitor Sports and G2CS Messenger	1962	70163A	54680850					
			*later †Airflow ‡12 volt ††650cc only	*2 off	*later †Airflow ‡Lighting and ignition	*Escutcheon plate †later	*later †Airflow ‡Non-starter version only	*Escutcheon plate	*When fitted

124

SWITCHES

	STOP LAMP	SPRING, STOP LAMP	HORN PUSH & DIPPER	HORN PUSH	DIPPER	PANEL
(1)	34448B					
(2)	34448B					
(3)	34257A					
(4)	34257A					
(5)	34257A	31563D				
(6)	31437B					
(7)	34257A					
(8)	34448B					
(9)	34448B					
(10)	34448B					
(11)	34448B					
(12)	34448B					
(13)						
(14)	34448B			76204D	31620F	
(15)	34448B					
(16)	34448B					
(17)	31688A			76204D	31549B	
(18)	31437D	315714	31563D		‡31549B	
(19)	31688A		31563D	‡76204D	‡31549B	
(20)	31688A		31563D	‡76204D	‡31549B	
(21)	31437D	315714	31563D			
(22)	31688A		31563D			
(23)	31688A/B			‡76204D	31549B	
(24)	31437D *31688A	315714	31563D			
(25)	31688A		31563D			
(26)			31563D	‡76204D	‡31549B	
(27)			31563D	‡76204D	‡31549B	
(28)	31688A/B		31563D		31549B	
(29)			31563D			
(30)	31688A/B		31563D			
	31688A/B		31563D			
	31688A/B		31563D			
(31)	31688B		31563D			
	31688B		31563D			
(32)	31688B		31563D			
(33)						
(34)						
	*later		*later	*Optional †Clubman ‡Sports	‡Sports †Starter Motor	

1960-1968 SPECIFICATIONS

HORN | SWITCHES

	MAKE AND MODEL	YEAR	HORN	BRACKET	LIGHTING	KNOB, LIGHTING	IGNITION	COVER OR KNOB (IGNITION)	CUTOUT
	MATCHLESS (Continued)								
(1)	350cc G3C Maestro	1960-61	069446	703232	31754A				
(2)	350cc G3C Maestro	1962-65	70163A	54680850	31754A	351815			
(3)	500cc G80 Major	1960-61	70137A	701851	54033109		54033027		
(4)	500cc G80 Major	1962-65	70163A/B	54680850	34289A	54330934	34427B	54336178	
(5)	500cc G80CS Marksman	1960-61	70137A	701851	31784A				
(6)	500cc G80CS Marksman	1962-63	70163A	54680850	31784D	351815			
(7)	500cc G80CS Marksman	1964	70163A/B	54680850	34289A	54330934			
(8)	500cc G80CS Marksman	1965-66	70163D	54680850	31784D				
(9)	500cc G80CS Marksman	1967-68	70196A		31784D				76204D
(10)	650cc G12 Majestic	1960-61	70137A	701851	54033028		54033056		
(11)	650cc G12 Majestic	1962-63	70163A	54680850	34289A	54330934	34287B	54332498	*76204D
(12)	650cc G12 Majestic and 750cc G15CS	1964-65	70159B/D		34289A	54330934	34427B	54336178	*76204D
(13)	650cc G12 Majestic	1966	70163D		34289A	54330934	34427B	54336178	
(14)	650cc G12 De Luxe	1960-61	70137A	701851	54033028				76204A
(15)	650cc G12CS and G12CSR Monarch	1960-61	70137A	701851	31754A				76204A
(16)	650cc G12CS and G12CSR Monarch	1962-63	70163A	54680850	34289A *31784D	54330934			76204D
(17)	650cc G12CSR Monarch	1964-65	70159B/D		34289A	54330934			76204D
(18)	650cc G12CSR Monarch	1966	70163D		34289A	54330934			
(19)	750cc G15CS and G15 Mk II	1965	70159B/D		34289A	54330934			76204D
(20)	750cc G15, G15CS and G15 Mk II	1966	70159B/D		34289A	54330934			
(21)	750cc G15, G15CS and G15 Mk II	1967-68	70197A		34289A	54330934			76204D
(22)	750cc G15CSR	1966-67	70197A		34289A	54330934			
(23)	750cc Commando	1968	54068152	*54680686	35710A		31899B		
	NORTON								
(24)	350cc Navigator	1961	70136A	701851					
(25)	350cc Navigator	1962-65	70163B	54680850					
(26)	350 50 Mk II	1965	70163B	54680850	34289A	54330934	34427B	54336178	
(27)	397cc Electra	1963	70164B	54680850					
(28)	397cc Electra	1964-65	70164B	54680850					
(29)	500cc Nomad, Dominator 88, ES2 and 600cc Dominator 99	1960-61	70140A	700776	31443E				
(30)	600 Nomad and 650cc Manxman	1960-61	70140A	700776	31784A				
(31)	500cc ES2, Dominator 88, 600cc Dominator 99 and 650cc Dominator 650	1962	70163A	54680850	†31443E	318346			
(32)	500cc Dominator 88SS, 600cc Dominator 99SS, 650cc Dominator 650SS and Manxman	1962	70163A	54680850	31784D	351815			76204D
(33)	500cc ES2, Dominator 88 and 650cc Dominator 650	1963	70163A	54680850	‡31443E *34289A	318346 †54330934	34427B *34287A	54332498	
(34)	500cc Dominator 88SS, 650cc Dominator 650SS, Manxman and 750cc Atlas	1963	70163A	54680850	34289A	54330934			76204D
(35)	500cc Dominator 88SS, 650cc Dominator 650SS, Manxman and 750cc Atlas	1964-65	70159D		34289A	54330934			76204D
(36)	500cc ES2 Mk II	1965	70163B	54680850	34289A	54330934	34427B	54336178	
(37)	500cc Dominator 88SS and 650cc Dominator 650SS	1966-67	70197A		34289A	54330934			76204D
(38)	650cc Manxman, 750cc Atlas, N15 and N15CS	1966-67	70197A		34289A	54330934			76204D
(39)	650cc Manxman, 750cc N15CS	1968	70197A		34289A	54330934			76204D
(40)	750cc Atlas and Commando	1968	54068152	*54680686	35710A		31899B		
(41)	750cc P.11	1967-68	70197D		34289A		‡31899B		
	TRIUMPH								
(42)	200cc T20 Tiger Cub	1960-62			‡31443E	318346			
(43)	200cc T20S, T20SC, T20SL, T20SR, T20SS and T20T (E.T. condition) Tiger Cub	1960-62	70145D		31276A				76204D
(44)	200cc T20SH Tiger Cub	1962	70163A	54680850	34289A	54330934	34427A	54336178	
(45)	200cc T20 Tiger Cub	1963	70178A	54680850	34289A	54330662	34427A	54336307	
(46)	200cc T20 Tiger Cub – later	1963-65	70169B	54680850	34289A	54330934 *54330576	34427B	54336178 *54330576	
(47)	200cc T20SH Tiger Cub	1963-65	70163D	54680850	34289A	54330934 *54330576	34427B	54336178 *54330576	
(48)	200cc T20SC and T20SR Riger Cub	1963	70145D		31356A				76204D
			*later †Airflow ‡12 volt ††650cc only	*2 off	*later †Airflow ‡Lighting and ignition	*Escutcheon plate †later	*later †Airflow ‡Non-starter version only	*Escutcheon plate	*When fitted

SWITCHES

	STOP LAMP	SPRING, STOP LAMP	HORN PUSH & DIPPER	HORN PUSH	DIPPER	PANEL
(1)	31384B	315543		76204A	31482A	
(2)	31384B	315543	31563D			
(3)	31384B	315543	31563D			
(4)	31383A/B		31563D			
(5)	31384B	315543		76204A	31620A	
(6)	31384B	315543	31563D			
(7)	31384B	315543	31563D			
(8)	54033235		31563D			
(9)	31384B	315543	31563D			
(10)	31384B	315543	31563D			
(11)	31384B *31383A	315543	31563D			
(12)	31383A/B		31563D			
(13)	31383A/B		31563D			
(14)	31384B	315543	31563D			
(15)	31384B	315543		76204A	31482A	
(16)	31384B	315543	31563D			
(17)	31383A/B		31563D			
(18)	31383A/B		31563D			
(19)	31383A/B		31563D			
(20)	31383A/B		31563D			
(21)	31383B		31563D			
(22)	34815A		*31563D			
(23)	34815A					
(24)						
(25)						
(26)	31383B		31563D			
(27)					†31872A	
(28)						
(29)	31383B		31563D			
(30)	31383B		31563D			
(31)	31383B		31563D			
(32)	31383B		31563D			
(33)	31383B		31563D			
	31383B		31563D			
(34)	31383B		31563D			
(35)	31383B		31563D			
(36)	31383B		31563D			
(37)	31383B		31563D			
(38)	31383B		31563D			
(39)	31383B		31563D			
(40)	34815A					
(41)	34815A					
(42)	31437B	315738			31549B	
(43)	31437B	315738		76204D	31620B	
(44)					31620B	
(45)	31437B	315738		76234A	31549B	
(46)	31437B	315738	31563D			
(47)	31437B	315738		76204D	31620B	
(48)	31437B	315738		76204D	31620B	
	*later		*late	*Optional †Clubman ‡Sports	‡Sports †Starter Motor	

1960-1968 SPECIFICATIONS

HORN | SWITCHES

	MAKE AND MODEL	YEAR	HORN	BRACKET	LIGHTING	KNOB, LIGHTING	IGNITION	COVER OR KNOB (IGNITION)	CUTOUT
	TRIUMPH (Continued)								
(1)	200cc T20R Trials and T20S Scrambler	1964	70145D		31356A				31071D
(2)	200cc T20SM and T20SS Tiger Cub	1965			31356B				76204D
(3)	200cc T20 Tiger Cub	1966-67	70169D	54680850	34289A	54330934 *54330576	34427B	54336178 *54330576	
(4)	200cc T20SH and T20SR Tiger Cub	1966	70169D	54680850	34289A	54330934 *54330576	34427B	54336178 *54330576	
(5)	200cc T20SM Tiger Cub	1966-67			31356B				76204D
(6)	200cc T20TR Tiger Cub	1966							76204D
(7)	500cc TR5A-C	1961	70145D		31276A				76204D
(8)	500cc TR5A-R	1961	70155B		‡31460A	318346			76204D
(9)	500cc TR5A-R – E.T. condition	1961	70155B		31784A/D				76204D
(10)	500cc T100SS Tiger	1962	70163A	54680850	‡31443E	318346			
(11)	500cc T100SC Tiger	1962	70145D		31276A				76204D
(12)	500cc T100SS Tiger	1963	70163A	54680850	34289A	54330934	34427A	54336178	
(13)	500cc T100SC Tiger	1963	70145D		31356A				76204D
(14)	500cc T100SC Tiger	1964	70145D		31356A/B				31071D
(15)	500cc 5TA Speed Twin and 650cc 6T Thunderbird	1960	70048J	701851	‡31460A	318346			
(16)	500cc 5TA Speed Twin and 650cc 6T Thunderbird	1961	70048J	701851	‡31460A	318346			
(17)	500cc 5TA Speed Twin and 650cc 6T Thunderbird	1962	70163A	54680850	‡31443E	318346			
(18)	500cc T100A Tiger	1960-61	70048J	701851	‡31460A	318346			31376B
(19)	650cc T110 Tiger	1960-61	70048J	701851	31784B				31376B
(20)	650cc TR6 Trophy and T120 Bonneville	1960-61	70048J	701851	31784B				76210A
(21)	650cc TR6SS Trophy and T120 Bonneville	1962	70163A	54680850	34289A	54330934			76210A
(22)	650cc 6T Thunderbird, TR6SS Trophy and T120 Bonneville	1963	70163A	54680850	34289A	54330934	34427A	54336178	
(23)	650cc 6T Thunderbird	1964	70164A/B	54680850	34289A	54330934	34427A	54336178	
(24)	650cc TR6 Trophy and T120 Bonneville	1964	70163A/B	54680850	34289A	54330934	34427A	54336178	
(25)	650cc 6T Thunderbird	1965	70164D	54680850	34289A	54330934 *54330576	34427A	54336178 *54330576	
(26)	650cc TR6 Trophy and T120 Bonneville	1965	70163D	54680850	34289A	54330934 *54330576	34427A	54336178 *54330576	
(27)	500cc 5TA Speed Twin	1963	70163A	54680850	‡31443A	318346			
(28)	500cc 5TA Speed Twin and T100 Tiger	1964-65	70163D	54680850	34289A	54330934 *54330576	34427B	54336178 *54330576	
(29)	500cc T100SC Tiger	1965			31356B				31071D
(30)	500cc 5TA Speed Twin and 650cc 6T Thunderbird	1966	70169D	54680850	34289A	54330934 *54330576	34427B	54336178 *54330576	35601A
(31)	500cc T100, T100R Tiger, 650cc TR6, TRTR6R Trophy, T120 and T120R Bonneville	1966	70164D	54680850	34289A	54330934 *54330576	31899B		35601A
(32)	500cc T100, T100R T100S Tiger, T100T Daytona Tiger, 650cc TR6, TR6R Trophy, T120 and T120R Bonneville	1967	‡70197A		34289A	54330934	31899B	54336178	35601A
(33)	500cc T100R Daytona Super Sports, 650cc T120R Bonneville and 650cc TR6R Trophy	1968	70197		35710		31899B		
(34)	500cc T100C Tiger, 650cc TR6C Trophy and T120TT Special	1966-67			31356B				31107D
(35)	500C T-100C Tiger, 650cc TR6C Trophy	1968	70197		35710A		31899B		35835A

*later
†Airflow
‡12 volt
††650cc only

*2 off

*later
†Airflow
‡Lighting and ignition

*Escutcheon plate
†later

*later
†Airflow
‡Non-starter version only

*Escutcheon plate

*When fitted

SWITCHES

	STOP LAMP	SPRING, STOP LAMP	HORN PUSH & DIPPER	HORN PUSH	DIPPER	PANEL
(1)	31437B	315738		76204D	31620B	
(2)	31437B	315738			31620B	
(3)	54033234	315738	31563D			
(4)	54033234	315738		76204D	31620F	
(5)	54033234	315738			31620F	
(6)						
(7)	34381A			76204D	31620B	
(8)	34381A			76204D	31549B	
(9)	34381A			76204D	31549B	
(10)	34381B		31563D			
(11)	34381B			76204D	31620B	
(12)	31383A		31563D			
(13)	31383A			76204D	31620B	
(14)	31383A			76204D	31620B	
(15)	31688A		31563D			
(16)	34381A		31563D			
(17)	34381B		31563D			
(18)	31688 *34381		31563D			
(19)	31688 *34381		31563D			
(20)	31688A			76210A		
(21)	34381B		31563D			
(22)	31383A		31563D			
(23)	31383A		31563D			
(24)	31383A		31563D			
(25)	31437B	315738	31563D			
(26)	31437B	315738	31563D			
(27)	31383A		31563D			
(28)	31383A		31563D			
(29)	31437B	315738			31620B	
(30)	54033234		31563D			
(31)	54033234	315738	31563D			
(32)	54033234		31563D			
(33)	31437B	315738			31563D	
(34)	54033234	315738			31620F	
(35)	31437B	315738			31620F	
	*later		*later	*Optional †Clubman ‡Sports	‡Sports †Starter Motor	

HEADLAMP AND PARTS

1960-1968 SPECIFICATIONS

	MAKE AND MODEL	YEAR	HEAD LAMP	LIGHT UNIT	RIM OR DOOR	WIRE, LIGHT UNIT FIXING	SCREW, RIM FIXING	GROMMET, CABLE ENTRY OR GASKET RUBBER	SCREW, LAMP FIXING	SLEEVE TERMINAL
	A.J.S.									
(1)	350cc 16C Experts	1960-61	58224D	516798	553248	504665	144921		112201	188818
(2)	350cc 16C Experts	1962-63	58224D	516798	553248	504665	144921		112201	555910
(3)	350cc 16C Experts – later	1963	58859A	516798	553248	504665	144921		112201	555910
(4)	500cc 18 Statesman	1960-61	58409A	516798	553248	504665	144921	54942783	112201	188818
(5)	500cc 18 Statesman	1962	58409A	516798	553248	504665	144921	54942783	112201	555910
(6)	500cc 18 Statesman – later	1962-63	58702A/B	516798	553248	504665	144921		112201	555910
(7)	500cc 18 Statesman	1964-65	59171A	516798	553248	504665	144921	199001	112201	555910
(8)	500cc 18 Statesman – Alternative, Magneto Ignition	1965	59252A	516798	553248	504665	144921	199001	112201	555910
(9)	500cc 18CS Southerner	1960-61	58586A	516798	553248	504665	144921		112201	555910
(10)	500cc 18CS Southerner	1962	58829A	516798	553248	504665	144921	199002	112201	555910
(11)	500cc 18CS Southerner	1963-65	58829A/B	516798	553248	504665	144921	199002	112201	555910
(12)	500cc 18CS Southerner	1966	59667A	516798	553248	504665	144921	199002	112201	555910
(13)	650cc 31 Swift	1960-61	58432A	516798	553248	504665	144921	54942783	112201	188818
(14)	650cc 31 Swift	1962	58432A	516798	553248	504665	144921		112201	555910
(15)	650cc 31 Swift – later	1962-63	58702A/B	516798	553248	504665	144921		112201	555910
(16)	650cc 31 Swift – Alternative, Magneto Ignition	1962-63	58704A/B	516798	553248	504665	144921		112201	555910
(17)	650cc 31 Swift and 31 Tourer	1964-66	59237A	516798	553248	504665	144921	199001	112201	555910
(18)	650cc 31 Swift – Alternative, Magneto Ignition	1964-65	59252A	516798	553248	504665	144921	199001	112201	555910
(19)	650cc 31 De Luxe	1960-61	58477A	516798	553248	504665	144921	54942783	112201	188818
(20)	650cc 31CS and 31CSR Hurricane	1960	58224D	516798	553248	504665	144921		112201	188818
(21)	650cc 31CS and 31CSR Hurricane	1961	58556A	516798	553248	504665	144921	199002	112201	188818
(22)	650cc 31CS and 31CSR Hurricane	1962-63	58704A/B	516798	553248	504665	144921		112201	555910
(23)	650cc 31CS and 31CSR Hurricane – Alternative	1962-63	58258B	516798	554440		198898			555910
(24)	650cc 31CS and 31CSR Hurricane – Sports	1962	58829A	516798	553248	504665	144921	199002	112201	555910
(25)	650cc 31CS and 31CSR Hurricane – Tourer	1962-63	58556A	516798	553248	504665	144921	199002	112201	555910
(26)	650cc 31CSR Hurricane – Tourer, later	1963	58878A	516798	553248	504665	144921	199002	112201	555910
(27)	650cc 31CSR Hurricane, 750cc 33 and 33CS	1964-65	59281A	516798	553248	504665	144921	199001	112201	555910
(28)	650cc 31CSR Hurricane, 750cc 33 and 33CS	1966-67	59666A	516798	553248	504665	144921	199001	112201	555910
	B.S.A.									
(29)	250cc C15 Star	1960	58234D	516828	534343	504665	144921			188818
(30)	250cc C15 Star SS80 Sports Star, 350cc B40 Star and SS90 Sports Star	1961-64	58234D	516828	534343	504665	144921			555910
(31)	250cc C15 Star, SS80 Sports Star, 350cc B40 Star and SS90 Sports Star	1965	59344A	516828	534343	504665	144921	199005	112201	555910
(32)	250cc C15 Star and 350cc B40 Star	1966-67	58234D	516828	534434	504665	144921			555910
(33)	250cc Starfire 250	1967	59658A/B	516798	553248	504665	144921		112201	555910
(34)	250cc Starfire 250	1968	59872A	516798	553248	504665	144921		112201	555910
(35)	250cc C15S, C15T Competition and 350cc B40ES	1960-65	58395E/F	54520452	534348	504665	144921	199003	112201	555910
(36)	250cc C15S Sportsman	1966	59616A	516828	534343	504665	144921	199005	112201	555910
(37)	350cc B32 Gold Star and Competition and 500cc B34 Gold Star and Competition	1960	58224B	516798	553248	504665	144921		112201	188818
(38)	350cc B32 Gold Star and Competition and 500cc B34 Gold Star and Competition	1961-62	58224D	516798	553248	504665	144921		112201	555910
(39)	350cc B32 Gold Star and Competition and 500cc B34 Gold Star and Competition – later	1962	58859A	516798	553248	504665	144921		112201	555910
(40)	441cc B44 Victor Special	1967	58395L	54520452	534343	504665	144921	199003	112201	555910
(41)	441cc B44 Victor Special	1968	59887A	516828	534343	504665	144921		112201	555910
(42)	441cc Shooting Star 441	1967	59658A/B	516798	553248	504665	144921		112201	555910
(43)	441cc Shooting Star 441	1968	59872A	516798	553248	504665	144921		112201	555910
(44)	500cc B34 Gold Star and Competition	1963	58224D	516798	553248	504665	144921		112201	555910
(45)	500cc B34 Gold Star and Competition – later	1963	58859A	516798	553248	504665	144921		112201	555910
(46)	500cc A7 Shooting Star and 650cc A10 Golden Flash	1960-61	58159B	516810	553248	504665	144921			555910
(47)	500cc A7 Shooting Star, A50 Star, 650cc A10 Golden Flash and A65 Star	1962	58208D	516798	553248	504665	144921		112201	555910
(48)	500cc A50 Star, 650cc A10 Golden Flash and A65 Star	1963	58873A	516798	553248	504665	144921		112201	555910
(49)	500cc A50 Star and 650cc A65 Star	1964	59141A	516810	553248	504665	144921	†Grommet, trip cable		555910
			*–later							

HEADLAMP AND PARTS

| | PLUG AND CABLE OR SOCKET | BULB HOLDERS OR ADAPTORS ||| WARNING LIGHT | PARKING LAMP | PILOT LAMP LENS | BULBS ||| Ammeter or Warning Light | AMMETER |
		MAIN	PARKING	INTERIOR PARKING				MAIN	PARKING	PARKING LAMP		
(1)	809795 *54941768	554602	554710	553780				312	988			36084F
(2)	54941768	554602	554710	553780				312	988			36084F
(3)	54941768	554602	554710	553780				312	988			36296A
(4)		554602	554710	553780				312	988			36084F
(5)		554602	554710	553780				312	988			36084F
(6)		554602	554710	553780				312	988			36084F
(7)		554602	554710	553780				312	988			36296A
(8)		554602	554710	553780				446	989			36296A
(9)	809795 *54946012	554602	554710	553780				312	988			36084F
(10)	54946012	554602	554710	553780				312	988			36084F
(11)	54944387	554602	554710	553780				312	988			36296A
(12)	54944387	554602	554710	553780	38189A			312	988		282	36296A
(13)		554602	554710	553780				312	988			36084F
(14)		554602	554710	553780				312	988			36084F
(15)		554602	554710	553780				312	988			
(16)		554602	554710	553780				312	988			36084F
(17)		554602	554710	553780				446	989			36296A
(18)		554602	554710	553780				446	989			36296A
(19)		554602	554710	553780				312	988			36084F
(20)	809795 *54941768	554602	554710	553780				312	988			36084F
(21)	54944387	554602	554710	553780				312	988			36084F
(22)		554602	554710	553780				312	988			36084F
(23)		554602	554710	553780				312	988			36084F
(24)	54944387	554602	554710	553780				312	988			36084F
(25)	54944387	554602	554710	553780				312	988			36084F
(26)	54944387	554602	554710	553780				312	988			36296A
(27)		554602	554710	553780				446	989			36296A
(28)		554602	554710	553780	38189A			446	989		281	
(29)		554602	554710	553780				312	988			36084F
(30)		554602	554710	553780				312	988			36084F
(31)		554602	554710	553780				312	988			36084F
(32)		554602	554710	553780				312	988			36084F
(33)		554602	554710	553780	38189A			446	989		281	36296A
(34)		554602	54573590	553780	38189A			446	989		281	36403A
(35)		554602						166				36084F
(36)		554602	554710	553780				312	988			36084F
(37)		554602	554710	553780				312	988			36084F
(38)		554602	554710	553780				312	988			36084F
(39)		554602	554710	553780				312	988			36296A
(40)		554602	554710	553780	38189A			166			282	36296A
(41)		554602	54573590	553780	38189A			446	989		281	
(42)		554602	554710	553780	38189A			446	989		281	36296A
(43)		554602	54573590	553780	38189A			446	989		281	36403A
(44)		554602	554710	553780				312	988			36084F
(45)		554602	554710	553780				312	988			36296A
(46)		554602	554710	553780				312	988			36084F
(47)	54941699	554602	554710	553780				312	988			36084F
(48)	54941699	554602	554710	553780				312	988			36296A
(49)		554602	554710	553780				312	988			36296A
	*Plug and cable				*Optional ‡later. †Also 38191A (green)	*When fitted			*When fitted	*When fitted	*When fitted	

HEADLAMP AND PARTS (Continued)

1960-1968 SPECIFICATIONS

	MAKE AND MODEL	YEAR	HEAD LAMP	LIGHT UNIT	RIM OR DOOR	WIRE, LIGHT UNIT FIXING	SCREW, RIM FIXING	GROMMET, CABLE ENTRY OR GASKET RUBBER	SCREW, LAMP FIXING	SLEEVE TERMINAL
	B.S.A. (Continued)									
(1)	500cc A50 Cyclone and 650cc A65 Spitfire Hornet	1964	58395F	54520452	534343	504665	144921	199003	112201	555910
(2)	500cc A50 Star and 650cc A65 Star	1965	59171A	516798	553248	504665	144921	199001	112201	555910
(3)	500cc A50C Cyclone and A50CC Cyclone Clubman	1965	59355A	516798	553248	504665	144921		112201	555910
(4)	500cc A502C Cyclone Road	1965	59357A	516798	553248	504665	144921	199001	112201	555910
(5)	500cc A502CC Cyclone Competition and 650cc A65 Spitfire Hornet	1965	58395A	54520452	534343	504665	144921	199003	112201	555910
(6)	500cc A50 Royal Star	1966	59580A	516798	553248	504665	144921		112201	555910
(7)	500cc A50 Royal Star	1967	59658A/B	516798	553248	504665	144921		112201	555910
(8)	500cc A50 Royal Star	1968	59872A	516798	553248	504665	144921		112201	555910
(9)	650cc A10 Super Rocket	1960-61	58208B	516798	553248	504665	144921		112201	188818
(10)	650cc A10 Super Rocket (later) and Rocket Gold Star	1961-62	58208D	516798	553248	504665	144921		112201	555910
(11)	650cc A10 Super Rocket and Rocket Gold Star	1963	58873A	516798	553248	504665	144921		112201	555910
(12)	650cc A65 Lightning Rocket and A65R Rocket (with Speedo Aperture)	1964	59171A	516798	553248	504665	144921	199001	122201	555910
(13)	650cc A65 Lightning Rocket and A65R Rocket (less Speedo Aperture)	1964	59137A	516798	553248	504665	144921		112201	555910
(14)	650cc A65L Lightning and A65LC Lightning Clubman	1965	59355A	516798	553248	504665	144921		112201	555910
(15)	650cc A65lT Thunderbolt Rocket and A65R Rocket (6 volt)	1965	59357A	516798	553248	504665	144921	199001	112201	555910
(16)	650cc A65R Rocket (12 volt)	1965	59237A	516798	553248	504665	144921	199001	112201	555910
(17)	650cc A652L Lightning Rocket	1965	59137A	516798	553248	504665	144921		112201	555910
(18)	650cc A65 Thunderbolt, A65L Lightning and A65 Spitfire Mk II Special	1966	59580A	516798	553248	504665	144921		112201	555910
(19)	650cc A65 Thunderbolt, A65L Lightning and A65 Spitfire Mk II Special	1967	59658A/B	516798	553248	504665	144921		112201	555910
(20)	650cc A65 Thunderbolt, Lightning and Spitfire Mk IV	1968	59872A	516798	553248	504665	144921		112201	555910
(21)	650cc A65 Firebird	1968	59881A	516828	534343	504665	144921		112201	555910
	ENFIELD									
(22)	All models (except Airflow)	1960	50943E	553925	553248	504665	144921			188818
(23)	All models (with Airflow)	1960	58258A	516798	554440		198898			188818
(24)	All models (Except Airflow and Fury Scrambler)	1961-62	50943E	553925	553248	504665	144921			555910
(25)	All models (with Airflow)	1961-62	58258A	516798	554440		198898	555415		555910
(26)	500cc Fury Scrambler	1961	51751A	553925	553248	504665	144921		112201	188818
(27)	500cc Sports Twin (except Airflow) and 700cc Constellation - 6 volt (except Airflow)	1963	50943E	553925	553248	504665	144921			555910
(28)	500cc Sports Twin (with Airflow) and 700cc Constellation - 6 volt (with Airflow)	1963	58258B	516798	554440		198898	555415		555910
(29)	700cc Constellation (except Airflow) - 12 volt	1963	59118A	553921	553248	504665	144921			555910
(30)	700cc Constellation (with Airflow) - 12 volt	1963	59119A	555309	554440		198898			555910
(31)	736cc Interceptor (6 volt)	1963-66	58937A	516798	553248	504665	144921	199002	112201	555910
(32)	736cc Interceptor (12 volt)	1964	50943E	553925	553248	504665	144921			555910
(33)	736cc Interceptor (12 volt) – later	1964	59176A	516810	553248	504665	144921			555910
(34)	736cc Interceptor (12 volt)	1965-66	59345A	516798	553248	504665	144921	199002	112201	555910
(35)	736cc Interceptor (12 volt)	1967-68	59529A	516798	553248	504665	144921		112201	555910
	MATCHLESS									
(36)	350cc G3C Maestro	1960-61	58224D	516798	553248	504665	144921		112201	188818
(37)	350cc G3C Maestro	1962-63	58224D	516798	553248	504665	144921		112201	555910
(38)	350cc G3C Maestro – later	1963	58859A	516798	553248	504665	144921		112201	555910
(39)	500cc G50CSR	1962	58937A	516798	553248	504665	144921	199002	112201	555910
(40)	500cc G80 Major	1960-61	58409A	516798	553248	504665	144921	54942783	112201	188818
(41)	500cc G80 Major	1962	58409A	516798	553248	504665	144921	54942783	112201	555910
(42)	500cc G80 Major – later	1962-63	58702A	516798	553248	504665	144921		112201	555910
(43)	500cc G80 Major	1964-65	59171A	516798	553248	504665	144921	199001	112201	555910
(44)	500cc G80 Major – Alternative Magneto Ignition	1965	59252A	516798	553248	504665	144921	199001	112201	555910
(45)	500cc G80CS Marksman	1960-61	58586A	516798	553248	504665	144921		112201	188818
(46)	500cc G80CS Marksman	1962	58829A	516798	553248	504665	144921	199002	112201	555910
(47)	500cc G80CS Marksman	1963-65	58829A/B	516798	553248	504665	144921	199002	112201	555910
(48)	500cc G80CS Marksman	1966-68	59667A	516798	553248	504665	144921	199002	112201	555910
(49)	650cc G12 Majestic	1960-61	58432A	516798	553248	504665	144921		112201	188818
				*-later				†Grommet, trip cable		

HEADLAMP AND PARTS (Continued)

	PLUG AND CABLE OR SOCKET	BULB HOLDERS OR ADAPTORS			WARNING LIGHT	PARKING LAMP	PARKING LAMP LENS	BULBS				AMMETER
		MAIN	PARKING	INTERIOR, PARKING				MAIN	PARKING	PARKING LAMP	Ammeter or Warning Light	
(1)		554602						166				
(2)		554602	554710	553780				312	988			36296A
(3)		554602	554710	553780				312	988			36296A
(4)		554602	554710	553780				312	988			36296A
(5)		554602						166				
(6)		554602	554710	553780				446	989			36296A
(7)		554602	554710	553780	38189A			446	989		281	36296A
(8)		554602	54573590	553780	38189A			446	989		281	36403A
(9)	54940037	554602	554710	553780				312	988			36084F
(10)	54941699	554602	554710	553780				312	988			36084F
(11)	54941699	554602	554710	553780				312	988			36084F
(12)		554602	554710	553780				312	988			36296A
(13)		554602	554710	553780				312	988			36296A
(14)		554602	554710	553780				312	988			36296A
(15)		554602	554710	553780				312	988			36296A
(16)		554602	554710	553780				446	989			36296A
(17)		554602	554710	553780				312	988			36296A
(18)		554602	554710	553780				446	989			36296A
(19)		554602	554710	553780	38189A			446	989		281	36296A
(20)		554602	54573590	553780	38189A			446	989		281	36403A
(21)		554602	54573590	553780	38189A			446	989		281	
(22)		554602				*52234A	573615	312	*988	*988		36084F
(23)		554602	554710	553780		*52234A	573615	312	*988	*988		36084F
(24)		554602				*52234A	573615	312	*988	*988		36084F
(25)		554602	554710	553780		*52234A	573615	312	*988	*988		36084F
(26)		554602						312				36084F
(27)		554602				*52234A	573615	312	*988	*988		36084F
(28)		554602	554710	553780		*52234A	573615	312	*988	*988		36084F
(29)		554602				*52414A	573615	414	*989	*989		36296A
(30)		554602	554710	553780				414	989			36296A
(31)	54944389	554602	554710	553780		*52234A	573615	312	*988	*988		36296A
(32)		554602				*52414A	573615	446	*989	*989		36296A
(33)		554602	554710	553780		*52414A	573615	446	*989	*989		36296A
(34)	54944387	554602	554710	553780				446	989			36296A
(35)		554602	554710	553780				446	989			36296A
(36)	809795 *54941768	554602	554710	553780				312	988			36084F
(37)	54941768	554602	554710	553780				312	988			36084F
(38)	54941768	554602	554710	553780				312.	988			36296A
(39)	54944387	554602	554710	553780				312	988			36084F
(40)		554602	554710	553780				312	988			36084F
(41)		554602	554710	553780				312	988			36084F
(42)		554602	554710	553780				312	988			36084F
(43)		554602	554710	553780				312	988			36296A
(44)		554602	554710	553780				446	989			36296A
(45)	809795 *54946012	554602	554710	553780				312	988			36084F
(46)	54946012	554602	554710	553780				312	988			36084F
(47)	54944387	554602	554710	553780				312	988			36296A
(48)	54944387	554602	554710	553780	38189A			312	988		282	36296A
(49)		554602	554710	553780				312	988			36084F
	*Plug and cable				*Optional ‡later. †Also 38191A (green)	*When fitted			*When fitted	*When fitted	*When fitted	

HEADLAMP AND PARTS (Continued)

1960-1968 SPECIFICATIONS

	MAKE AND MODEL	YEAR	HEAD LAMP	LIGHT UNIT	RIM OR DOOR	WIRE, LIGHT UNIT FIXING	SCREW, RIM FIXING	GROMMET, CABLE ENTRY OR GASKET RUBBER	SCREW, LAMP FIXING	SLEEVE TERMINAL
	MATCHLESS (Continued)									
(1)	650cc G12 Majestic	1962	58432A	516798	553248	504665	144921		112201	555910
(2)	650cc G12 Majestic – later	1962-63	58702A/B	516798	553248	504665	144921		112201	555910
(3)	650cc G12 Majestic – Alternative, Magneto Ignition	1962-63	58704A/B	516798	553248	504665	144921		112201	555910
(4)	650cc G12 and G12 Majestic	1964-66	59237A	516798	553248	504665	144921	199001	112201	555910
(5)	650cc G12 Majestic – Alternative, Magneto Ignition	1964-65	59252A	516798	553248	504665	144921	199001	112201	555910
(6)	650cc G12 De Luxe	1960-61	58477A	516798	553248	504665	144921	54942783	112201	188818
(7)	650cc G12CS and G12CSR Monarch	1960	58224D	516798	553248	504665	144921		112201	188818
(8)	650cc G12CS and G12CSR Monarch	1961	58556A	516798	553248	504665	144921	199002	112201	188818
(9)	650cc G12CS and G12CSR Monarch	1962-63	58704A/B	516798	553248	504665	144921		112201	555910
(10)	650cc G12CS and G12CSR Monarch – Alternative	1962-63	58258B	516798	554440		198898			555910
(11)	650cc G12CS and G12CSR Monarch – Sports	1962	58829A	516798	553248	504665	144921	199002	112201	555910
(12)	650cc G12CS and G12CSR Monarch – Tourer	1962-63	58556A	516798	553248	504665	144921	199002	112201	555910
(13)	650cc G12CSR Monarch – Tourer (later)	1963	58878A	516798	553248	504665	144921	199002	112201	555910
(14)	650cc G12CSR Monarch, 750cc G15, G15 Mk II and G15CS	1964-65	59281A	516798	553248	504665	144921	199001	112201	555910
(15)	650cc G12CSR Monarch, 750cc G15, G15 Mk II and G15CS	1966-68	59666A	516798	553248	504665	144921		112201	555910
(16)	750cc G15CSR	1966	59529A	516798	553248	504665	144921	199001	112201	555910
(17)	750cc G15CSR	1967-68	59579A	516798	553238	504665	144921		112201	555910
(18)	750cc Commando	1968	59872A	516798	553248	504665	144921		112201	555910
	NORTON									
(19)	350cc 50 Mk II	1965	59171A	516798	553248	504665	144921	199001	112201	555910
(20)	350cc 50 Mk II – Optional (when Magneto fitted)	1965	59252A	516798	553248	504665	144921	199001	112201	555910
(21)	500cc ES2	1960-63	58404A	516798	553248	504665	144921	862217 †517239	112201	555910
(22)	500cc ES2 – later	1963	58702A	516798	553248	504665	144921		112201	555910
(23)	500cc ES2 Mk II	1965	59171A	516798	553248	504665	144921	199001	112201	555910
(24)	500cc ES2 Mk II – Optional (when Magneto fitted)	1965	59252A	516798	553248	504665	144921	199001	112201	555910
(25)	500cc Nomad and 600cc Nomad	1960	58241B	516798	553248	504665	144921	862217 †517239	112201	188818
(26)	500cc Dominator 88 and 600cc Dominator 99 (blue)	1960	58157B	516798	553248	504665	144921	862217 †517239	112201	188818
(27)	500cc Dominator 88 and 600cc Dominator 99 (gray)	1960	58125B	516798	553248	504665	144921	862217 †517239	112201	188818
(28)	500cc Dominator 88 and 600cc Dominator 99 (black)	1960	58197A	516798	553248	504665	144921	862217 †517239	112201	188818
(29)	500cc Dominator 88 and 600cc Dominator 99 (red)	1960	58156B	516798	553248	504665	144921	862217 †517239	112201	188818
(30)	500cc Dominator 88, 600cc Dominator 99 and 650cc Dominator 650 (blue)	1961-62	58157B	516798	553248	504665	144921	862217 †517239	112201	555910
(31)	500cc Dominator 88, 600cc Dominator 99 and 650cc Dominator 650 (gray)	1961-62	58125B	516798	553248	504465	144921	862217 †517239	112201	555910
(32)	500cc Dominator 88, 600cc Dominator 99 and 650cc Dominator 650 (black)	1961-62	58197A	516798	553248	504665	144921	862217 †517239	112201	555910
(33)	500cc Dominator 88, 600cc Dominator 99 and 650cc Dominator 650 (red)	1961-62	58156B	516798	553248	504665	144921	862217 †517239	112201	555910
(34)	500cc Dominator 88 and 650cc Dominator 650	1963	58702A/B	516798	553248	504665	144921		112201	555910
(35)	500cc Dominator 88SS and 650 Dominator 99SS	1962	58885A	516798	553248	504665	144921	862217 †517239	112201	555910
(36)	650cc Dominator 650SS	1962	58241B	516798	553248	504665	144921	862217 †517239	112201	555910
(37)	500cc Dominator 88SS and 650cc Dominator 650SS	1963	58704A/B	516798	553248	504665	144921		112201	555910
			*–later					†Grommet, trip cable		

HEADLAMP AND PARTS (Continued)

	PLUG AND CABLE OR SOCKET	BULB HOLDERS OR ADAPTORS			WARNING LIGHT	PARKING LAMP	PARKING LAMP LENS	BULBS				AMMETER
		MAIN	PARKING	INTERIOR, PARKING				MAIN	PARKING	PARKING LAMP	Ammeter or Warning Light	
(1)		554602	554710	553780				312	988			36084F
(2)		554602	554710	553780				312	988			36084F
(3)		554602	554710	553780				312	988			36084F
(4)		554602	554710	553780				446	989			36296A
(5)		554602	554710	553780				446	989			36296A
(6)		554602	554710	553780				312	988			36084F
(7)	809795 *54941768	554602	554710	553780				312	988			36084F
(8)	54944387	554602	554710	553780				312	988			36084F
(9)		554602	554710	553780				312	988			36296A
(10)		554602	554710	553780				312	988			36084F
(11)	54944387	554602	554710	553780				312	988			36084F
(12)	54944387	554602	554710	553780				312	988			36296A
(13)	54944387	554602	554710	553780				312	988			36084F
(14)		554602	554710	553780				446	989			36296A
(15)		554602	554710	553780	38189A			446	989		281	36296A
(16)		554602	554710	553780				446	989			36296A
(17)		554602	554710	553780	38189A			446	989		281	36296A
(18)		554602	54573590	553780	38189A			446	989		281	36403A
(19)		554602	554710	553780				312	988			36296A
(20)		554602	554710	553780				446	989			36296A
(21)		554602	554710	553780				312	988			36084F
(22)		554602	554710	553780				312	988			36084F
								312	988			
(23)		554602	554710	553780				312	988			36296A
(24)		554602	554710	553780				446	989			36296A
(25)		554602	554710	553780				312	988			36084F
(26)		554602	554710	553780				312	988			36084F
(27)		554602	554710	553780				312	988			36084F
(28)		554602	554710	553780				312	988			36084F
(29)		554602	554710	553780				312	988			36084F
(30)		554602	554710	553780				312	988			36084F
(31)		554602	554710	553780				312	988			36084F
(32)		554602	554710	553780				312	988			36084F
(33)		554602	554710	553780				312	988			36084F
(34)		554602	554710	553780				312	988			36084F
(35)		554602	554710	553780				312	988			36084F
(36)		554602	554710	553780				312	988			36084F
(37)		554602	554710	553780				312	988			36084F
	*Plug and cable				*Optional ‡later †Also 38191A (green)	*When fitted			*When fitted	*When fitted	*When fitted	

HEADLAMP AND PARTS (Continued)

1960-1968 SPECIFICATIONS

	MAKE AND MODEL	YEAR	HEAD LAMP	LIGHT UNIT	RIM OR DOOR	WIRE, LIGHT UNIT FIXING	SCREW, RIM FIXING	GROMMET, CABLE ENTRY OR GASKET RUBBER	SCREW, LAMP FIXING	SLEEVE TERMINAL
	NORTON (Continued)									
(1)	500cc Dominator 88SS and 650cc Dominator 650SS	1964-66	59252A	516798	553248	504665	144921		112201	555910
(2)	650cc Dominator 650SS	1967	59666A	516798	553248	504665	144921		112201	555910
(3)	650cc Manxman	1961-62	58761A	516798	553248	504665	144921	862217 †517239	112201	555910
(4)	750cc Atlas	1962	58241B	516798	553248	504665	144921	862217 †517239	112201	555910
(5)	650cc Manxman and 750cc Atlas	1963	58704A/B	516798	553248	504665	144921		112201	555910
(6)	650cc Manxman and 750cc Atlas	1964-65	59281A	516798	553248	504665	144921	199001	112201	555910
(7)	650cc Manxman and 750cc Atlas	1966-67	59666A	516798	553248	504665	144921		112201	555910
(8)	650cc Manxman	1968	59666A	516798	553248	504665	144921		112201	555910
(9)	750cc Atlas and Commando	1968	59872A	516798	553248	504665	144921		112201	555910
(10)	750cc N15 and N15CS	1965	59281A	516798	553248	504665	144921	199001	112201	555910
(11)	750cc N15, N15CS, P11	1966-68	59666A	516798	553248	504665	144921		112201	555910
	TRIUMPH									
(12)	200cc T20 Tiger Cub	1960-62	51548D	516659	516723	500291	516710			555910
(13)	200cc T20 Tiger Cub	1963-66	59004B	54520452	516723	500291	516710			555910
(14)	200cc T20 Tiger Cub	1967	59629A	516828	534343	504665	144921	199005	112201	555910
(15)	200cc T20S, T20SC, T20SH, T20SL, T20SR, T20SS, T20T Tiger Cub	1960-62	58395B	54520452	534343	504665	144921	199003	112201	555910
(16)	200cc T20R Trials, T20S Scrambler, T20SC, T20SM, T20SR and T20SS Tiger Cub	1963-65	58395B	54520452	534343	504665	144921	199003	112201	555910
(17)	200cc T20SM and T20SR (1966 only) Sports Cub	1963-66	58935B/D	516828	534343	504665	144921		112201	555910
(18)	200cc T20SM Tiger Cub	1966-67	58395F/L	54520452	534343	504665	144921	199003	112201	555910
(19)	500cc T100SS Tiger	1962	58878A	516798	553248	504665	144921	199002	112201	555910
(20)	500cc T100SS Tiger – later	1962-63	58934A	516798	553248	504665	144921	199002	112201	555910
(21)	500cc T100C and T100SC Tiger	1962-66	58395B/F	54520452	534343	504665	144921	199003	112201	555910
(22)	500cc T100C Tiger	1967	59699A	54520452	534343	504665	144921	199003	112201	555910
(23)	500cc T100C Tiger	1968	59882A	516828	534343	504665	144921		112201	555910
(24)	500cc T100 Tiger	1964-65	58934A	516798	553248	504665	144921		112201	555910
(25)	500cc T100 Tiger and T100R Tiger	1966	59579A	516798	553248	504665	144921		112201	555910
(26)	500cc T100 T100R, T100S Tiger and T100T Daytona Tiger	1967	59734A	516798	553248	504665	144921	199002	112201	555910
(27)	500cc T100R Daytona Super Sports	1968	59883A	516798	553248	504665	144921		112201	555910
(28)	500cc T100A Tiger, 5TA Speed Twin 650cc 6T Thunderbird and T110 Tiger	1960-63	51756E	516810	553248	504665	144921			188818
(29)	500cc 5TA Speed Twin	1964-65	51756E	516810	553248	504665	144921			555910
(30)	500cc 5TA Speed Twin	1966	59176A	516810	553248	504665	144921			555910
(31)	500cc TR5A-C	1961	58395B	54520452	534343	504665	144921	199003	112201	555910
(32)	500cc TR5A-R 650cc TR6 Trophy and T120 Bonneville	1960-61	58556A	516798	553248	504665	144921		112201	188818
(33)	650cc 6T Thunderbird	1964-66	59176A	516810	553248	504665	144921			555910
(34)	650cc TR6 and TR6SS Trophy and T120 Bonneville	1962	58900A	516798	553248	504665	144921	199002	112201	555910
(35)	650cc TR6 and TR6SS Trophy and T120 Bonneville – later	1962-65	58934A	516798	553248	504665	144921	199002	112201	555910
(36)	650cc TR6, TR6R Trophy, T120 and T120R Bonneville	1966	59579A	516798	553248	504665	144921		112201	555910
(37)	650cc TR6, TR6R Trophy, T120 and T120R Bonneville	1967	59734A	516798	553248	504665	144921	199002	112201	555910
(38)	650cc TR6R Trophy and T120R Bonneville	1968	59883A	516798	553248	504665	144921		112201	555910
(39)	650cc TR6C Trophy and T120TT Special	1966	58395F	54520452	534343	504665	144921	199003	112201	555910
(40)	650cc TR6C Trophy	1967	59699A	54520452	534343	504665	144921	199003	112201	555910
(41)	650cc TR6C Trophy	1968	59882A	516828	534343	504665	144921		112201	555910

*-later

†Grommet, trip cable

HEADLAMP AND PARTS (Continued)

	PLUG AND CABLE OR SOCKET	BULB HOLDERS OR ADAPTORS			WARNING LIGHT	PARKING LAMP	PARKING LAMP LENS	BULBS				AMMETER
		MAIN	PARKING	INTERIOR PARKING				MAIN	PARKING	PARKING LAMP	Ammeter or Warning Light	
(1)		554602	554710	553780				446	989			36296A
(2)		554602	554710	553780	38189A			446	989		281	36296A
(3)		554602	554710	553780				312	988			36084F
(4)		554602	554710	553780				312	988			36084F
(5)		554602	554710	553780				312	988			36084F
(6)		554602	554710	553780				446	989			36296A
(7)		554602	554710	553780	38189A			446	989		281	36296A
(8)		554602	554710	553780	38189A			446	989		281	36296A
(9)		554602	54573590	553780	38189A			446	989		281	36403A
(10)		554602	554710	553780				446	989			36296A
(11)		554602	554710	553780	38189A			446	989		281	36296A
(12)		554946						312				
(13)		554602						312				
(14)		554602	554710	553780	*38189A			312	988		*282	
(15)		554602						166				
(16)		554602						166				
(17)		554602	554710	553780				166	988			
(18)		554602	*54945643		‡38189A			166			*282	
(19)	54944387	554602	554710	553780				312	988			36084F
(20)		554602	554710	553780				312	988			36296A
(21)		554602						166				
(22)		554602			38189A			166			282	
(23)		554602	54573590	553780	†38189A(red)			446	989		281	
(24)		554602	554710	553780				312	988			36296A
(25)		554602	554710	553780	38189A			446	989		281	36296A
(26)		554602	554710	553780	†38189A(red)			446	989		281	36296A
(27)		554602	54573590	553780	†38189A(red)			446	989		281	36403A
(28)		554602	554710	553780				312	988			36189A
(29)		554602	554710	553780				312	988			36296A
(30)		554602	554710	553780				312	988			36296A
(31)		554602						166				36084F
(32)		554602	554710	553780				312	988			36084F
(33)								446	989			36296A
(34)		554602	554710	553780				312	988			36296A
(35)		554602	554710	553780				312	988			36296A
(36)		554602	554710	553780	38189A			446	989		281	36296A
(37)		554602	554710	553780	†38189A(red)			446	989		281	36296A
(38)		554602	54573590	553780	†38189A(red)			446	989		281	36403A
(39)		554602						166				
(40)		554602			38189A			166			282	
(41)		554602	54573590	553780	†38189A(red)			446	989		281	
	*plug and cable		*Warning light bulb holder		*Optional ‡later. †Also 38191A (green)	*When fitted			*When fitted	*When fitted	*When fitted	

STOP TAIL AND LICENSE PLATE LAMP

1960-1968 SPECIFICATIONS

	MAKE AND MODEL	YEAR	LAMP	LENS	WINDOW	NUT OR SCREW, LENS OR RIM FIXING	GASKET, LENS SEATING
	A.J.S.						
(1)	250cc 14 Sapphire and 14CS Scorpion	1960-62					
(2)	250cc 14CS Scorpion – optional	1960-62	*57116			*54570241	
(3)	350cc 16C Experts	1960-62	53429A	526404	526406	133551	
(4)	350cc 16C Experts – optional	1960-62	*57116			*54570241	
(5)	350cc 16C Experts	1963	53432B	573839	575200	575219	575208
(6)	500cc 18 Statesman, 650cc 31 Swift and 31 De Luxe	1960-61	53432B	573839	575200	575219	575208
(7)	500cc 18 Statesman and 650cc 31 Swift	1962-63	53432B	573839	575200	575219	575208
(8)	500cc 18CS Southerner, 650cc 31CS and 31CSR Hurricane	1960-61	53429A	526404	526406	133551	
(9)	500cc 18CS Southerner, 650cc 31CS and 31CSR Hurricane – optional	1960-61	*57116			*54570241	
(10)	500cc 18CS Southerner	1962	53429A	526404	526406	133551	
(11)	500cc 18CS Southerner – optional	1962	*57116			*54570241	
(12)	500cc 18CS Southerner	1963	53432B	573839	575200	575219	575208
(13)	500cc 18 Statesman	1964-65	53432B/D	54576001		575219	575208
(14)	500cc 18CS Southerner	1964-66	53972A/B	54572932		572289	54571677
(15)	650cc 31CS and 31CSR Hurricane	1962	53429A	526404	526406	133551	
(16)	650cc 31CS and 31CSR Hurricane – optional	1962	*57116			*54570241	
(17)	650cc 31 Swift and 31 Tourer	1964-66	53454B/D	54576001		575219	575208
(18)	650cc 31CSR Hurricane	1963	53432B	573839	575200	575219	575208
(19)	650cc 31CSR Hurricane, 750cc 33 and 33CS	1964-67	53973A/B	54572932		572289	54571677
	B.S.A.						
(20)	125cc D.1 Bantam, 175cc D7 Bantam Major, Super Bantam, D10 Bantam De Luxe and Bantam Silver	1960-66					
(21)	175cc D10 Bantam Silver, Supreme, Sports and Bushman	1967-68	53972D	54577109		114921	54571677
(22)	250cc C15 Star and C15S and C15T Competition	1960	53394B	573839	575200	575219	575208
(23)	250cc C15 Star and C15S and C15T, Competition – alternative	1960	53825A	573839	575200	575219	575208
(24)	250cc C15 Star and SS80 Sports Star	1961-63	53394B	573839	575200	575219	575208
(25)	250cc C15 Star and SS80 Sports Star	1964-65	53972A/B	54572932		572289	54571677
(26)	250cc C15S and C15T Competition	1961-62	53432B	573839	575200	575219	575208
(27)	250cc C15S and C15T Competition	1963-64	†53825A	573839	575200	575219	575208
(28)	250cc C15S and C15T Competition – optional	1964	53432B	573839	575200	575219	575208
(29)	250cc C15S and C15T Competition and 350cc B40ES	1965	53972A/B	54572932		572289	54571677
(30)	250cc C15 Star and C15S Sportsman	1966-67	53972B	54572932		572289	54571677
(31)	250cc Starfire 250 and 441cc Shooting Star 441	1967-68	53973D	54577109		144921	54571677
(32)	350cc B32, 500cc B34, A7 and 650cc A10 – all models	1960	53432B	573839	575200	575219	575208
(33)	350cc B32 Gold Star and Competition and 500cc B34 Gold Star and Competition	1961-63	53432B	573839	575200	575219	575208
(34)	350cc B40, SS90, 500cc A7, A50, 650cc A65 and Rocket Gold Star – all models	1961-63	53432B	573839	575200	575219	575208
(35)	350cc B40, SS90, 650cc Thunderbolt Rocket, Lightning Rocket and A65R Rocket (6 volt)	1964-65	53972A/B	54572932		572289	54571677
(36)	350cc B40 Star	1966	53432D	54576001		575219	575208
(37)	441cc B44 Victor Special	1967	53972D	54577109		144921	54571677
(38)	441cc B44 Victor Special	1968	53973D	54577109		144921	54571677
(39)	500cc A50 Star and 650cc A65 Star	1964-65	53972B	54572932		572289	54571677
(40)	500cc A50 Cyclone and 650cc A65 Spitfire Hornet	1964	53972A/B	54572932		572289	54571677
(41)	500cc A50 Cyclone Competition and 650cc A65 Spitfire Hornet	1965	53972B	54572932		572289	54571677
(42)	500cc A50 Cyclone, Cyclone Clubman, Cyclone Road, 650cc A65 Lightning and Lightning Clubman	1965	53972A/B	54572932		572289	54571677
(43)	650cc A65R Rocket (12 volt)	1965	53454D	54576001		575219	575208
(44)	500cc A50 Royal Star 650cc A65 Thunderbolt, Lightning and Spitfire Mk II Special	1966	53973B	54572932		572289	54571677
(45)	500cc A50 Royal Star, 650cc A65 Thunderbolt, Lightning, Spitfire Mk III, Spitfire Mk IV, Hornet and Firebird	1967-68	53973D	54577109		144921	54571677
	ENFIELD						
(46)	250cc Hounds Crusader	1960-61	53394B	573839	575200	575219	575208
(47)	500cc and 700cc – All models	1960	53432B	573839	575200		575208
(48)	500cc – All models	1961-63	53432B	573839	575200	575219	575208
(49)	700cc – All models	1961-62	53432B	573839	575200	575219	575208
(50)	700cc Constellation – (6 volt)	1963	53432B	573839	575200	575219	575208
(51)	700cc Constellation – (12 volt)	1963	53454B	573839	575200	575219	575208
(52)	736cc Interceptor – (6 volt)	1963-64	53432B	573839	575200	575219	575208
(53)	736cc Interceptor – (12 volt)	1964	53454B	573839	575200	575219	575208
(54)	736cc Interceptor (6 volt)	1965	53432D	54576001		575219	575208
(55)	736cc Interceptor – (12 volt)	1965	53454D	54576001		575219	575208

*Reflex reflector
†tail & number plate

*Rim reflex

STOP TAIL AND LICENSE PLATE LAMP | BATTERY

	BASE	GROMMET, BULB HOLDER	INTERIOR, BULB HOLDER	SHELL, BULB HOLDER	CABLE GROMMET	NUT, LAMP FIXING	REFLEX REFLECTOR	BULB	BATTERY
(1)								384	PUZ7E-11
(2)	54570242						575878	384	
(3)	526421		573828 *526418			166103		384	PUZ7E-11
(4)	54570242						575878	384	
(5)	576002	575207	573828	575209	573825	166014		384	PUZ7E-11
(6)	576002	575207	573828	575209	573825	166014		384	MLZ9E
(7)	576002	575207	573828	575209		166104		384	PUZ7E-11
(8)	526421		573828 *526418			166103		384	MLZ9E
(9)	54570242						575878	384	
(10)	526421		573828 *526418			166103		384	MLZ9E
(11)	54570242						575878	384	
(12)	576002	575207	573828	575209	573825	166014		384	MLZ9E
(13)	54573881	575207	573828	575209	573825	166014		384	PUZ7E-11
(14)	54571319		573828	*54574348		*127684		384	MLZ9E
(15)	526421		573828 *526418			166108		384	PUZ7E-11
(16)	54570242						575878	384	
(17)	575964	575207	573828	575209	573825			380	MKZ9E(2)
(18)	576002	575207	573828	575209	573825	166014		384	PUZ7E-11
(19)	54571319		573828	*54574348		*127684		380	MKZ9E(2)
(20)									PUZ5E-11
(21)	54577139		573828	*54574348		*110714		384	PUZ5E-11
(22)	576002	575207	573828	575209	573825	166014		352	MLZ9E
(23)	54571053	575207	573832	54571021	573825	166014		205	MLZ9E
(24)	576002	575207	573828	575209	573825	166014		350 *352	MLZ9E
(25)	54571319		573828	*54574348				384	MLZ9E
(26)	576002	575207	573832	575209	573825	166014		384	MLZ9E
(27)	54571053	575207	573832	54571021	573825	166014		205	
(28)	54573881	575207	573828	575209		166014		205	
(29)	54571319		573828	*54574348				384	
(30)	54571319		573828	*54574348		*127684		384	MLZ9E
(31)	54577139		573828	*54574348		*110714		380	PUZ5A
(32)	576002	575207	573828	575209	573825	166014		384	PUZ7E-10
(33)	576002	575207	575828	575209	573825	166014		384	PUZ7E-10
(34)	576002	575207	573828	575209	573825	166014		384	MLZ9E
(35)	54571319		573828	*54574348				384	MLZ9E
(36)	54573851	575207	573828	575209	573825	166019		384	MLZ9E
(37)	54577139		573828	*54574348		*110714		384	
(38)	54577139		573828	*54574348		*110714	*57111(red)	380	PUZ5A
(39)	54571319		573828	*54574348				384	MLZ9E
(40)	54571319		573828	*54574348				384	
(41)	54571319		573828	*54574348				384	
(42)	54571319		573828	*54574348				384	MLZ9E
(43)	575964	575207	573828	575209	573825	166014		380	MKZ9E(2)
(44)	54571319		573828	*54574348		*127684		380	MKZ9E(2)
(45)	54577139		573828	*54574348		*110714		380	PUZ5A
(46)	576002	575207	573828	575209	573825	166014		352	PUZ7E-11
(47)	576002	575207	573828	575209	573825	166014		384	PUZ7E-11
(48)	576002	575207	573828	575209	573825	166014		384	PUZ7E-11
(49)	576002	575207	573828	575209	573825	166014		384	MLZ9E
(50)	576002	575207	573828	575209	573825	166014		384	PUZ7E-11
(51)	575964	575207	573828	575209	573825	161014		384	MLZ9E(2)
(52)	54573881	575207	573828	575209	573825	166014		384	MLZ9E
(53)	575964	575207	573828	575209	573825	166014		380	MLZ9E(2)
(54)	54573881	575207	573828	575209	573825	166014		384	MLZ9E
(55)	575964	575207	573828	575209	573825	166014		380	MLZ9E(2)
			*Bulb holder complete.	*Bulb holder with reflector.		*Screw	*Also 57162 (amber)	*later	*later (2) Quantity 2

STOP TAIL AND LICENSE PLATE LAMP (Continued)

1960-1968 SPECIFICATIONS

	MAKE AND MODEL	YEAR	LAMP	LENS	WINDOW	NUT OR SCREW, LENS OR RIM FIXING	GASKET, LENS SEATING
	ENFIELD (Continued)						
(1)	736cc Interceptor – (6 volt)	1966	53432D	54576001		575219	575208
(2)	736cc Interceptor – (12 volt)	1966	53454D	54576001		575219	575208
(3)	736cc Interceptor – (12 volt)	1967-68	53973D	54577109		144921	54571677
	MATCHLESS						
(4)	250cc G2 Monitor and G2CS Messenger	1960-62					
(5)	250cc G2CS Messenger – optional	1960-62	*57116			*54570241	
(6)	350cc G3C Maestro	1960-62	53429A	526404	526406	133551	
(7)	350cc G3C Maestro – optional	1960-62	*57116			*54570241	
(8)	350cc G3 Maestro	1963	53432B	573839	575200	575219	575208
(9)	500cc G80 Major, 650cc G12 Majestic and G12 De Luxe	1960-61	53432B	573839	575200	575219	575208
(10)	500cc G50CSR, G80 Major and 650cc G12 Majestic	1962-63	53432B	573839	575200	575219	575208
(11)	500cc G80CS Marksman, 650cc G12CS and G12CSR Monarch	1960-61	53429A	526404	526406	133551	
(12)	500cc G80CS Marksman, 650cc G12CS and G12CSR Monarch – optional	1960-61	*57116			*54570241	
(13)	500cc G80CS Marksman	1962	53429A	526404	526406	133551	
(14)	500cc G80CS Marksman – optional	1962	*57116			*54570241	
(15)	500cc G80CS Marksman	1963	53432B	573839	575200	575219	575208
(16)	500cc G80 Major	1964-65	53432B/D	54576001		575219	575208
(17)	500cc G80CS Marksman	1964-66	53972A/B	54572932		572289	54571677
(18)	650cc G12CS and G12CSR Monarch	1962	53429A	526404	526406	133551	
(19)	650cc G12CS and G12CSR Monarch – optional	1962	*57116			*54570241	
(20)	650cc G12 Majestic	1964-66	53454B/D	54576001		575219	575208
(21)	650cc G12CSR Monarch	1963	53432B	573839	575200	575219	575208
(22)	500cc G80CS, 650cc G12CSR Monarch, 750cc G15 Mk II, G15CS and G15CSR	1964-67	53973A/B	54572932		572289	54571677
(23)	750cc Commando	1968	53973D	54577109		144921	54571677
	NORTON						
(24)	350cc Navigator	1961	53432B	573839	575200	575219	575208
(25)	350cc Navigator	1962	53432B	573839	575200	575219	575208
(26)	350cc Navigator	1963	53432B	573839	575200	575219	575208
(27)	350cc Navigator 50 Mk II and 500cc ES2 Mk II	1964-65	53432B	573839	575200	575219	575208
(28)	All models over 350cc (except Nomad, Manxman and Electra)	1960-63	53432B	573839	575200	575219	575208
(29)	397cc Electra	1963	53973A/B	54572932		572289	54571677
(30)	397cc Electra	1964-65	53973A/B	54572932		572289	54571677
(31)	500cc Nomad and 600cc Nomad	1960	53432B	573839	575200	575219	575208
(32)	650cc Manxman	1961	53432B	573839	575200	575219	575208
(33)	650cc Manxman	1962-63	53432B	573839	575200	575219	575208
(34)	500cc Dominator 88SS and 650cc Dominator 650SS	1964	53454B	573839	575200	575219	575208
(35)	500cc Dominator 88SS and 650cc Dominator 650SS	1965	53454D	54576001		575219	575208
(36)	500cc Dominator 88SS and 650cc Dominator 650SS	1966-67	53454D	54576001		575219	575208
(37)	650cc Manxman and 750cc Atlas	1964	53973A/B	54572932		572289	54571677
(38)	650cc Manxman 750cc Atlas, N15 and N15CS	1965	53973B	54572932		572289	54571677
(39)	650cc Manxman, 750cc Atlas, N15 and N15CS	1966-67	53973B/D	54572932		572289	54571677
(40)	750cc P.11	1967	53973B/D	54572932		572289	54571677
(41)	650cc Manxman, 750cc N15CS, Atlas, Commando and P.11	1968	53973D	54577109		144921	54571677
	TRIUMPH						
(42)	200cc T20 Tiger Cub	1960-61	53331A	526404	526406	133551	
			*57080A			*575481	
(43)	200cc T20 and T20SH Tiger Cub	1962-64	53394B	573839	575200	575219	575208
(44)	200cc T20S Tiger Cub Scrambler	1960	53428B	526404	526406	133551	
			*57080A			*575481	
(45)	200cc T20S Scrambler, T20SL Tiger Cub and T20T Trials	1961	53429A	526404	526406	133551	
			*57080A			*575481	
(46)	200cc T20R Trials, T20S Scrambler, T20SC, T20SR and T20SS Tiger Cub	1962-64	53394B	573839	575200	575219	575208
(47)	200cc T20 Tiger Cub and T20SH Sports Cub	1965	53972B	54572932		572289	54571677
(48)	200cc T20SS Tiger Cub	1965	53432D	54576001		575219	575208
(49)	200cc T20SM Tiger Cub – optional	1965	53394B	54576001		575219	575208
(50)	200cc T20 Tiger Cub, T20SH and T20SR Sports Cub	1966	53972D	54577138		572289	54571677
(51)	200cc T20 Tiger Cub	1967	53432B	54576001		575219	575208

*Reflex reflector.
†tail & number plate.
*Rim reflex

STOP TAIL AND LICENSE PLATE LAMP (Continued) | BATTERY

	BASE	GROMMET, BULB HOLDER	INTERIOR, BULB HOLDER	SHELL, BULB HOLDER	CABLE GROMMET	NUT, LAMP FIXING	REFLEX REFLECTOR	BULB	BATTERY
(1)	54573881	575207	573828	575209	573825	166019		384	MLZ9E
(2)	575964	575207	573828	585209	573825	166019		380	MLZ9E(2)
(3)	54577139		573828	*54574348		*110714		380	PUZ5A
(4)								384	PUZ7E-11
(5)	54570242						575878	384	
(6)	526421		573828 *526418			166103		384	
(7)	54570242						575878	384	
(8)	576002	575207	573828	575209	573825	166014		384	PUZ7E-11
(9)	576002	575207	573828	575209	573825	166014		384	MLZ9E
(10)	576002	575207	573828	575209	573825	166014		384	PUZ7E-11
(11)	526421		573828 *525418			166103		384	MLZ9E
(12)	54570242						575878	384	
(13)	526421		573828 *526418			166103		384	MLZ9E
(14)	54570242						575878	384	
(15)	576002	575207	573828	575209	573825	166014		384	MLZ9E
(16)	54573881	575207	573828	575209	573825	166014		384	PUZ7E-11
(17)	54571319		573828	*54574348		*127684		384	MLZ9E
(18)	526421		573828 *526418			166103		384	PUZ7E-11
(19)	54570243						575878	384	
(20)	575964	575207	573828	575209	573825			380	MKZ9E(2)
(21)	576002	575207	573828	575209	573825	166014		384	PUZ7E-11
(22)	54571319		573828	*54574348		*127684		380	MKZ9E(2)
(23)	54577139		573828	*54574348		*110714	57162A	380	PUZ5A
(24)	576002	575207	573828	575209	573825	166014		384	PUZ7E-11
(25)	576002	575207	573828	575209	573825	166014		384	
(26)	576002	575207	573828	575209	573825	166014		384	PUZ7E-11
(27)	54573881	575207	573828	575209	573825	166014		384	
(28)	576002	575207	573828	575209	573825	166014		384	PUZ7E-11
(29)	54571319		573828	*54574348				380	MSLZ11E(2)
(30)	54571319		573828	*54574348				380	MSLZ11E(2)
(31)	576002	575207	573828	575209	573825	166014		384	
(32)	576002	575207	573828	575209	573825	166014		384	
(33)	576002	575207	573828	575209	573825	161014		384	PUZ7E-11
(34)	575964	575207	573828	575209	573825	166014		380	MKZ9E(2)
(35)	575964	575207	573828	575209	573825			380	MKZ9E(2)
(36)	575964	575207	573828	575209	573825	166019		380	MKZ9E(2)
(37)	54571319		573828	*54574348				380	MKZ9E(2)
(38)	54571319		573828	*54574348				380	MKZ9E(2)
(39)	54571319		573828	*54574348	573825	166019		380	MKZ9E(2)
(40)	54571319		573828	*54574348		*110714		380	PU5A
(41)	54571319		573828	*54574348		*110714	57162A	380	PUZ5A
(42)	526421	526415	573828 *526418			166103		352	PUZ5E-11
	575480					175300	574749		
(43)	54573881	575207	573828	575209	573825	166014		352	PUZ5E-11
(44)	526408		553780 *554719			166103		951	
	575480					175300	574749		
(45)	526421		573828 *526418			166103		951	PUZ5E-11
	575480					175300	574749		
(46)	54573881	575207	573828	575209	573825	166014		352	PUZ5E-11
(47)	54571319		573828	*54574348				384	PUZ5E-11
(48)	54573881	575207	573828	575209	573825	166014		384	
(49)	54573881	575207	573828	575209	573825	166014		352	
(50)	54577139		573828	*54574348				384	PUZ5E-11
(51)	54573881	575207	573828	575209	573825	166019		384	MLZ9E
			*Bulb holder complete.	*Bulb holder with reflector.		*Screw		*later	*later (2) Quantity 2

STOP TAIL AND LICENSE PLATE LAMP (Continued)

1960-1968 SPECIFICATIONS

	MAKE AND MODEL	YEAR	LAMP	LENS	WINDOW	NUT OR SCREW, LENS OR RIM FIXING	GASKET, LENS SEATING
	TRIUMPH (Continued)						
(1)	200cc T20SM Tiger Cub	1966-67	53972B	54577138		575219	54571677
(2)	500cc 5TA Speed Twin, T100A and T100SC Tiger	1960-64	53432B	573839	575200	575219	575208
(3)	500cc T100SS Tiger and 650cc 6T Thunderbird	1960-63	53432B	573839	575200	575219	575208
(4)	500cc T100 Tiger	1964	53432B	573839	575200	575219	575208
(5)	500cc 5TA Speed Twin T100 and T100SC Tiger	1965	53972B	54572932		572289	54571677
(6)	500cc T100 Tiger	1966	53454D	54576001		575219	575208
(7)	500cc T100 Tiger – later	1966	53454D	54576001		575219	575208
(8)	500cc T100C Tiger	1966-67	53972B	54572932		572289	54571677
(9)	500cc T100C Tiger (1968), 5TA Speed Twin, T100R Tiger and Daytona Super Sports.	1966-68	53973D	54577109		572289	54571677
(10)	500cc T100S Tiger and T100T Daytona Tiger	1967	53454D	54576001		575219	575208
(11)	650cc 6T Thunderbird	1964	53454D	573839	575200	575219	575208
(12)	650cc 6T Thunderbird	1965-66	53973B	54572932		572289	54571677
(13)	650cc T110 Tiger	1960-61	53432B	573839	575200	575219	575208
(14)	650cc TR6, TR6SS Trophy and T120 Bonneville	1960-62	53432B	573839	575200	575219	575208
(15)	650cc TR6, TR6SS Trophy and T120 Bonneville	1963-64	53432B	573839	575200	575219	575208
(16)	650cc TR6 Trophy and T120 Bonneville	1965	53972B	54572932		572289	54571677
(17)	650cc TR6 Trophy and T120 Bonneville	1966-68	53454D	54576001		575219	575208
(18)	650cc TR6C Trophy and T120TT Special	1966-67	53972B	54572932		572289	54571677
(19)	650cc TR6C Trophy (1968), TR6R Trophy and T120R Bonneville	1966-68	53973D	54577109		572289	54571677
			*Reflex reflector. †tail & number plate.			*Rim reflex	

STOP TAIL AND LICENSE PLATE LAMP (Continued) | BATTERY

	BASE	GROMMET, BULB HOLDER	INTERIOR, BULB HOLDER	SHELL, BULB HOLDER	CABLE GROMMET	NUT, LAMP FIXING	REFLEX REFLECTOR	BULB	BATTERY
(1)	54577139		573828	*54574348				384	
(2)	54573881	575207	573828	575209	573825	166014		384	PUZ7E-11
(3)	576002	575207	573828	575209	573825	166014		384	MLZ9E
(4)	54573881	575207	573828	575209	573825	166014		384	MLZ9E
(5)	54571319		573828	*54574348				384	MLZ9E
(6)	54573881	575207	573828	575209	573825	166019		380	MKZ9E (2)
(7)	54573881	575207	573828	575209	573825	166019		380	PUZ5A
(8)	54571319		573828	*54574348				384	
(9)	54577139		573828	*54574348			57161A	380	MKZ9E (2) *PUZ5A
(10)	54573881	575207	573828	575209	573825	166019	57161A	380	PUZ5A
(11)	575964	575207	573828	575209	573825	166014		380	MKZ9E (2)
(12)	54571319		573828	*54574348				380	MKZ9E (2)
(13)	576002	575207	573828	575209	573825	166014		384	MLZ9E
(14)	576002	575207	573828	575209	573825	166014		384	PUZ7E-10
(15)	54573881	575207	573828	575209	573825	166014		384	MLZ9E
(16)	54571319		573828	*54574348				384	MLZ9E
(17)	54573881	575207	573828	575209	573825	166019	57161A	380	MKZ9E (2) *PUZ5A
(18)	54571319		573828	*54574348				380	
(19)	54577139		573828	*54574348			57161A	380	PUZ5A
			*Bulb holder complete.	*Bulb holder with reflector.		*Screw		*later	*later (2) Quantity 2

MAGNETO AND PARTS
(REFER ALSO TO PAGES 26 and 27)

1960-1968 SPECIFICATIONS

	MAKE AND MODEL	YEAR	MAGNETO	CLIP ASSEMBLY, PICK-UP	RUBBER COVER, PICK-UP	PICK-UP ASSEMBLY Right Hand	PICK-UP ASSEMBLY Left Hand	BRUSH AND SPRING PICK-UP
	A.J.S.							
(1)	250cc 14CS Scorpion, 350cc 16C Experts and 500cc 18CS Southerner	1960-66	42347E	455733	457810		456794	451260
(2)	250cc 14 Sapphire, 14S Sapphire Sports and 500cc 18 Statesman	1960-65	42371B	455733	457810		456794	451260
(3)	500cc 18 Statesman	1964-66	42272B			463066		451260
(4)	650cc 31 De Luxe	1960-61	42230E	455734	458658	458367	458368	451260
(5)	650cc 31CS Swift Sports and 31CSR Hurricane	1960	42264B	455734	458658	458367	458368	451260
(6)	650cc 31 Swift (optional) 31CS Swift Sports and 31CSR Hurricane – later	1960-66	42264D	455734	458658	458367	458368	451260
(7)	750cc 33 and 33CS	1965-67	42453A			458367	458368	451260
	B.S.A.							
(8)	350cc B32 and 500cc B34 – Gold Star Models	1960-63	46048A	See Magdyno				
(9)	350cc B32 and 500cc B34 – Competition models	1960-63	42348E	457333	457810		456794	451260
(10)	350cc B32 and 500cc B34 – Racing Models	1960-63	42123M	455733	457810		456794	451260
(11)	500cc A7 and 650cc A10 Golden Flash	1960-61	42379A			458865	458866	451260
(12)	500cc A7 and 650cc A10 Golden Flash – later	1961-63	42379B/D			458865	458866	451260
(13)	500cc A7 Shooting Star and 650cc A10 Super Rocket	1960	42380B			459190	459190	451260
(14)	500cc A7 Shooting Star, 650cc A10 Super Rocket and Rocket Gold Star	1961-63	42413A			459190	459190	451260
	ENFIELD							
(15)	500cc Bullet	1960-61	*42330B					
(16)	500cc Fury Scrambler	1961	42272B			463066		451260
(17)	700cc Super Meteor	1960	†42364D					
(18)	700cc Constellation	1960	42369A			458367	458368	451260
(19)	700cc Constellation (later) and 736cc Interceptor	1960-63	42369B		458658	458367	458368	451260
(20)	736cc Interceptor	1964-66	42442A		458658	458367	458368	451260
	MATCHLESS							
(21)	250cc G2CS Messenger, 350cc G3C Maestro and G80CS Marksman	1960-68	42347E	455733	457810		456794	451260
(22)	250cc G2 Monitor, G2S Monitor Sports and 500cc G80 Major	1960-63	42371B	455733	457810		456794	451260
(23)	500cc G80 Major	1966-65	42272B			463066		451260
(24)	650cc G12 De Luxe	1960-61	42230E	455734	458658	458367	458368	451260
(25)	650cc G12CS Majestic Sports and G12CSR Monarch	1960	42264B	455734	458658	458367	458368	451260
(26)	650cc G12 Majestic (optional) G12CS Majestic Sports and G12CSR Monarch (later)	1960-66	42264D	455734	458658	458367	458368	451260
(27)	750cc G15, G15 Mk II G15CS and G15CSR	1965-68	42453A			458367	458368	451260
	NORTON							
(28)	350cc 50 Mk II and 500cc ES2 Mk II (optional)	1965	42272B			463066		451260
(29)	500cc Dominator 88SS, Nomad, 600cc Dominator 99SS and Nomad	1960-62	42350F/H	455734	458658	458876	458876	451260
(30)	650cc Dominator 650SS, Manxman and 750cc Atlas	1961-62	42368D	455734	458658	458876	458876	451260
(31)	500cc Dominator 88SS, 650cc Dominator 650SS, Manxman and 750cc Atlas	1963-64	42368D	455734	458658	458876	458876	451260
(32)	750cc Atlas (first 150 machines built in 1964)	1964	42452A	455734	458658	458367	458368	451260
(33)	500cc Dominator 88SS, 650cc Dominator 650SS Manxman and 750cc Atlas – later	1964	42379B/D			458865	458866	451260
(34)	500cc Dominator 88SS, 650 Dominator 650SS, Manxman, 750cc Atlas, N15 and N15CS	1965-67	42453A			458367	458368	451260
(35)	650cc Manxman and 750cc N15CS	1968	42453A			458367	458368	451260
	TRIUMPH							
(36)	650cc TR6 Trophy	1960	42298D		458658	458876	458876	451260
(37)	650cc TR6 Trophy (later), TR6SS Trophy, T110 Tiger and T120 Bonneville	1960-62	42344E		458658	458876	458876	451260
(38)	650cc TR6, TR6SS, T110 and T120 – alternative Competition	1960-62	42350H	455734	458658	458876	458876	451260
(39)	650cc TR6, TR6SS, T110 and T120 – alternative Competition	1960-62	42368D	455734	458658	458876	458876	451260
(40)	650cc TR6SS Trophy and T120 Bonneville	1962	42368D	455734	458658	458876	458876	451260

*Alternative Ignition
†'Meteor' for sidecar use only

MAGNETO AND PARTS
(REFER ALSO TO PAGES 26 and 27)

	NUT, H.T. CABLE	COVER CONTACT BREAKER	CONTACT BREAKER	CONTACT SET	SPRINGS, ACUATING	BRUSH AND SPRING, C.B. EARTHING	CONTROL PARTS, SET	RUBBER COVER, CONTROL SET	CAM	SPRING AND PIN, C.B. COVER	PLATE, C.B. HOUSING
(1)	410600	459199	492854	54440888			459305	454475	459321		459313
(2)	410600	459205	492854	54440888			459305	454475	459321		459313
(3)	410600	460061	460051	484098			463107	454475	493178		464317
(4)	410600	459037	492854	54440888			458364	454475	458725		459036
(5)	410600	458619	470534	470609	470688	470537	463107	454475	458725	458613	458726
(6)	410600	458619	492854	54440888			463107	454475	458725	458613	458726
(7)	410600	459269	492854	54440888					459130		54440096
(8)											
(9)	410600	459199	492854	54440888			459305	454475	459321		459313
(10)	455791	459199	470924			470537	457117	454475			
(11)	410600	459269	470534	470609	470688	470537			459130		54440096
(12)	410600	459269	492854	54440888					459130		54440096
(13)	410600	459269	492854	54440888			463107	454475	458725		54440090
(14)	410600	459269	492854	54440888			463107	454475	458725		54440090
(15)				458053					458020		
(16)	410600	460061	460051	484098			463107	454475	493178	451315	464317
(17)				458053					458021		
(18)	410600	458619	470533	470608	470688	470537	463107	454475	458855	458613	493747
(19)	410600	458619	493836	54440887			463107	454475	458855	458613	493747
(20)	410600	458619	493836	54440887					459131	458613	459105
(21)	410600	459199	492854	54440888			459305	454475	459321		459313
(22)	410600	459205	492854	54440888			459305	454475	459321		459313
(23)	410600	460061	460051	484098			463107	454475	493178		464317
(24)	410600	459037	492854	54440888			458364	454475	458725		459036
(25)	410600	458619	470534	470609	470688	470537	463107	454475	458725	458613	458726
(26)	410600	458619	492854	54440888			463107	454475	458725	458613	458726
(27)	410600	459269	492854	54440888					459130		54440096
(28)	410600	460051	460051	484098			463107	454475	493178		464317
(29)	410600	459205	470534 *492854	470609 *54440888	470688	470537	459305	454475	458725		459271
(30)	410600	459205	492854	54440888	455190				459130		493716
(31)	410600	459205	492854	54440888	455190				459130		493716
(32)	410600	458619	492854	54440888	455190				459130		
(33)	410600	459269	492854	54440888	455190				459130		
(34)	410600	459269	492854	54440888					459130		54440096
(35)	410600	459269	492854	54440888					459130		54440096
(36)	410600	459269	492854	54440888			492195	454475	458725		459271
(37)	410600	459269	492854	54440888					459130		493716
(38)	410600	459205	492854	54440888			459305	454475	458725		459271
(39)	410600	459205	492854	54440888	455190				459130		493716
(40)	410600	459205	492854	54440888	455190				459130		493716
			*Later	*Later							

BREAKDOWN OF PARTS CONTINUED ON PAGES 26 AND 27

MAGNETO AND PARTS (Continued)
(REFER ALSO TO PAGES 24 and 25)

1960-1968 SPECIFICATIONS

	MAKE AND MODEL	YEAR	MAGNETO	CUP, INSULATING, BEARING	NUT, SHAFT	ARMATURE	SLIP RING	CONDENSER
	A.J.S.							
(1)	250cc 14CS, Scorpion, 350cc 16C Experts and 500cc 18CS Southerner	1960-66	42347E	463932	170109	493176	464277	454415
(2)	250cc 14 Sapphire, 14S Sapphire Sports and 500cc 18 Statesman	1960-63	42371B	463932	170109	493176	464277	454415
(3)	500cc 18 Statesman	1964-65	42272B	451379	170109	454385	454496	454415
(4)	650cc 31 De Luxe	1960-61	42230E	451379	170109	459004	455361	458339
(5)	650cc 31CS Swift Sports and 31CSR Hurricane	1960	42264B	451379	170109	459004	455361	458339
(6)	650cc 31 Swift (optional) 31CS Swift Sports and 31CSR Hurricane – later	1960-66	42264D	451379	170109	459004	455361	458339
(7)	750cc 33 and 33CS	1965-67	42453A	451379		459004	455361	458339
	B.S.A							
(8)	350cc B32 and 500cc B34 – Gold Star Models	1960-63	46048A	See Magdyno				
(9)	350cc B32 and 500cc B34 – Competition Models	1960-63	42348E	563932	170109	493176	464277	454415
(10)	350cc B32 and 500cc B34 – Racing Models	1960-63	42123M		170109			
(11)	500cc A7 and 650cc A10 Golden Flash	1960-61	42379A			459004	455361	458339
(12)	500cc A7 and 650cc A10 Golden Flash – later	1961-63	42379B/D	451379		459004	455361	458339
(13)	500cc A7 Shooting Star and 650cc A10 Super Rocket	1960	42380B	451379		459004	455361	458339
(14)	500cc A7 Shooting Star 650cc A10 Super Rocket and Rocket Gold Star	1961-63	42413A	451379		459004	455361	458339
	ENFIELD							
(15)	500cc Bullet	1960-61	*42330B	451378	170109			492342
(16)	500 Fury Scrambler	1961	42272B	451379	170109	454385	454496	454415
(17)	700cc Super Meteor	1960	†42364D	451378	170109			492342
(18)	700cc Constellation	1960	42369A	451379	170109	459142	454479	458339
(19)	700cc Constellation (later) and 736cc Interceptor	1960-63	42369A	451379	170109	459142	454497	458339
(20)	736cc Interceptor	1964-66	42442A	451379	170109	459142	454497	458339
	MATCHLESS							
(21)	250cc G2CS Messenger 350cc G3c Maestro and G80CS Marksman	1960-68	42347E	463932	170109	493176	464277	454415
(22)	250cc G2 Monitor, G2S Monitor Sports and 500cc G80 Major	1960-63	42371B	463932	170109	493176	464277	454415
(23)	500cc G80 Major	1964-65	42272B	451379	170109	454385	454496	454415
(24)	650cc G12 De Luxe	1960-61	42230E	451379	170109	459004	455361	458339
(25)	650cc G12CS Majestic Sports and G12CSR Monarch	1960	42264B	451379	170109	459004	455361	458339
(26)	650cc G12 Majestic (optional), G12CS Majestic Sports and G12CSR Monarch (later)	1960-66	42264D	451379	170109	459004	455361	458339
(27)	750cc G15, G15 Mk II, G15CS and G15CSR	1965-68	42453A	451379		459004	455361	458339
	NORTON							
(28)	350cc 50 Mk II and 500cc ES2 Mk II (optional)	1965	42272B	451379	170109	454385	454496	454415
(29)	500cc Dominator 88SS, Nomad, 600cc Dominator 99SS and Nomad	1960-62	42350F/H	463932	170109	459376	456727	
(30)	650cc Dominator 650SS, Manxman and 750cc Atlas	1961-62	42368D	463932	170109	459376	456727	
(31)	500cc Dominator 88SS, 650cc Dominator 650SS, Manxman and 750cc Atlas	1963-64	42368D	463932	170109	459376	456727	
(32)	750cc Atlas (first 150 machines built in 1964)	1964	42452A	451379	170109	459004	455361	458339
(33)	500cc Dominator 88SS, 650cc Dominator 650SS, Manxman and 750cc Atlas – later	1964	42379B/D	451379		459004	455361	458339
(34)	500cc Dominator 88SS, 650cc Dominator 650SS, Manxman, 750cc Atlas, N15 and N15CS	1965-67	42453A	451379		459004	455361	458339
(35)	650cc Manxman and 750cc N15CS	1968	42453A	451379		459004	455361	458339
	TRIUMPH							
(36)	650cc TR6 Trophy	1960	42298D	463932	170109	459004	455361	458339
(37)	650cc TR6 Trophy (later), TR6SS Trophy, T110 Tiger and T120 Bonneville	1960-62	42344E	463932	170109	459004	455361	458339
(38)	650cc TR6, TR6SS, T110 and T120 – alternative Competition	1960-62	42350H	463932	170109	459376	456727	
(39)	650cc TR6, TR6SS, T110 and T120 – alternative Competition	1960-62	42368D	463932	170109	459376	456727	
(40)	650cc TR6SS Trophy and T120 Bonneville	1963	42368D	463932	170109	459376	456727	

*Alternative Ignition
†'Meteor' for sidecar use only.

(CONTINUATION OF PAGES 24 AND 25)

MAGNETO AND PARTS (Continued)
(REFER ALSO TO PAGES 24 and 25)

	BEARING, C.B. END	BEARING, DRIVE END	BRUSH, SPRING & HOLDER, EARTHING	BRUSH & SPRING, EARTHING	SPRING AND PIN, PICK-UP	OIL SEAL	CUP, INSUL., D.E. BEARING	BODY GASKET	SUNDRY PARTS SET	AUTO-ADVANCE UNIT	SPRINGS SET A.-A. UNIT
(1)	189294	189294	455191	455190		459033	463932		454697		
(2)	189294	189294	455191	455190		459033	463932		454697		
(3)	189291	189291	455191	455190			451379		454697		
(4)	189291	189244	455191	455190	458370	459002	459005		458675		
(5)	189291	189244	455191	455190	458370	459002	459005		458675		
(6)	189291	189244	455191	455190	458370	459002	459005		458675		
(7)	189291	189244	455191	455190	458370	459002	459005		458675	47508D	498157/S
(8)											
(9)	189294	189294	455191	455190		459033	463932		454697		
(10)			455191	455190					458869		
(11)	189291	189244	455191	455190	458370	459002	459005		458675	47503E	498157/S
(12)	189291	189244	455191	455190	458370	459002	459005		458675	47503E	498157/S
(13)	189291	189244	455191	455190	458370	459002	459005		458675		
(14)	189291	189244	455191	455190	458370	459002	459005		458675		
(15)	189289	189291				459033	451379	458194	490663	47556B	498157/S
(16)	189291	189291	455191	455190		458375	451379		454697		
(17)	189289	189291				459033	451379	458194	490665	47553B	498157/S
(18)	189291	189244	455191	455190	458370	459002	459005		458675		
(19)	189291	189244	455191	455190	458370	459002	459005		458675		
(20)	189291	189244	455191	455190	458370	459002	459005		458675	47613A	498157/S
(21)	189294	189294	455191	455190		459033	463932		454697		
(22)	189294	189294	455191	455190		459033	463932		454697		
(23)	189291	189291	455191	455190			451379		454697		
(24)	189291	189244	455191	455190	458370	459002	459005		458675		
(25)	189291	189244	455191	455190	458370	459002	459005		458675		
(26)	189291	189244	455191	455190	458370	459002	459005		458675		
(27)	189291	189244	455191	455190	458370	459002	459005		458675	47508D	498157
(28)	189291	189291	455191	455190			451379		454697		
(29)	189294	189244	455191	455190		459002	459005		458675		
(30)	189294	189244	455191	455190		459002	459005		458675	47508D	498157/S
(31)	189294	189244	455191	455190		459002	459005		458675	47508D	498157/S
(32)	189291	189244	455191	455190	458370	459002	459005		458675	47508D	498157/S
(33)	189291	189244	455191	455190	458370	459002	459005		458675	47508D	498157/S
(34)	189291	189244	455191	455190	458370	459002	459005		458675	47508D	498157
(35)	189291	189244	455191	455190	458370	459002	459005		458675	47508D	498157
(36)	189294	189244	455191	455190		459002	459005		458675		
(37)	189294	189244	455191	455190		459002	459005		458675		
(38)	189294	189244	455191	455190		459002	459005		458675		
(39)	189294	189244	455191	455190		459002	459005		458675	47502B	498157/S
(40)	189294	189244	455191	455190		459002	459005		458675	47502B	498157/S

BREAKDOWN OF PARTS CONTINUED ON PAGES 24 AND 25

GENERATOR AND PARTS

1960-1968 SPECIFICATIONS

MAKE AND MODEL	YEAR	GENERATOR	BRUSH SET	BRACKET, C.E.	BEARING, C.E.	INSUL. PLATE WITH Brushgear	BRUSH SPRING	C.E. COVER	BEARING, D.E.
A.J.S.									
(1) 350cc 16C 'Experts'	1960-61	20038B	200737	200713/S	189210	200911	220197	200924	189307
(2) 350cc 16C 'Experts'	1962-63	20038B	200737	200713/S	189210	200911	220197	200924	189307
(3) 650cc 31 De Luxe, 31CS and 31CSR	1960	20035A	200737	200910	189210	200911	220197	200924	189307
(4) 650cc 31 De Luxe, 31CS and 31CSR – later	1960-61	20035A	200737	200910	189210	200911	220197	200924	189307
(5) 650cc 31 De Luxe, 31CS and 31CSR	1962	20035A	200737	200910	189210	200911	220197	200924	189307
B.S.A									
(6) 350cc B32 and 500cc B34 Gold Star and Competition	1960	20034B	200737	200713/S	189210	200911	220197	200923	189307
(7) 350cc B32 and 500cc B34 Gold Star and Competition	1961-63	20034B	200737	200713/S	189210	200911	220197	200923	189307
(8) 500cc A7, 650cc A10 and 650cc Rocket Gold Star	1960	20036A	200737	200713/S	189210	200911	220197	200924	189307
(9) 500cc A7, 650cc A10 and 650cc Rocket Gold Star	1961-63	20036A	200737	200713/S	189210	200911	220197	200924	189307
MATCHLESS									
(10) 350cc G3C 'Maestro'	1960-61	20038B	200737	200713/S	189210	200911	220197	200924	189307
(11) 350cc G3C 'Maestro'	1962-63	20038B	200737	200713/S	189210	200911	220197	200924	189307
(12) 650cc G12 De Luxe, G12CS, G12CSR	1960	20035A	200737	200910	189210	200911	220197	200924	189307
(13) 650cc G12 De Luxe, G12CS and G12CSR – later	1960-61	20035A	200737	200910	189210	200911	220197	200924	189307
(14) 650cc G12 De Luxe, G12CS, G12CSR and G50CSR	1962	20035A	200737	200910	189210	200911	220197	200924	189307

GENERATOR AND PARTS — CONTROL BOX AND PARTS

	BRACKET, D.E.	OIL SEAL	SHAFT NUT SCREW, GEAR RETAINING	GEAR, DRIVING	ARMATURE	FIELD COIL	THROUGH BOLT	SUNDRY PARTS SET	CONTROL BOX	COVER
(1)	200805				200802	200188	200227	200806	37232	54380803
(2)	200805				200802	200188	200227	200806	37232	54381655
(3)	200760	188614	111704		200712	200731	200732	200806	37252	226546
(4)	200760	188614	111704		200712	200731	200732	200806	37252	54380805
(5)	200760	188614	111704		200712	200731	200732	200806	37232	54381655
(6)	200912		111704	454495	200754	200731	200732	200806	37225	54380806
(7)	200912		111704	454495	200754	200731	200732	200806	37221	54380803 *54381655
(8)	200382	*200378	111704		200752	200731	200732	200806	37225	54380806
(9)	200382	*200378	111704		200752	200731	200732	200806	37221	54380803 *54381655
(10)	200805				200802	200188	200227	200806	37232	54380803
(11)	200805				200802	200188	200227	200806	37232	54381655
(12)	200760	188614	111704		200712	200731	200732	200806	37252	226546
(13)	200760	188614	111704		200712	200731	200732	200806	37252	54380805
(14)	200760	188614	111704		200712	200731	200732	200806	37232	54381655

*Oil thrower

*-later

MAGDYNO AND PARTS

1960-1968 SPECIFICATIONS		MAGDYNO	GENER-ATOR	MAGNETO PORTION	STRAP ASSEMBLY	PICK-UP	NUT, MOULDED	COVER, CONTACT BREAKER	CONTACT BREAKER	CONTACT SET
MAKE AND MODEL	YEAR									
B.S.A (1) 350cc B32 and 500cc B34 – Gold Star and Competition Models	1960-63	46048A	20034A	464247	460056	463066	410600	460061	460051	484098

STARTER AND PARTS

1960-1968 SPECIFICATIONS		STARTER	BOLT	BRUSH SET	C.E. BRACKET	BEARING BUSH	THRUST PAD
MAKE AND MODEL	YEAR						
NORTON (1) 397cc 'Electra'	1963-65	26509A	54254142	54252361	54254127	261233	542252180

MAGDYNO AND PARTS

	JUMP RING	CAM	CONTROL PARTS SET	SPRING PIN	END PLATE, C.B.	CUP, INSUL., C.E. & D.E.	BEARING, C.B. & D.E.	END PLATE, D.E.	GEAR SET	ARMATURE	SLIP RING	BRUSH, SPRING & HOLDER	BRUSH & SPRING
(1)	455347	493181	463107	463899	464255	*451379 †463932	*189291 †189294	463989	462863	464205	454496	455191	455190
						*Contact breaker end †Drive end	*Contact breaker end †Drive end						

STARTER AND PARTS

	LINER INSUL.	PLATE, BRUSH BOXES	SPRING SET	BRACKET, D.E.	BEARING BUSH	ARMATURE	FIELD COIL	FIELD TERMINAL	SUNDRY PARTS, SET	SWITCH OR SOLENOID
(1)	54251728	54251740	54252360	54255890	54255274	54255281	54251462	54251387	54252417	76464E

DISTRIBUTOR AND PARTS AND CONTACT BREAKER UNIT AND PARTS

1960-1968 SPECIFICATIONS

NOTE: Do not order Contact Breaker Unit part numbers shown in brackets, as they are serviced separately by the Auto Advance unit and the Contact Breaker Assembly.

	MAKE AND MODEL	YEAR	Distributor	Contact Breaker Unit	Auto Advance Unit	Contact Breaker Assembly	Contact Set	Condenser or Capacitor	Base, Contact Breaker	A.A. Springs	A.A. Weights	Shaft & Action Plate
	A.J.S.											
(1)	500cc 18 Statesman	1960-63		47579			420196	54413002	465958	416136	415729	425733
(2)	500cc 18 Statesman	1964-66		(47615A)*	54416405	54415296	54415803	425377	425370	54416405		
(3)	650cc 31 Swift	1960-63	40589D				425219	54410823	423113	54412732		
(4)	650cc 31 Swift	1964-66		(47617B)*	54417710	425379	54415803	425377	425370	54413020		
	B.S.A.											
(5)	250cc C15 Star	1960	40621B				421106	421327		54412731	421056/S	421054
(6)	250cc C15T and C15S Competition	1960	40669A/B				421106	421327		54412018	421056/S	421054
(7)	250cc C15T and C15S Competition – later	1960-62	40702A				421106	421327		54412018	421056/S	421054
(8)	250cc C15 Star and Sports Star and 350cc B40 Star	1961-62	40701A				421106	421327		54412731	421056/S	421054
(9)	250cc C15 Star and Sports Star and 350cc B40 Star and Sports Star	1963-64	40867A				421106	421327		54412018	421056	421054
(10)	250cc C15T and C15S Competition	1963-64	40868A				421106	421327		54412018	421056	421054
(11)	250cc C15 Star and Sports Star and 350cc B40 Star and Sports Star	1965		(47621A)*	54416405	54415296	54415803	425377	425370	54415640		
(12)	250cc C15 Star and Sports Star and 350cc B40 Star and Sports Star – later	1965		(47615B)*	54416405	54415296	54415803	425377	425370	54415640		
(13)	250cc C15T, C15S Competition and 350cc B40 E.S.	1965		(47603D)*	54415748	54415296	54415803	425377	425370	54415640		
(14)	250cc C15 Star, C15S Sportsman, Starfire 250 and 350cc B40 Star	1966-67		(47621D)*	54416405	54415296	54415803	425377	425370	54415640		
(15)	250cc Starfire 250	1968		(47635)*	54419653	54419645	54419827	54441582		54415638		
(16)	441cc B44 Victor Special	1966-67		(47624A)*	54417989	54415296	54415803	425377	425370	54417992		
(17)	441cc Shooting Star 441	1966-67		(47621D)*	54416405	54415296	54415803	425377	425370	54415640		
(18)	441cc Shooting Star and Victor Special	1968		(47635)*	54419653	54419645	54419827	54441582		54415638		
(19)	500cc A50 Star and 650cc A65 Star	1963		(47583)*	54440028	425379	54415803	425377	425370	54413020		
(20)	500cc A50 Star	1964		(47583B)*	54440028	425379	54415803	425377	425370	54413020		
(21)	500cc A50 Star – later	1964		(47583B)*	54440028	425379	54415803	425377	425370	54413020		
(22)	500cc A50 Cyclone	1964		(47612A)*	54416150	425379	54415803	425377	425370	54415641		
(23)	500cc A50 Star, A50 Cyclone, Cyclone Clubman and Cyclone Road	1965		(47583B)*	54440028	425379	54415803	425377	425370	54413020		
(24)	500cc A50CC Cyclone Competition	1965		(47612A)*	54446150	425379	54415803	425377	425370	54415641		
(25)	500cc A50 Royal Star	1966-67		(47583F)*	54440028	425379	54415803	425377	425370	54413020		
(26)	500cc A50 Royal Star	1968		(47630)*	54419344	54419097	54419827	*54418527 †54418528		54415642		
(27)	500cc A50 Wasp	1966-67		(47612E)*	54416150	425379	54415803	425377	425370	54415641		
(28)	650cc A65 Star (6V), Lightning, Lightning Clubman, Lightning Rocket (6V), Thunderbolt Rocket and Rocket (6V)	1964-65		(47583B)*	54440028	425379	54415803	425377	425370	54413020		
(29)	650cc A65 Star (12V), Rocket (12V) and Lightning Rocket (12V)	1964-65		(47583B)	54440028	425379	54415803	425377	425370	54413020		
(30)	650cc A65 Spitfire Hornet	1964-65		(47612A)*	54416150	425379	54415803	425377	425370	54415641		
(31)	650cc A65 Spitfire Hornet	1966-67		(47612E)*	54416150	425379	54415803	425377	425370	54415641		

*Capacitors (2 off).
†Cover for capacitor pack.

DISTRIBUTOR AND PARTS AND CONTACT BREAKER UNIT AND PARTS | IGNITION COIL

	Cam	Clamping Plate	Cover	Brush & Spring	Grommet, Rubber	Clip, Cable Contact	Rotor Arm	Terminal	Bush, Terminal Insul.	Clip, Cover	Bush or Bearing	Ignition Coil
(1)	465939											45077B
(2)												45152B
(3)	425284	420151	425049	404435	421554	421863	423486	123154	423110	424158	425498	45077E *45152B
(4)												45110A
(5)	421047		421112					405314	421109	421561		45077B
(6)	54412727		421112					405314	421109	421561		45112A
(7)	54412727		54411737					405314	421109			45112A
(8)	421047		54411737					405314	421109	421561		45077E
(9)	421206		54411737					405314	421109			45077E *45152A
(10)	54415051		54411737					405314	421109			45112A/D *45149B
(11)												45152B
(12)												45152B
(13)												45149B
(14)												45152B
(15)												45110D
(16)												45149A
(17)												45149A
(18)												45110D
(19)												45077E *45152A
(20)												45077E
(21)												45152B
(22)												45149B (right hand) 45150A (left hand)
(23)												45152B
(24)												45149B (right hand) 45150A (left hand)
(25)												45110D
(26)												45110D
(27)												45149B (right hand) 45150A (left hand)
(28)												45152B
(29)												45110A
(30)												45149B (right hand) 45150A (left hand)
(31)												45149B (right hand) 45150A (left hand)

*later
†Suitable Lucas replacement.

DISTRIBUTOR AND PARTS AND CONTACT BREAKER UNIT AND PARTS (CONTINUED)

1960-1968 SPECIFICATIONS

NOTE: Do not order Contact Breaker Unit part numbers shown in brackets, as they are serviced separately by the Auto Advance unit and the Contact Breaker Assembly.

	MAKE AND MODEL	YEAR	Distributor	Contact Breaker Unit	Auto Advance Unit	Contact Breaker Assembly	Contact Set	Condenser or Capacitor	Base, Contact Breaker	A.A. Springs	A.A. Weights	Shaft & Action Plate
	B.S.A. (Continued)											
(1)	650cc A65 Thunderbolt, Lightning and Spitfire Mk II Special	1966-67		(47583F)*	54440028	425379	54415803	425377	425370	54413020		
(2)	650cc A65 Firebird, Thunderbolt, Lightning and Spitfire Mk IV	1968		(47630)*	54419344	54419097	54419827	*54418527 †54418528		54415642		
	ENFIELD											
(3)	500cc Bullet	1960	40466B				421106	421327		422655/S	421056/S	422584
(4)	500cc Bullet	1961-62	40712A				421106	421327		422655/S	421056/S	422584
(5)	500cc Meteor Minor, Sports Twin, 700cc Super Meteor and Constellation (6 volt)	1960-63	40610A				425219	54410823	423113	54412732	421056/S	425596
(6)	700cc Constellation (12 volt)	1963	40610A				425219	54410823	423113	54412732	421056/S	425596
(7)	736cc Interceptor	1967-68		(47628)*	54419167	425379	54415803	425377	425370	54413020		
	MATCHLESS											
(8)	500cc G80 Major	1960-63		47579			420196	54413002	465958	416136	415729	425733
(9)	500cc G80 Major	1964-66		(47615A)*	54416405	54415296	54415803	425377	425370	54415640		
(10)	650cc G12 Swift	1960-63	40589D				425219	54410823	423113	54412732	421056/S	425444
(11)	650cc G12 Swift	1964-66		(47617B)*	54417710	425379	54415803	425377	425370	54413020		
(12)	750cc Commando	1968		(47643)*	54419340	54419097	54419827	*54420128 †54418528		54415642		
	NORTON											
(13)	350cc 50 Mk II	1965		(47618A/B)*	54416286	54415296	54415803	425377	425370	54413020		
(14)	500cc ES2	1960-63	40628B				425219	54410823	423113	425398/S	421056/S	544105
(15)	500cc ES2 MkII			(47615A)*	54416405	54415296	54415803	425377	425370	54415640		
(16)	500cc, 600cc and 650cc Dominator Models	1960-63	40589D				425219	54410823	423113	54412732	421056/S	425444
(17)	750cc P.11	1967-68		(47627A)*	54418910	425379	54415803	425377	425370	54415642		
(18)	750cc P.11 (later), Atlas and Commando	1968		(47643)*	54419340	54419097	54419827	*54420128 †54418528		54415642		
	TRIUMPH											
(19)	200cc T20 and T20SH Tiger Cub	1960-62	40699A				421106	421327		54412731	421056/S	421054
(20)	200cc T20S Tiger Cub	1960	40664B				421106	421327		421415	421056/S	421054
(21)	200cc T20S (later), T20SC, T20SL, T20SR, T20SS and T20T Tiger Cub	1960-62	40700A				421106	421327		421415	421056/S	421054
(22)	200cc T20SC and T20SR Tiger Cub	1963		(47603B)*	54415748	54415296	54415803	425377	425370	54415640		
(23)	200cc T20 and T20SH Tiger Cub	1963-64		(47604B)*	54415658	54415296	54415803	425377	425370	425768		
(24)	200 T20 and T20SH Tiger Cub – later	1964-65		(47615A)*	54416405	54415296	54415803	425377	425370	54415640		
(25)	200cc T20R and T20S	1964		(47603B)*	54415748	54415296	54415803	425377	425370	54415640		
(26)	200cc T20 and T20S (later), T20SM, T20SS and TS20 Tiger Cub	1964-65		(47603B)*	54415748	54415296	54415803	425377	425370	54415640		
(27)	200cc T20, T20SH and T20SR Tiger Cub	1966-67		(47621A/D)*	54416405	54415296	54415803	425377	425370	54415640		
(28)	200cc T20SM Tiger Cub	1966-67		(47624A)*	54417989	54415296	54415803	425377	425370	54417992		
(29)	200cc T20TR Tiger Cub	1966		(47625A)*	54415748	54415296	54415803	425377	425370	54415640		

*Capacitors (2 off).
†Cover for capacitor pack.

DISTRIBUTOR AND PARTS AND CONTACT BREAKER UNIT AND PARTS (CONTINUED) | IGNITION COIL

	Cam	Clamping Plate	Cover	Brush & Spring	Grommet, Rubber	Clip, Cable Contact	Rotor Arm	Terminal	Bush, Terminal Insul.	Clip, Cover	Bush or Bearing	Ignition Coil
(1)												45110D
(2)												45110D
(3)	422659	406105	421112					405314	421109	421561		45077E
(4)	422659	406105	54411737					605314	421109			45077E
(5)	425598	420151	425049	404435	421554	421863	423486	123154	423110	424158	432121	45077E *45152B
(6)	425598	420151	425049	404435	421554	421863	423486	123154	423110	424158	432121	45110A/D
(7)												45110D
(8)	465939											45077B
(9)												45152B
(10)	425284	420151	425049	404435	421554	421863	423486	123154	423110	424158	425498	45077E *45152B
(11)												45110A/D
(12)												†45110A
(13)												45152B
(14)	425746	420151	424151					123154	423110	424158	423121	45077E *45152B
(15)												45152B
(16)	425284	420151	425049	404435	421554	421863	423486	123154	423110	424158	425498	45077E *45152B
(17)												
(18)												†45110A
(19)	423759		54411737					405314	421109			45077E
(20)	54411249		421112					405314	421109	421561		45112B
(21)	54411249		54411737					405314	421109			45112B
(22)												45112D / 45149B
(23)												45152A
(24)												45152B
(25)												45112D
(26)												45149B
(27)												45152B
(28)												45149B (right hand) / 45150A (left hand)
(29)												45149B (right hand) / 45150A (left hand)

*later
†Suitable Lucas replacement.

DISTRIBUTOR AND PARTS AND CONTACT BREAKER UNIT AND PARTS (CONTINUED)

1960-1968 SPECIFICATIONS

MAKE AND MODEL	YEAR	Distributor	Contact Breaker Unit	Auto Advance Unit	Contact Breaker Assembly	Contact Set	Condenser or Capacitor	Base, Contact Breaker	A.A. Springs	A.A. Weights	Shaft & Action Plate
*NOTE: Do not order Contact Breaker Unit part numbers shown in brackets, as they are serviced separately by the Auto Advance unit and the Contact Breaker Assembly											
TRIUMPH (continued)											
(1) 500cc 5TA Speed Twin, TR5A-R, T100A Tiger and T100SS Tiger	1960-62	40646B				425219	54410823	423113	54420895	421056/S	424967
(2) 500cc 5TA Speed Twin	1963	40646B				425219	54410823	423113	54410895	421056/S	424967
(3) 500cc 5TA Speed Twin	1964		(47606B)*	54415752	425379	54415803	425377	425370	425105		
(4) 500cc 5TA Speed Twin — later	1964-65		(47605B)*	54415750	425379	54415803	425377	425370	54415642		
(5) 500cc T100A Tiger (E.T. condition) and TR5A-C and TR5A-R (E.T. condition)	1961	40710B				425219	54441582	54410498	422655/S	421056/S	424967
(6) 500cc T100SC Tiger	1962	40820A				425219	54441582	54410498	422655/S	421056/S	424967
(7) 500cc T100C and T100SC Tiger	1963-67		(47602B)*	54415746	425379	54415803	425377	425370	54415641		
(8) 500cc T100 and T100SS Tiger	1963-64		(47606B)*	54415752	425379	54415803	425377	425370	425105		
(9) 500cc T100 Tiger	1964-65		(47605B)*	54415750	425379	54415803	425377	425370	54415642		
(10) 500cc 5TA Speed Twin, T100 and T100R Tiger	1966-67		(47605B)*	54415750	425379	54415803	425377	425370	54415642		
(11) 500cc T100C Tiger and T100R Daytona Super Sports	1968		(47632A)*	54419340	54419097	54419827	*54418527 †54418528		54415642		
(12) 650cc 6T Thunderbird	1960-62	40690B				425219	54410823	423113	425398/S	421056/S	425444
(13) 650cc 6T Thunderbird	1963		(47605B)*	54415750	425379	54415803	425377	425370	54415642		
(14) 650cc 6T Thunderbird	1964-67		(47605B)*	54415750	425379	54415803	425377	425370	54415642		
(15) 650cc TR6 and TR6SS Trophy and T120 Bonneville	1963-65		(47605B)*	54415750	425379	54415803	425377	425370	54415642		
(16) 650cc TR6 and TR6R Trophy and T120 and T120R Bonneville	1966-67		(47605B)*	54415750	425379	54415803	425377	425370	54415642		
(17) 650cc TR6C Trophy and T120TT Special	1966-67		(47602D)*	54415746	425379	54415803	425377	425370	54415641		
(18) 650cc TR6C, TR6R Trophy and T120R Bonneville	1968		(47632A)*	54419340	54419097	54419827	*54418527 †54418528		54415642		

*Capacitors (2 off)
†Cover for capacitor pack.

DISTRIBUTOR AND PARTS AND CONTACT BREAKER UNIT AND PARTS (CONTINUED) | IGNITION COIL

	Cam	Clamping Plate	Cover	Brush & Spring	Grommet, Rubber	Clip, Cable Contact	Rotor Arm	Terminal	Bush, Terminal Insul.	Clip, Cover	Bush or Bearing	Ignition Coil
(1)	424972		425049	404435	421554	421863	423486	123154	423110	424158	423571	45077E
(2)	424972		425049	404435	421554	421863	423486	123154	423110	424158	423571	45077E
(3)												45152A
(4)												45152A
(5)	54412359		425049	404435	421554	421863	423486	123154	423110	424158	423571	45112D
(6)	54414381		425049	404435	421554	421863	423486	123154	423110	424158	423571	45112D
(7)												45149B (right hand) 45150A (left hand)
(8)												45152A
(9)												45152B
(10)												45152B
(11)												45110D
(12)	425284		425049	404435	421554	421863	423486	123154	423110	424158	425498	45077E
(13)												45152A
(14)												45110D
(15)												45152A
(16)												45110D
(17)												45149B (right hand) 45150A (left hand)
(18)												45110D

*later
†Suitable Lucas replacement.

ALTERNATOR AND PARTS | CAPACITOR | DIODE, ZENER

1960-1968 SPECIFICATIONS

	MAKE AND MODEL	YEAR	ROTOR	STATOR	CABLE CLIP	RECTIFIER	CAPACITOR	DIODE, ZENER
	Note: Alternators serviced by Rotor and Stator							
	A.J.S.							
(1)	500cc 18 Statesman, 18CS Southerner and 650cc 31 Swift	1960-61	423506	47122A	54211509	47132B		
(2)	500cc 18 Statesman and 650cc 31 Swift	1962	423506	47122	54211509	47132		
(3)	500cc 18CS Southerner, 650cc 31CS and 31CSR Hurricane	1962	423506	47154	54211509	47132		
(4)	500cc 18 Statesman and 650cc 31 Swift	1963	423506	47122A	54211509	49072A		
(5)	500cc 18 Statesman and 650cc 31 Swift – later	1963	54213901	47164A	54210167	49072A		
(6)	500cc 18CS Southerner 650cc 31CS and 31CSR Hurricane	1963	423506	47154A	54211509	49072A		
(7)	500cc 18CS Southerner, 650cc 31CS and 31CSR Hurricane – later	1963-66	54213901	47162A	54210167	49072A		49345A
(8)	500cc 18 Statesman and 650cc 31 Swift	1964	54213901	47181	54210167	49072A		49345A
(9)	650cc 31 Swift (magneto ignition)	1964	54213901	47162A	54210167	49072A		49345A
(10)	500cc 18 Statesman, 650cc 31 Swift, 750cc 33 and 33CS	1965-67	54213901	47162A	54210167	49072A		49345A
	B.S.A.							
(11)	250cc C15 Star	1960-61	466125	47134A	54210167	47132B		
(12)	250cc C15S and C15T Competition (less stop light)	1969-61	466125	47176	54210167	47132B		
(13)	250cc C15S and C15T Competition (with stop light)	1960-61	466125	47177A	54210167	47132B		
(14)	250cc C15 Star and SS80 Sports Star	1962	54213903	47161	54210167	47132		
(15)	250cc C15S and C15T Competition	1962	54213901	47173	54210167	47132		
(16)	250cc C15 Star and SS80 Sports Star	1963-65	54213903	47161	54213907	49072A		
(17)	250cc C15S and C15T Competition and 350cc B40ES	1963-65	54213901	47173	54310167			
(18)	250cc C15 Star and C15S Sportsman	1966-67	54213903	47161	54213907	49072A		
(19)	250cc Starfire 250 and 441cc Shooting Star 441	1967	54213901	47162A	54210167	49072A		
(20)	250cc Starfire 250 and 441cc Shooting Star 441	1968	54213901	47204A		49072A		49345A
(21)	350cc B40 Star	1960-62	423506	47134	54210167	47132		
(22)	350cc B40 Star and SS90 Sports Star	1963	54213901	47164A	54210167	49072A		
(23)	350cc B40 Star and SS90 Sports Star	1964	54213901	47181	54210167	49072A		
(24)	350cc B40 Star and SS90 Sports Star	1965-66	54213901	47162	54210167	49072A		
(25)	441cc B44 Victor Special	1966	54213901	47173	54210167	49072A		
(26)	441cc B44 Victor Special	1967	54213901	47197A				
(27)	441cc B44 Victor Special	1968	54213901	47204A		49072A	54170009 †54483156	49345A
(28)	500cc A50 Star and 650cc A65 Star	1962	54213901	47164	54210167	47132		
(29)	500cc A50 Star and 650cc A65 Star	1963	54213901	47164A	54210167	49072A		
(30)	500cc A50 Star 650cc A65 Star, Rocket and Lightning Rocket	1964	54213901	47181	54210167	49072A		*49345A
(31)	500cc A50 Cyclone and 650cc A65 Spitfire Hornet	1964	54213901	47188	54211644			
(32)	500cc A50 Star, Royal Star, Cyclone, Cyclone Clubman and Cyclone Road	1965-67	54213901	47162	54210167	49072A		*49345A
(33)	500cc A50 Cyclone Competition, Wasp and 650cc A65 Spitfire Hornet	1965-66	54213901	47188	54211644	~~49072A~~		
(34)	650cc A65 Star, Lightning, Lightning Clubman, Thunderbolt, Thunderbolt Rocket, Rocket and Spitfire Mk II Special	1965-67	54213901	47162	54210167	49072A		*49345A
(35)	500cc A50 Royal Star, 650cc A65 Thunderbolt, Lightning and Spitfire Mk IV	1968	54213901	47204A		49072A		49345A
(36)	650cc A65 Hornet	1967	54213901	47197A				
(37)	650cc A65 Firebird	1968	54213901	47204A		49072A		49345A
	ENFIELD							
(38)	500cc and 700cc – All models	1960-62	423506	469427	54211509	47132		
(39)	500cc Sports Twin 700cc Constellation and 736cc Interceptor	1963	423506	469427	54211509	49072A		
(40)	500cc Sports Twin, 700cc Constellation and 736cc Interceptor – later	1963	54213901	47164A	54210167	49072A		
(41)	736cc Interceptor	1964	54213901	47181	54210167	49072A		*49345A
(42)	736cc Interceptor	1965-67	54213901	47162	54210167	49072A		*49345A
(43)	736cc Interceptor	1968	54213901	47205A		49072A		49345A
	MATCHLESS							
(44)	500cc G80 Major G80CS Marksman and 650cc G12 Majestic	1960-61	423506	47122A	54211509	47132B		
(45)	500cc G80 Major and 650cc G12 Majestic	1962	423506	47122	54211509	47132		
(46)	500cc G80CS Marksman, 650cc G12CS and G12CSR Monarch	1962	423506	47154	54211509	47132		
(47)	500cc G80 Major and 650cc G12 Majestic	1963	423506	47122A	54211509	49072A		
(48)	500cc G80 Major and 650cc G12 Majestic – later	1963	54213901	47164A	54210167	49072A		
(49)	500cc G80CS Marksman 650cc G12CS and G12CSR Monarch	1963	423506	47154A	54211509	49072A		
(50)	500cc G80CS Marksman, 650cc G12CS and G12CSR Monarch – later	1963-68	54213901	47162A	54210167	49072A		49345A
							*P.11 †Mounting Spring	*12 volt machines

ALTERNATOR AND PARTS (Continued)

1960-1968 SPECIFICATIONS

	MAKE AND MODEL	YEAR	ROTOR	STATOR	CABLE CLIP	RECTIFIER	CAPACITOR	DIODE, ZENER
	Note: Alternators serviced by Rotor and Stator							
	MATCHLESS (Continued)							
(1)	500cc G80 Major and 650cc G12 Majestic	1964	54213901	47181	54210167	49072A		49345A
(2)	650cc G12 Majestic (magneto ignition)	1964	54213901	47162A	54210167	49072A		49345A
(3)	500cc G80 Major 650cc G12 Majestic, 750cc G15, G15CS, G15CSR and G15 Mk II	1965-67	54213901	47162A	54210167	49072A		49345A
(4)	750cc Commando	1968	54213901	47205A		49072A	54170009 †54483156	49345A
	NORTON							
(5)	350cc 50 Mk II	1965	54213901	47162	54210167	49072A		
(6)	500cc Nomad and 600cc Nomad	1960	423506	468678	54210167	47132B		
(7)	500cc ES2, Dominator 88 and 600cc Dominator 99	1960-61	423506	47122A	54211509	47132B		
(8)	500cc ES2, Dominator 88 and 600cc Dominator 99	1962	54213901	47181	54211644	47132		
(9)	500cc Dominator 88SS and 600cc Dominator 99SS	1962	54213901	47182	54210167	47132		
(10)	500cc ES2 and Dominator 88	1963	54213901	47181A	54210167	49072A		
(11)	500cc Dominator 88 – later	1963	54213901	47164A	54210167	49072A		
(12)	500 Dominator 88SS	1963	54213901	47162A		49072A		
(13)	500cc ES2 Mk II and Dominator 88SS	1964-67	54213901	47162A	54210167	49072A		49345A
(14)	650cc Manxman, Dominator 650 and Dominator 650SS	1961-62	423506	468678	54210167	47132		
(15)	650cc Dominator 650	1963	54213901	47181A	54210167	49072A		
(16)	650cc Dominator 650 – later	1963	54213901	47164A	54210167	49072A		
(17)	650cc Dominator 650SS	1963	54213901	47162A		49072A		
(18)	750cc Atlas	1962	54213901	47162		47132		
(19)	650cc Manxman and 750cc Atlas	1963	54213901	47183A	54210167	49072A		
(20)	650cc Manxman, Dominator 650SS, 750cc Atlas, N15, N15CS, P.11	1964-67	54213901	47162	54210167	49072A	*54170009 *†54483155	49345A
(21)	650cc Manxman, 750cc P.11	1968	54213901	47162	54210167	49072A	*54170009 †54483155	49345A
(22)	750cc P.11 – later	1968	54213901	47204A		49072A	54170009 †54483156	49345A
(23)	750cc Atlas and Commando	1968	54213901	47205A		49072A	54170009 †54483156	49345A
	TRIUMPH							
(24)	200cc T20 Tiger Cub	1960-62	466124	47137	54210167	47132		
(25)	200cc T20 Tiger Cub – later	1962	54213903	47161	54210167	47132		
(26)	200cc T20 and T20SH Tiger Cub	1963-67	54213903	47161	54213907	49072A		
(27)	200cc T20S Tiger Cub	1962	466124	47175A	54210167	47132B		
(28)	200cc T20S, T20SC, T20SL, T20SR, T20SS and T20T Tiger Cub	1961-62	466124	47177	54210167	47132		
(29)	200cc T20SC, T20SR and T20SS Tiger Cub – later	1962	54213901	47173	54210167	47132		
(30)	200cc T20R, T20S, T20SC and T20SR Tiger Cub	1963-64	54213901	47173	54210167			
(31)	200cc T20SM, T20SS, TR20, TS20 and T20TR Tiger Cub	1965-66	54212006	47173	54210167			
(32)	200cc T20SR Tiger Cub	1966-67	54213903	47161	54213907	49072A		
(33)	200cc T20SM and T20TR	1967	54213901	47173B	54210167			
(34)	200cc T20SM and T20TR – later	1967	54213901	47197A	54210167			
(35)	500cc 5TA Speed Twin	1960-61	423506	468973	54210167	47132B		
(36)	500cc TR100A Tiger	1960	54211596	47149A		47132B		
(37)	500cc TR5A-R and T100A Tiger	1961	54211596	468973		47132B		
(38)	500cc TR5A-R and T100A Tiger (E.T. condition)	1961	54211596	47149A		47132B		
(39)	500cc TR5A-C	1961	54211596	47165A				
(40)	500cc 5TA Speed Twin and T100SS Tiger	1962	54213901	47164	54210167	47132		
(41)	500cc 5TA Speed Twin and T100SS Tiger	1963	54213901	47164	54210167	49072A		
(42)	500cc 5TA Speed Twin and T100 Tiger	1964	54213901	47181	54210167	49072A		
(43)	500cc 5TA Speed Twin, T100, T100R and T100S Tiger and T100T Daytona Tiger	1965-67	54213901	47162	54210167	49072A		*49345A
(44)	500cc T100, T100R and T100S Tiger and T100T Daytona Tiger – later	1967	54213901	47204A	54210167	49072A		*49345A
(45)	500cc T100SC Tiger	1962-63	54214272	47173	54210167			
(46)	500cc T100C, T100SC Tiger, 650cc TR6C, Trophy and T120TT Special	1963-67	54213901	47188A	54211644			*49345A
(47)	500cc T100C Tiger 650cc TR6C Trophy and T120TT Special – later	1967	54213901	47197A	54210167			*49345A
(48)	500cc T100C Tiger and 650cc TR6C Trophy	1968	54213901	47204A		49072A	54170009 †54483156	49345A
(49)	500cc T100R Daytona Super Sports	1968	54213901	47204A		49072A	54170009 ‡54483156 ‡‡54953455	49345A

*P. 11
‡Optional fitment
†Mounting Spring
‡Conversion cable (required when fitting capacitor)

*12 volt machines

ALTERNATOR AND PARTS (Continued)

1960-1968 SPECIFICATIONS

	MAKE AND MODEL	YEAR	ROTOR	STATOR	CABLE CLIP	RECTIFIER	CAPACITOR	DIODE, ZENER
	TRIUMPH (Continued)							
(1)	650cc 6T Thunderbird	1960-61	423506	469427	54211509	47132B		
(2)	650cc 6T Thunderbird	1962	54213901	47164	54210167	47132		
(3)	650cc 6T Thunderbird	1963	54213901	47164	54210167	49072A		
(4)	650cc TR6 Trophy, T110 Tiger and T120 Bonneville	1960	423506	47134A	54210167	47132B		
(5)	650cc TR6 Trophy, T110 Tiger and T120 Bonneville	1961	423506	47178A	54210167	47132B		
(6)	650cc TR6SS Trophy and T120 Bonneville	1962	54213901	47183	54210167	47132		
(7)	650cc TR6SS Trophy and T120 Bonneville	1963	54213901	47183	54210167	49072A		
(8)	650cc 6T Thunderbird, TR6, TR6R Trophy, T120 and T120R Bonneville	1964-67	54213901	47162	54210167	49072A		*49345A
(9)	650cc TR6, TR6R Trophy, T120 and T120R Bonneville – later	1967	54213901	47204A	54210167	49072A		*49345A
(10)	650cc TR6R Trophy and T120R Daytona Super Sports	1968	54213901	47204A		49072A	‡54170009 ‡†54483156 ‡:54953455	49345A

*P.11
‡ Optional fitment
† Mounting Spring
: Conversion cable (required when fitting capacitor)

*12 volt machines

GIRLING EQUIPMENT (Suspension Units and Parts)

1960-1968 SPECIFICATIONS

	MAKE AND MODEL	YEAR	SUSPENSION UNIT	FERRULE TUBE AND BUSH ASSEMBLY	SPRING	OUTER DIRT SHIELD
	A.J.S.					
(1)	250cc 14 Sapphire, 14S Sapphire Sports and 350cc 16C Experts	1960-65	64053911	64533658	9054/277	64533025A
(2)	250cc 14CS Scorpion	1960-62	64054000	64533658	9054/58	64533025A
(3)	500cc 18 Statesman	1960-61	64053049	64533645 (top) 9054/307-8 (sleeves) 9054/219 (bottom)	9054/312	64533389A
(4)	500cc 18 Statesman	1962	64054389	64533645 (top) 64533658 (bottom)	9054/277	64533025A
(5)	500cc 18 Statesman – later	1962-63	64054391	64533645 (top) 64533658 (bottom)	9054/277	9054/151H
(6)	500cc 18 Statesman – later	1963-65	64054493	64533645	64532786	64533025A
(7)	500cc 18CS Southerner	1960-61	64053046	64533645 (top) 9054/307-8 (sleeves) 9054/219 (bottom)	9054/58	64533389A
(8)	500cc 18CS Southerner	1962-64	64054393	64533645 (top) 64533658 (bottom)	9054/277	9054/151H
(9)	500cc 18CS Southerner	1965-66	64054392	64533645 (top) 64533658 (bottom)	9054/277	64533025A
(10)	650cc 31 Swift and 31 DeLuxe	1960-61	64053049	64533645 (top) 9054/307-8 (sleeves) 9054/219 (bottom)	9054/312	64533389A
(11)	650cc 31CS	1960-61	64053046	64533645 (top) 9054/307-8 (sleeves) 9054/219 (bottom)	9054/58	64533389A
(12)	650cc 31CSR Hurricane	1960-61	64054353	64533645 (top) 9054/307-8 (sleeves) 9054/219 (bottom)	9054/280	64533025H
(13)	650cc 31 Swift	1962-64	64054391	64533645 (top) 64533658 (bottom)	9054/277	9054/151H
(14)	650cc 31CSR Hurricane	1962-64	64054393	64533645 (top) 64533658 (bottom)	9054/277	9054/151H
(15)	650cc 31CS	1962	64054392	64533645 (top) 64533658 (bottom)	9054/277	64533025A
(16)	650cc 31 Swift, 31 Tourer and 31CSR Hurricane	1965-66	64054493	64533645	64532786	64533025A
(17)	750cc 33	1965-67	64054493	64533645	64532786	64533025A
(18)	750cc 33CS	1965	64054493	64533645	64532786	64533025A
(19)	750cc 33CS and 33CSR	1966-67	64054590	64533645	9054/94	64532981A
	B.S.A.					
(20)	175cc D.7 Bantam Major, Super and DeLuxe and D.10 Bantam Silver and Supreme	1960-68	64053983	64533645 (top) 64533654 (bottom)		
(21)	175cc D.10 and D.14 Bantam Sports	1967-68	64054911	64533645 (top) 64533654 (bottom)	64543553	
(22)	175cc D.10 and D.14 Bantam Bushman	1967-68	64054957	64533645 (top) 64533654 (bottom)		
(23)	250cc C15 Star	1960-62	64053974	64533645 (top) 64533654 (bottom)		
(24)	250cc C15 Star	1963-67	64053973	64533645 (top) 64533654 (bottom)		
(25)	250cc C15SS80 Sports Star	1962-65	64054445	64533645 (top) 64533654 (bottom)	9054/58	64533025A
(26)	250cc C15S Scrambles	1960-62	64054127	64533645 (top) 64533654 (bottom)		
(27)	250cc C15S Scrambles	1963-65	64054545	64533645 (top) 64533654 (bottom)	64541530	64541113
(28)	250cc C15T Competition	1960-62	64054129	64533645 (top) 64533654 (bottom)		
(29)	250cc C15T Competition	1963-65	64054445	64533645 (top) 64533654 (bottom)	9054/58	64533025A
(30)	250cc Starfire 250	1967-68	64054927	64533645 (top) 64533654 (bottom)	64543626	64532778
(31)	350cc B32 Gold Star and Competition	1960-62	64053804	64533645	9054/59	64533025A
(32)	350cc B40 Star	1961	64053983	64533645 (top) 64533654 (bottom)		
(33)	350cc B40 Star Competition	1961	64054445	64533645 (top) 64533654 (bottom)	9054/58	64533025A
(34)	350cc B40 Star	1962	64054129	64533645 (top) 64533654 (bottom)		
(35)	350cc B40 Star	1963-66	64054404	64533645 (top) 64533654 (bottom)		
(36)	350cc B40SS90 Sports Star and B40 E.S.	1963-65	64054445	64533645 (top) 64533654 (bottom)	9054/58	64533025A
(37)	441cc B44 Victor Special	1966-67	64054545	64533645 (top) 64533654 (bottom)	64541530	64541113
(38)	441cc B44 Victor Special	1968	64054927	64533645 (top) 64533654 (bottom)	64543626	64532778
(39)	441cc B44 Shooting Star	1967-68	64054927	64533645 (top) 64533654 (bottom)	64543626	64532778

GIRLING EQUIPMENT (Suspension Units and Parts)
(Continued)
1960-1968 SPECIFICATIONS

	MAKE AND MODEL	YEAR	SUSPENSION UNIT	FERRULE TUBE AND BUSH ASSEMBLY	SPRING	OUTER DIRT SHEILD
	B.S.A. (continued)					
(1)	500cc B34 Gold Star and Competition	1960-63	64053804	64533645	9054/59	64533025A
(2)	500cc A7	1960-62	64053805	64533645	9054/70	64533025A
(3)	500cc A7SS Shooting Star	1960-62	64053806	64533645	9054/63	64533025A
(4)	500cc A50 Star and Royal Star	1962-66	64054475	64533645	9054/94	64532981A
(5)	500cc A50 Royal Star	1967	64054970	64533645	64543735	64532778
(6)	500cc A50 Royal Star	1968	64054376	64533645	64541530	64532778
(7)	500cc A50, A50C Cyclone, A50CC Cyclone Clubman, A502C Cyclone Road and A502CC Cyclone Competition	1964-65	64054475	64533645	9054/94	64532981A
(8)	500cc A50 Wasp	1966	64054475	64533645	9054/94	64532981A
(9)	650cc A10 Super Rocket, A10 Golden Flash and Rocket Gold Star	1960-63	64053805	64533645	9054/70	64533025A
(10)	650cc A65 Star, A65L2 Lightning Rocket and A65R Rocket	1962-65	64054475	64533645	9054/94	64532981A
(11)	650cc A652L, Lightning Rocket (later), A65L Lightning, A65LC Lightning Clubman, A65 Thunderbolt, A651T Thunderbolt Rocket, A65 Spitfire MK II, MK III and MK IV	1965-67	64054970	64533645	64543735	64532778
(12)	650cc A65 Thunderbolt	1968	64054376	64533645	64541530	64532778
(13)	650cc A65 Lightning and Spitfire MK IV	1968	64054970	64533645	64543735	64532778
(14)	650cc A65 and A65SPH Spitfire Hornet	1964	64054475	64533645	9054/94	64532981A
(15)	650cc A65 and A65SPH Spitfire Hornet	1965	64054970	64533645	64543735	64532778
(16)	650cc A65 and A65SPH Spitfire Hornet	1966	64052009	64533645	64542879	64532778
(17)	650cc A65 Hornet and Firebird	1967-68	64052009	64533645	64542879	64532778
	ENFIELD					
(18)	250cc Hounds Crusader	1960	64053811	64533652	9054/312	645330752
(19)	250cc Hounds Crusader	1961	64054090	64533652	9054/277	64533075A
(20)	250cc Hounds Crusader – later	1961	64054502	64533652	9054/312	64532778
(21)	500cc Meteor Minor, Meteor Minor DeLuxe, Meteor Minor Sports and Sports Twin	1960-63	64054090	64533652	9054/277	64533075A
(22)	750cc Interceptor	1963-67	64054604	64533652	64539963	64533025A
(23)	750cc Interceptor	1968	64054968	64533652	64539963	64533032A
	MATCHLESS					
(24)	250cc G2 Monitor, G2S Monitor Sports	1960-62	64053911	64533658	9054/277	64533025A
(25)	250cc G2CS Messenger	1960-62	64054000	64533658	9054/58	64533025A
(26)	350cc G3C Maestro	1960-62	64053911	64533658	9054/277	64533025A
(27)	350cc G3C Maestro	1963-65	64054493	64533645	64532786	64533025A
(28)	500cc G80 Major and G80CS Marksman	1960-61	64053046	64533645 (top) 9054/307-8 (sleeves) 9054/219 (bottom)	9054/58	64533389A
(29)	500cc G80 Major	1962-64	64054391	64533645 (top) 64533658 (bottom)	9054/277	9054/151H
(30)	500cc G80CS Marksman	1962-64	64054393	64533645 (top) 64533658 (bottom)	9054/277	9054/151H
(31)	500cc G80 Major	1965	64054493	64533645	64532786	64533025A
(32)	500cc G80CS Marksman	1965-68	64054392	64533645 (top) 64533658 (bottom)	9054/277	64533025A
(33)	500cc G85CS	1966-67	64054834	64533645	64541530	64533025A
(34)	650cc G12 Majestic and G12 DeLuxe	1960-61	64053049	64533645 (top) 9054/307-8 (sleeves) 9054/219 (bottom)	9054/312	64533389A
(35)	650cc G12 Majestic	1962-64	64054391	64533645 (top) 64533658 (bottom)	9054/277	9054/151H
(36)	650cc G12CSR Monarch	1960-64	64054393	64533645 (top) 64533658 (bottom)	9054/277	9054/151H
(37)	650cc G12CS	1960-62	64053046	64533645 (top) 9054/307-8 (sleeves) 9054/219 (bottom)	9054/58	64533389A
(38)	650cc G12 Majestic and G12CSR Monarch	1965-66	64054493	64533645	64532786	64533025A
(39)	750cc G15 and G15 MK II	1964-68	64054493	64533645	64532786	64533025A
(40)	750cc G15CS	1964	64054493	64533645	64532786	64533025A
(41)	750cc G15CS	1965-67	64054590	64533645	9054/94	64532981A
(42)	750cc G15CS	1968	64054392	64533645 64533658	9054/277	64533025A
(43)	750cc G15CSR	1966-68	64054763	64533645	64543114	64533025A
(44)	750cc P.11	1968	64054590	64533645	9054/94	64532981A

GIRLING EQUIPMENT (Suspension Units and Parts)
(Continued)
1960-1968 SPECIFICATIONS

	MAKE AND MODEL	YEAR	SUSPENSION UNIT	FERRULE TUBE AND BUSH ASSEMBLY	SPRING	OUTER DIRT SHIELD
	NORTON					
(1)	350cc Navigator	1961-64	64054359	64533656	9054/58	64533025AV
(2)	350cc Navigator	1965	64053939	64533656	9054/58	64533025A
(3)	350cc 50 – MK II	1965	64054423	64533656 (top) 64533651 (bottom)	9054/277	64533025A
(4)	400cc Electra	1963-64	64054423	64533656 (top) 64533651 (bottom)	9054/277	64533025A
(5)	400cc Electra – later	1963-64	64053939	64533656	9054/58	64533025A
(6)	400cc Electra	1965	64054423	64533656 (top) 64533651 (bottom)	9054/277	64533025A
(7)	500cc E.S.2	1960	64054313	64533651	SA193/57	64533025A
(8)	500cc E.S.2	1961-63	64054174	64533656 (top) 64533651 (bottom)	9054/277	64533025AV
(9)	500cc E.S.2. MK II	1965	64054423	64533656 (top) 64533651 (bottom)	9054/277	64533025A
(10)	500cc Nomad	1960	64053875	64533651	64532786	9054/151A
(11)	500cc Dominator 88	1960	64053075	64533651	9054/70	64533025F
(12)	500cc Dominator 88	1961	64054174	64533656 (top) 64533651 (bottom)	9054/277	64533025AV
(13)	500cc Dominator 88	1962-63	64054423	64533656 (top) 64533651 (bottom)	9054/277	64533025A
(14)	500cc Dominator 88SS Sports Special	1962-64	64053075	64533651	9054/70	64533025F
(15)	500cc Dominator 88SS Sports Special	1965-66	64054423	64533656 (top) 64533651 (bottom)	9054/277	64533025A
(16)	600cc Nomad	1960	64054313	64533651	SA193/57	64533025A
(17)	600cc Dominator 99	1960	64053075	64533651	9054/70	64533025F
(18)	600cc Dominator 99	1961	64054174	64533656 (top) 64533651 (bottom)	9054/277	64533025AV
(19)	600cc Dominator 99 and 99SS Sports Special	1962	64054423	64533656 (top) 64533651 (bottom)	9054/277	64533025A
(20)	650cc Dominator 650 and 650SS Sports Special	1962-64	64053075	64533651	9054/70	64533025F
(21)	650cc Dominator 650SS Sports Special	1965-67	64054423	64533656 (top) 64533651 (bottom)	9054/277	64533025A
(22)	650cc Manxman	1961-68	64053080	64533651	9054/66	64532778
(23)	750cc Atlas	1963-68	64054423	64533656 (top) 64533651 (bottom)	9054/277	64533025A
(24)	750cc N-15 and N1-15	1965-67	64054493	64533645	64532786	64533025A
(25)	750cc N15CS and P.11	1965-68	64054590	64533645	9054/94	64532981A
	TRIUMPH					
(26)	200cc T20, T20S, T20SC, T20SH, T20SL, T20SR and T20T Tiger Cub	1960-67	64053112	64533645 (top) 64533654 (bottom)		
(27)	200cc T20C Tiger Cub Competition	1960-61	64053112	64533645 (top) 64533654 (bottom)		
(28)	200cc T20C Tiger Cub Competition	1962	64054441	64533645 (top) 64533654 (bottom)	9054/317	64533025A
(29)	200cc T20C Tiger Cub Competition, (later), T20SS and TS20 Tiger Cub	1962-66	64054523	64533645 (top) 64533654 (bottom)	9054/312	64533075A
(30)	200cc T20R, TR20 and T20SM Tiger Cub	1965-67	64054441	64533645 (top) 64533654 (bottom)	9054/317	64533025A
(31)	200cc T20 SuperCub	1968	64053983	64533645 (top) 64533654 (bottom)		
(32)	500cc 5TA Speed Twin	1960-62	64053946	64533645	64539963	64533025AW
(33)	500cc 5TA Speed Twin	1963-66	64053946	64533645	64539963	64533025A
(34)	500cc T100, T100A, T100S, T100SS Tiger and T100T Daytona Tiger	1960-67	64053946	64533645	64539963	64533025A
(35)	500cc TR5A-C, TR5A-R, T100C, T100SC, T100R Tiger and T100R Daytona Super Sports	1962-68	64054164	64533645	9054/280	9054/151A
(36)	650cc – All models (except 6T Thunderbird)	1960-68	64054164	64533645	9054/280	9054/151A
(37)	650cc 6T Thunderbird	1960	64053093	64533645	9054/280	64533025A
(38)	650cc 6T Thunderbird – later	1960-62	64054164	64533645	9054/280	9054/151A
(39)	650cc 6T Thunderbird – later	1962-66	64054506	64533645	SA235/5	64533025A

NOTES

INDEX

	Page No.
MOTORCYCLE EQUIPMENT SPECIFICATIONS 1969-1977.	4-21
HEADLAMPS	23-24-25
STOPLAMPS	23-25
TURN SIGNAL LAMPS	25
STARTER	23
SPARK PLUGS	26
GIRLING SUSPENSION UNITS	26-27
BULBS	28
WIRING HARNESS CONNECTORS	29
STATOR GUIDE - MISC. INFO	30
ACCESSORIES	31

Lucas Service

MOTORCYCLE APPLICATIONS

BSA		Page No.
B25 Starfire	1969-70	4
B25SS Goldstar	1971-72	4
B25T Victor Trail	1971-72	4
B44 Victor Special	1969-70	4-5
A50 Royal Star	1969-70	
B50MX Victor	1971-72	5
B50MX	1973-on	5
B50SS Goldstar	1971-72	4
B50T Victor Trail	1971-72	
A65FS Firebird Scrambler	1969-71	5-6
A65L Lighting	1969-on	6
A65T Thunderbolt	1969-on	6
A75R Rocket 3	1969-on	7

BULTACO		
All with Lucas	1969-on	7

CZ		
Enduro 250	1976	8

DALESMAN		
All with Lucas	1970-On	8

ENFIELD		
Interceptor III	1969-70	8

LAVERDA		
All with Lucas	1973-on	8

MZ		
TS150 Street Model	1974	9
TS250 Street Model	1974	9

MONTESA		
King Scorpion	1972-73	9

MOTO-GUZZI		
All with Lucas Turn Signals		9

NORTON		Page No.
Commando, All Models	1969	9-10
Commando All Models	1970	10
Commando All Models	1971-72	10-11
Commando All Models	1973-74	11
Commando All Models	1975-on	11-12
John Player Special	1975	11-12

RICKMAN		
125 Enduro	1971	13
125 Six Days	1973	13

TRIUMPH		
TR5MX See BSA B50MX	1973-on	5
TR25W Trophy	1969-70	13
T25T Trail Blazer	1971	13-14
TR25SS Blazer	1971	13-14
T100C Trophy	1971-72	14
T100R Daytona	1971-72	14
T100R Daytona	1973-on	15
TR5T Trophy Trail	1973-74	15
TR6C Trophy	1969-70	16
T100C Trophy	1969-70	14
TR6R Tiger	1969-70	16
T100R Daytona	1969-70	16
T120R Bonneville	1969-70	16
TR6C Trophy	1971-72	16-17
TR6R Tiger	1971-72	16-17
T120R Bonneville	1971-72	16-17
TRX75 Hurricane	1973	17
T140V Bonneville Twin	1973-75	18
TR7RV Tiger	1973-75	18
T140V Bonneville Twin	1976-77	18
TR7RV Tiger	1976-77	18
T150 Trident	1969-70	19
T150T Trident	1971-72	19
T150V Trident	1973-on	20
T160 Trident Electric Start	1975-76	20-21

BSA B25 Starfire (250 cc Single Cyl.) 1969-70

Unit	Year	Part No.	Page	Unit	Year	Part No.	Page
ALTERNATOR				LAMPS (Cont'd.)			
Rotor	1969-70	54213901		Rim	1969-70	553248	
Stator	1969-70	47205		Bulb Main	1969-70	446	
AMMETER	1969-70	36403		Bulb Pilot	1969-70	989	
BATTERY	1969-70	PUZ5A		Bulb Warning	1969-70	281	
BULBHOLDER				Stop Tail Lamp Assembly	1969-70	53973	25
Instruments	1969-70	554710		Lens	1969-70	54577109	
Bulb	1969-70	643		Bulb	1969-70	384	
CONDENSER, IGNITION	1969-70	54441582		RECTIFIER	1969-70	49072	
COIL, IGNITION	1969-70	45223		REFLECTOR			
CONTACT BREAKER				Amber	1969-70	57162	
Plate Assembly	1969-70	54419645		Red	1969-70	57111	
Points Set	1969-70	54419827		SWITCHES			
Eccentric Adjustment Screw	1969-70	54419220		Ignition	1969-70	31899	
Auto Advance Assembly	1969-70	54419653		Lighting	1969-70	35710	
Auto Advance Springs	1969-70	54417992		Stop Rear	1969-70	34515	
LAMPS				WIRING HARNESS	1969-70	54957239	
Head Lamp Assembly	1969-70	59883	24	ZENER DIODE	1969-70	49345	
Light Unit	1969-70	516798					

BSA B25SS & B50SS Goldstar B25T & B50T Victor (250 cc & 500 cc Single Cyl.) 1971 on

Unit	Year	Part No.	Page	Unit	Year	Part No.	Page
ALTERNATOR				LAMPS (Cont'd.)			
Rotor	1971-on	54213901		Stop Lamp Assembly	1971-on	53973	25
Stator		47205		Lens		54577109	
BATTERY		PUZ5A		Bulb		380	
BULBHOLDER				Turn Signal Lamp (Less Stanchions)	1971-on	56147	25
Speedo & Tacho	1971-on	554710		Lens		54581638	
Bulb		643		Bulb		382	
CAPACITOR	1971-on	54170009		Stanchions		60600092	
Rubber Moulding		54422860		RECTIFIER		49072	
CONDENSER (IGNITION)	1971-on	54420128		REFLECTORS			
COIL	1971-on	45223		Amber		57160	
CONTACT BREAKER				Red		575189	
Plate Assy	1971-on	54419645		RUBBER MOULDING			
Points		54419827		(Electric Box)		54422860	
Adjustment Pin		54419220		SWITCHES			
Auto Advance		54423215		L.H. Dip-Horn	1971-on	54033666	
A.A. Springs		54417992		L.H. Casting, Lever Pivot	1971-on	54343791	
FLASHER UNIT	1972-on	35048		R.H. Cut-Out Turn Signal	1971-on	54033667	
Clip		54385091		R.H. Casting, Lever Pivot	1971-on	54343792	
Mounting Spring		54386637		Lighting	1971-on	31356	
FUSE HOLDER	1971-on	544190387		Master (Ignition)	1971-on	39784	
Fuse		188218		Stop		34815	
HORN	1971-on	70228		WIRING HARNESS			
LAMPS				Headlamp	1971	54959532	
Headlamp Assembly	1971-on	60262	24	Headlamp	1972-on	54960713	
Light Unit		54525272		Main	1971	54954980	
Rim		534343		Main	1972-on	54960721	
Bulb Main		370		Electric Box	1971	54959680	
Bulb Parking		989		Electric Box	1972-on	54960720	
Bulb Warning		281		ZENER DIODE	1971-on	49345	

BSA B44 Victor Special (441 cc Single Cyl.) 1969-70

Unit	Year	Part No.	Page	Unit	Year	Part No.	Page
ALTERNATOR				CONDENSER			
Rotor	1969-70	54213901		Ignition	1969-70	54441582	
Stator	1969-70	47205		COIL			
BATTERY	1969-70	PUZ5A		Ignition	1969-70	45223	
BULBHOLDER				CONTACT BREAKER			
Instruments	1969-70	554710		Complete C.B. Plate Assembly	1969-70	54419645	
Bulb	1969-70	643					

BSA B44 VICTOR SPECIAL (441cc Single Cyl.) 1969-70 (Cont'd.)

Unit	Year	Part No.	Page	Unit	Year	Part No.	Page
CONTACT BREAKER (Cont'd.)				**LAMPS (Cont'd.)**			
Points Set	1969-70	54419827		Bulb	1969-70	384	
Eccentric Adjustment Screw	1969-70	54419220		**RECTIFIER**	1969-70	49072	
Auto Advance Assembly	1969-70	54419653		**REFLECTORS**			
Auto Advance Springs	1969-70	54417992		Amber	1969-70	57162	
LAMPS				Red	1969-70	57111	
Head Lamp Assembly	1969-70	60037	24	**SWITCHES**			
Light Unit	1969-70	54524526		Ignition	1969-70	31899	
Rim	1969-70	534343		Horn Push	1969-70	76204	
Bulb Main	1969-70	446		Lighting	1969-70	35710	
Bulb Parking	1969-70	989		Stop Rear	1969-70	34815	
Bulb Warning	1969-70	281		**WIRING HARNESS**	1969-70	54955718	
Stop Tail Lamp Assembly	1969-70	53973	25	**ZENER DIODE**	1969-70	49345	
Lens	1969-70	54577109					

BSA B50 MX Victor With E.T. Ignition (500 cc Single Cyl.) 1971 on

Unit	Year	Part No.	Page	Unit	Year	Part No.	Page
ALTERNATOR				**CONTACT BREAKER**			
Rotor	1971-on	54213901		Assembly	1971-on	54419645	
Stator	1971-on	47226		Points Set	1971-on	54419827	
CONDENSER				Eccentric Adjustment Screw	1971-on	54419220	
Ignition	1971-on	54441582		Auto Advance Assembly	1971-on	54423215	
COIL				Auto Advance Springs	1971-on	54417992	
(E.T.)	1971-on	45149		**WIRING HARNESS**	1971-on	54959649	

BSA & TRIUMPH-BSA B50 MK Victor 500 cc 1973 on, Triumph TR5MX (1974) 500 cc (Capacitor Ignition Single Cyl.)

Unit	Year	Part No.	Page	Unit	Year	Part No.	Page
ALTERNATOR				**CONTACT BREAKER**			
Rotor	1973-on	54213901		Complete C.B. Plate Assembly	1973-on	54425458	
Stator	1973-on	47205		Points Set	1973-on	60600271	
CAPACITOR	1973-on	54170009		Eccentric Adjustment Screw	1973-on	54419220	
Mounting Spring	1973-on	54481355		Auto Advance Assembly	1973-on	54425655	
CONDENSER				Auto Advance Springs	1973-on	54417992	
Ignition	1971-on	54441582		**RECTIFIER**	1973-on	49072	
COIL				**WIRING HARNESS**	1973-on	54961599	
Ignition	1973-on	45223		**ZENER DIODE**	1973-on	49345	

BSA A65 Firebird Scrambler (650 cc Twin Cyl.) 1969 on

Unit	Year	Part No.	Page	Unit	Year	Part No.	Page
ALTERNATOR				**CONTACT BREAKER**			
Rotor	1969-on	54213901		Contact Breaker Assy.	1969-on	54419097	
Stator	1969-on	47205		Points	1969-on	54419827	
BATTERY	1969-on	PUZ5A		Adjustment Pin	1969-on	54419220	
BULBHOLDER				Auto Advance	1969-on	54419344	
Instruments	1969-70	554710		AA Springs	1969-on	54415642	
Bulb	1969-70	643		**FLASHER UNIT**	1971	35048	
Bulb Holder	1971	863511		Mounting Clip	1971	54385091	
Bulb	1971	643		Mounting Spring	1971	54386637	
CONDENSER				**FUSE HOLDER**	1971	54190387	
Ignition	1969-71	54420128		Fuse	1971	188218	
Cover	1969-71	54418528		**HORN**	1971	70216	
Base Plate	1969-71	54418526		**LAMPS**			
COIL				Head Lamp Assembly	1969	60037	24
IGNITION	1969-on	45223		Light Unit	1969	54524526	

BSA A65 Firebird Scrambler (650 cc Twin Cyl.) 1969 on (Cont'd.)

Unit	Year	Part No.	Page	Unit	Year	Part No.	Page
LAMPS (Cont'd.)				RECTIFIER	1969-71	49072	
Rim	1969	534343		REFLECTORS			
Bulb Main	1969	446		Amber	1969-70	57162	
Bulb Parking	1969	986		Red	1969-70	57111	
Bulb Warning	1969	281		Amber	1971	57183	
Head Lamp Assembly	1970	59965	24	Red	1971	575189	
Light Unit	1970	54524526		SWITCHES			
Rim	1970	534343		L.H. Dip-Horn	1971	54033666	
Bulb Main	1970	464		L.H. Casting Lever Pivot	1971	54340882	
Bulb Parking	1970	989		R.H. Cutout, Turnsignal	1971	54033667	
Bulb Warning	1970	281		R.H. Casting Lever Pivot	1971	54340883	
HeadLamp Assembly	1971	60262	24	Horn	1969-70	76204	
Light Unit	1971	54525272		Ignition	1969-70	31899	
Rim	1971	534343		Lighting	1969-70	35710	
Bulb Main	1971	370		Lighting	1971	31356	
Bulb Parking	1971	989		Master Ignition	1971	39565	
Bulb Warning	1971	281		Stop. Rear	1969-70	34448	
Stop Tail Lamp Assembly	1969-71	53973	25	Stop. Rear	1971	34815	
Lens	1969-71	54577109		WIRING HARNESS			
Bulb	1969-71	384		Main	1969-70	54955270	
Turn Signal Lamps (Less				Headlamp	1971	54959535	
Stanchions)	1971	56147	25	Main	1971	54959629	
Lens	1971	54581638		ZENER DIODE	1969-71	49345	
Bulb	1971	382					
Stanchions	1971	60600092					

BSA A65L Lightning (650 cc Twin Cyl.) A65T Thunderbolt (650 cc) A50R Royal Star (500 cc) 1969 on

Unit	Year	Part No.	Page	Unit	Year	Part No.	Page
ALTERNATOR				LAMPS (Cont'd.)			
Rotor	1969-on	54213901		Bulb Parking	1971-on	989	
Stator	1969-on	47205		Bulb Warning	1971-on	281	
AMMETER	1969-on	36403		Stop Tail Lamp Assembly	1969-on	53973	25
BATTERY	1969-on	PUZ5A		Lens	1969-on	54577109	
BULBHOLDER				Bulb	1969-on	380	
Instruments	1969-70	554710		Turn Signal Lamps (Less			
Bulb		643		Stanchions)	1972-on	56147	25
Bulbholder	1971-on	863511		Lens	1972-on	54581638	
Bulb		643		Bulb	1972-on	382	
CONDENSER IGNITION	1969-on	54420128		Stanchions		60600092	
Cover		54418528		RECTIFIER	1969-on	49072	
Base Plate		54418526		REFLECTORS			
COILS				Amber	1969-70	57183	
Ignition	1969-on	45223		Red	1969-70	575189	
CONTACT BREAKER				Amber	1971-on	57162	
Complete C.B. Plate Assembly	1969-on	54419097		Red	1971-on	57111	
Points Set	1969-on	54419827		RELAY			
Eccentric Adjustment Screw	1969-on	54419220		(Lightning) Horn	1969-70	33188	
Auto Advance Assembly	1969-on	54419344		SWITCHES			
Auto Advance Springs	1969-on	54415642		L.H. Dip-Horn	1971-72	54033666	
FLASHER UNIT	1971-on	35048		L.H. Casting Lever Half	1971-72	54340882	
Mounting Clip	1971-on	54385091		R.H. Cutout Turn Signal	1971-72	54036667	
Mounting Spring	1971-on	54386637		R.H. Casting Lever Half	1971-72	54340883	
FUSEHOLDER	1971-on	54190387		Ignition	1969-70	31899	
Fuse		188218		Ignition, Lighting Master	1971-on	39784	
HORN	1971-on	70216		Lighting	1969-70	35710	
LAMPS				Lighting	1971-on	31356	
Head Lamp Assembly	1969-70	59883	24	Stop Rear	1971-on	34448	
Light Unit	1969-70	516798		Stop Rear	1969-70	34815	
Rim	1969-70	553248		WIRING HARNESS			
Bulb Main	1969-70	446		Main	1969-70	54955258	
Bulb Parking	1969-70	989		Headlamp	1971	54959535	
Bulb Warning	1969-70	281		Headlamp	1972	54960711	
Head Lamp Assembly	1971-on	60260	24	Main	1971	54959629	
Light Unit	1971-on	54525927		Main	1972	54960710	
Rim	1971-on	553248		ZENER DIODE	1969-on	49345	
Bulb Main	1971-on	370					

BSA A75 Rocket 3 (750 cc Three Cyl., 1969 on

Unit	Year	Part No.	Page
ALTERNATOR			
Rotor	1969-on	54213902	
Stator	1969	47209	
Stator	1970-on	47205	
AMMETER	1969-on	36421	
BATTERY	1969-on	PUZ5A	
BULBHOLDER			
Instruments	1969	554743	
Bulb	1969	989	
Bulbholder	1970	554710	
Bulb	1970	643	
Bulbholder	1971-72	863511	
Bulb	1971-72	643	
CONDENSER			
Ignition	1969-on	54420128	
Rubber Cover	1969-on	54418528	
Base Plate	1969-on	54418526	
COIL			
Ignition	1969-on	45223	
CONTACT BREAKER			
Complete C.B. Breaker Assembly	1969-on	54419327	
Points Set	1969-on	54419828	
Adjustment Screw	1969-on	54419220	
Auto Advance Assembly	1969-on	54419867	
Auto Advance Springs	1969-on	54417992	
FLASHER UNIT	1971-on	35048	
Mounting Clip	1971-on	54385091	
Mounting Spring	1971-on	54386637	
FUSE HOLDER	1971-on	54190387	
Fuse	1971-on	188218	
HORN	1971-72	70216	
LAMPS			
Headlamp Assembly	1969-70	59892	24
Light Unit	1969-70	516798	
Rim	1969-70	553248	
Bulb Main	1969-70	446	
Bulb Parking	1969-70	989	
Headlamp Assembly	1971-on	60260	24
Light Unit	1971-on	54525927	
Rim	1971-on	553248	
Bulb Main	1971-on	370	
Bulb Parking	1971-on	989	
Bulb Warning	1971-on	281	
Stop Tail Lamp Assembly	1969-on	53973	25

Unit	Year	Part No.	Page
LAMPS (Cont'd.)			
Lens	1969-on	54577109	
Bulb	1969-on	380	
Turn Signal Lamp (Less Stanchions)	1971-on	56147	25
Lens	1971-on	54581638	
Bulb	1971-on	382	
Stanchions			
Front	1971-on	60600091	
Rear	1971-on	60600092	
RECTIFIER	1969-on	49072	
REFLECTOR			
Amber	1969-70	57161	
Red	1969-70	57111	
Amber	1971-72	57160	
Red	1971-72	575189	
RELAY			
Horn	1969-70	33188	
SWITCHES			
L.H. Dip-Horn Switch	1971-on	54033666	
L.H. Casting Lever Half	1971-on	54343791	
R.H. Cut-Out, Turn Signal Switch	1971-on	54033667	
R.H. Casting Lever Half	1971-on	54343792	
Engine Stop	1969-70	35835	
Horn Switch & Dip	1969-70	31563	
Ignition	1969-70	31899	
Ignition	1971-on	39784	
Lighting	1969-70	31788	
Lighting	1971-on	31356	
Stop Light Rear	1969-on	34815	
WARNING LIGHTS			
Amber	1969-on	54363453	
Green	1969-on	54363455	
Red	1969-on	54363454	
Bulbholder	1969-on	54955043	
Bulb	1969-on	281	
WIRING HARNESS			
Main	1969	54954246	
Main	1970	54958880	
Head Lamp	1971	54959640	
Main	1971	54959638	
Headlamp	1972-on	54960712	
Main	1972-on	54960717	
ZENER DIODE	1969-on	49345	

BULTACO 250 cc (Fitted With Lucas Lamps) 1969 on

Unit	Year	Part No.	Page
LAMPS			
Head Lamp Assembly	1969-72	60067	24
Light Unit	1969-72	54524526	
Rim	1969-72	534343	
Bulb Main	1969-72	403	
Bulb Parking	1969-72	951	
Bulb Warning	1969-72	282	
Head Lamp Assembly	1973-on	60289	24
Light Unit	1973-on	54524526	
Rim	1973-on	534343	
Bulb Main	1973-on	403	
Bulb, Parking	1973-on	951	
Bulb, Warning	1973-on	282	
Stop Lamp Assembly	1969-72	53972	25
Lens	1969-72	54577109	
Bulb	1969-72	384	
Stop Lamp Assembly	1973-on	56512	25
Lens		54584930	
Bulb		384	

Unit	Year	Part No.	Page
REFLECTORS			
Amber	1969-72	57162	
Red	1969-72	57111	
Amber	1973-on	57183	
Red	1973-on	57079	
SWITCHES			
Engine-Stop	1969	76204	
Horn Push and Dip	1969	31563	
Lighting	1969	31780	

CZ Enduro 250 (250 cc Single Cyl.) 1976

Unit	Year	Part No.	Page	Unit	Year	Part No.	Page
LAMPS				**LAMPS (Cont'd.)**			
*Head Lamp Assembly	1976	60835	25	Bulb	1976	384	
Light Unit	1976	54525927		Turn Signal Lamps (Less Mounting			
Rim	1976	553248		Brackets or Stanchions)	1976	56606	25
Bulb, Main	1976	403		Lens	1976	54581638	
Bulb, Parking	1976	293		Bulb (Order Seperate)	1976	317	
Stop Lamp Assembly	1976	56754	25	**SWITCH**			
Lens	1976	54584930		Turnsignal, Horn-Dip	1976	30707	

* Assembly serviced by vehicle manufacturer

DALESMAN Models Fitted with Lucas Lamps 1970 on

Unit	Year	Part No.	Page	Unit	Year	Part No.	Page
HORN	1970-on	70196		**LAMPS (Cont'd.)**			
LAMPS				Lens	1970-on	54577109	
Head Lamp Assembly	1970-on	60327	24	Bulb	1970-on	384	
Light Unit	1970-on	54523513		**REFLECTOR**			
Rim	1970-on	534343		Amber	1970-on	57183	
Bulb, Main	1970-on	312		Red	1970-on	57079	
Bulb, Parking	1970-on	951		**SWITCH**			
Bulb, Warning	1970-on	282	25	Lighting	1970-on	31356	
Stop Lamp Assembly	1970-on	53972					

ENFIELD Interceptor SERIES II (750cc) 1969-70

Unit	Year	Part No.	Page	Unit	Year	Part No.	Page
ALTERNATOR				**LAMPS**			
Rotor	1969-70	54213901		Head Lamp Assembly	1969-70	59883	24
Stator	1969-70	47205		Light Unit	1969-70	516798	
AMMETER	1969-70	36403		Rim	1969-70	553248	
BATTERY	1969-70	PUZ5A		Bulb, Main	1969-70	446	
BULBHOLDER				Bulb, Parking	1969-70	989	
Instruments	1969-70	54945043		Bulb Warning	1969-70	281	
Bulb	1969-70	283		Stop Lamp Assembly	1969-70	53973	25
CAPACITOR				Lens	1969-70	54577109	
(2MC)	1969-70	54170009		Bulb	1969-70	380	
Mounting Spring	1969-70	54483156		**RECTIFIER**	1969-70	49072	
CONDENSER				**REFLECTORS**			
Ignition	1969-70	425377		Amber	1969-70	57162	
COIL				Red	1969-70	57110	
Ignition	1969-70	45223		**SWITCHES**			
CONTACT BREAKER				Horn Push & Dip	1969-70	31563	
Complete C.B. Plate Assembly	1969-70	54419097		Ignition	1969-70	31899	
Points Set	1969-70	54419827		Lighting	1969-70	31788	
Eccentric Adjustment Screw	1969-70	54419220		Stop Light, Rear	1969-70	31688	
Auto Advance Assembly	1969-70	54420472		**WIRING HARNESS**			
Auto Advance Springs	1969-70	54413020		Main	1969-70	54954557	
HORN	1969-70	70183		**ZENER DIODE**	1969-70	49345	

LAVERDA Models Fitted with Lucas Turn Signals (750 Twin Cyl.) 1973 on

Unit	Year	Part No.	Page	Unit	Year	Part No.	Page
FLASHER UNIT	1973-on	35048		**SWITCHES**			
Mounting Clip	1973-on	54385091		Dip, Horn Combination	1973-on	54033666	
LAMPS				Turn-Signal, Engine	1973-on	54033667	
Turn Signal Lamp (Less Stanchions)	1973-on	56147	25	Stop Combination	1973-on	54343791	
Lens	1973-on	54581638					
Bulb	1973-on	382					
Stanchions	1973-on	60600092					

MZ TS150 (150 cc Single Cyl.) TS250 (250 cc Single Cyl.) 1974

Unit	Year	Part No.	Page	Unit	Year	Part No.	Page
FLASHER UNIT	1974	35013		LAMPS (Cont'd.)			
LAMPS				Bulb	1974	384	
Head Lamp Assembly	1974	60818	25	Turn Signal Lamp (Less Stanchions)	1974	56757	25
Light Unit	1974	54525927		Lens	1974	54581638	
Rim	1974	553248		Bulb	1974	317	
Bulb, Main	1974	403		Stanchions	1974	60600313	
Bulb, Parking	1974	988		REFLECTOR			
Bulb, Warning	1974	282		Amber	1974	57183	
Stop Lamp Assembly	1974	56754	25	SWITCHES			
Lens	1974	54584930		Handlebar Combination	1974	30683	

MONTESA King Scorpion (250 cc Single Cyl.) 1972-73

Unit	Year	Part No.	Page	Unit	Year	Part No.	Page
FLASHER UNIT	1972-73	35013		LAMPS (Cont'd.)			
Mounting Spring	1972-73	54380121		Stanchions			
LAMPS				Front	1972-73	60600313	
Head Lamp Assembly	1972-73	60533	24	Rear	1972-73	60600312	
Light Unit	1972-73	54525272		REFLECTORS			
Rim	1972-73	534343		Amber	1972-73	57183	
Bulb Main	1972-73	403		SWITCHES			
Bulb Parking	1972-73	281		L.H. Dip	1972-73	54033666	
Bulb Warning	1972-73	989		Casting Lever Pivot	1972-73	54340882	
Turn Signal Lamps (Less Stanchions)	1972-73	56559	25	R.H. Turn Signal	1972-73	39951	
Lens	1972-73	54581638		Casting Lever Pivot	1972-73	54343792	
Bulb	1972-73	317		Lighting		35710	

MOTO GUZZI (Models Fitted with Lucas Turn Signals)

Unit	Year	Part No.	Page	Unit	Year	Part No.	Page
LAMPS				REFLECTOR			
Turn Signal Lamp (Less Stanchions)		56147	25	Amber		57183	
Lens		54581638		Red		57079	
Bulb		382					
Stanchions		60600169					

NORTON COMMANDO (750 cc Twin Cyl.) All 1969 Models

Unit	Year	Part No.	Page	Unit	Year	Part No.	Page
ALTERNATOR				CONTACT BREAKER (Cont'd.)			
Rotor	1969	54213901		Auto Advance Assembly	1969	54419340	
Stator	1969	47205		Auto Advance Springs	1969	54415642	
AMMETER	1969	36403		HORN	1969	69219	
BATTERY	1969	PUZ5A		Mounting Bracket	1969	54680686	
BULBHOLDER				LAMPS			
Instruments	1969	554710		Head Lamp Assembly	1969	59883	24
Bulb	1969	643		Light Unit	1969	516798	
CAPACITOR (2MC)	1969	54170009		Rim	1969	553248	
Mounting Spring	1969	54483156		Bulb Main	1969	446	
CONDENSER				Bulb Parking	1969	989	
Ignition	1969	54420128		Bulb Warning	1969	281	
Rubber Cover	1969	54418528		Stop Lamp Assembly	1969	53973	25
Base Plate	1969	54418526		Lens	1969	54577109	
CONTACT BREAKER				Bulb	1969	380	
Complete C.B. Plate Assembly	1969	54419097		RECTIFIER	1969	49072	
Points Set	1969	54419827		REFLECTORS			
Eccentric Adjustment Screw	1969	54419220		Amber	1969	57162	
				Red	1969	57110	

NORTON Commando (750 cc Twin Cyl.) All Models For 1969 (Cont'd.)

Unit	Year	Part No.	Page	Unit	Year	Part No.	Page
SWITCHES				**WIRING HARNESS**	1969	54954277	
Ignition	1969	31899		**ZENER DIODE**	1969	49345	
Lighting	1969	35710					
Stop, Rear	1969	34815					

NORTON Commando (750 cc Twin Cyl.) All Models For 1970

Unit	Year	Part No.	Page	Unit	Year	Part No.	Page
ALTERNATOR				**LAMPS**			
Rotor	1970	54213901		Head Lamp Assembly	1970	59969	24
Stator	1970	47205		Light Unit	1970	516798	
AMMETER	1970	36403		Rim	1970	553248	
BATTERY	1970	PUZ5A		Bulb Main	1970	446	
BULBHOLDER				Bulb Parking	1970	989	
Instruments	1970	554710		Bulb Warning	1970	281	
Bulb	1970	643		Stop Lamp Assembly	1970	53973	25
CAPACITOR (2MC)	1970	54170009		Lens	1970	54577109	
Mounting Spring	1970	54483155		Bulb	1970	380	
CONDENSER				**RECTIFIER**	1970	49072	
Ignition	1970	425377		**REFLECTORS**			
COIL				Amber	1970	57162	
Ignition	1970	45223		Red	1970	57110	
CONTACT BREAKER				**SWITCHES**			
Complete C.B. Plate Assembly	1970	54419097		Ignition	1970	31899	
Points Set	1970	54419827		Lighting	1970	35710	
Eccentric Adjustment Screw	1970	54419220		Stop, Rear	1970	34815	
Auto Advance Assembly	1970	54419344		**WIRING HARNESS**	1970	54956250	
Auto Advance Springs	1970	54415642		**ZENER DIODE**	1970	49345	
HORN	1970	60219					
Mounting Bracket	1970	54680686					

NORTON Commando (750 cc Twin Cyl.) All Models 1971-72

Unit	Year	Part No.	Page	Unit	Year	Part No.	Page
ALTERNATOR				**LAMPS**			
Rotor	1971-72	54213901		Head Lamp Assembly	"All Commando Models"	60263	24
Stator	1971-72	47205		Light Unit	1971-72	54525927	
BALLAST RESISTOR IGNITION	1971-72	47225		Rim	1971-72	553248	
BATTERY	1971-72	PUZ5A		Bulb, Main	1971-72	370	
BULBHOLDER				Bulb, Parking	1971-72	989	
Instruments	1971-72	554710		Bulb, Warning	1971-72	281	
Bulb	1971-72	643		Head Lamp Assembly	"Hi Rider"	60261	24
CAPACITOR (2MC)	1971-72	54170009		Light Unit	1971-72	54525272	
Mounting Spring	1971-72	54483155		Rim	1971-72	534343	
CONDENSER				Bulb, Main	1971-72	370	
Ignition	1971-72	54420128		Bulb, Parking	1971-72	989	
Rubber Cover	1971-72	54418528		Bulb, Warning	1971-72	281	
Base Plate	1971-72	54418526		Stop Lamp Assembly	1971-72	53973	25
COIL				Lens	1971-72	54577109	
Ignition	1971-72	45222		Bulb	1971-72	380	
Mounting Bracket	1971-72	54419974		Turn Signal Assembly (Less Stanchions)	1971-72	56147	25
CONTACT BREAKER							
Complete C.B. Plate Assembly	1971-72	54419097		Lens	1971-72	54581638	
Points Set	1971-72	54419827		Bulb	1971-72	382	
Eccentric Adjustments Screw	1971-72	54419220		Stanchions	1971-72	60600091	
Auto Advance Assembly	1971-72	54419344		**RECTIFIER**	1971-72	49072	
Auto Advance Springs	1971-72	54415642		**REFLECTORS**			
FLASHER UNIT	1971-72	35048		Amber	1971-72	575189	
Mounting Clip	1971-72	54385091		Red	1971-72	57183	
HORN	1971-72	60219		**SIMULATOR WARNING LIGHT**	1971-72	38706	
Mounting Bracket	1971-72	54680686					

NORTON Commando (750 cc Twin Cyl.) All Models For 1971-72 (Cont'd.)

Unit	Year	Part No.	Page	Unit	Year	Part No.	Page
SWITCHES				SWITCHES (Cont'd.)			
R.H. Dip Horn Combination	1971-72	54033666		Lighting	1971-72	34660	
R.H. Casting Lever Pivot	1971-72	54343792		Stop Light Rear	1971-72	34815	
L.H. Cut-Out, Turn Signal				Stop Light, Front (Disc Brakes)	1971-72	34619	
Combination	1971-72	54033667		WIRING HARNESS			
L.H. Casting Lever Pivot	1971-72	54343791		Head Lamp	1971-72	54959633	
(Note Blackfinish Switches No				Main	1971-72	54959643	
Longer Available)	Late 1972	—		ZENER DIODE	1971-72	49345	
Ignition, Master	1971-72	39784					

NORTON Commando (750 - 850 cc Twin Cyl. Except John Player 850 cc) 1973-74

Unit	Year	Part No.	Page	Unit	Year	Part No.	Page
ALTERNATOR				LAMPS (Cont'd.)			
Rotor	1973-74	54213901		Bulb Main		370	
Stator	1973-74	47205		Bulb Parking		989	
BALLAST RESISTOR IGNITION	1973-74	47225		Bulb Warning		281	
BATTERY	1973-74	PUZ5A		Head Lamp Assembly	"Hi Rider		
BULBHOLDER					III"	60942	25
Instruments	1973-74	554710		Light Unit		54525272	
Bulb	1973-74	643		Rim		534343	
CAPACITOR (2MC)	1973-74	54170009		Bulb		370	
CONDENSER				Bulb		233	
Ignition	1973-74	54420128		Stop Lamp Assembly	1973-74	56513	25
Rubber Cover	1973-74	54418528		Lens	1973-74	54584930	
Base Plate	1973-74	54418526		Bulb	1973-74	380	
COIL				Turn Signal Assembly (Less			
Ignition	1973-74	45222		Stanchions)	1973-74	56147	25
Mounting Bracket	1973-74	54419974		Lens	1973-74	54581638	
CONTACT BREAKER				Bulb	1973-74	382	
Complete C.B. Plate Assembly	1973-74	54425160		Stanchions	1973-74	60600091	
Points Set	1973-74	60600271		RECTIFIER	1973-74	49072	
Eccentric Adjustment Screw	1973-74	54419220		REFLECTORS			
Auto Advance Assembly	1973-74	54425656		Front	1973-74	57183	
Auto Advance Springs	1973-74	54412229		SIMULATOR WARNING LIGHT	1973-74	38717	
FLASHER UNIT	1973-74	35048		SWITCHES			
Mounting Clip	1973-74	54385091		R.H. Cutout, Turn Signal			
HORN	1973-74	69219		Combination	1973-74	39951	
Mounting Bracket	1973-74	54680686		R.H. Casting Lever Pivot (Drum			
LAMPS				Brakes)	1973-74	54343792	
Head Lamp Assembly	"All Commando			L.H. Dip-Horn Combination	1973-74	39949	
	Models"	60263	24	Ignition Master	1973-74	39784	
Light Unit		54525927		Lighting	1973-74	34660	
Rim		553248		Stop Light Rear	1973-74	34815	
Bulb Main		370		Stop Light Front (Disc Brakes)	1973-74	34619	
Bulb Parking		989		WIRING HARNESS			
Bulb Warning		281		Head Lamp	1973	54960724	
Head Lamp Assembly	"Hi-Rider"	60261	24	Head Lamp	1974	54962265	
Light Unit		54525272		Main	1973-74	54961586	
Rim		534343		ZENER DIODE	1973-74	49345	

NORTON Commando-John Player (850 cc Twin Cylinder) 1975

Unit	Year	Part No.	Page	Unit	Year	Part No.	Page
ALTERNATOR				CAPACITOR (2MC)	1975	54170009	
Rotor	1975	60600444		Mounting Spring	1975	54483156	
Stator	1975	47239		CONDENSER			
BALLAST RESISTOR IGNITION	1975	47225		Ignition	1975	54420128	
BATTERY	1975	PUZ5A		Rubber Cover	1975	54418528	
BULBHOLDER				Base Plate	1975	54418526	
Instruments	1975	51271406		COIL			
Bulb	1975	504		Ignition	1975	45222	
				Mounting Bracket	1975	54419974	

NORTON Commando-John Player (850 cc Twin Cylinder) 1975 (Cont'd.)

Unit	Year	Part No.	Page	Unit	Year	Part No.	Page
CONTACT BREAKER				STANCHIONS			
Complete C.B. Plate Assembly	1975	54425160		Front	1975	60600313	
Points Set	1975	60600271		Rear	1975	60600312	
Eccentric Adjustment Screw	1975	54419220		RECTIFIER	1975	49181	
Auto Advance Assembly	1975	54426429		REFLECTOR			
Auto Advance Springs	1975	54412229		Amber	1975	57183	
FLASHER UNIT	1975	35048		SIMULATOR, WARNING LIGHT	1975	38717	
Mounting Clip	1975	54387043		Mounting Spring	1975	54387043	
HORN	1975	69219		SWITCHES			
Mounting Bracket	1975	54680686		L.H. Dip-Horn Combination	1975	39949	
LAMPS				L.H. Casting Lever Pivot	1975	54343791	
Head Lamp Assembly	1975	Not Available		R.H. Cut-Out, Turn Signal Combination	1975	39951	
Note: Parts Listed below must be ordered separately				Ignition	1975	39784	
Rim, Outer	1975	534343		Lighting	1975	35710	
Light Unit	1975	54525272		Stop Light, Rear	1975	34815	
Bulb, Main	1975	370		Stop Light, Front	1975	34619	
Bulb Parking	1975	989		WARNING LIGHTS			
Bulb Holder, Main	1975	553738		Amber	1975	54363453	
Bulb Holder Parking	1975	54573590		Green	1975	54363455	
Light Unit Fixing Wire	1975	504665		Red	1975	54363454	
Clip, Outer Rim	1975	534296		Bulb	1975	281	
Screw, Clip, Outer Rim	1975	144921		Bulbholder	1975	54945043	
Stop Lamp Assembly	1975	56513	25	Sealing Washer	1975	54140331	
Lens	1975	54584930		Shield	1975	54525212	
Bulb	1975	380		WIRING HARNESS			
Turn Signal Lamps (Less Stanchions)	1975	56559	25	Main	1975	54961586	
Lens	1975	54581638		ZENER DIODES	1975	49345	
Bulb	1975	382					

NORTON-Commando MK.III Electric Start (850 cc Twin Cyl.) 1975 on

Unit	Year	Part No.	Page	Unit	Year	Part No.	Page
ALTERNATOR				LAMPS (Cont'd.)			
Rotor	1975-on	60600444		Stop Lamp Assembly	1975-on	56513	25
Stator	1975-on	47239		Lens	1975-on	54584930	
BALLAST RESISTOR	1975-on	47225		Bulb	1975-on	380	
BATTERY	1975-on	MCZ9-B		Turn Signal Lamp (Less Stanchions)	1975-on	56559	25
BULBHOLDER				Lens	1975	54581638	
Instruments	1975-on	51271406		Bulb	1975	382	
Bulb	1975-on	504		Stanchions			
CAPACITOR (2MC)	1975-on	54170009		Front	1975-on	60600313	
Mounting Spring	1975-on	54483156		Rear	1975-on	60600312	
CONDENSER				RECTIFIER	1975-on	49181	
Ignition	1975-on	54420128		REFLECTOR			
Rubber Cover	1975-on	54418528		Amber	1975-on	57183	
Base Plate	1975-on	54418526		SIMULATOR, WARNING LIGHT	1975-on	38717	
COIL				Mounting Spring	1975-on	54387043	
Ignition	1975-on	45222		SWITCHES			
Mounting Bracket	1975-on	54419974		L.H. Handlebar Combination	1975-on	30663	
CONTACT BREAKER				R.H. Handlebar Combination	1975-on	30664	
Complete C.B. Plate Assembly	1975-on	54425160		Ignition, Master	1975-on	39784	
Points Set	1975-on	60600271		Neutral	1975-on	30702	
Eccentric Adjustment Screw	1975-on	54419220		Solenoid, Starter (Suitable Replacement)	1975-on	76771	
Auto Advance Assembly	1975-on	54426429		Stop Light, Front & Rear	1975-on	34619	
Auto Advance Springs	1975-on	54412229		WIRING HARNESS			
FLASHER UNIT	1975-on	35048		Head Lamp, Ignition & Main	1975-on	54962258	
Mounting Clip	1975-on	54387043		ZENER DIODES	1975-on	49345	
HORN	1975-on	69219					
Mounting Bracket	1975-on	54680686					
LAMPS							
Head Lamp Assembly	1975-on	60867	25				
Light Unit	1975-on	54525927					
Rim	1975-on	553248					
Bulb, Main	1975-on	370					
Bulb, Parking	1975-on	233					

RICKMAN 125 Enduro (125 cc Single Cyl.) 1971

Unit	Year	Part No.	Page	Unit	Year	Part No.	Page
HORN	1971	70196		LAMPS (Cont'd)			
LAMPS				Lens	1971	54577109	
Head Lamp Assembly	1971	60327	24	Bulb	1971	384	
Light Unit	1971	54523513		REFLECTOR			
Rim	1971	534343		Amber	1971	57183	
Bulb Main	1971	312		Red	1971	59079	
Bulb Parking	1971	951		SWITCH			
Bulb Warning	1971	282		Lighting	1971	31356	
Stop Lamp Assembly	1971	53973	25				

RICKMAN 125 Six Days (125 cc Single Cyl.) 1973

Unit	Year	Part No.	Page	Unit	Year	Part No.	Page
DIODE, HEAD LAMP	1973	83205		LAMPS (Cont'd)			
FLASHER UNIT (REPLACEMENT)	1973	35013		Lens	1973	54584930	
LAMPS				Bulb	1973	384	
Head Lamp Assembly	1973	60488	24	Turn Signal Lamp (Less Stanchions)	1973	56559	25
Light Unit	1973	54523513		Lens	1973	54581638	
Rim	1973	534343		Bulb	1973	317	
Bulb, Main	1973	403		Stanchions	1973	60600312	
Bulb, Parking	1973	988		SWITCHES			
Bulb, Warning	1973	282		Lighting	1973	34419	
Stop Lamp Assembly	1973	56512	25				

TRIUMPH TR25W Trophy (250 cc Single Cyl.) 1969-70

Unit	Year	Part No.	Page	Unit	Year	Part No.	Page
ALTERNATOR				LAMPS (Cont'd)			
Rotor	1969-70	54213901		Rim	1969-70	534343	
Stator	1969-70	47205		Bulb, Main	1969-70	446	
BATTERY		PUZ5A		Bulb, Parking	1969-70	989	
BULBHOLDER				Bulb Warning	1969-70	281	
Instruments	1969-70	54945043		Stop Lamp Assembly	1969-70	53973	25
Bulb	1969-70	281		Lens	1969-70	54577109	
CONDENSER				Bulb	1969-70	380	
Ignition	1969-70	54441582		RECTIFIER	1969-70	49072	
COIL				REFLECTORS			
Ignition	1969-70	45223		Amber	1969-70	57173	
CONTACT BREAKER				Red	1969-70	57111	
Complete C.B. Plate Assembly	1969-70	54419645		SWITCHES			
Points Set	1969-70	54419827		Ignition	1969-70	35710	
Eccentric Adjustment Screw	1969-70	54419220		Lighting	1969-70	31899	
Auto Advance Assembly	1969-70	54419653		Stop Lamp Rear	1969-70	34815	
Auto Advance Springs	1969-70	54417992		WIRING HARNESS			
LAMPS				Main	1969	54955718	
Head Lamp Assembly	1969-70	60037	24	Main	1970	54957308	
Light Unit	1969-70	54524526		ZENER DIODE	1969-70	49345	

TRIUMPH T25T Trail Blazer T25SS Blazer (250 cc Single Cyl.) 1971

Unit	Year	Part No.	Page	Unit	Year	Part No.	Page
ALTERNATOR				CAPACITOR (2MC)	1971	54170009	
Rotor	1971	54213901		Rubber Mounting	1971	54422860	
Stator	1971	47205		CONDENSER			
BATTERY	1971	PUZ5A		Ignition	1971	54420128	
BULBHOLDER				COIL			
Instruments	1971	54933910		Ignition	1971	45223	
Bulb	1971	281		CONTACT BREAKER			
				Complete C.B. Plate Assembly	1971	54419645	

TRIUMPH T25T Trail Blazer T25SS Blazer (250 cc Single Cyl.) 1971 (Cont'd.)

Unit	Year	Part No.	Page	Unit	Year	Part No.	Page
CONTACT BREAKER (Cont'd.)				**LAMPS (Cont'd.)**			
Points Set	1971	54419827		Lens	1971	54581638	
Eccentric Adjustment Screw	1971	54419220		Bulb	1971	382	
Auto Advance Assembly	1971	54419653		Stanchions	1971	60600092	
Auto Advance Springs	1971	54417992		**RECTIFIER**	1971	49072	
FLASHER UNIT	1971	35048		**REFLECTORS**			
Mounting Clip	1971	54385091		Amber	1971	57160	
Mounting Spring	1971	54386637		Red	1971	575189	
FUSE HOLDER	1971	54190387		**SWITCHES**			
Fuse	1971	188218		L.H. Dip-Horn Combination	1971	54033666	
HORN	1971	70228		L.H. Casting Lever Pivot	1971	54343791	
LAMPS				R.H. Cut-out Turn Signal	1971	54033667	
Head Lamp Assembly	1971	60262	24	R.H. Casting Lever Pivot	1971	54343792	
Light Unit	1971	54525272		Ignition, Lighting Master	1971	39784	
Rim	1971	534343		Lighting	1971	31356	
Bulb Main	1971	370		Stop Light, Rear	1971	34815	
Bulb Parking	1971	989		**WIRING HARNESS**			
Bulb Warning	1971	281		Electric Box	1971	54959680	
Stop Lamp Assembly	1971	53973	25	Head Lamp	1971	54959532	
Lens	1971	54577109		Main	1971	54959480	
Bulb	1971	380		**ZENER DIODE**	1971	49345	
Turn Signal Lamp (Less Stanchions)	1971	56147	25				

TRIUMPH T100C Trophy T100R Daytona (500 cc Twin Cyl.) 1971-72

Unit	Year	Part No.	Page	Unit	Year	Part No.	Page
ALTERNATOR				**LAMPS (Cont'd.)**			
Rotor	1971-72	54213901		Bulb, Main	1971-72	370	
Stator	1971-72	47205		Bulb, Parking	1971-72	989	
BATTERY	1971-72	PUZ5A		Bulb, Warning Light	1971-72	281	
BULBHOLDER				Stop Lamp Assembly	1971-72	53973	25
Instruments	1971	554710		Lens	1971-72	54577109	
Bulb	1971	643		Bulb	1971-72	380	
BULBHOLDER				Turn Signal Lamp (Less Stanchions)	1971-72	56147	25
Instruments	1972	863511		Lens	1971-72	54581638	
Bulb	1972	643		Bulb	1971-72	382	
CAPACITOR (2MC) OPTIONAL	1971-72	54710009		Stanchions	1971-72	60600092	
Mounting Spring	1971-72	54483156		**RECTIFIER**	1971-72	49072	
CONDENSER				**REFLECTORS**			
Ignition	1971-72	54420128		Amber	1971-72	57183	
Rubber Cover	1971-72	54418528		Red	1971-72	575189	
Base Plate	1971-72	54418526		**SWITCHES**			
COIL				L.H. Dip. Horn Combination	1971-72	54033666	
Ignition	1971-72	45223		L.H. Casting, Lever Pivot	1971-72	54343791	
CONTACT BREAKER				R.H. Cut-Out, Turn-Signal Combination	1971-72	54033667	
Complete C.B. Plate Assembly	1971-72	54419097		R.H. Casting, Lever Pivot	1971-72	54343792	
Points Set	1971-72	54419827		Ignition	1971-72	31899	
Eccentric Adjustment Screw	1971-72	54419220		Lighting	1971-72	35710	
Auto Advance Assembly	1971-72	54419340		Stop Light, Rear	1971-72	54033234	
Auto Advance Springs	1971-72	54415642		Spring, Stoplight Rear	1971-72	315738	
FLASHER UNIT	1971-72	35048		**WIRING HARNESS**			
Mounting Clip	1971-72	54385091		Head Lamp	1971-72	54959531	
Mounting Spring	1971-72	54386637		Main	1971-72	54959628	
FUSE HOLDER	1971-72	54190387		**ZENER DIODE**	1971-72	49345	
Fuse	1971-72	188218					
HORN	1971	70216					
HORN	1972	70228					
LAMPS							
Head Lamp Assembly (T100C)	1971-72	60261	24				
Light Unit	1971-72	54525272					
Rim	1971-72	534343					
Bulb Main	1971-72	370					
Bulb, Parking	1971-72	989					
Bulb, Warning Light	1971-72	281					
Head Lamp Assembly (T100R)	1971-72	60263	24				
Light Unit	1971-72	54525927					
Rim	1971-72	553248					

TRIUMPH T100R Daytona (500 cc Twin Cyl.) 1973 on

Unit	Year	Part No.	Page	Unit	Year	Part No.	Page
ALTERNATOR				LAMPS (Cont'd.)			
Rotor	1973-on	54213901		Bulb, Warning Light	1973-on	281	
Stator	1973-on	47205		Stop Lamp Assembly	1973-on	56513	25
BULBHOLDER				Lens	1973-on	54584930	
Instruments	1973-on	863511		Bulb	1973-on	380	
Bulb	1973-on	643		Turn Signal Lamp (Less Stanchions)	Early 1973	56147	25
CAPACITOR (2MC) OPTIONAL	1973-on	54170009		Lens		54581638	
Mounting Spring	1973-on	54483156		Bulb		382	
CONDENSER				Stanchions		60600092	
Ignition	1973-on	54420128		Turn Signal Lamps (Less			
Rubber Cover	1973-on	54418528		Stanchions)	Late		
Base Plate	1973-on	54418526			1973-on	56559	25
COIL				Lens		54581638	
Ignition	1973-on	45223		Bulb		382	
CONTACT BREAKER				Stanchions Front		60600320	
Complete C.B. Plate Assembly	Early 1973	54419097		Rear		60600312	
Points Set		54419827		RECTIFIER	1973-on	49072	
Eccentric Adjustment Screw		54419220		REFLECTOR			
Complete C.B. Plate Assembly	Late			Amber	1973-on	57183	
	1973-on	54425160		RELAY			
Points Set		60600271		Horn	1973-on	33213	
Eccentric Adjustment Screw		54419220		SWITCHES			
Auto Advance Assembly	1973-on	54425657		L.H. Cut-Out Turn Signal			
Auto Advance Springs	1973-on	54412229		Combination	1973-on	54033667	
FLASHER UNIT	1973-on	35048		L.H. Casting, Lever Pivot	1973-on	54343791	
Mounting Clip	1973-on	54385091		R.H. Dip, Horn Combination	1973-on	54033722	
Mounting Spring	1973-on	54386637		R.H. Casting, Lever Pivot	1973-on	54343793	
FUSE HOLDER	1973-on	54190387		Ignition	1973-on	31899	
Fuse	1973-on	188218		Lighting	1973-on	34419	
HORN	1973-on	70228		Stop Light, Rear	1973-on	54033234	
LAMPS				Spring, Stop Light Rear	1973-on	315738	
Head Lamp Assembly	1973-on	60512	24	WIRING HARNESS			
Light Unit	1973-on	54525927		Head Lamp	1973-on	54959531	
Rim	1973-on	553248		Main	1973-on	54959268	
Bulb, Main	1973-on	370		ZENER DIODE	1973-on	49345	
Bulb, Parking	1973-on	989					

TRIUMPH TR5T Trophy Trail (500 cc Twin Cyl.) 1973-74

Unit	Year	Part No.	Page	Unit	Year	Part No.	Page
ALTERNATOR				LAMPS			
Rotor	1973-74	54213901		Head Lamp Assembly	1973-74	60514	24
Stator	1973-74	47205		Light Unit	1973-74	54524526	
BATTERY	1973-74	PUZ5A		Rim	1973-74	534343	
CAPACITOR (2MC)	1973-74	54170009		Bulb, Main	1973-74	370	
Mounting Spring	1973-74	54483155		Bulb, Parking	1973-74	989	
CONDENSER				Bulb, Warning	1973-74	281	
Ignition	1973-74	54420128		Stop Lamp Assembly	1973-74	56513	25
Rubber Cover	1973-74	54418528		Lens	1973-74	54584930	
Base Plate	1973-74	54418526		Bulb	1973-74	380	
COIL				Turn Signal Lamps (Less			
Ignition	1973-74	45223		Stanchions)	1973-74	56147	25
CONTACT BREAKER				Lens	1973-74	54581638	
Complete C.B. Plate Assembly	1973-74	54425160		Bulb	1973-74	382	
Point Set	1973-74	60600271		Stanchions, Rear	1973-74	60600269	
Eccentric Adjustment Screw	1973-74	54419220		RECTIFIER	1973-74	49072	
Auto Advance Assembly	1973-74	54425657		REFLECTORS			
Auto Advance Springs	1973-74	54412229		Amber	1973-74	57183	
FLASHER UNIT	1973-74	35048		SWITCHES			
Mounting Clip	1973-74	54385091		Engine Cut-Out	1973-74	35835	
Mounting Spring	1973-74	54386637		Ignition	1973-74	31899	
HORN	1973-74	70228		Lighting	1973-74	34419	
				Stop Light (Rear)	1973-74	34815	
				WIRING HARNESS	1973-74	54961591	
				ZENER DIODE	1973-74	49345	

TRIUMPH TR6C (650 cc Twin Cyl.) T100C (500 cc Twin Cyl.) 1969-70

Unit	Year	Part No.	Page	Unit	Year	Part No.	Page
ALTERNATOR				LAMPS (Cont'd)			
Rotor	1969-70	54213901		Bulb, Main	1969-70	446	
Stator	1969-70	47205		Bulb, Parking	1969-70	989	
BATTERY		PUZ5A		Bulb, Warning Light	1969-70	281	
CAPACITOR (2MC) OPTIONAL	1969-70	54170009		Stop Lamp Assembly	1969-70	53973	25
Mounting Spring	1969-70	54483156		Lens	1969-70	54577109	
CONDENSER				Bulb	1969-70	380	
Ignition	1969-70	54420128		RECTIFIER	1969-70	49072	
Rubber Cover	1969-70	54418528		REFLECTORS			
Base Plate	1969-70	54418526		Amber	1969-70	57161	
COIL				Red	1969-70	57111	
Ignition	1969-70	45223		SWITCHES			
CONTACT BREAKER				Engine Stop	1969-70	35835	
Complete C.B. Plate Assembly	1969-70	54419097		Ignition	1969-70	31899	
Points Set	1969-70	54419827		Lighting	1969-70	35710	
Eccentric Adjustment Screw	1969-70	54419220		Stop Light Rear	1969-70	54033234	
Auto Advance	1969-70	54419340		Spring, Stop Light Rear	1969-70	315738	
Auto Advance Springs	1969-70	54415642		WIRING HARNESS			
HORN	1969-70	70183		Main	1969	54955719	
LAMPS				Main	1970	54957096	
Head Lamp Assembly	1969-70	60037	24	Capacitor (2MC) Optional Cable	1970	54953455	
Light Unit	1969-70	54524526		ZENER DIODE	1969-70	49345	
Rim	1969-70	534343					

TRIUMPH TR6R Tiger (650 cc Twin Cyl.) T100R Daytona (500 cc Twin Cyl.) T120R Bonneville (650 cc Twin Cyl.) 1969-70

Unit	Year	Part No.	Page	Unit	Year	Part No.	Page
ALTERNATOR				LAMPS (Cont'd)			
Rotor	1969-70	54213901		Rim	1969-70	553248	
Stator	1969-70	47205		Bulb, Main	1969-70	446	
AMMETER	1969-70	36403		Bulb, Parking	1969-70	989	
BATTERY	1969-70	PUZ5A		Bulb, Warning Light	1969-70	281	
BULBHOLDER				Stop Lamp Assembly	1969-70	53973	25
Instruments	1969-70	554710		Lens	1969-70	54577109	
Bulb	1969-70	643		Bulb	1969-70	380	
CAPACITOR (2MC) OPTIONAL	1969-70	54710009		RECTIFIER	1969-70	49072	
Mounting Spring	1969-70	54483156		REFLECTORS			
CONDENSER				Amber	1969-70	57161	
Ignition	1969-70	54420128		Red	1969-70	57111	
Rubber Cover	1969-70	54418528		RELAY			
Base Plate	1969-70	54418526		Horn (T120R)	1969-70	33188	
COIL				SWITCHES			
Ignition	1969-70	45223		Horn Push & Dip	1969-70	31563	
CONTACT BREAKER				Ignition	1969-70	31899	
Complete C.B. Plate Assembly	1969-70	54419097		Lighting	1969-70	35710	
Points Set	1969-70	54419827		Stop Light Rear	1969-70	54033234	
Eccentric Adjustment Screw	1969-70	54419220		Spring, Stop Light Rear	1969-70	315738	
Auto Advance Assembly	1969-70	54419340		WIRING HARNESS			
Auto Advance Springs	1969-70	54415642		Main	1969	54955256	
HORN	1969-70	70183		Main	1970	54957095	
LAMPS				Capacitor (2MC) Optional Cable	1969-70	54953455	
Head Lamp Assembly	1969-70	59883	24	ZENER DIODE	1969-70	49345	
Light Unit	1969-70	516798					

TRIUMPH TR6C Trophy (650 cc Twin Cyl.) TR6R Tiger (650 cc Twin Cyl.) T120R Bonneville (650 cc Twin Cyl.) 1971-72

Unit	Year	Part No.	Page	Unit	Year	Part No.	Page
ALTERNATOR				BULBHOLDER			
Rotor	1971-72	54213901		Instruments	1971-72	863511	
Stator	1971-72	47205		Bulb	1971-72	643	
BATTERY	1971-72	PUZ5A					

TRIUMPH TR6C Trophy (650 cc Twin Cyl.) TR6R Tiger (650 cc Twin Cyl.) T120R Bonneville (650 cc Twin Cyl.) 1971-72 (Cont'd.)

Unit	Year	Part No.	Page	Unit	Year	Part No.	Page
CONDENSER				**LAMPS (Cont'd.)**			
Ignition	1971-72	54420128		Bulb, Parking	1971-72	989	
Rubber Cover	1971-72	54418528		Bulb, Warning Light	1971-72	281	
Base Plate	1971-72	54418526		Stop Lamp Assembly	1971-72	53973	25
COIL				Lens	1971-72	54577109	
Ignition	1971-72	45223		Bulb	1971-72	380	
CONTACT BREAKER				Turn Signal Lamp (Less Stanchions)	1971-72	56147	25
Complete C.B. Plate Assembly	1971-72	54419097		Lens	1971-72	54581638	
Points Set	1971-72	54419827		Bulb	1971-72	382	
Eccentric Adjustment Screw	1971-72	54419220		Stanchions	1971-72	60600092	
Auto Advance Assembly	1971-72	54419340		**RECTIFIER**	1971-72	49072	
Auto Advance Springs	1971-72	54415642		**REFLECTORS**			
FLASHER UNIT	1971-72	35048		Amber	1971-72	57183	
Mounting Clip	1971-72	54385091		Red	1971-72	575189	
Mounting Spring	1971-72	54386637		**SWITCHES**			
FUSE HOLDER	1971-72	54190387		L.H. Dip-Horn Combination	1971-72	54033666	
Fuse	1971-72	188218		L.H. Casting Lever Pivot	1971-72	54340882	
HORN	1971-72	70216		R.H. Cut-Out, Turn Signal Combination	1971-72	54033667	
LAMPS				R.H. Casting, Lever Pivot	1971-72	54340883	
Head Lamp Assembly (TR6C)	1971-72	60262	24	Ignition, Lighting Master	1971-72	39784	
Light Unit	1971-72	54525272		Lighting	1971-72	31356	
Rim	1971-72	534343		Stop Light, Rear	1971-72	34815	
Bulb, Main	1971-72	370		**WIRING HARNESS**			
Bulb, Parking	1971-72	989		Head Lamp	1971	54959535	
Bulb, Warning Light	1971-72	281		Head Lamp	1972	54967011	
Head Lamp Assembly (TR6R & T120R)	1971-72	60260	24	Main	1971	54959629	
Light Unit	1971-72	54525927		Main	1972	54960710	
Rim	1971-72	553248		**ZENER DIODE**	1971-72	49345	
Bulb, Main	1971-72	370					

TRIUMPH TRX75 Hurricane (750 cc Three Cyl.) 1973

Unit	Year	Part No.	Page	Unit	Year	Part No.	Page
ALTERNATOR				**LAMPS (Cont'd.)**			
Rotor	1973	54213902		Bulb, Parking	1973	989	
Stator	1973	47205		Bulb, Warning	1973	281	
BATTERY	1973	PUZ5A		Stop Lamp Assembly	1973	53973	25
CONDENSER				Lens	1973	54577109	
Ignition	1973	54420128		Bulb	1973	380	
Rubber Cover	1973	54418528		**RECTIFIER**	1973	49072	
Base Plate	1973	54418526		**REFLECTORS**			
COIL				Amber	1973	575189	
Ignition	1973	45223		Red	1973	57160	
CONTACT BREAKER				**SWITCHES**			
Complete C.B. Plate Assembly	1973	54419327		Engine Stop	1973	35835	
Points Set	1973	54419828		Horn Push & Dip	1973	31563	
Eccentric Adjustment Screw	1973	54419220		Ignition	1973	31899	
Auto Advance Assembly	1973	54419867		Lighting	1973	35710	
Auto Advance Springs	1973	54417992		Stop Light Rear	1973	34815	
LAMPS				**WIRING HARNESS**			
Head Lamp Assembly	1973	60263	24	Head Lamp	1973	54960707	
Light Unit	1973	54525927		Main	1973	54960708	
Rim	1973	553248		**ZENER DIODE**	1973	49345	
Bulb, Main	1973	370					

TRIUMPH T140V Bonneville TR7RV Tiger (750 cc Twin Cylinder) 1973-75

Unit	Year	Part No.	Page	Unit	Year	Part No.	Page
ALTERNATOR				**LAMPS (Cont'd.)**			
Rotor	1973-75	54213901		Bulb, Parking	1973-75	989	
Stator	1973-75	47205		Bulb, Warning	1973-75	281	
BATTERY	1973-75	PUZ5A		Stop Lamp Assembly	1973-75	56513	25
BULBHOLDER				Lens	1973-75	54584930	
Instruments	1973-75	54959626		Bulb	1973-75	380	
Bulb	1973-75	643		Turn Signal Lamp (Less Stanchions)	1973-75	56147	25
CONDENSER				Lens	1973-75	54581638	
Ignition	1973-75	54441582		Bulb	1973-75	382	
COIL				Stanchions			
Ignition	1973-75	45223		Front	1973-75	60600091	
CONTACT BREAKER				Rear	1973-75	60600269	
Complete C B Plate Assembly	1973-75	54425160		**RECTIFIER**	1973-75	49072	
Points Set	1973-75	60600271		**REFLECTOR**			
Eccentric Adjustment Screw	1973-75	54419220		Amber	1973-75	57183	
Auto Advance Assembly	1973-75	54425657		**SWITCHES**			
Auto Advance Springs	1973-75	54412229		Dip Horn Combination	1973-75	54033666	
FLASHER UNIT	1973-75	35048		L.H. Casting, Lever Pivot	1973-75	54340882	
Mounting Clip	1973-75	54385091		R.H. Cut-Out Turn Signal			
Mounting Spring	1973-75	54386637		Combination	1973-75	54033751	
HORN	1973-75	70228		Ignition	1973-75	31899	
LAMPS				Lighting	1973-75	34419	
Head Lamp Assembly	1973-75	60512	24	Stop Lamp (Rear)	1973-75	34815	
Light Unit	1973-75	54525927		**WIRING HARNESS**			
Rim	1973-75	553248		Main	1973-75	54961593	
Bulb, Main	1973-75	370		**ZENER DIODE**	1973-75	49345	

TRIUMPH T140V Bonneville TR7RV Tiger (750 cc Twin Cylinder) 1976-77

Unit	Year	Part No.	Page	Unit	Year	Part No.	Page
ALTERNATOR				**LAMPS (Cont'd.)**			
Rotor	1976-77	54213901		Rim	1976-77	553248	
Stator	1976-77	47205		Bulb, Main	1976-77	370	
BATTERY	1976-77	PUZ5A		Bulb, Parking	1976-77	989	
BULBHOLDER				Bulb, Warning	1976-77	281	
Instruments	1976-77	51271406		Stop Lamp Assembly	1976-77	56513	25
Bulb	1976-77	643		Lens	1976-77	54584930	
CONDENSER				Bulb	1976-77	380	
Ignition	1976-77	54420128		Turn Signal (Less Stanchions)	1976-77	56559	25
COIL				Lens	1976-77	54581638	
Ignition	1976-77	45223		Bulb	1976-77	382	
CONTACT BREAKER				Stanchions			
Complete C.B. Plate Assembly	1976-77	54425160		Front	1976-77	60600313	
Points Set	1976-77	60600271		Rear	1976-77	60600312	
Eccentric Adjustment Screw	1976-77	54419220		**RECTIFIER**	1976-77	49072	
Auto Advance Assembly	1976-77	54425657		**REFLECTORS**			
Auto Advance Springs	1976-77	54412229		Amber	1976-77	57183	
DIODE				**SWITCHES**			
Head Lamp (Canada)	1976-77	83205		L.H. Handle Bar Combination	1976-77	30447	
FLASHER				R.H. Handle Bar Combination	1976-77	30781	
Unit	1976-77	35048		Ignition	1976-77	31899	
Mounting Clip	1976-77	54385091		Lighting	1976-77	34419	
Mounting Spring	1976-77	54386637		Stop. Lamp (Rear)	1976-77	34815	
HORN	1976-77	70228		**WIRING HARNESS**			
LAMPS				Main	1976-77	54962258	
Head Lamp Assembly	1976-77	60512	24	**ZENER DIODE**	1976-77	49345	
Light Unit	1976-77	54525927					

TRIUMPH T150 Trident (750 cc Three Cyl.) 1969-70

Unit	Year	Part No.	Page	Unit	Year	Part No.	Page
ALTERNATOR				**LAMPS (Cont'd)**			
Rotor	1969-70	54213902		Bulb, Warning	1969-70	281	
Stator	1969-70	47209		Stop Lamp Assembly	1969-70	53973	25
AMMETER	1969-70	36421		Lens	1969-70	54577109	
BATTERY	1969-70	PUZ5A		Bulb	1969-70	380	
BULBHOLDER				**RECTIFIER**	1969-70	49072	
Instruments	1969	554734		**REFLECTORS**			
Bulb	1969	987		Amber	1969-70	57160	
Instruments	1970	863511		Red	1969-70	57111	
Bulb	1970	643		**RELAY**			
CONDENSER				Horn	1969-70	33188	
Ignition	1969-70	54420128		**SWITCH**			
Rubber Cover	1969-70	54418528		Engine-Stop	1969-70	35835	
Base Plate	1969-70	54418526		Horn Push-Dip	1969-70	31563	
COIL				Ignition	1969-70	31899	
Ignition	1969-70	45223		Lighting	1969-70	31788	
CONTACT BREAKER				Stop Light Rear	1969-70	34815	
Complete C.B. Plate Assembly	1969-70	54419327		**WARNING LIGHTS**			
Points Set	1969-70	54419828		Green	1969-70	38191	
Eccentric Adjustment Screw	1969-70	54419220		Red	1969-70	38189	
Auto Advance Assembly	1969-70	54419867		Bulbholder	1969-70	54945043	
Auto Advance Springs	1969-70	54415642		Bulb	1969-70	281	
LAMPS				**WIRING HARNESS**			
Head Lamp Assembly	1969-70	59892	24	Main	1969	54954246	
Light Unit	1969-70	516798		Main	1970	54955732	
Rim	1969-70	553248		Ignition C.B. 3 Core	1969-70	54939169	
Bulb, Main	1969-70	446		**ZENER DIODE**	1969-70	49345	
Bulb, Parking	1969-70	989					

TRIUMPH T150 Trident (750 cc Three Cylinder) 1971-72

Unit	Year	Part No.	Page	Unit	Year	Part No.	Page
ALTERNATOR				**LAMPS (Cont'd)**			
Rotor	1971-72	54213902		Bulb, Warning	1971-72	281	
Stator	1971-72	47205		Stop Lamp Assembly	1971-72	53973	25
BATTERY	1971-72	PUZ5A		Lens	1971-72	54577109	
BULBHOLDER				Bulb	1971-72	380	
Instruments	1971-72	863511		Turn Signal Lamp (Less Stanchions)	1971-72	56147	25
Bulb	1971-72	643		Lens	1971-72	54581638	
CONDENSER				Bulb	1971-72	382	
Ignition	1971-72	54420128		Stanchions	1971-72	60600092	
Rubber Cover	1971-72	54418528		**RECTIFIER**	1971-72	49072	
Base Plate	1971-72	54418526		**REFLECTORS**			
COIL				Amber	1971-72	57160	
Ignition	1971-72	45223		Red	1971-72	575189	
CONTACT BREAKER				**RELAY**			
Complete C.B. Plate Assembly	1971-72	54419327		Horn	1971-72	33213	
Points Set	1971-72	54419828		**SWITCHES**			
Eccentric Adjustment Screw	1971-72	54419220		L.H. Dip-Horn Combination	1971-72	54033666	
Auto Advance Assembly	1971-72	54419867		L.H. Casting, Lever Pivot	1971-72	54340883	
Auto Advance Springs	1971-72	54417992		R.H. Cut-Out Turn Signal	1971-72	54033667	
FLASHER				R.H. Casting, Lever Pivot	1971-72	54340884	
Unit	1971-72	35048		Ignition, Lighting Master	1971-72	39565	
Mounting Clip	1971-72	54385091		Lighting	1971-72	31356	
FUSE HOLDER	1971-72	54190387		Stop Light, Rear	1971-72	34815	
Fuse	1971-72	188218		**WIRING HARNESS**			
LAMPS				Head Lamp	1971	54959640	
Head Lamp Assembly	1971-72	60260	24	Main	1971	54959638	
Light Unit	1971-72	516801		Head Lamp	1972	54960712	
Rim	1971-72	553248		Main	1972	54960717	
Bulb, Main	1971-72	370		Ignition, C.B. 3 Core	1971-72	54939169	
Bulb, Parking	1971-72	989		**ZENER DIODE**	1971-72	49345	

TRIUMPH T150V Trident (750 cc Three Cylinder) 1973 on

Unit	Year	Part No.	Page
ALTERNATOR			
Rotor	1973-on	54213902	
Stator	1973-on	47205	
BATTERY	1973-on	PUZ5A	
BULBHOLDER			
Instruments	1973	54953387	
Bulb	1973	643	
BULBHOLDER			
Instruments	1974-on	51271406	
Bulb	1974-on	504	
CONDENSER			
Ignition	1973-on	54420128	
Rubber Cover	1973-on	54418528	
Base Plate	1973-on	54418526	
COIL			
Ignition	1973-on	45223	
CONTACT BREAKER			
Complete C.B. Plate Assembly	1973-on	54419327	
Points Set	1973-on	54419328	
Eccentric Adjustment Screw	1973-on	54419220	
Auto Advance Assembly	1973-on	54419867	
Auto Advance Springs	1973-on	54417992	
FLASHER UNIT	1973-on	35048	
Mounting Clip	1973-on	54385091	
FUSE HOLDER	1973-on	54190387	
Fuse	1973-on	188218	
HORN	1973-on	70235	
LAMPS			
Head Lamp Assembly	1973-on	60260	24
Light Unit	1973-on	54525927	
Rim	1973-on	553248	
Bulb, Main	1973-on	370	
Bulb, Parking	1973-on	989	
Bulb, Warning	1973-on	281	
Stop Lamp Assembly	1973-on	56513	25
LAMPS (Cont'd.)			
Lens	1973-on	54584930	
Bulb	1973-on	380	
Turn Signal Lamp (Less Stanchions)	Early 1973	56147	25
Lens		54581638	
Bulb		382	
Stanchions	Early 1973	60600092	
Turn Signal Lamp (Less Stanchions)	Late 1973-on	56559	25
Lens		54581638	
Bulb		382	
Stanchions			
Front		60600313	
Rear		60600312	
RECTIFIER	1973-on	49072	
REFLECTORS			
Amber	1973-on	57183	
RELAY			
Horn	1973-on	33213	
SWITCHES			
L.H. Dip-Horn Combination	1973	54033666	
L.H. Casting, Lever Pivot	1973	54340882	
L.H. Turn-Signal-Cut-Out	1974-on	39951	
L.H. Casting, Lever Pivot	1974-on	54343791	
R.H. Dip-Horn Combination	1973	54033751	
R.H. Dip-Horn Combination	1974-on	39949	
Ignition	Early 1973	31899	
Ignition, & Lighting	Late 1973-on	39565	
Lighting	1973-on	31356	
Stop Light Rear	1973-on	34815	
WIRING HARNESS	1973-on	54961595	
Ignition, C.B. 3 Core	1973-on	54939169	
ZENER DIODE		49345	

TRIUMPH T160 Trident (750 cc Three Cylinder Electric Start) 1975-76

Unit	Year	Part No.	Page
ALTERNATOR			
Rotor	1975-76	54202275	
Stator	1975-76	47205	
BALLAST RESISTOR IGNITION	1975-76	47190	
BATTERY	1975-76	MCZ9-8	
BULBHOLDER			
Instruments	1975-76	51271406	
Bulb	1975-76	504	
CONDENSER			
Ignition	1975-76	54420128	
Rubber Cover	1975-76	54418528	
Base Plate	1975-76	54418526	
COIL			
Ignition	1975-76	45220	
CONTACT BREAKER			
Complete C.B. Plate Assembly	1975-76	54419327	
Points Set	1975-76	54419828	
Eccentric Adjustment Screw	1975-76	54419220	
Auto Advance Assembly	1975-76	54419867	
Auto Advance Springs	1975-76	54417992	
FLASHER UNIT	1975-76	35048	
Mounting Clip	1975-76	54385091	
Mounting Spring	1975-76	54386637	
FUSE HOLDER	1975-76	54190387	
Fuse	1975-76	188218	
HORN	1975-76	70235	
LAMPS			
Head Lamp Assembly	1975-76	60646	24
LAMPS (Cont'd)			
Light Unit	1975-76	54525927	
Rim	1975-76	553248	
Bulb, Main	1975-76	370	
Bulb, Parking	1975-76	989	
Stop Lamp Assembly	1975-76	56513	25
Lens	1975-76	54584930	
Bulb	1975-76	380	
Turn Signal Lamp (Less Stanchions)	1975-76	56559	25
Lens	1975-76	54581638	
Bulb	1975-76	382	
Stanchions			
Front	1975-76	60600313	
Rear	1975-76	60600312	
RECTIFIER	1975-76	49072	
REFLECTOR			
Amber	1975-76	57183	
RELAY			
Starter	1975-76	33336	
STARTER	1975-76	L26518	25
Note: Following Parts not supplied with starter			
Drive (Includes Jump Ring & Thrust Washer)	1975-76	54246123	
Intermediate Shaft Assembly	1975-76	54246003	
Lever Assembly	1975-76	54247153	
Solenoid	1975-76	76849	
Spring & Spacers (Between Lever & Drive)	1975-76	54245340	

TRIUMPH T160 Trident (750 cc Three Cylinder Electric Start) 1975-76 (Cont'd.)

Unit	Year	Part No.	Page	Unit	Year	Part No.	Page
SWITCHES				**WARNING LAMPS (Cont'd.)**			
L.H. Dip-Turn-Signal & Horn				Green	1975-76	54363455	
Combination	1975-76	30707		Red	1975-76	54363454	
R.H. Engine Cut-Out & Starter				Bulbholder	1975-76	54933910	
Combination	1975-76	30723		Bulb	1975-76	281	
Ignition & Lighting Master	1975-76	39784		**WIRING HARNESS**			
Lighting	1975-76	34660		Head Lamp	1975-76	54962252	
Neutral	1975-76	30702		Main	1975-76	54964675	
Stop Rear	1975-76	34815		Ignition C.B. 3 Core	1975-76	54939169	
WARNING LIGHTS				Cable-Relay to Solenoid	1975-76	54962253	
Amber	1975-76	54363453		Cable Battery to Ground	1975-76	54962257	
Blue	1975-76	54361250		**ZENER DIODE**	1975-76	49345	

NOTES

Lucas Service

HEAD LAMPS

Part No.	Page No.	Part No.	Page No.	Part No.	Page No.
59666	24	60261	24	60533	24
59883	24	60262	24	60646	24
59892	24	60263	24	60818	25
59965	24	60289	24	60835	25
59969	24	60327	24	60867	25
60037	24	60488	24	60942	25
60067	24	60512	24		
60260	24	60514	24		

STARTER

Starter No.	Page No.
L26518	25

STOP & TURN SIGNAL LAMPS

Lamp No.	Page No.	Lamp No.	Page No.	Lamp No.	Page No.
53972	25	56513	25	56606	25
53973	25	56559	25	56754	25
56147	25	56605	25	56757	25
56512	25				

Spark Plug Application Chart	Pg. 26
Girling Shock Info	Pgs. 26-27
Bulb Chart	Pg. 28
Wiring Harness Connectors	Pg. 29
Miscellaneous Info	Pg. 30
Accessories	Pgs. 31-32

HEADLAMPS

UNIT NO.	59666	59883	59892	59965	59969	60037
Wire Reflector Fixing	504665	504665	504665	504665	504665	504665
Screw Rim Fixing	144921	144921	144921	144921	144921	144921
Plate Rim Fixing	534296	534296	534296	534296	534296	534296
Warning Light Amber	—	—	—	—	—	—
Warning Light Green	—	—	—	38191	38191	38191
Warning Light Red	38189	38189	—	—	38189	38189
Warning Light Shield	—	—	—	—	—	—
Warning Light Sealing Washer	54140331	54140331	—	54140331	54140331	54140331
Switch-Lighting	—	35710	—	35710	35710	35710
Screw-Lamp Fixing	112201	112201	112201	112201	112201	112201
Washer-Lamp Fixing	137498	137498	137498	137498	137498	137498
Grommet or Cover	—	—	54524048	—	—	—
Bulbholder-Main	554602	554602	554602	553738	554602	554602
Bulbholder-Parking	554710	54573590	54573590	54573590	54573590	54573590
Bulbholder-Warning	54945043	54945043	—	54945043	54945043	54945043
Interior Bulbholder Parking	553780	553780	553780	553780	553780	553780
Ring Parking Bulbholder	554354	554354	554354	554354	554354	554354
Ammeter	36403	36403	—	—	36403	—
Switch-Dip	—	—	—	31620	—	—
Diode-Clipper	—	—	—	—	—	—

UNIT NO.	60067	60260	60261	60262	60263	60289
Wire Reflector Fixing	504665	504665	504665	504665	504665	504665
Screw Rim Fixing	144921	144921	144921	144921	144921	144921
Plate Rim Fixing	534296	534296	534296	534296	534296	534296
Warning Light Amber	—	54363453	54363453	5436453	—	—
Warning Light Green	—	54363455	54363455	54363455	54363455	—
Warning Light Red	38189	54363454	54363454	54363454	54363454	54363454
Warning Light Shield	—	—	54525212	—	54525212	54525212
Warning Light Sealing Washer	54140331	54140331	54140331	54140331	54140331	54140331
Switch-Lighting	31780	31356	35710	31356	35710	31780
Screw-Lamp Fixing	112201	54115106	54115106	54115106	54115106	54115106
Washer-Lamp Fixing	137498	143086	143086	143086	143086	143086
Grommet or Cover	—	54524048	—	—	862217	—
Bulbholder-Main	54523241	554602	554602	—	554602	554602
Bulbholder-Parking	54573590	54573590	54573590	54573590	54573590	—
Bulbholder-Warning	54945043	54945043	54945043	54945043	54945043	54945043
Interior Bulbholder Parking	553780	553780	553780	553780	553780	—
Ring Parking Bulbholder	554354	554354	554354	554354	554354	—
Ammeter	—	—	—	—	—	—
Diode-Clipper	—	—	—	—	—	49934

UNIT NO.	60327	60488	60512	60514	60533	60646
Wire Reflector Fixing	504665	504665	504665	504665	504665	504665
Screw Rim Fixing	144921	144921	144921	144921	144921	144921
Plate Rim Fixing	534296	534296	534296	534296	534296	534296
Warning Light Amber	54363453	—	54363453	54363453	54363453	—
Warning Light Green	54363455	—	54363455	54363455	54363455	—
Warning Light Red	—	54363454	54363454	54363454	54363454	—
Warning Light Shield	54525212	—	—	—	—	—
Warning Light Sealing Washer	54140331	54140331	54140331	54140331	54140331	—
Switch-Lighting	31356	34419	34419	34419	—	34660
Screw-Lamp Fixing	54115106	54115106	54104506	54104506	—	54115106
Washer-Lamp Fixing	143086	143086	143086	143086	—	143086
Grommet	—	862217	862217	862217	—	862217
Bulbholder-Main	554602	554602	554602	554602	554602	554602
Bulbholder-Parking	54573590	—	54573590	54573590	54573590	—
Bulbholder-Warning	54945043	54945043	54945043	54945043	54945043	—
Interior Bulbholder Parking	553780	—	553780	553780	553780	—
Ring, Parking Bulbholder	554354	—	554354	554354	554354	—

HEADLAMPS (Cont'd.)

UNIT NO.	60818	60835	60867	60942
Wire Reflector Fixing	504665	504665	504665	504665
Screw-Rim Fixing	144921	144921	144921	144921
Plate Rim Fixing	534296	534296	534296	534296
Warning Light Amber	54363453	—	—	—
Warning Light Green	—	—	—	—
Warning Light Red	—	—	—	—
Warning Light Blue	54361250	—	—	—
Warning Light Sealing Washer	54140331	—	—	—
Switch-Lighting	—	—	—	—
Screw-Lamp Fixing	—	54115106	54115106	—
Washer-Lamp Fixing	—	143086	143086	—
Grommet	862217	862217	862217	—
Bulbholder-Main	554602	554602	554602	554602
Bulbholder-Parking	54573590	54573590	54573590	54573590
Bulbholder-Warning	—	—	—	—
Interior Bulbholder Parking	553780	553780	553780	553780
Ring, Parking Bulbholder	554354	554354	554354	554354

STOP LAMPS AND TURN SIGNAL LAMPS

UNIT NO.	53972	53973	56147	56512	56513	56559
Bulbholder	54578213	54578213	54580322	—	—	—
Interior Bulbholder	573828	573828	573832	573828	573828	573828
Gasket	54571677	54571677	—	54583924	54583924	54583924
Base Assembly	54578212	54578212	—	54584931	54584931	54584931

UNIT NO.	56605	56606	56754	56757
Bulbholder	54580322	54580322	—	54580322
Interior Bulbholder	573832	573832	573828	573832
Gasket	—	—	54583924	—
Base Assembly	—	—	54584931	—

STARTER

STARTER NO.	L26518
Armature	54249341
Bolt, Through Fixing	54254142
Bracket, Commutator End	54260204
Bushing Commutator End	261233
Thrust Pad	54252180
Bracket, Drive End	54249344
Bushing, Drive End	54244545
Brushes, Set	54255887
Field Coils	54256043
Terminal Field Coils	54256040
Liner, Insulating	54251728
Plate, Complete With Brush	
Boxes and Springs	54251727
Spring Set, Brush	54252360
Sundry Parts Set	54252417

SPARK PLUG APPLICATION CHART

BSA

	Displacement c.c.	Regular	Gold Palladium
Starfire, Goldstar, Victor Trail	250	N3	N3G
Victor Special	440	N4	N4G
Goldstar, Victor, MX	500	N3	N3G
Royal Star	500	N3	N3G
Lighting, Thunderbolt.	650	N3	N3G
Firebird	650	N3	N3G
Rocket 3	750	N3	N3G

DALESMAN

	Displacement c.c.	Regular	Gold Palladium
Trail & MX 1970-72	125	N3	N3G
Enduro, MX, Trails	125	L81/L82	L6G

NORTON

	Displacement c.c.	Regular	Gold Palladium
High Rider	750	N6Y	N3G
Commando, Fastback, S. SS	750	N7Y	N4G
Roadster (Gap .025")	750	N7Y	N4G
Commando, MK III	850	N7Y	N4G

RICKMAN

	Displacement c.c.	Regular	Gold Palladium
Enduro, Six Day, 125 MX	125	L81/L82	L6G

TRIUMPH

	Displacement c.c.	Regular	Gold Palladium
All Models	All	N3	N3G

GIRLING TWIN-TUBE SUSPENSION UNITS

Unit	Year	Part No.	Page	Unit	Year	Part No.	Page
BSA				**RICKMAN**			
B25 Starfire	1969-70	2110		125 Enduro	1971	2508	
B25SS Goldstar	1971-72	2483		125 Six Days	1973	2574	
B25T Victor Trail	1971-72	2483					
B44 Victor Special	1969-70	2110		**TRIUMPH**			
A50 Royal Star	1969-70	2108		TR5MX	1973-on	2487	
B50MX Victor	1971-72	2487		TR5T Trophy Trail	1973-74	2453	
B50MX	1973-on	2487		TR6C Trophy	1969-70	2107	
B50SS Goldstar	1971-72	2483		TR6C Trophy	1971-72	2497	
B50T Victor Trail	1971-72	2483		TR6R Tiger	1969-70	2107	
A65FS Firebird Scrambler	1969-71	2497		TR6R Tiger	1971-72	2497	
A65L Lighting	1969-on	2497		TR7RV Tiger	1973-75	2564	
A65T Thunderbolt	1969-on	2497		TR7RV Tiger	1976-77	2564	
A75R Rocket 3	1969-on	2105		TR25SS Blazer	1971	2453	
				T25T Trail Blazer	1971	2453	
DALESMAN				TR25W Trophy	1969-70	2110	
Enduro	1971-on	2517		TRX75 Hurricane	1973	2510	
Trails	1970-on	4341		T100C Trophy	1969-70	2107	
				T100C Trophy	1971-72	2107	
ENFIELD				T100R Daytona	1969-70	2107	
Interceptor III	1969-on	4969		T100R Daytona	1971-72	2107	
				T100R Daytona	1973-on	2107	
NORTON				T120R Bonneville	1969-70	2107	
All Commando Models	1969- Early 1975	2311		T120R Bonneville	1971-72	2497	
				T140V Bonneville Twin	1973-75	2564	
				T140V Bonneville Twin	1976-77	2564	
				T150 Trident	1969-71	2341	
All Models	Late 1975-on	2936		T150V Trident	1972-on	2564	
				T160 Trident Electric Start	1975-76	2564	

SUSPENSION UNIT
REPAIR PARTS

Part No. Complete Suspen'n Unit	Length Ins. Ex-tended	Length Ins. Com-pressed	Bushings	Spring Part No.	Spring Rate lbs./in.	Spring Lgth in	Dirt Shield	Shock Absorber Only
2105	13.3	11.2	64533645	64544235	110	9.4	64532778	2211
2107	12.9	10.7	64533645	64543708	100	8.4	—	2090
2108	13.3	10.7	64533645	64543735	90	9.4	—	4971
2110	12.9	10.3	T64533645 B64533654	64543708	100	8.4	—	4644
2311	12.9	10.2	64533658	64544621	126	8.4	—	2149
2341	12.9	10.7	64533645	64544754	110	8.4	—	2090
2453	12.9	10.3	64533645	64543708	100	8.4	—	2455
2483	12.9	10.3	64533645	64543708	100	8.4	—	2484
2487	12.9	9.9	64533645	64543626	70/100	8.4	—	2488
2497	12.9	10.7	64533645	64545350	88	8.4	—	2090
2508	12.9	9.9	64533645	9054/317	75	8.0	—	2507
2510	13.4	12.1	64533645	64544235	110	9.4	—	2511
2517	11.9	8.9	64533645	64541788	60/90	8.0	—	4814
2564	12.4	10.4	64533645	64543708	100	8.4	—	2563
2574	12.5	9.4	64533647	9054/317	75	8.0	—	2578
2936	12.9	10.2	T64533658 B64541661	64544621	126	8.4	—	2935
4341	11.9	9.3	64533645	9054/58	90	8.0	—	4459
4969	11.9	9.7	64533652	64543764	132	8.0	—	4646

Other Parts

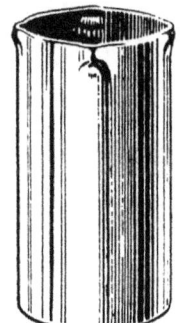

Chrome Dirt Shield
For all Twin Tube Shocks
64532778

SB Unit Adjuster Wrench
64947081

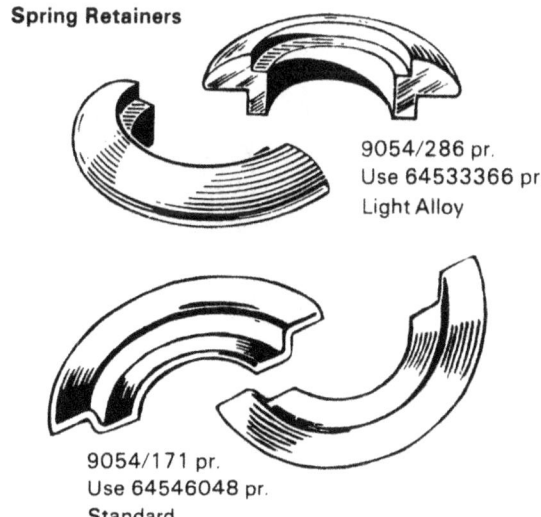

Spring Retainers

9054/286 pr.
Use 64533366 pr.
Light Alloy

9054/171 pr.
Use 64546048 pr.
Standard

BULBS

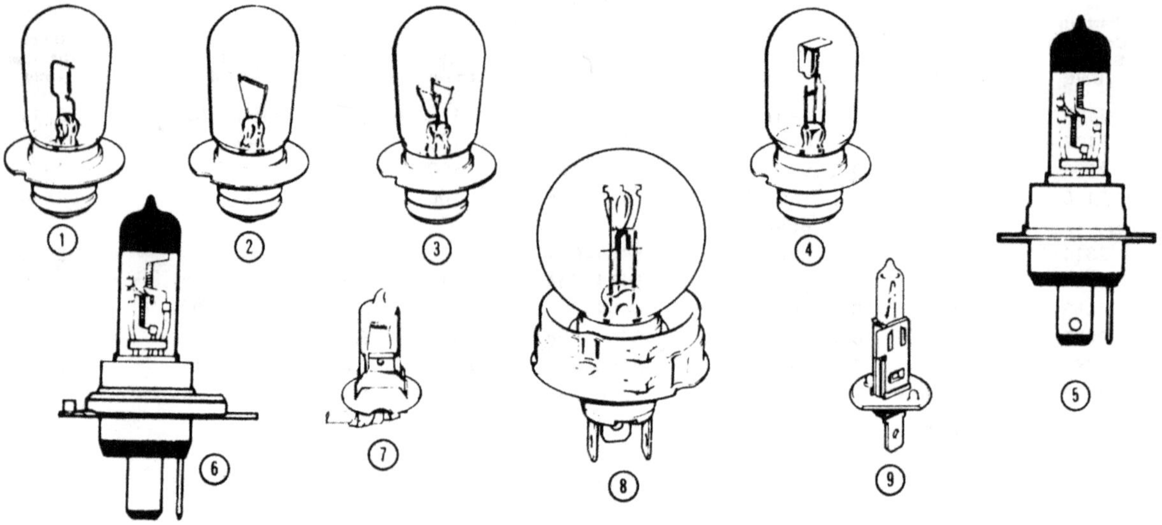

Illus. No.	Volts	Watts	Part No.	Notes	Illus. No.	Volts	Watts	Part No.	Notes
1	6	36	172		6	12	60/55	472	Quartz H4
1	12	48	185		7	6	55	455	Quartz H3
2	6	36	173		7	12	55	453	Quartz H3
2	12	48	323		8	6	45/40	423	
3	6	30/24	312		8	12	60/40	417	
3	12	50/40	446		9	6	55	465	Quartz H1
4	6	35/35	403		9	12	55	448	Quartz H1
4	12	45/40	370						
5	12	60/50	463	Quartz					

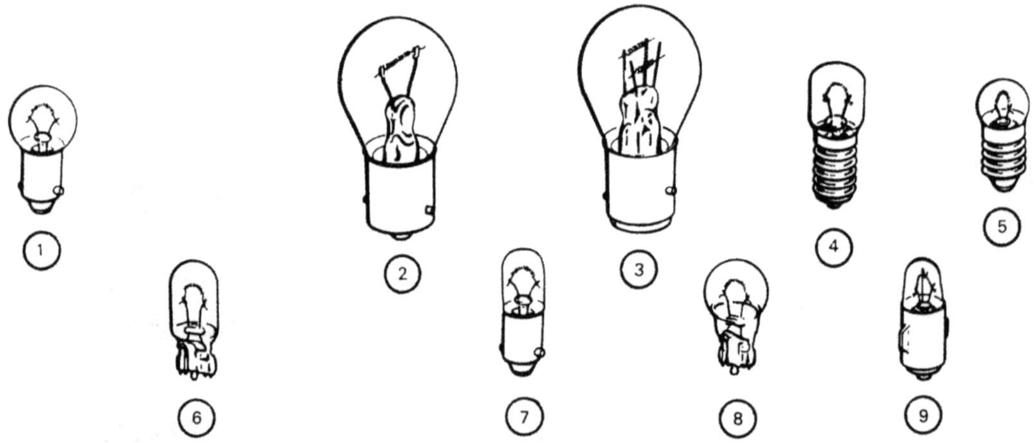

Illus. No.	Volts	Watts	Part No.	Notes	Illus. No.	Volts	Watts	Part No.	Notes
1	6	6	951		4	12	1.5	280	
1	12	2.2	643		5	6	3	990	
1	12	6	989		5	12	2.2	987	
2	6	18	317		6	12	2.2	504	Capless
2	12	21	382		7	12	4	233	
3	6	21/5	384		8	12	5	501	Capless
3	12	21/6	380		9	6	0.6	282	
3	12	21/6	381	Straight Pins	9	12	2	281	

Wiring Harness Connectors

FEMALE TERMINALS AND SLEEVES

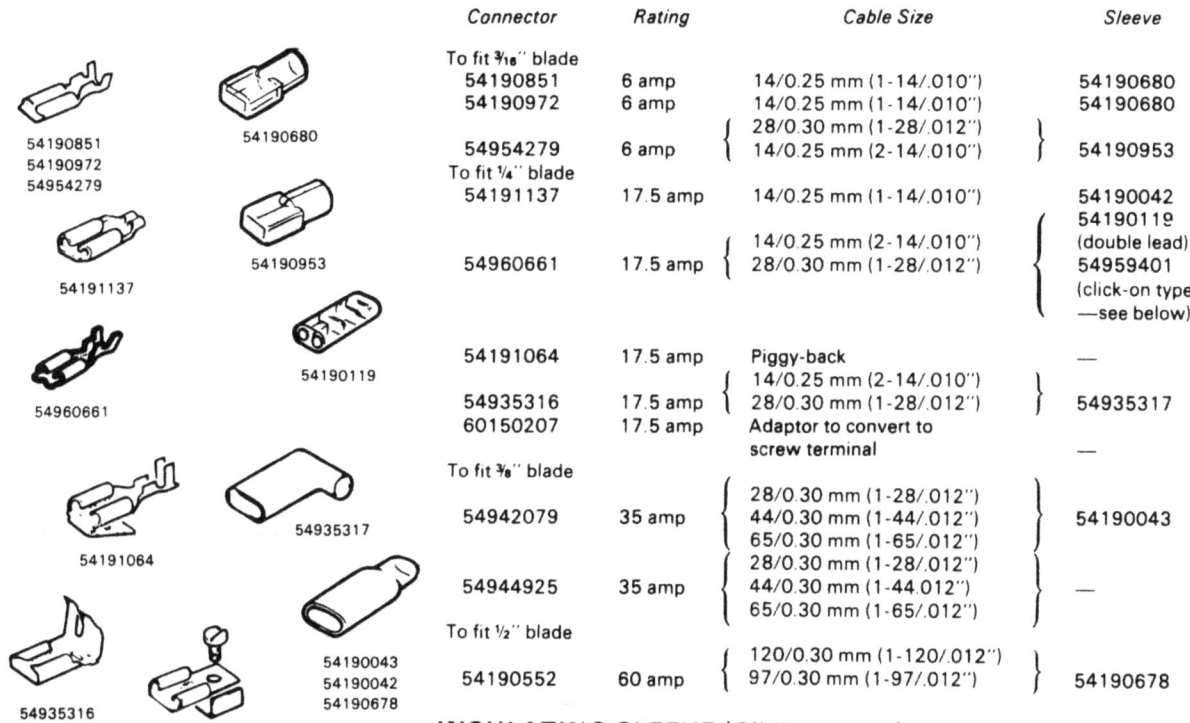

Connector	Rating	Cable Size	Sleeve
To fit ³⁄₁₆" blade			
54190851	6 amp	14/0.25 mm (1-14/.010")	54190680
54190972	6 amp	14/0.25 mm (1-14/.010")	54190680
54954279	6 amp	28/0.30 mm (1-28/.012") / 14/0.25 mm (2-14/.010")	54190953
To fit ¼" blade			
54191137	17.5 amp	14/0.25 mm (1-14/.010")	54190042
54960661	17.5 amp	14/0.25 mm (2-14/.010") / 28/0.30 mm (1-28/.012")	54190119 (double lead) 54959401 (click-on type —see below)
54191064	17.5 amp	Piggy-back	—
54935316	17.5 amp	14/0.25 mm (2-14/.010") / 28/0.30 mm (1-28/.012")	54935317
60150207	17.5 amp	Adaptor to convert to screw terminal	—
To fit ⅜" blade			
54942079	35 amp	28/0.30 mm (1-28/.012") / 44/0.30 mm (1-44/.012") / 65/0.30 mm (1-65/.012")	54190043
54944925	35 amp	28/0.30 mm (1-28/.012") / 44/0.30 mm (1-44.012") / 65/0.30 mm (1-65/.012")	—
To fit ½" blade			
54190552	60 amp	120/0.30 mm (1-120/.012") / 97/0.30 mm (1-97/.012")	54190678

INSULATING SLEEVE (Click-on type)

Part No. 54959401

Completely insulates the full range of ¼" straight Lucar terminals, crimped, welded or soldered types covering conductor sizes 14/.010" (14/0.25 mm) to 44/.012" (44/0.30 mm). A locking device ensures proper contact with the mating blade and prevents displacement of the cover.

Cable Connectors

Description	Part No.
2-way snap-in cable connector (may be used with ⁹⁄₃₂" single cable clip Pt. No. 187042)	900288
4-way cable connector (common contact)	850641
6-way cable connector (insulated)	850844
6-way cable connector (common contact)	54948105
10-way cable connector (insulated)	850832

Cable Eyelet

Fixing hole	Number of leads	Part No.
⅛"	1	187700
³⁄₁₆"	1	187009
¼"	1	187736
³⁄₁₆"	2	850405
¼"	2	850406
⁵⁄₁₆"	2	900450
⅜"	2	850402
³⁄₁₆"	1	187704
¹¹⁄₆₄"	1	187709

Cable Eyelet (Typical)

Snap-in Bullet Terminal Ends

(For use with cable connectors)

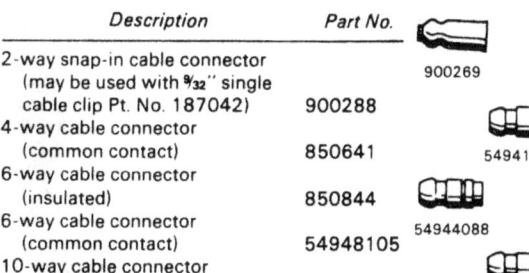

Description	Overall dia.	Part No.
Soldered type	4.75 mm (0.187)"	900269
Crimp type, suitable for cable 14/0.25 mm (14/.010") Pt and SPT	4.75 mm (0.187")	54941384
Crimp type, suitable for cable 14/0.30 mm (14/.012") PT	4.75 mm (0.187")	54944088
Crimp type, suitable for cable 28/0.30 mm (28/.012") PT	4.75 mm (0.187")	54944095
Crimp type, suitable for cable 44/0.30 mm (44/.012") PT	4.75 mm (0.187")	54946098
Sleeve terminal ³⁄₁₆" dia.	—	188818

In-line Fuseholders

Fuseholder	54190387
With 35 amp fuse and 14/0.25 cable with eyelets	54938986

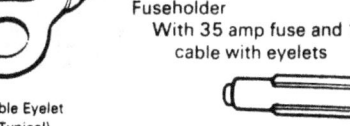

Fuse holder

MISCELLANEOUS INFORMATION

Stator Guide

Part Number	Number Wires	Wire Color Code	Notes
47105	3	GW-GB-GY	12 volt
47127	3	GW-GB-GY	
47177	4	NU-BW-R-U	
47197	5	R-BY-NU-BW-B	E.T. ign.
47204	3	GB-GY-GW	6 volt
47205	2	GY-WG	12 volt
47209	3	GW-GB-GY	12 volt
47226	2	Racing Half Stator	
47239	2	GY-GY	High Output

Color Code
- B Black   G Green
- U Blue   W White
- N Brown   Y Yellow

When a cable has two color code letters, the first denotes the main color and the second denotes the tracer color.

Contact Breaker Wiring Harness

Part Number	Motorcycle	Year
54956251	Twin Cylinders	1970-on
54939169	Three Cylinder	1970-on

Fuses (glass cartridge)

Identification	Fusing Value	Part No.
1 5/32" long		
Blue on White	2 amp	188202
Red strip on Yellow	5 amp	188206
Blue on Green	8 amp	188209
Green on Black	10 amp	188211
Light Brown	15 amp	188220
Blue on Yellow	20 amp	188215
Pink	25 amp	188216
White	35 amp	188218
Purple and Yellow	50 amp	188219

Fast Moving Parts

49072 Rectifier

49345 Zenner

54170009 Capacitor

Ignition Switches

31899 2-position

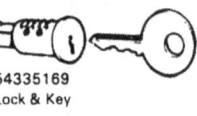
54335169 Lock & Key

39565 4-position

Stop Light Switches

34815

54033234

Lighting Switches

31276

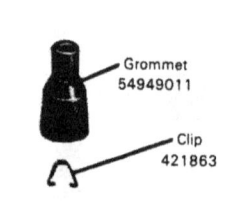
35710

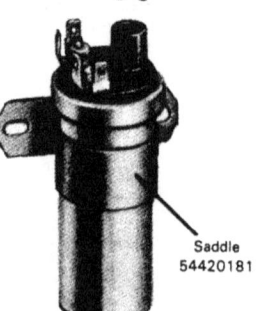
Grommet 54949011
Clip 421863
Saddle 54420181
12 volt. 45223
6 volt. 45222

Lens 54584930
Lens assembly 54581638

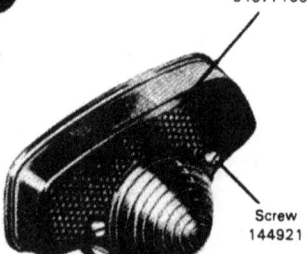
Lens 54577109
Screw 144921

LUCAS ACCESSORIES

NO BATTERY

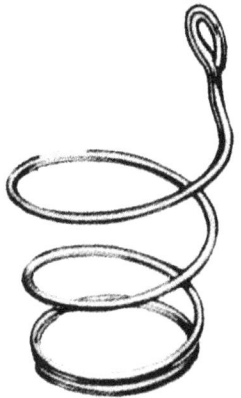

MOTOR CYCLE CAPACITOR MODEL 2MC

One of the many motorcycling problems which Lucas has successfully tackled is that of the enthusiast who wants to use his road machine for occasional competition work. Obviously, he doesn't want to run with a battery in circuit, but he still needs an adequate supply of power for lighting and starting. And, after the meeting, he wants to be able to re-fit his battery for normal road use.

Lucas answer all these needs— and more—with their 2MC Capacitor Ignition System, incorporating the standard 12 volt battery coil ignition components with zener diode charge control.

This shows many advantages over the A.C. and coil ignition systems. It has been fully proved in trials work and has led the way to many important successes.

How it works The capacitor stores energy to supply the ignition coil, as required, to ensure easy starting and smoother running at all speeds. Magnetic timing is less critical than with A.C. ignition systems. Auto advance mechanisms with a greater rate of advance, such as are used on battery-operated coil ignition systems, can be employed.

How it is fitted If your machine is already fitted with Lucas 12 volt equipment, you only need the 2 MC capacitor complete with mounting spring. The alternator should be re-connected to give full output in all lighting switch positions and the zener diode should be mounted on a heat sink of sufficient size to cope with this output. Minimum recommended heat sink size is 6" x 6" x 1/8" aluminium plate. (The shape is not important but there must be at least 72 square inches of surface area). The heat sink must be mounted in an adequate airstream.

Earlier machines, wired to give only part generator output in "Off" and "Pilot" positions, will not have heat sinks of sufficient size and replacement will be necessary.

Your machine is a 6 volt? You can enjoy the benefits of Lucas Capacitor Ignition, together with many other advantages, by converting your machine to 12 volts.

A.C. ignition equipped machines will, in addition, require a battery-charging alternator stator, a new wiring harness and lighting and ignition switches.

54170009

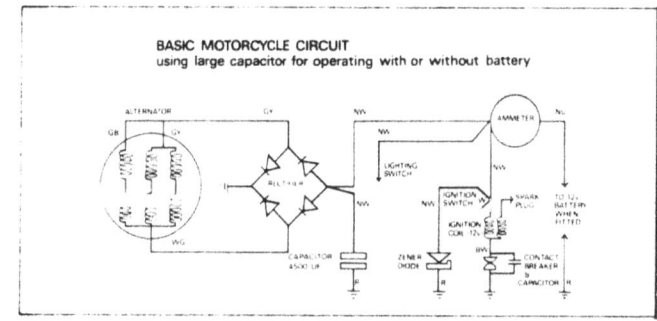

BASIC MOTORCYCLE CIRCUIT using large capacitor for operating with or without battery

SOMETHING NEW in motorcycle ignition coils

45276A

45275A

The new Lucas 17P12 and 17P6 coils have been introduced as replacements for the 17M12 and 17M6 versions and incorporate the techniques used and learned in car and motor cycle coil production since the early 1950's.

Providing that the system in which they are used is capable of supplying the increased power requirements, the 17P12 and 17P6 coils will make for ease of starting, improved performance, and extended plug life.

Two new features incorporated into the design have meant that the coil size has not been increased. Firstly, the insulating top of the coil is treated with a track resistant paint to improve its insulatory properties. Secondly, the case of the coil is anodised in distinctive dark colours, not only to improve its appearance, but to increase the thermal dissipation allowing the same size of coil to handle more power.

Powerful looks with powerful performance—the new Lucas 17P12 and 17P6 coils.

VELOCEPRESS MANUALS - MOTORCYCLE

1930'S BRITISH MOTORCYCLE CARBS & ELEC COMPONENTS (BOOK OF)
1930'S BRITISH MOTORCYCLE ENGINES (OVERHAUL & MAINTENANCE)
1930'S BRITISH MOTORCYCLE GEARBOXES & CLUTCHES (BOOK OF)
AJS 1932-1948 SINGLES & TWINS 250cc THRU 1000cc (BOOK OF)
AJS 1945-1960 SINGLES 350cc & 500cc MODELS 16 & 18 (BOOK OF)
AJS 1955-1965 SINGLES 350cc & 500cc (BOOK OF)
ARIEL UP TO 1932 (BOOK OF)
ARIEL 1932-1939 PREWAR MODELS (BOOK OF)
ARIEL 1933-1951 (WORKSHOP MANUAL)
ARIEL 1939-1960 4 STROKE SINGLES (BOOK OF)
ARIEL 1958-1964 LEADER & ARROW (BOOK OF)
BMW R26 R27 (1956-1967) FACTORY WORKSHOP MANUAL
BMW R50 R50S R60 R69S (1955-1969) FACTORY WORKSHOP MANUAL
BRIDGESTONE 90 SERIES FACTORY WSM & PARTS CATALOGUE
BRIDGESTONE 175 SERIES FACTORY WSM & PARTS CATALOGUE
BRIDGESTONE 350 SERIES FACTORY WSM & PARTS CATALOGUES
BSA BANTAM ALL MODELS FROM 1948 ONWARDS (BOOK OF)
BSA SINGLES & V-TWINS UP TO 1927 (BOOK OF)
BSA SINGLES & V-TWINS UP TO 1930 (BOOK OF)
BSA SINGLES & V-TWINS UP TO 1935 (BOOK OF)
BSA SINGLES & V-TWINS 1936-1939 (BOOK OF)
BSA OHV & SV SINGLES 250-600cc 1945-1959 (BOOK OF)
BSA OHV & SV SINGLES 250cc (ONLY) 1954-1970 (BOOK OF)
BSA OHV SINGLES 350 & 500cc 1955-1967 (BOOK OF)
BSA TWINS 1948-1962 (BOOK OF)
BSA TWINS 1962-1969 (SECOND BOOK OF)
CYCLEMOTOR (BOOK OF)
DOUGLAS 1929-1939 PREWAR ALL MODELS (BOOK OF)
DOUGLAS 1948-1957 POSTWAR ALL MODELS FACTORY SHOP MANUAL
DUCATI 160cc, 250cc & 350cc OHC MODELS FACTORY SHOP MANUAL
HONDA 50 ALL MODELS UP TO 1970 INC MONKEY & TRAIL (BOOK OF)
HONDA 90 ALL MODELS UP TO 1966 (BOOK OF)
HONDA 125-150cc TWINS C/CS/CB/CA FACTORY WORKSHOP MANUAL
HONDA 250-305 TWINS C/CS/CB FACTORY WORKSHOP MANUAL
HONDA 450 CB/CL 1965-1974 K0 TO K7 WORKSHOP MANUAL
HONDA C100 SUPER CUB FACTORY WORKSHOP MANUAL
HONDA C110 SPORT CUB 1962-1969 FACTORY WORKSHOP MANUAL
HONDA TWINS & SINGLES 50cc THRU 305cc 1960-1966 (BOOK OF)
HONDA TWINS ALL MODELS 125cc THRU 450cc UP TO 1968 (BOOK OF)
INDIAN PONYBIKE, BOY RACER & PAPOOSE ILL PARTS LIST & SALES LIT
J.A.P. ENGINES 1927-1952 & MOTORCYCLES 1934-1952 (BOOK OF)
LAMBRETTA 1947-1957 ALL 125 & 150cc MODELS (BOOK OF)
LAMBRETTA 1957-1970 LI & TV MODELS (SECOND BOOK OF)
MATCHLESS 1931-1939 ALL MODELS 250cc THRU 990cc (BOOK OF)
MATCHLESS 1945-1956 350 & 500cc SINGLES (BOOK OF)
MATCHLESS 1955-1966 350 & 500cc SINGLES (BOOK OF)
NEW IMPERIAL ALL SV & OHV FROM 1935 ONWARDS (BOOK OF)
NORTON 1932-1939 PREWAR MODELS (BOOK OF)
NORTON 1932-1947 (BOOK OF)
NORTON 1938-1956 (BOOK OF)
NORTON 1955-1963 MODELS 19, 50 & ES2 (BOOK OF)
NORTON 1955-1965 DOMINATOR TWINS (BOOK OF)
NORTON 1957-1970 TWINS FACTORY WORKSHOP MANUAL
NSU PRIMA 1956-1964 ALL MODELS (BOOK OF)
NSU QUICKLY 1953-1963 ALL MODELS (BOOK OF)
PANTHER 1932-1958 LIGHTWEIGHT MODELS 250 & 350cc (BOOK OF)
PANTHER 1938-1966 HEAVYWEIGHT MODELS 600 & 650cc (BOOK OF)
RALEIGH MOPEDS 1960-1969 (BOOK OF)
RALEIGH MOTORCYCLES 1919-1933 (BOOK OF)
ROYAL ENFIELD 1934-1946 SINGLES & V TWINS (BOOK OF)
ROYAL ENFIELD 1937-1953 SINGLES & V TWINS (BOOK OF)
ROYAL ENFIELD 1946-1962 SINGLES (BOOK OF)
ROYAL ENFIELD 1958-1966 250cc & 350cc SINGLES (SECOND BOOK OF)
ROYAL ENFIELD 736cc INTERCEPTOR FACTORY WORKSHOP MANUAL
RUDGE 1933-1939 (BOOK OF)
SUNBEAM 1928-1939 (BOOK OF)
SUNBEAM 1946-1957 S7 & S8 (BOOK OF)
SUZUKI 50cc & 80cc UP TO 1966 (BOOK OF)
SUZUKI T10 1963-1967 FACTORY WORKSHOP MANUAL
SUZUKI T20 & T200 1965-1969 FACTORY WORKSHOP MANUAL
SUZUKI TWINS 1962 ONWARDS 125-500cc WORKSHOP MANUAL
TRIUMPH 1935-1939 PREWAR MODELS (BOOK OF)
TRIUMPH 1935-1949 (BOOK OF)
TRIUMPH 1937-1951 (WORKSHOP MANUAL)
TRIUMPH 1945-1955 FACTORY WORKSHOP MANUAL
TRIUMPH 1945-1958 TWINS (BOOK OF)
TRIUMPH 1956-1969 TWINS (BOOK OF)
VELOCETTE 1925-1970 ALL SINGLES & TWINS (BOOK OF)
VESPA 1951-1961 (BOOK OF)
VESPA 1955-1963 125 & 150cc & GS MODELS (SECOND BOOK OF)
VESPA 1955-1968 GS & SS (BOOK OF)
VESPA 1963-1972 90, 125 & 150cc (THIRD BOOK OF)
VILLIERS ENGINE UP TO 1959 INC. 3 WHEELERS (BOOK OF)
VILLIERS ENGINE UP TO 1969 (BOOK OF)
VINCENT 1935-1955 (WORKSHOP MANUAL)
YAMAHA 1961-1967 YA5 & YA6 (WORKSHOP MANUAL & ILL PARTS LIST)
YAMAHA 1971-1972 JT1 & JT2 (WORKSHOP MANUAL & ILL PARTS LIST)

VELOCEPRESS TECHNICAL BOOKS – MOTORCYCLE

CATALOG OF BRITISH MOTORCYCLES (1951 MODELS)
LUCAS ELECTRONICS BRITISH M/CYCLES REPAIR & PARTS (1950-1977)
MOTORCYCLE ENGINEERING (P.E. Irving)
MOTORCYCLE ROAD TESTS 1949-1953 (Motor Cycle Magazine UK)
SPEED AND HOW TO OBTAIN IT (Motor Cycle Magazine UK)
TUNING FOR SPEED (P.E. Irving)

VELOCEPRESS MANUALS - THREE WHEELER'S

BSA THREE WHEELER (BOOK OF)
VINTAGE MORGAN THREE WHEELER (BOOK OF)

VELOCEPRESS MANUALS - AUTOMOBILE

ALFA ROMEO GIULIA WORKSHOP MANUAL 1300 TO 2000cc 1962-1975
ALFA ROMEO GIULIA TECH MANUAL CARBURETED CARS FROM 1962
ALFA ROMEO GIULIA TECH MANUAL FUEL INJECTED CARS FROM 1969
ALFA ROMEO GIULIETTA & GIULIA 750 & 101 SERIES 1955-1965 WSM
AUSTIN-HEALEY SPRITE & MG MIDGET WORKSHOP MANUAL 1958-1971
BMW 600 LIMOUSINE FACTORY WORKSHOP MANUAL
BMW 600 LIMOUSINE OWNERS HAND BOOK & SERVICE MANUAL
BMW 2000 & 2002 1966-1976 WORKSHOP MANUAL
BMW ISETTA FACTORY WORKSHOP MANUAL
CORVAIR 1960-1969 WORKSHOP MANUAL
CORVETTE V8 1955-1962 WORKSHOP MANUAL
FIAT 500 FACTORY WORKSHOP MANUAL 1957-1973
FIAT 600, 600D & MULTIPLA FACTORY WORKSHOP MANUAL 1955-1969
JAGUAR E-TYPE 3.8 & 4.2 SERIES 1 & 2 WORKSHOP MANUAL
JAGUAR MK 7, 8, 9 & XK120, 140, 150 WORKSHOP MANUAL 1948-1961
METROPOLITAN FACTORY WORKSHOP MANUAL
MGA & MGB OWNERS HANDBOOK & WORKSHOP MANUAL
MG MIDGET TC, TD, TF & TF1500 WORKSHOP MANUAL
PORSCHE 356 1948-1965 WORKSHOP MANUAL
PORSCHE 911 2.0, 2.2, 2.4 LITRE 1964-1973 WORKSHOP MANUAL
PORSCHE 911 2.7, 3.0, 3.2 LITRE 1973-1989 WORKSHOP MANUAL
PORSCHE 912 WORKSHOP MANUAL
TRIUMPH TR2, TR3, TR4 1953-1965 WORKSHOP MANUAL
VOLKSWAGEN TRANSPORTER, TRUCKS & WAGONS 1950-1979 WSM
VOLVO 1944-1968 ALL MODELS WORKSHOP MANUAL

VELOCEPRESS TECHNICAL BOOKS - AUTOMOBILE

FERRARI 250/GT SERVICE AND MAINTENANCE
FERRARI GUIDE TO PERFORMANCE
FERRARI OWNER'S HANDBOOK
FERRARI TUNING TIPS & MAINTENANCE TECHNIQUES
HOW TO BUILD A FIBERGLASS CAR
HOW TO BUILD A RACING CAR
HOW TO RESTORE THE MODEL 'A' FORD
MASERATI OWNER'S HANDBOOK
OBERT'S FIAT GUIDE
PERFORMANCE TUNING THE SUNBEAM TIGER
SOUPING THE VOLKSWAGEN
SOLEX CARBURETORS (EMPHASIS ON UK & EU AUTOMOBILES)
SU CARBURETORS (EMPHASIS ON UK AUTOMOBILES)
WEBER CARBURETORS (EMPHASIS ON ALFA & FIAT)

VELOCEPRESS BOOKS & GUIDES - AUTOMOBILE

ABARTH BUYERS GUIDE
COMPLETE CATALOG OF JAPANESE MOTOR VEHICLES
FERRARI 308 SERIES BUYER'S AND OWNER'S GUIDE
FERRARI BERLINETTA LUSSO
FERRARI BROCHURES AND SALES LITERATURE 1946-1967
FERRARI BROCHURES AND SALES LITERATURE 1968-1989
FERRARI OPP, MAINTENANCE & SERVICE H/BOOKS 1948-1963
FERRARI SERIAL NUMBERS PART I - ODD NUMBERS TO 21399
FERRARI SERIAL NUMBERS PART II - EVEN NUMBERS TO 1050
FERRARI SPYDER CALIFORNIA
HENRY'S FABULOUS MODEL "A" FORD
MASERATI BROCHURES AND SALES LITERATURE

VELOCEPRESS BOOKS – RACING

CARRERA PANAMERICANA - MEXICAN ROAD RACE (BOOK OF)
DIALED IN - THE JAN OPPERMAN STORY
IF HEMINGWAY HAD WRITTEN A RACING NOVEL
VEDA ORR'S NEW REVISED HOT ROD PICTORIAL

AUTOBOOKS WORKSHOP MANUALS & BROOKLANDS ROAD TEST PORTFOLIOS

FOR A COMPLETE LISTING OF THE AUTOBOOKS & BROOKLANDS TITLES THAT WE CURRENTLY HAVE AVAILABLE, PLEASE VISIT OUR WEBSITE.

www.VelocePress.com